SO-DUU-395

Ordinary Mind as the Way

Ordinary Mind as the Way

The Hongzhou School and the Growth of Chan Buddhism

MARIO POCESKI

OXFORD
UNIVERSITY PRESS

2007

Oxford University Press, Inc., publishes works that further
Oxford University's objective of excellence
in research, scholarship, and education.

Oxford   New York
Auckland   Cape Town   Dar es Salaam   Hong Kong   Karachi
Kuala Lumpur   Madrid   Melbourne   Mexico City   Nairobi
New Delhi   Shanghai   Taipei   Toronto

With offices in
Argentina   Austria   Brazil   Chile   Czech Republic   France   Greece
Guatemala   Hungary   Italy   Japan   Poland   Portugal   Singapore
South Korea   Switzerland   Thailand   Turkey   Ukraine   Vietnam

Copyright © 2007 by Oxford University Press, Inc.

Published by Oxford University Press, Inc.
198 Madison Avenue, New York, New York 10016

www.oup.com

Oxford is a registered trademark of Oxford University Press

Library of Congress Cataloging-in-Publication Data
Poceski, Mario.
Ordinary mind as the way : the Hongzhou school and the growth of Chan Buddhism /
Mario Poceski.
    p. cm.
Includes bibliographical references and index.
ISBN 978-0-19-531996-5
1. Hongzhou (Sect)—History.   2. Zen Buddhism—China—History.   I. Title.
BQ9550.H652P63   2007
294.3'927—dc22   2006021028

9 8 7 6 5 4 3 2 1

Printed in the United States of America
on acid-free paper

Acknowledgments

The origins of this book go back about two decades, to my early monastic years in East Asia. The recorded sayings of Mazu, Huangbo, and other medieval Chan monks were among the first Chinese texts I ever read. My ongoing engagement with the Hongzhou school's literature led to the publication of my first book, which contained translations from the records of Mazu and his disciples. Following my entry into the academic world, initially as a graduate student in Buddhist studies at the University of California, Los Angeles, I received invaluable help and support from a number of excellent teachers and colleagues. I am especially indebted to Robert Buswell, who guided my doctoral research at UCLA. I also want to acknowledge the supervision I received from the other members of my dissertation committee: Benjamin Elman, William Bodiford, and David Schaberg.

Much of the initial research for the book was conducted at Komazawa University, Japan, between 1997 and 1999, with generous financial support in the form of Charlotte W. Newcombe and Fulbright-Hays fellowships. During my stay at Komazawa, I especially benefited from the immense knowledge and outstanding scholarship of Ishii Shūdō, who generously answered a host of questions, assisted me with the procurement of research materials, and helped me socialize into Japanese academic life. I also wish to thank Ogawa Takashi, who extended his friendship to make my stay in Tokyo more pleasurable, and who kindly proofread an early draft of the bibliography of East Asian works. I offer special thanks to Tennei-ji temple in Kyoto for the photographic image and permission to use the painting of Mazu that appears on the cover, and to Kanazawa Bunko in Yokohama for their kind permission to take and use the pictures of ancient Chan manuscripts from their collection that appear as figures 2.1 and 5.1.

Albert Welter and John McRae read early drafts of the manuscript and offered valuable feedback that I incorporated into the book. The same applies to the two readers who reviewed the manuscript for Oxford University Press. I also thank Steven Heine for his friendship and helpful professional advice, as well as for commenting on a draft version of the introduction. Among my colleagues at the University of Florida, I am indebted to Richard Wang for checking the Chinese characters in the glossary and the bibliography. I would also like to acknowledge the support I received from my colleagues in the Religion Department, especially David Hackett, Manuel Vásquez, Vasudha Narayanan, and Jason Neelis. I am appreciative of the financial support I received from the College of Liberal Arts and Sciences at the University of Florida, which provided a generous summer grant that enabled me to go back to Komazawa in 2002 for follow-up research. I am especially grateful to Ruth Sheng for the Chinese calligraphy that graces the title pages, and for proofreading the Chinese text in the glossary and the bibliography.

I extend special thanks to Cynthia Read and Oxford University Press for their interest in my project and the skilled work on the manuscript. I would especially like to acknowledge the work of Linda Donnelly and Julia TerMaat. Finally, I wish to express gratitude to my wife, Hiroko Poceski, for her love, patience, and support.

Contents

Abbreviations and Conventions, xi

Introduction, 3

    Mazu and the Hongzhou School, 4
    The Study of Chan History, 7
    Images of the Hongzhou School, 8
    About this Volume, 11
    Summary of the Chapters, 14

PART I   History

1. The Life and Times of Mazu Daoyi, 21

    Early Years in Sichuan, 22
    Formative Monastic Training, 23
    Travel East, 25
    Study with Huairang, 26
    Initial Teaching in Fujian and Jiangxi, 29
    Training of Disciples in Hongzhou, 30
    Final Days and Passing Away, 32

2. Regional Spread of the Hongzhou School, 45

    Backgrounds of Mazu's Disciples, 45
    Xitang Zhizang, 47
    Baizhang Huaihai, 49

Other Monks Active in Jiangxi and the South, 52
Spread to Central China, 55
Growth in the Lower Yangtze Region, 56
Expansion to the North, 60
Mazu's Disciples in Chang'an, 61
Ruman and Chan in Luoyang, 68

3. The Hongzhou School and Mid-Tang Chan, 85

Pattern of Growth, 86
Literati Associations and Networks of Patronage, 89
Interactions with other Chan Lineages, 95
Contours of the Chan Movement, 99
Lineage and Religious Identities, 103
Reconfiguration of Chan Orthodoxy, 106
Influence on the Spread of Chan in Korea, 108
Transitions in Tang Chan, 110
Later Developments, 111

PART II   Doctrine and Practice

4. Doctrinal Contexts and Religious Attitudes, 125

The Traditions and Doctrines of Tang Buddhism, 126
Doctrinal Taxonomies, 129
Monastic Mores and Ideals, 131
Attitudes toward Meditation, 135
Canonicity and Attitudes toward Scriptural Authority, 139
Use of Scriptures, 144

5. Mind, Buddha, and the Way, 157

Detachment, 159
Expedient Means, 163
Mind and Buddha, 168
Some Critiques, 172
"It Is Not a Thing," 177
Ordinary Mind, 182

6. Path of Practice and Realization, 193

The "Sudden" and "Gradual" Paradigms, 194
A Vanishing Paradigm, 199

A Gradual Path of Practice, 203
Stages of the Path, 207
Comparable Conceptual Models, 212
Awakening and Realization, 215

Conclusion, 225

Appendix, 233

Glossary, 249

Bibliography, 257

Index, 275

Abbreviations and Conventions

BGL	*Baizhang guanglu* 百丈廣錄
BLZ	*Baolin zhuan* 寶林傳
CDL	*Jingde chuandeng lu* 景德傳燈錄
IBK	*Indogaku bukkyōgaku kenkyū* 印度學佛教學研究
JTS	*Jiu tangshu* 舊唐書
K	*Koryŏ taejanggyŏng* 高麗大藏經
KDBR	*Komazawa daigaku bukkyō gakubu ronshū* 駒澤大學佛教學部論集
MY	*Mazu yulu* 馬祖語錄
QTW	*Quan tang wen* 全唐文
SGSZ	*Song gaoseng zhuan* 宋高僧傳
SK	*[Komazawa daigaku] Shūgaku kenkyū* [駒澤大學]宗學研究
T	*Taishō shinshū daizōkyō* 大正新修大藏經
TG	*Tōhō gakuhō* 東方學報
TGDL	*Tiansheng guangdeng lu* 天聖廣燈錄
WYYH	*Wenyuan yinghua* 文苑英華
XTS	*Xin tangshu* 新唐書
XZJ	*Xu zangjing* 續藏經 (reprint of *Dai Nihon zokuzōkyō* 大日本續藏經)
ZBKK	*Zen bunka kenkyūjo kiyō* 禪文化研究所紀要
ZG	*Zen no goroku* 禪の語錄
ZJL	*Zongjing lu* 宗鏡錄
ZK	*Zengaku kenkyū* 禪學研究
ZTJ	*Zutang ji* 祖堂集

Chinese words are transliterated according to the Pinyin system, with the exception of names that are better known in another transcription, and in cases of citations of other works that use the Wade-Giles system; for Japanese, I use the Revised Hepburn Romanization system. References to classical Chinese texts include the title, followed by fascicle and page number; when they are included in larger collections, such as the *Taishō* and *Zokuzōkyō* editions of the Buddhist canon, I also include the abbreviated title of the collection, followed by the volume, page, and column number (a, b, or c). For example, CDL 14, T 51.310c, stands for *Jingde chuandeng lu*, fascicle 14, in the *Taishō* canon, volume 51, page 310, bottom column. The translations from Chinese texts are my own, unless otherwise noted. When using the translations of others, I have often revised them, sometimes considerably. When referring to the geographical locations of various monasteries, mountains, and other sites, I use present-day provincial boundaries.

Ordinary Mind as the Way

Introduction

The emergence of Chan and its establishment as a major school of Chinese Buddhism were significant events in the religious history of the Tang dynasty (618–907), part of an ongoing transformation of Buddhism in late medieval China that reflected the Sinification of its beliefs, doctrines, practices, and institutions. At the center of these changes were the new Buddhist schools of the Sui (581–618) and Tang periods: Chan, Huayan, and Tiantai, as well as the Pure Land (Jingtu) tradition, which, although it was not a "school" in the same sense as the other three, introduced popular beliefs and practices that were widely diffused throughout Chinese Buddhism. The emergence of these new schools involved a rethinking of received teachings and traditions and the production of new religious paradigms whose doctrinal systems and soteriological models remain crowning achievements of Chinese Buddhism. The growth of Chan during this period paved the way for its dominant position within elite Chinese Buddhism and had significant ramifications for the later history of Buddhism throughout East Asia.

This book is concerned with a key phase in the history of Tang Chan. It focuses on the Hongzhou school, which, under the leadership of Mazu Daoyi (709–788) and his disciples, replaced the various traditions of early Chan and dominated the Chan movement for nearly a century, from around the aftermath of the An Lushan rebellion (755–763) until after the Huichang-era (841–845) persecution of Buddhism.[1] As Mazu and his leading disciples came to occupy central positions in the pantheon of Chan worthies, stories about their spiritual exploits became prominent fixtures in traditional Chan lore.

Ever since those records assumed canonical status during the Song period (960–1281), generations of devotees and other admirers have venerated them as models of Chan wisdom and as normative statements of orthodoxy.

But the romanticized image of the Hongzhou school as an iconoclastic tradition expressed in later Chan texts—and widely reproduced in popular and scholarly works on Chan/Zen—is at odds with the historical realities of Tang Chan. A starting point for studying the Hongzhou school, therefore, is the apparent gap between its history and the pseudo-history or mythology presented in Song-era (or later) records and chronicles. The two are intertwined and often hard to disentangle, but nonetheless they are two separate issues. Accordingly, we need to treat them as distinct (even if related) topics of scholarly inquiry, pertinent to two different historical periods. Within that framework, this book is primarily about certain aspects of Tang religious history, rather than about how later generations of Chan historians and adherents appropriated and reworked that history to meet their ideological objectives and religious predilections.

The emergence of the Linji school as the bearer of Chan orthodoxy during the Song period reinforced the Hongzhou school's prominent status within Chan history. Because its putative founder, Linji Yixuan (d. 866), was Mazu's third-generation disciple, Linji Chan assumed the role of the direct heir and main representative of the Hongzhou school.[2] As the Linji school maintained its dominant position during the subsequent epochs—not only in China but also spreading to Korea, Japan, and Vietnam—the Hongzhou school gained additional acceptance. For over a millennium, the legacy of the Hongzhou school—real and imagined—continued to shape the religious and social identities of the Chan/Zen traditions in East Asia. Even today, it continues to serve as an article of faith and a reference point for the demarcation of orthodoxy.

In view of the Hongzhou school's prominent place in Buddhist history, a scholarly treatment of its formative period has long been overdue. This book attempts to fill that lacuna in Buddhist studies by presenting a comprehensive study of the Hongzhou school's history and doctrines.

Mazu and the Hongzhou School

The focus of the book is on Mazu and his first-generation disciples, a period that constitutes the main phase of the Hongzhou school's growth. In terms of Tang chronology, it coincides with the dynasty's middle period and covers the reigns of four emperors: Daizong (r. 762–779), Dezong (r. 779–805), Shunzong (r. 805), and Xianzong (r. 805–820). The analysis of the Hongzhou school's development presented here is set against the larger backdrop of Tang religious history, including developments in early Chan. Consequently, it takes into account both the patterns of continuity and the points of divergence between the Hongzhou school and the rest of Tang Buddhism.

The Hongzhou school established an identity that revolved around the principles of discipleship and membership in Mazu's lineage, which were reinforced by the espousal of common religious attitudes and teachings. The epitaphs of Mazu's disciples explicitly affirm these intimate links among various monks—as students of Mazu and members of the same Chan lineage—suggesting that they were conscious of being members of a distinct tradition. In these epitaphs, we repeatedly find statements to the effect that monk so-and-so was a disciple of Mazu and a member of his lineage, which was part of a larger Chan tradition. On the other hand, we need to be careful not to reify their group identity and construe it in narrow sectarian terms. As we will see, that identity was flexible and lacked an independent institutional basis. It also overlapped with other religious identities, including those of memberships in the monastic order and the larger Chan movement.[3] Thus, although we speak in terms of such distinctions—Hongzhou school versus Chan versus Buddhism—we need to keep in mind that within the Tang context the lines of demarcation among them were porous and easily crossed.

In contrast to the traditional image of a radical movement that grew on the margins of Tang Buddhism, the Hongzhou school quickly evolved from a regional into an empire-wide tradition, occupying a position at the center and representing the mainstream. Numerous disciples of Mazu secured prominent clerical positions throughout China, including the two capitals. They attracted scores of disciples, some coming from as far away as Korea, and received support and approbation from famous literati, powerful officials, and the imperial court. Many of them were well educated and from gentry families. They were versed in canonical literature, and in their sermons they frequently quoted and alluded to scriptural passages. As part of the religious establishment, they upheld the norms of monastic life and acted in accord with their priestly status.

The emergence of the Hongzhou school on the Tang religious scene coincided with the gradual decline and disappearance of the diverse schools of early Chan. Given that by the early ninth century Mazu's disciples had become bearers of Chan orthodoxy, the Hongzhou school supplanted the earlier Chan traditions, a development that had notable unifying and consolidating effects on the previously fragmented Chan movement. We can even speculate that if it were not for the ascendancy of the Hongzhou school, with the fading of the early schools the nascent Chan movement faced the prospect of a precipitous decline, perhaps even sinking into oblivion, with lasting ramifications for the subsequent history of Chan and Chinese Buddhism.

In their unifying and stabilizing roles, Mazu and his followers furthered the integration of Chan into the Buddhist mainstream, even as, paradoxically, they also reinforced their tradition's distinct identity. They presented an inclusive and expansive version of Chan as a tradition within Buddhism, putting forward their teachings as the essence of Buddhist spirituality. As a result, they nudged the Chan school toward a central course, away from antinomian extremes such as those of the Baotang school in Sichuan or the divisive sectarianism epitomized by Shenhui's (684–758) acrimonious campaigns against the Northern school. In that sense, the rise of the Hongzhou school represented a consolidation and maturation of the Chan movement, a culmination of its evolution during the Tang period.

The Hongzhou school's successful growth was largely predicated on its ability to mediate tensions arising from its engagement with established teachings and traditions. That is to say, its success in becoming the dominant tradition of Chan depended primarily on its capacity to balance adherence to established norms and ideals, on the one hand, with the need to forge an identity by selecting and reformulating aspects of received traditions on the other. The emergence of the Hongzhou school therefore represents a significant stage in the complex and protracted evolution of Chan, one that involved neither a drastic paradigm shift driven by an iconoclastic ethos, nor merely a predictable continuation of received traditions.

That balancing act is evident in the Hongzhou school's doctrinal formulations, whose considerable appeal was a significant factor in its growth and popularity. Mazu and his disciples introduced innovative doctrinal formulations and fresh perspectives on spiritual cultivation. Their sermons and discussions are among the most lucid and engaging records of religious teachings from the Tang period. The sermons exemplify a direct approach to doctrine and practice, divested of superfluous embellishments and extraneous elements. They are presented in a distinct Chan idiom, and yet they are identifiable as products of the broader intellectual and religious milieus of medieval Chinese Buddhism. As part of their recasting of Mahāyāna doctrine, monks associated with the Hongzhou school took rarefied concepts and ideals commonly accepted as key elements of Buddhism and expressed them in distinctive ways that appealed to monks with contemplative interests. For example, canonically inspired notions about the inherence of Buddhahood and the immediacy of practice and awakening were crystallized into such well-known Chan adages as "mind is Buddha" and "ordinary mind is the Way."

Mazu and his disciples were also adept at presenting their teachings in ways that appealed to sophisticated officials and literati. An ability to catch the imagination of the sociopolitical and cultural elites was crucial, since they were key supporters and the institutional viability of Buddhist groups depended on their patronage. As can be seen from poems and documents composed by Tang writers, many of them were attracted to the Chan teachers' religious personalities and teachings, and captivated by the prospect of being able to obtain a glimpse of the ineffable realm of awakening.

The Study of Chan History

Mazu and his leading disciples receive cursory treatment in a number of works on the history of Chinese Chan, and the records of key figures—Mazu, Bai-zhang Huaihai (749–814), Dazhu Huihai (fl. 8th c.), and Huangbo Xiyun (d. 850?)—are available in English translations, although all of them in a non-scholarly format and directed toward a general audience.[4] Specialized studies of Chan that deal with various aspects of its history, literature, and doctrines also consider the Hongzhou school;[5] particularly notable is the putative establishment of a unique system of Chan monasticism, traditionally attributed to Baizhang, which has been treated in a number of publications.[6]

While the Hongzhou school has not received the attention it deserves, scholarship has made substantial progress in other areas of Chan studies. Significant contributions have been made by scholars such as Yanagida Seizan, Shiina Kōyū, and Ishii Shūdō in Japan, and John R. McRae, Robert Buswell, Bernard Faure, and others in the West. In contrast to the elegant simplicity of the traditional genealogical narrative about the early transmission of Chan, modern research presents a different picture of the formative period, characterized by greater complexity and diversity. Much of our new knowledge about the early phase of the Chan school's development was made possible by the redis-covery of early Chan records that had been lost for centuries. Most of these texts were among the Dunhuang manuscripts, discovered during the early twenti-eth century.[7] Other long-lost texts, such as *Zutang ji* (Hall of the Patriarchs' Collection), were rediscovered in monastic libraries in Korea and Japan.[8]

The scholarly focus on researching early Chan documents recovered from Dunhuang and elsewhere was a response to the excitement generated by the discovery of long-forgotten texts that shed light on a poorly understood phase of Chan history. By utilizing these documents and critically reexamining other extant sources, we are now in a better position to draw a balanced out-line of early Chan history and to reassess the Chan school's position vis-à-vis other traditions of Chinese Buddhism. For example, we now have two English-language books on the Northern school—which traditional historians glossed over as a collateral lineage—along with other studies published by Japanese scholars.[9]

The study of the Dunhuang manuscripts exposed fundamental problems with traditional conceptions of early Chan history as a straight line of trans-mission stemming from Bodhidharma and the early patriarchs. Instead, re-search into early Chan texts revealed a remarkable diversity. Examples of such texts include *Lengqie shizi ji* (Record of the Teachers and Disciples of the Laṅkāvatāra), *Lidai fabao ji* (Record of the Dharma Jewel through Successive Generations, compiled c. 774), the records of Heze Shenhui (684–758), and the

TABLE I.I. Schools/Lineages of Early Chan

School/lineage	Leader/"founder"	Main location
East Mountain (Dongshan)	Hongren (601–674)	Hubei
Northern	Shenxiu (606?–706)	Chang'an, Luoyang
Heze	Shenhui (684–758)	Luoyang
Niutou (Ox Head)	Farong (594–657)	Jiangsu, other
Jingzhong	Wuxiang (684–762)	Sichuan
Baotang	Wuzhu (714–774)	Sichuan

writings of Guifeng Zongmi (780–841). From them we learn that the various lineages formed during the early Tang period (shown in table I.1) espoused a plurality of doctrinal standpoints and soteriological approaches. They included those of the Northern school, the Niutou school, the Jingzhong and Baotang schools in Sichuan, and the Heze lineage of Shenhui.[10] All of them staked claims to socioreligious legitimacy by introducing their versions of Chan orthodoxy and asserting the authenticity of their dharma transmission.

Besides the research on early Chan, there have also been advances in the study of Song Chan, reflecting a general trend toward greater scholarly interest in that period.[11] In contrast, there is a shortage of studies of Chan history that cover the second half of the Tang era or the Five Dynasties period (907–960),[12] even though the subsequent Chan/Zen traditions throughout East Asia came to consider this to be the golden age or classical period of Chan.[13] This study attempts to begin redressing that imbalance, thereby contributing to the scholarly reassessment of the Chan school's far-reaching and multifaceted transformation during the Tang-Song transition.

Images of the Hongzhou School

The normative account of early Chan history—generally still accepted by the Chan/Zen traditions—is deceptively straightforward. The narrative of Chan's formative development tends to follow a linear pattern, framed around a lineage of patriarchs. According to this approach, the tradition began in China with the Indian monk Bodhidharma, the first Chinese "patriarch" (*zu* or *zushi*, sometimes translated as "ancestor"), whose transmission of the essence of Buddhist enlightenment was passed on from teacher to disciple until it reached Huineng (638–713), the legendary "sixth patriarch." Although the transmission of a single Chan lineage supposedly ended with Huineng, the Southern school that descended from him prospered and had an undisputed claim to orthodoxy. After branching into two lineages under Huineng's two prominent second-generation disciples, Mazu and Shitou Xiqian (700–790), the Southern school entered its classical period or golden age. Ever since, all traditions of Chan/Zen throughout East Asia have traced their origins to it.

Traditionalist accounts of Chan history place Mazu and his disciples at the center of novel developments that ushered the Chan tradition into a period of remarkable growth and innovation. According to these accounts, the Hongzhou school was a revolutionary movement that rejected mainstream mores, teachings, and institutions, thereby charting a new path for the Chan school's independent growth as a principal tradition of Chinese Buddhism. The classical form of these depictions was formulated during the Song dynasty, as is evident in the Chan "histories" compiled at the time, the most influential of which was *Jingde chuandeng lu* (Jingde [Era] Record of the Transmission of the Lamp; composed in 1004). These texts—which came to epitomize Chan's supposedly unique approach and independent spirit—conveyed an iconoclastic image of the Hongzhou school that persists to this day. Here we find portrayals of Mazu and his disciples as iconoclasts par excellence, who transgress established norms and subvert received traditions. A well-known example of such radical representations is the story about Mazu's disciple Nanquan (748–834) killing a cat. Later versions of the story, such as the following, also involve Zhaozhou (778–897), Nanquan's leading disciple:

> [One day] Nanquan came across the monks from the eastern and western halls of the monastery, who were quarreling over a cat. He told the assembled monks, "If you are able to say something [that will accord with the truth], then you will save the cat. If you cannot say anything, then I will kill the cat." The monks had no response, and Nanquan killed the cat. [Later, when] Zhaozhou returned from outside, Nanquan told him about what had happened. Zhaozhou then took off his shoes, put them on the top of his head, and went out. Nanquan said, "If you were here earlier, you would have saved the cat."[14]

According to tradition, stories of this kind exemplify the unique style and ethos of the Hongzhou school, which at times seem to border on antinomianism. Examples of similar stories include those of Mazu kicking his disciple Shuilao into a puddle of water[15] and the burning of a Buddha image by Danxia (739–824), another disciple of Mazu, who supposedly performed this sacrilegious act in order to warm himself on a cold winter day.[16] This kind of story is by far the best-known part of traditional Chan lore. These dramatic anecdotes are behind the romanticized images of Mazu and his disciples as unconventional spiritual virtuosi, leaders of a radical movement that with its idiosyncratic teaching methods—which included shouts and beatings—flouted the established standards of religious behavior.

Scholars who pioneered the field of Chan/Zen studies gave academic credence to the iconoclastic image of the Hongzhou school. Early scholars presented a romanticized view of Tang Chan that privileged the iconoclastic stories as key records of Chan's inimitable wisdom. In spite of their contrasting views about Chan history, in their pioneering studies both D. T. Suzuki and Hu Shih portrayed the emergence of Chan as a rupture with previous Buddhist traditions, a decisive event in the development of a distinctly Chinese form of Buddhism. According to Hu Shih, "Chinese Chan" became properly established only with Mazu and his disciples.[17] Mazu's disciples did away with "the medieval ghosts, the gods, the bodhisattvas and the Buddhas"; eighth-century Chan was "no Chan at all, but a Chinese reformation or revolution within Buddhism."[18]

The writings of the next generation of Chan/Zen scholars, such as Yanagida and Heinrich Dumoulin, are products of better informed and more sophisticated scholarship.[19] Nonetheless, they too largely accept an image of Tang Chan as a totally new tradition whose formation represented a culmination of the Chinese transformation of Buddhism. According to Yanagida, the Hongzhou school formed its religious identity by a wholesale repudiation of established beliefs and practices.[20] The actual creation of the Chan school, in Yanagida's view, occurred under Mazu and his great disciples. This was tantamount to the establishment of a completely new and distinctively Chinese religious tradition that reflected the cultural ethos and spiritual sentiments of the Chinese people:

> The Chan transmitted from India escaped from the confines of
> the mysterious practice of meditation and samādhi, and melted into
> everyday life as a religion of the pragmatic Chinese people from
> about the ninth century. That meant the onset of a new Chan
> school that did not exist in Indian Buddhism. The leading actors in
> the establishment of that new Chan school, who appear in the
> genealogical chart presented on the left, were Mazu of Jiangxi and
> Shitou of Hunan.[21]

While in accord with tradition Yanagida mentions Shitou, he makes it clear that Mazu was the main figure in this historical process. I discuss Yanagida's assessment of the Hongzhou school in more detail in the appendix; here it will suffice to say that, notwithstanding his huge contributions to the study of early Chan history and literature, his views about the Hongzhou school reflect the influence of traditional Zen perspectives. They are still based on a problematic reading of misleading primary sources, especially the apocryphal "encounter dialogue" (*kien mondō* in Japanese, or *jiyuan wenda* in Chinese) stories presented in Song collections (such as Nanquan's anecdote cited previously), and exemplify an uncritical acceptance of normative interpretations of their meaning and significance.[22]

As I have shown elsewhere, an unreflective reliance on the Song texts—especially the iconoclastic stories contained in them—is problematic because we cannot trace any of the encounter dialogues back to the Tang period.[23] No source from the Tang period indicates that there was even an awareness of the existence of the encounter-dialogue format, let alone that it was the main medium of instruction employed in Chan circles. The radicalized images of Mazu, Nanquan, and other Chan teachers from the mid-Tang period make their first appearance in the middle of the tenth century, well over a century after their deaths. The earliest text that contains such anecdotes is *Zutang ji* (compiled in 952), and the iconoclastic stories became normative only during the Song period.[24] Accordingly, we can best understand such records as apocryphal or legendary narratives. They were a focal element of imaginative Chan lore created in response to specific social and religious circumstances and served as a centerpiece of an emerging Chan ideology. By means of these stories, novel religious formulations and nascent orthodoxies were retroactively imputed back to the great Chan teachers of the Tang period. The connection with the glories of the bygone Tang era bestowed a sense of sanctity and was a potent tool for legitimizing the Chan school in the religious world of Song China.

Nanquan's story and similar anecdotes thus have little to tell us about Chan during the mid-Tang period. Once we move beyond this sort of "evidence" and look instead at extant Tang sources, the unabashed iconoclasm habitually associated with the Hongzhou school gives way to a more complex and nuanced historical reality. The historical image of Mazu and his disciples we are confronted with is not simply that of a radical religious movement bent on subverting established norms and traditions. Instead, as we will see, the Hongzhou school comes across as being much closer to the mainstream of Buddhism—and to early Chan—than Zen apologetics would have us believe.

About This Volume

In the chapters that follow, I paint as detailed and nuanced picture of the Hongzhou school's history and teachings as possible on the basis of the extant sources, and within the confines of a volume of manageable size. I rely on Tang-period materials as much as possible, especially for ascertaining the broader historical trajectories and the basic character of the Hongzhou school's teachings.[25] Considering the relative paucity of primary sources, at times I also make selective use of later sources, typically to fill gaps in the narrating of specific events, to illustrate basic principles, or to help establish issues of secondary importance. Considering the time frame of the subject matter and the quantity and nature of the available sources, I am aware that any study of this kind is by definition tentative, and inevitably some ambiguities will remain. A comprehensive portrayal of something as intricate and multifarious as a religious tradition is an open-ended interpretative endeavor that is intrinsically contestable. This is true of any kind of historical or cultural analysis, including those of contemporary cultures or religious traditions, to which we have direct access and manifold avenues for gathering research data.[26] But it is especially the case with a tradition, such as the Hongzhou school, that flourished over a millennium ago and that we can approach only through fragmentary literary artifacts. An analysis of this kind thus unavoidably entails making sense of fragmented sets of data and ascertaining their relations to complex conceptual structures and elusive historical contexts.

In the process of decoding ancient texts and unraveling intricate historical processes and ideas, one inevitably has to make debatable interpretative decisions, often without the full benefit of collaborating sources or irrefutable proofs. That, however, cannot serve as an excuse for paralysis, indecision, and endless self-reflection. Considering the importance of the subject matter, we have no choice but to forge ahead and make the best use of the available materials. Notwithstanding the problems of sources and interpretations, the available texts, when used carefully, make it possible to ascertain the overall pattern of the Hongzhou school's growth and its place in Tang Buddhism. It is also possible to arrive at a general understanding of the doctrinal outlooks and religious attitudes adopted by Mazu and his disciples, as depicted in the extant records, even if specific issues might be open to interpretation. I hope that this study will stimulate a renewed interest and appreciation of the Hongzhou school and the Tang era, and contribute to our general knowledge of the history of Buddhism in late medieval China.

The notion that the Hongzhou school's teaching constituted a kind of systematic whole, evident in the doctrinal analysis presented in Part II, does not preclude an appreciation of the fact that individual texts adopt peculiar perspectives and exhibit distinctive features. Nevertheless, overall the early stratum of the Hongzhou school's records assumes a shared outlook and conveys a general sense of doctrinal coherence. The various texts adopt a common idiom, deal with analogous themes and issues, embrace joint perspectives, incorporate cross-references, and invoke familiar sources of authority, including canonical texts and the teachings of Mazu. Moreover, the earliest sources, such as the stele inscriptions, make it clear that individual monks associated with the Hongzhou school saw themselves as followers of Mazu and his teachings, even if they did not draw sharp lines of demarcation between those and other religious identities, including their membership in the Buddhist monastic order. All of these point to close personal ties, collective religious attitudes, and shared intellectual frames of reference among Mazu's disciples, who saw and described themselves as members of a distinct lineage that was part of the larger Chan movement. This is especially evident in the case of the disciples active in the Tang capital, who took specific steps to bolster the authority and prestige of the Hongzhou school, such as securing a posthumous title for Mazu from the imperial court and commissioning an inscription for his relatively obscure teacher, Nanyue Huairang (677–744).[27]

In the light of these considerations, Part II of this volume aims at uncovering the common elements and sketching the Hongzhou school's theoretical stances and practical approaches to spiritual cultivation, as presented in the main sources. The approach to the subject matter is thematic, focusing on key themes and issues derived from the extant sources, with chapter 5 largely revolving around Mazu's sermons, while in chapter 6 the focus is on Baizhang's record. I have selected this holistic approach, instead of dealing with individual texts separately, in part because the main texts are available in English translations (even if some of them are dated and in need of more exacting scholarly treatment). The reader is thus able to compare the doctrinal analysis presented here against the Chinese originals and/or the English translations of the main sources.

In my examination of the Hongzhou school's teachings, I have been careful to let the original texts guide my doctrinal analysis. I have deliberately avoided selecting parts of the texts that support a predetermined doctrinal position or point of view. Even so, there are unavoidable elements of interpretation in my study, evident in my use and analysis of the original sources. The accounts of the Hongzhou school's history and doctrines presented in this volume are therefore based on my reading and analysis of the extant sources in relation to the pertinent religious and historical contexts, and I make no claim that they are the only possible interpretations. In fact, ample evidence of alternative explanations is discernible in the treatments of the Hongzhou school's teachings throughout subsequent Chan/Zen history, which was largely a series of interpretative distortions that privileged an iconoclastic ethos represented by the encounter-dialogue model. Notwithstanding these caveats, I am confident that the analysis presented here serves as a much-needed historical reassessment and a corrective to popular images and stereotypical depictions of Mazu and his disciples as leaders of an anticonventional, iconoclastic tradition. In contrast to traditionalist interpretations, this study takes into account the original mid-Tang context; moreover, it is based on careful analysis, judicious use, and critical assessment of the provenance of the Chan records of sayings and other pertinent sources.

The book is divided into two parts, each consisting of three chapters. Part I is a study of the Hongzhou school's history, while part II examines its doctrines and practices. While this arrangement of the material is introduced for the sake of convenience and follows a familiar organizational pattern, it is not meant to suggest an artificial barrier or division between the study of history and the study of thought. The two parts of the book are closely related and mutually reinforcing. Shedding light on each other, they both support my basic interpretation of the Hongzhou school as a culmination of developments set in motion by early Chan. Within that interpretative scheme, the Hongzhou school functioned as a catalyst for the consolidation of the whole Chan movement, which furthered an ongoing integration of Chan into the Buddhist mainstream and reflected the broader social and religious predicaments of the mid-Tang period. Accordingly, the formation of the Hongzhou school's teachings described in Part II should be read in the light of the social and historical backgrounds described in Part I and vice versa.

Summary of the Chapters

The study of the Hongzhou school's historical growth begins with a biographical overview of Mazu's life. The first chapter covers his entire monastic career, starting with his initial engagement with Buddhism as a young man and his monastic ordination in his native Sichuan. It then takes us through his early travels and studies, his establishment of monastic communities in Fujian and Jiangxi, his gradual rise to fame, and eventually his death in Hongzhou as a revered religious leader with large monastic and lay followings. The exploration of Mazu's monastic life situates his activities within the context of the local communities where he resided and his interactions with other monastic and lay individuals.

The second chapter focuses on Mazu's immediate disciples and surveys the regional growth of the Hongzhou school during the late eighth and early ninth centuries. The discussion is organized according to regional boundaries, encompassing four main geographical areas: Jiangxi and the rest of southern China, central China or the middle Yangtze area, the lower Yangtze area, and the North. Xitang (735–817) and Baizhang receive individual treatment as Mazu's leading disciples. I also consider separately the spread of the Hongzhou school into the two Tang capitals. The activities of Mazu's disciples in Chang'an and Luoyang form an important chapter in the Hongzhou school's history. By overlooking these monks and their activities, traditional and modern historians misconstrued the pattern of the Hongzhou school's growth and its place in Tang Buddhism.

The third chapter concludes the study of the Hongzhou school's history by exploring the pattern of its expansion, situating its growth in relation to the broader framework of mid-Tang Chan, and surveying its impact on the historical evolution of the Chan tradition. It begins with a discussion of the Hongzhou school's regional growth and the networks of patronage that facilitated it, thereby challenging the prevalent view of it as a regional tradition that shied away from seeking patronage from those in high places. That is followed by a survey of the Hongzhou school's interactions with other Chan traditions and its position within the wider milieu of early-ninth-century Chan. The remaining sections explore the function of ancestral lineage in the construction of religious identities within the context of Tang Chan, the key transitions occasioned by the rise of the Hongzhou school, its impact on the growth of Chan on the Korean peninsula, and its effect on the subsequent development of the Chan movement.

The fourth chapter initiates the study of the Hongzhou school's teachings. Its first part surveys the religious and intellectual milieus of Tang Buddhism, which formed the backdrop for the development of the Hongzhou school's doctrines and its approaches to spiritual cultivation. The second part offers an analysis of the Hongzhou school's attitudes in four key areas of medieval religious life: monastic mores and ideals, meditative praxis, canonicity and religious authority, and the use of scriptures. My exploration of their basic doctrinal and ethical frameworks shows that Mazu and his disciples were engaged in the creative reformulation of age-old monastic ideals and outlooks, which helped situate the Hongzhou school within a larger nexus of canonically inspired traditions of contemplative monasticism.

The fifth chapter explores key themes in the Hongzhou school's doctrinal formulations. It draws attention to the relentless attacks on all form of dogmatism, including reifying conceptualizations of the mind derived from Chinese interpretations of the Buddha-nature theory, which forms a central theme that links together the main sources. A substantial part of the chapter is concerned with the flexible and context-sensitive interpretive strategies employed in discussions of famous Chan adages associated with Mazu, especially "mind is Buddha" and "ordinary mind is the Way."

The final chapter examines the Hongzhou school's conception of a Chan path of practice and realization. Based primarily on Baizhang's record, it focuses on that text's explication of a path of spiritual practice defined in terms of three distinct stages that represent increasingly subtle forms of detachment and deeper insight into the nature of reality. The investigation of the three stages is followed by an analysis of comparable conceptual schemata formulated by the scholastic traditions of medieval Chinese Buddhism. The chapter ends with a note on Baizhang's intimations of the realm of awakening, which he conceptualized as a consummate perfection of detachment and transcendence, and a fulfillment of the Bodhisattva's selfless activity of helping others.

NOTES

1. The term "Hongzhou school" comes from the name of the Tang prefecture, located in the northern part of present-day Jiangxi province—the area around Nanchang, the provincial capital—where Mazu taught during the final years of his life. Because a number of his disciples, including Xitang and Baizhang, were also active in the same prefecture, Hongzhou came to be perceived as the geographical center of their tradition, although it is unclear whether they actually used the term to refer to themselves.

2. In the strict sense of the word, Linji was not the "founder" of the Linji school; later generations of disciples and writers affixed this designation to him retroactively, long after he passed away. We can say the same of the "founders" of various Chan schools/lineages, starting with Bodhidharma as the founder of Chinese Chan and Huineng as the founder of the Southern school. A similar situation exists among the other schools of medieval Chinese Buddhism; for example, neither Dushun nor Fazang (traditionally regarded as the first and third patriarch, respectively) actually established the Huayan school, which came to be recognized as a distinct school of Tang Buddhism only after their lifetimes.

3. For a more detailed discussion of the Hongzhou school's group identity, see "Lineage and Religious Identities" in chapter 3.

4. See Cheng-chien Bhikshu [Mario Poceski], *Sun-Face Buddha: The Teachings of Ma-tsu and the Hung-chou School of Ch'an*; Thomas Cleary, *Sayings and Doings of Pai-chang*; John Blofeld, *The Zen Teaching of Instantaneous Awakening* (originally published as *The Zen Teaching of Hui Hai on Sudden Illumination*) and *The Zen Teaching of Huang-po on the Transmission of Mind*. I have learned that a new English-language book by Jinhua Jia on the subject came out in print just as this volume was being readied for typesetting.

5. Most of these studies are in Japanese. Notable examples include Suzuki Tetsuo, *Tō-godai no zenshū: Konan, Kōsei hen* (information about monks associated with the Hongzhou school is scattered throughout the book) and *Tō-godai zenshū shi* (esp. 130–59, 259–72, 369–89); Yanagida Seizan, "Goroku no rekishi: Zen bunken no seiritsu shiteki kenkyū," 475–548. In English, a rare example of an article dealing with the Hongzhou school is Jia Jinhua, "Doctrinal Reformation of the Hongzhou School of Chan Buddhism," which is taken directly from her 1999 dissertation, "The Hongzhou School of Chan Buddhism and the Tang Literati." There are also the reflections on Huangbo in Dale S. Wright, *Philosophical Meditations on Zen Buddhism*. Additional relevant publications are cited in the following chapters as appropriate.

6. See "Baizhang Huaihai" in chapter 2, especially n. 50.

7. For comprehensive studies of the Chan manuscripts discovered in Dunhuang, see Tanaka Ryōshō, *Tonkō zenshū bunken no kenkyū*, and Shinohara Hisao and Tanaka Ryōshō, *Tonkō butten to zen*.

8. For more information on *Zutang ji*, see Albert Welter, "Lineage and Context in the *Patriarch's Hall Collection* and the *Transmission of the Lamp*," and Yanagida Seizan, "*Sodōshū* no shiryō kachi."

9. See Bernard Faure, *The Will to Orthodoxy: A Critical Genealogy of Northern Chan Buddhism*, and John R. McRae, *The Northern School and the Formation of Early Ch'an Buddhism*.

10. The occasionally interchangeable use of the terms "lineage" and "school" (and sometimes "tradition") reflects the ambiguity in the use of *zong* (and other related terms) in the primary sources. Generally speaking, the term "school" has wider connotations. However, as the notion of lineage usually functions as a key principle in establishing the distinctive identity of a given school of Chan, the distinction between the two meanings is often blurred. My use of these terms seeks to retain awareness of that ambiguity and avoid imputing to the original sources a sense of philological precision or rigid definitions that they lack.

11. An exemplary study of Song era Chan, focusing on the Caodong school, is Ishii Shūdō, *Sōdai zenshūshi no kenkyū: Chūgoku sōtōshū to dōgen zen*. For additional examples of studies of Song Buddhism, see the articles in Peter N. Gregory and Daniel A. Getz, Jr., *Buddhism in the Sung*, especially the articles on Chan by Griffith Foulk and Morten Schlütter.

12. Exceptions pertinent to the Five Dynasties period are Albert Welter, *The Meaning of Myriad Good Deeds: A Study of Yung-ming Yen-shou and Wan-shan t'ung-kuei chi*, and parts of the two volumes by Suzuki cited in n. 5. Also definitely worth consulting is Albert Welter's *Monks, Rulers, and Literati: The Political Ascendancy of Chan Buddhism*, which covers both the Five Dynasties and Song periods; unfortunately, the book came out after the work on this manuscript was completed, and I was unable to incorporate the invaluable research presented in it.

13. The view that the second half of the Tang and the Five Dynasties were the classical period of Chan is widely accepted by the Chan/Zen traditions in China, Korea, and Japan, and by many modern scholars, especially in East Asia. For example, see John R. McRae, "The Ox-head School of Chinese Ch'an Buddhism: From Early Ch'an to the Golden Age," 170, 207; and Henrich Dumoulin, *Zen Buddhism: A History*, vol. 1, 158–59. However, there are divergent opinions about the periodization of Chan history, and not everyone is in agreement with the use of the term "classical Chan." For example, Robert Buswell has argued that "classical Chan" should be used primarily to refer to the Northern Song tradition, when, he believes, Chan reached the pinnacle of its religious development, exemplified by the *kanhua* practice formulated by Dahui (1089–1163). See Robert Buswell, "The 'Short-cut' Approach of *K'an-hua* Meditation: The Evolution of Practical Subitism in Chinese Ch'an Buddhism," 327–28. See also the discussion of the phases of Chan history in John R. McRae, *Seeing through Zen: Encounter, Genealogy, and Transformation in Chinese Chan Buddhism*, 11–21 (esp. 19). Any periodization of this sort inevitably involves elements of arbitrariness, and it is essentially a scholarly exercise that relies on hindsight. With that in mind and with some reservations, I use the term "classical Chan" while keeping in mind the distinction between the historical realities of the Tang epoch and the mythologized and romanticized images of it created during the Song and subsequent periods.

14. CDL 8, T 51.258a; cf. Chang Chung-yuan, *Original Teachings of Chan Buddhism*, 156. This is the earliest version of the whole story, compiled 170 years after Nanquan's death. The first part of the story (up to Nanquan's killing of the cat) appears in Deshan's biography in ZTJ 5.130 and predates the CDL version by half a century. The story is often repeated in later Chan texts and can be found in the three main *gongan* (or *kōan* in Japanese) collections: as cases no. 63 and 64 in *Biyan lu*, T 48.194c–95b (for an English translation, see Thomas Cleary and J. C. Cleary, *The Blue Cliff Record*, 406–11); in *Wumen guan*, T 48.294c; and as case no. 9 in *Zongrong lu*, T 48.232b–33a.

15. MY, XZJ 119.408a; and Cheng Chien, *Sun-Face Buddha*, 16. There is a different version of this story in *Gu zunsu yulu*; see XZJ 118.80d, and Cheng Chien, *Sun-Face Buddha*, 92 n. 58.

16. ZTJ 4.96–97; CDL 14, T 51.310c. The story is illustrated in a painting by Yintuolou, with an inscription by Chushi Fengqi (1297–1371), from the Yuan dynasty (1271–1367) and now in the possession of Nanzenji temple in Kyoto.

17. Huang Xianian, *Hu Shi ji*, 60.

18. Hu Shih, "Ch'an/Zen Buddhism in China: Its History and Method," 17. See also Suzuki's rejoinder to Hu's article, "Zen: A Reply to Hu Shih"; John R. McRae, "Religion as Revolution in Chinese Historiography: Hu Shih (1891–1962) on Shenhui (684–758)"; and Bernard Faure's critique of Suzuki's and Hu's views in his *Chan Insights and Oversights: An Epistemological Critique of the Chan Tradition*, 53–67, 94–99.

19. For Henrich Dumoulin's presentation of Mazu, see his *Zen Buddhism: A History*, vol. 1, 161–66.

20. See Yanagida, "The 'Recorded Sayings' Texts of Chinese Ch'an Buddhism," 186–87. For similar views of Tang Chan as a powerful Chinese reaction against the Buddhist traditions inherited from India, see Arthur F. Wright, *Buddhism in Chinese History*, 77–79, and Kenneth Ch'en, *Buddhism in China: A Historical Survey*, 350–64.

21. Yanagida, "Chūgoku zenshū shi," 48–49. The genealogical chart referred to in the last sentence represents the normative ancestral genealogy of the two branches of the "orthodox" Southern school that supposedly began with Huineng (see figure 3.1 in chapter 3). In it, Huineng represents the first generation; his obscure disciples Nanyue Huairang (677–744) and Qingyuan Xingsi (d. 740) constitute the second generation and serve as links with the crucial third generation, represented by their disciples Mazu and Shitou.

22. The term "encounter dialogue" is John McRae's translation of *kien mondō*, a term coined by Yanagida. For its definition, see John R. McRae, "The Antecedents of Encounter Dialogue in Chinese Ch'an Buddhism," 47–48.

23. See Mario Poceski, "*Mazu yulu* and the Creation of the Chan Records of Sayings."

24. Griffith Foulk has argued that the image of Chan's golden age constructed on the basis of the records of sayings and transmission of the lamp chronicles was a product of Song Chan ideology. He believes that because the texts that supposedly depict the teachings of Tang Chan teachers were written during the Song period, they are most relevant for the study of Song Chan, although he provides little evidence in support of his contentions and glosses over the historical complexities and ambiguities that surround the provenance of the pertinent sources. Accordingly, he describes those records as "a body of religious mythology, a sacred history that served polemical, ritual, and didactic functions in the world of Song Chan." Foulk, "Myth, Ritual, and Monastic Practice in Sung Ch'an Buddhism," 149–50.

25. Documents of Tang origin, although not as extensive as one might hope, include numerous commemorative inscriptions and a few records of teachings, such as Dazhu's treatise and Baizhang's record. For more on the various sources, see the appendix. My notes provide additional information about the various sources, both Tang and post-Tang, as appropriate.

26. See Clifford Geertz, *The Interpretation of Cultures*, 29.

27. See "Mazu's Disciples in Chang'an" in chapter 2.

PART I

History

I

The Life and Times of Mazu Daoyi

In the Hongzhou school's history, Mazu Daoyi looms large as the dominant "founding" figure. This study of the Hongzhou school's historical growth therefore begins with a biographical overview of his life and career as a Chan teacher.[1] The story of Mazu's life takes us on an extended journey, in both space and time, through one of the most fascinating dynastic epochs in China's long history. Temporally, the story begins during the years of political turmoil that followed the usurpation of the Tang throne by Empress Wu Zetian and the end of her reign (r. 690–705). Its early and middle parts coincide with the long reign of Emperor Xuanzong (r. 712–756), which was marked by unparalleled economic prosperity, political stability, and cultural flourishing—abruptly brought to an end in 755 with the onset of the An Lushan rebellion. The final part of Mazu's life story takes us to the early post-rebellion period, a time of momentous political, social, economic, and intellectual change.

Spatially, the story of Mazu's life begins in the provincial world of Hanzhou in the northern part of the remote province of Jiannan (roughly corresponding to present-day Sichuan), at the western edge of the Tang empire on the border with the Tibetan highlands. Its middle part takes us on long travels over Jiangnan (literally "South of the [Long] River"), a large region of fertile valleys, mountains, lakes, and rivers, which corresponds roughly to the present-day provinces of Hunan, Jiangxi, Zhejiang, and parts of Jiangsu and Fujian.[2] During the early Tang, Jiangnan was still a relatively underdeveloped provincial region. However, around the time of Mazu's move to the area, and especially after the rebellion, it came to play an increasingly important role in the economic and cultural life of the empire. This change was partly related to the demographic shifts occasioned by large transfers of population from the North to the South during the An Lushan rebellion and its aftermath, when an influx of refugees (including monks) displaced by the fighting in the North arrived in the South. The change in Jiangnan's status was also due to the increasing importance of the southern provinces as the most reliable source of tax revenue for the central government after the loss of effective governmental control over great areas in the northeast. Mazu's life story ends in Hongzhou, the capital of the prefecture of the same name in the north of Jiangxi, where he passed his final years as a prominent religious leader and a successful Chan teacher surrounded by a large number of disciples.

Early Years in Sichuan

Mazu was born in 709, during the brief reign of emperor Zhongzong (r. 705–710), in Sifang county, Hanzhou prefecture.[3] Hanzhou was located in Jiannan province (as Sichuan was known during the early eighth century), just northeast of the provincial capital Chengdu.[4] His family's surname was Ma. Later, in recognition of his status as one of the greatest Chan teachers, he came to be called Mazu (literally "Patriarch Ma").[5] According to his stele inscription, composed by the prominent official Quan Deyu (759–818) in 791, Mazu's family had resided in the Hanzhou area for many generations.[6] We do not have reliable information about his family's socioeconomic background, but a mention in Quan's inscription about his study of the Confucian canon implies that he received a classical education during his youth (see below).[7] This suggests he came from a local gentry background.[8]

Biographical sources, starting with the stele inscription, depict Mazu as a precocious child. The inscription states that he had an exceptional physical appearance and was unlike an ordinary person. Even as a young child, we are told, he did not play any games. In a passage intended to suggest that he was destined for greatness from childhood, the inscription describes his appearance and character: "He stood as imposing as a mountain, and was as still as dammed water of a deep river. His tongue was so broad and long that it covered his nose. The soles of his feet were nicely shaped as if they had inscribed letters on them. He received his perfect character and [superior] spiritual abilities from heaven."[9]

As a large tongue and marks on the feet are two of the thirty-two physical marks of a Buddha, the text implies that Mazu inherited his saintly character and prodigious spiritual abilities from previous lives, during which he had cultivated the Buddhist path. Such stories or statements about a particular monk's childhood experiences that reveal his early predisposition for the important religious role he was later to assume are not uncommon in the hagiographies of noted Chan monks. The same trope also turns up in other monastic biographies, and its earliest origins go back to secular biographies contained in the official dynastic histories.

Mazu entered monastic life during his teens in Zizhong, in his native province, and at that time he received the monastic name Daoyi. A passage from his stele inscription suggests some of the motives and considerations that were behind his decision to enter monastic life: "While still young, he came to consider the [ancient] nine schools of thought and the six [Confucian] classics inadequate. Being, after all, [merely] tools for governing the world, how could they be methods that aid transcendence of the world? The correct awakening of the [Buddhist] method of liberation alone is the locale of the mind of those who possess supreme wisdom."[10]

According to this passage, during his youth Mazu studied the Confucian classics and the works of ancient Chinese thinkers as part of an educational curriculum typical for sons of families belonging to the gentry. The inscription suggests that he was disillusioned with his studies, since the texts he read offered little spiritual guidance of the kind necessary for transcendence of the mundane world, the avowed goal of Buddhism. Formulaic testimonials of this sort about formative experiences are emblematic of monastic biographies, so in that sense the passage offers only a limited insight into the circumstances that influenced Mazu's choice of religious vocation. Unfortunately, we have no additional data about his family's circumstances at the time of his departure from secular life, and we know nothing of changes in the family's social standing or financial situation, or whether his parents influenced his choice of vocation.

Formative Monastic Training

Mazu's first Buddhist teacher was Reverend Tang (684–734) of Zizhou.[11] A noted figure in the local Chan movement in Sichuan, Reverend Tang—so called because his family surname was Tang—was better known by his monastic name, Chuji.[12] He was a disciple of Zhishen (609–702) of Zizhou, one of the main disciples of the putative fifth Chan patriarch Hongren (601–674).[13] Although Zhishen appears in the list of Hongren's ten great disciples recorded in Jingjue's (683–750) Lengqie shizi ji as second after Shenxiu (606?–706),[14] the leader of the Northern school, there is not much information about him. We know little about Mazu's relationship with Chuji, but it is important to note that from the very beginning of his monastic career Mazu had a close connection with the early Chan movement.

Mazu was ordained as a monk in 728, when he reached the age of twenty according to traditional Chinese reckoning (which considers a person one year old at birth). That was the age when, according to the Vinaya, he could receive ordination as a full-fledged monk (*bhikṣu*).[15] The sources disagree about where his ordination took place. According to the *Song gaoseng zhuan* biography, Mazu's ordination took place in Yuzhou (present-day Ba county, Sichuan province), whereas his stele inscription states he was ordained in Baxi (present-day Minyang county, Sichuan province).[16] Mazu's preceptor was Vinaya teacher (*lüshi*) Yuan,[17] about whom nothing more is known.

According to Zongmi's commentary of the *Perfect Enlightenment Scripture*, *Yuanjuejing dashu chao*, Mazu also studied under Chuji's disciple Reverend Jin (or Kim in Korean, which was his family name), who is better known by his religious name, Wuxiang (or Musang in Korean).[18] While the connection between Mazu and Wuxiang appears only in Zongmi's writings, it is probable that the two met. Wuxiang (684–762) was born in the Korean kingdom of Silla (668–935) as a member of the royal family. He was Chuji's foremost disciple and was among the leaders of the Chan movement in Sichuan. Wuxiang arrived in the Chinese capital Chang'an from his native land in 728. According to his biography in *Song gaoseng zhuan*, during his stay there he met with Emperor Xuanzong.[19] Subsequently, probably in 730 or soon thereafter, he moved to Zizhong in Sichuan. There he met Chuji and studied with him for about two years.[20] Most likely Wuxiang stayed with Chuji from 732 until Chuji's death in 734, after which he went to reside at Tianyu mountain. A few years later, at the invitation of the provincial military governor Zhangqiu Jianqiong (dates of birth and death unknown), Wuxiang went to reside in Jingzhong monastery in Chengdu, the provincial capital and the largest and wealthiest city in the southwestern part of the Tang empire.[21] Zhangqiu, who rose to fame because of his successful role in the war against the Tibetans, held a post in Sichuan between 739 and 746,[22] which means that Wuxiang's move to Chengdu occurred at some point during that time.[23]

Jingzhong monastery was one of the important official monasteries in the provincial capital, and was also the site of monastic ordination ceremonies performed at regular intervals.[24] During his long stay at Jingzhong monastery, Wuxiang emerged not only as Chuji's leading disciple but also as arguably the leading figure of the Chan movement in Sichuan. His teachings also reached Tibet, where he was probably the best-known Chan teacher.[25] According to Zongmi, Wuxiang's main disciples were Shenhui (720–794) of Jingzhong monastery,[26] Suizhou, Tongquanxian Xiu, and Zhangsong Ma (dates unknown).[27]

Concerning the identity of Zhangsong Ma, the beginning of fascicle 4 of *Chuandeng lu* lists him as a disciple of Chuji, and it is plausible that he studied with both Chuji and Wuxiang.[28] Yanagida Seizan identifies this monk as none other than Mazu.[29] If this is correct, it would mean that after his study with Wuxiang, Mazu moved to Zhangsong mountain (located in the northwestern part of Qianzhou, not far from Chengdu) and started his teaching career at an unusually young age.[30]

Based on the available sources, it is impossible to either prove or refute Yanagida's identification of Zhangsong Ma as Mazu. The confusion arises mainly from the fact that Zhangsong Ma and Mazu were both students of Wuxiang whose surname was Ma, but that of course is nothing more than a simple co-incidence. Daoyuan, the compiler of *Chuandeng lu*, considered the two to be separate individuals and listed them as disciples of two separate teachers. It is improbable that Mazu assumed the role of a leader of his monastic community only a few years after his ordination, while he was still in his twenties. Moreover, there is absolutely no information in any of his early biographical sources that suggests that he was active as a teacher during his stay in Sichuan, nor is there any indication that he ever resided at Zhangsong mountain. All of these considerations lead me to believe that Zhangsong Ma was a different person.[31]

Travel East

Mazu left his home province not long after his ordination, while he was still in his twenties. The personal considerations that shaped this decision are unclear, but at that point in his monastic career such a course of action was not unusual, as it was not uncommon for monks from Sichuan to leave their native region and travel to Buddhist monasteries in other parts of the country. Monks had varied motives for such travels, including the desire to study with famous teachers or visit important pilgrimage sites. During the eighth century, Buddhism flourished in Sichuan and there were many monasteries where a young monk could study the scriptures or practice meditation. Nonetheless, Sichuan was on the periphery of the vast empire, far away from most of the main religious centers and holy sites. The chances for meeting famous teachers in Sichuan paled in comparison to the opportunities available in other parts of China. Sichuan monks were in a position somewhat similar to monks from the Korean peninsula, many of whom left their native land to travel to China in their search for better and more plentiful opportunities to meet qualified teachers and visit famous religious sites.

Mazu and Zongmi are the two best-known examples of monks born in Sichuan who left the province as young men and settled in other part of China, but there were many other monks associated with various Chan lineages who left the region during their young years. These monks include Shenhui's disciple Huanglong Weizhong (705–782), a native of Chengdu,[32] as well as Zhangle Farong (747–835) and Lingzhuo of Anguo Monastery (691–746),[33] two disciples of the famous Northern school teacher Puji (651–739). Mazu's disciples also included two monks from Sichuan, Lecturer Liang of Xishan (dates unknown) and Reverend Zechuan (dates unknown).[34] Even among Chuji's disciples, Mazu was not the only one who left Sichuan and headed east: Nanyue Chengyuan (712–802), who was Mazu's junior by three years and was also born in Hanzhou, left Sichuan after Chuji's death in 734 and arrived at the famous Yuquan monastery in Jingzhou (present-day Dang-yang county in Hubei province) in 735.[35]

Mazu probably left Sichuan about the same time as Chengyuan, namely around 735.[36] As they were both born in the same area, were roughly the same age, and were disciples of the same teacher, they presumably knew each other well and were aware of each other's travel plans. As they were also both headed in the same direction—Jingzhou in Shannan East (in present-day Hubei province)—it is conceivable that they left Sichuan together, al-though there is no evidence to verify that scenario. Zongmi writes that after his departure from Sichuan, Mazu resided at Mingyue mountain in Jingnan (i.e., Jingzhou) for an extended period, at a secluded site where he practiced meditation.[37] Jingzhou, an important point on the main road from the capi-tal to the South, was located on the land and river routes from Sichuan to south China, and Mazu mostly likely had to pass through the area on his eastward journey.[38]

Study with Huairang

Quan's inscription seems to suggests that Mazu had already heard about Huairang before they met at Nanyue, the famous mountain in Hunan where Huairang resided. He writes, "Later he heard that Chan master [Huai]rang at Hengyue received from the sixth patriarch [Huineng] at Caoxi the teaching that [directly] reaches the true mind, and is [thus] called the sudden approach. As soon as he heard [Huairang's] words, he was freed from mundane wor-ries."[39] The *Song gaoseng zhuan* biography goes a step further, implying that Mazu first heard about Huairang while he was still in Sichuan.[40] That is im-probable, however, since at that time Huairang was a little-known monk living at a mountain located far from Sichuan. It is more likely that Mazu heard about him after he arrived in Jingzhou, where Huairang was ordained a few decades earlier.

Although his name figures prominently in normative accounts of Chan history, during his lifetime Huairang was a little-known monk. The earliest extant version of *Liuzu dashi fabao tanjing* (hereafter referred to as the *Platform Scripture*), which lists the names of Huineng's leading disciples, makes no mention of Huairang.[41] If we exclude the brief mention of his meeting with Mazu in Mazu's stele inscription, the earliest information about Huairang's life dates from the early ninth century, over half a century after his death.[42] Huairang's subsequent rise to prominence in Chan circles came about solely because of his recognition as the teacher of Mazu, and by extension as a link between Huineng and Mazu.[43]

Huairang was born in 677 in the Du family in Jinzhou.[44] He entered monastic life in 692, at the age of fifteen.[45] He received monastic ordination on
the twelfth day of the fourth lunar month in 696 (first year of the Tongtian
era) at Yuquan monastery in Jingzhou.[46] This monastery became an important establishment during the Sui dynasty (581–618), when Zhiyi (538–597),
the great founder of the Tiantai tradition, resided there. During the Tang period, the monastery continued to function as an important center of Tiantai
studies.[47] Throughout the seventh century, it was also a center of meditation
practice, and from around 676 until 701 it was the residence of Shenxiu, the
leader of the Northern school of Chan.[48] In addition, the monastery was a hub
for Vinaya studies, and Huairang's preceptor Hongjing was one of the prominent Vinaya masters who resided there.[49] As Shenxiu was residing at Yuquan
monastery at the time Huairang was ordained there, it is probable that the two
met. It is even possible that Huairang studied under Shenxiu.

According to an extant fragment from *Baolin zhuan*'s lost tenth fascicle, after his ordination Huairang went to Song mountain, at the time a well-
established center of Chan practice, accompanied by a monk named Tanran.
There he studied with Lao'an (584?–709, also known as Hui'an), who was
among the most prominent Chan teachers at the time.[50] Some sources identify Lao'an as a student of Hongren, and his name appears among Hongren's
ten great disciples listed in *Lengqie shizi ji*. Together with Shenxiu and Faru
(638–689), he was among the leaders of the Chan school in the North.[51] Before going to Songshan, Lao'an had also resided at Yuquan monastery, and
Huairang must have heard about him during his stay there.[52]

According to his biography in *Zutang ji*, after visiting Songshan, Huairang
traveled south. Around 699 he arrived at Caoxi, in the northern part of Lingnan province (present-day Guangdong), where he met Huineng and studied
with him for twelve years.[53] If that is the case, it seems that he might have been
a student of three important Chan teachers: Shenxiu, Lao'an, and Huineng.
After his departure from Caoxi in 711, Huairang traveled north.[54] Around 720,
he reached Nanyue and settled on the mountain close to Buore (Prajñā) monastery, the same one where Zhiyi's teacher Huisi (515–577) had resided during the
sixth century. There Huairang led a quiet contemplative life until his death in
744. He did not have many disciples; in addition to Mazu, *Song gaoseng zhuan*
lists the name of one more disciple, an obscure monk called Daojun (dates unknown), while *Chuandeng lu* states that he had six main disciples.[55]

Later versions of the *Platform Scripture* and other Chan texts compiled
during the post-Tang period introduce apocryphal dialogues between Huairang and Huineng, created in order to elevate Huairang's status as one of
Huineng's main disciples, while glossing over his earlier connections with
other Chan teachers. One the one hand, this might well be an example of how
the images of Chan teachers were molded in response to the changing needs
of the Chan movement. On the other hand, Mazu's stele inscription already

mentions the teacher-disciple relationship between Huineng and Huairang, so it is apparent that during Mazu's lifetime Huairang was considered a disciple of Huineng and a teacher of Mazu.

Zongmi writes that after leaving Mingyue mountain, Mazu went on a pilgrimage. During his visit to Nanyue, Mazu met with Huairang and became his disciple.[56] The best-known account of Mazu's meeting with Huairang first appears in Huairang's biography in *Zutang ji*.[57] According to the *Chuandeng lu* version of the story, Huairang noticed Mazu while the latter was practicing meditation at Chuanfa temple on Nanyue mountain. In order to teach Mazu about the futility of his misguided attempts to achieve awakening by the practice of seated meditation, Huairang grabbed a tile and started to polish it. When the perplexed Mazu asked him what he was doing, Huairang explained that he was trying to make a mirror. When Mazu remonstrated that it was impossible to do that, Huairang explained that Mazu's meditation practice was as likely to make him a Buddha as polishing a brick was to turn it into a mirror. After Mazu realized his folly, Huairang offered him religious instruction. Here is the traditional account of that meeting:

> During the Kaiyuan period of the Tang [dynasty], Mazu was practicing meditation at Chuanfa temple in Hengyue.[58] There he met with Reverend Huairang, who immediately recognized him as a being worthy of receiving the teaching. Huairang asked him, 'Why are you sitting in meditation?" The Master replied, "Because I want to become a Buddha." Thereupon Huairang took a brick and started to polish it in front of Mazu's hermitage. Mazu asked him, "Why are you polishing that brick?" Huairang replied, "I am polishing it into a mirror." Mazu asked, "How can you make a mirror by polishing a brick?" Huairang said, "If I cannot make a mirror by polishing a brick, how can you become a Buddha by sitting in meditation?" Mazu asked, "Then what shall I do?" Huairang asked, "When an ox-carriage stops moving, do you hit the carriage or the ox?" Mazu had no reply.
>
> Huairang continued, "Are you practicing sitting in meditation, or practicing to sit like a Buddha? As to sitting in meditation, meditation is neither sitting nor lying. As to sitting like a Buddha, the Buddha has no fixed form. In the non-abiding Dharma, one should neither grasp nor reject. If you try to sit like a Buddha, you are just killing the Buddha. If you attach to the form of sitting, then you do not penetrate this principle."
>
> Upon hearing these instructions, Mazu felt as if he had tasted ghee. He bowed and asked, "How should one's mind be so that it will accord with the formless samādhi?" Huairang said, "Your study of the teaching of the mind-ground is like planting a seed. My teaching

of the essentials of the Dharma is like heavenly blessing [in the form of rain]. Because you have this opportunity [to encounter the teaching], you will perceive the Way (*Dao*)."

Mazu also asked, "The Way does not have the characteristics of form; how can it be perceived?" Huairang said, "The Dharma-eye of the mind-ground can perceive the Way.[59] It is same with the formless samādhi." Mazu asked, "Is that still subject to becoming and decay?" Huairang said, "If you see the Way through such concepts as becoming and decay, aggregating and disaggregating, then you do not truly see the Way. Listen to my verse:

> The mind-ground contains various seeds,
> With rain, they will come to sprout.
> The flower of samādhi is formless,
> How can it be subject to decay or becoming?[60]

The concluding verse symbolizes the transmission of the Buddha's enlightenment from Huairang to Mazu. The transmission verse became a key fixture of transmission narratives recorded in Chan chronicles, starting with *Baolin zhuan* during the early ninth century. Mazu is the only monk after Huineng accorded a transmission verse, which implies that he was the recipient of the "orthodox" patriarchal transmission. This dramatic depiction of Mazu's initial meeting with Huairang is one of the best-known stories of traditional Chan lore. However, it is unclear if the anecdote is an example of post-Tang literary creation in the "encounter dialogue" style, or evidence about events in Mazu's life.[61] Besides this story, there is hardly any information about Mazu's study with Huairang. Since there are no reliable records of Huairang's teachings, we do not know what he taught Mazu. We also cannot be sure about the length of time Mazu spent at Nanyue. Mazu left Huairang well before 744, the year of Huairang's death, and he could not have arrived there before 736.[62] A stay at Nanyue during the 736–740 period is a plausible conjecture, and his stay there might have been even shorter.[63]

Initial Teaching in Fujian and Jiangxi

After Mazu left Nanyue, he headed east.[64] Eventually he settled at Fojiyan in Jianyang (located in the northern part of present-day Fujian province, close to the border with Jiangxi), which at the time was a part of Jiangnan East province.[65] During his stay in Fojiyan, while he was in his early thirties, Mazu got his first disciples. The earliest information about the beginning of Mazu's teaching career comes from the biographies of two of his disciples,

Ziyu Daotong (731–813) and Ganquan Zhixian (dates unknown).[66] In addition to these two, disciples who studied with him at Fojiyan also included Tianmu Mingjue (d. 831?) and Dazhu Huihai, the author of *Dunwu yaomen*.[67]

According to the stele inscription, at some time during the Tianbao period (742–756) Mazu left Fujian and moved west to Jiangxi. There he initially re-sided at Xili mountain in Fuzhou (located in the western part of Linchuan county), and later moved further south to Gonggong mountain in Qianzhou. Mazu arrived in Linchuan around 743 and stayed there at least until 750.[68] On his move to Linchuan, Mazu was accompanied by his disciple Daotong, and soon after his arrival they were joined by Chaoan (dates unknown).[69] In 750, Xitang, who at the time was only twelve years old, also joined the expanding monastic congregation.[70]

Gonggong mountain was located in Nankang commandery, in the south-ern part of Jiangxi. Mazu moved to Nankang sometime after 750 but before 757.[71] His move roughly coincided with the outbreak of the An Lushan rebel-lion in 755, though there does not seem to be a direct connection between the two. His stay there lasted well over a decade, during which he gradually emerged as one of the leading Buddhist prelates in the region. In a somewhat dramatic fashion, the stele inscription describes the strong impact Mazu's charismatic personality and inspired religious teachings had on his disciples: "[Due to Mazu's teaching] the violent (*juebo*) were tamed and the cruel made benevo-lent. They all looked up to his [exemplary] conduct and their actions were greatly transformed."[72] Among the increasing number of spiritual seekers who came to Mazu's monastery during this period were Baizhang, Yanguan Qi'an (752–841), Ezhou Wudeng (749–830), and Funiu Zizai (741–841).

In addition to attracting a considerable number of monastic followers, during his stay at Gonggong mountain Mazu also began to cultivate close con-tacts with powerful government officials. The ability to gain the support of well-placed lay patrons was important for the growth and flourishing of his mo-nastic community. The establishment of a framework of personal relationships between Mazu and his disciples, on the one hand, and local literati and govern-ment officials on the other led to the formation of a stable framework of institu-tional support that during the subsequent decades enabled the Hongzhou school to flourish and expand. The first lay patron about whom we have information is the local prefect Pei Xu (719–793), who became Mazu's disciple during his stay at Gonggong mountain.[73] After assuming his local post in 766, Pei Xu met with Mazu on a number of occasions and received religious instructions from him.

Training of Disciples in Hongzhou

During the Dali period (766–779) of Emperor Daizong's reign, Mazu left Gonggong mountain and moved to Kaiyuan monastery, located in the prefectural capital of Hongzhou (present-day Nanchang, the capital of Jiangxi);[74] he probably left for Hongzhou around 770. According to his stele inscription, soon after Lu Sigong (711–781) assumed the post of civil governor of Jiangxi, he invited Mazu to stay at the official residence (lisuo) in Hongzhou.[75] It is not clear if Mazu was already in Hongzhou at the time, or if Lu's invitation led to his departure from Gonggong mountain.[76] As Lu became a governor in the first month of the seventh year of the Dali era (February 772)—or perhaps during the seventh month of the previous year (August 771), according to a different source—he probably extended his invitation to Mazu in 771 or 772.[77] When Mazu moved to Hongzhou, some of his close disciples, including Baizhang, followed him, but some disciples stayed at Gonggong mountain. Mazu entrusted the leadership of the community to Xitang, who by that time had emerged as his leading disciple.

Kaiyuan monastery was part of the network of state-sponsored monasteries established by emperor Xuanzong in 739, toward the end of the Kaiyuan era (713–741).[78] The monastery was located in the capital of Hongzhou prefecture, close to the border between Nanchang county and Xinjian county.[79] Originally the monastery was established during the reign of King Yuzhang (r. 551–552) of the Liang dynasty (502–557). Until the early eighth century, the name of the monastery was Dafo (Great Buddha) monastery. When Xuanzong's edict was enacted, the name was simply changed to Kaiyuan monastery.[80] The monastery still exists in the central area of Nanchang, although it is not certain if its present location is the same as the one during Mazu's time. The monastery was burned down during the late Tang era, and during its subsequent history its name changed a number of times. In the early twelfth century, the monastery was renamed Nengren monastery, and during the 1450s the name changed to Youqing monastery; its present name is Youmin monastery (figure 1.1).[81]

Kaiyuan was one of the principal monasteries in the area. As an official establishment, it had close connections with the local government. Presumably Mazu had the backing of powerful local officials, as he assumed the post of an abbot.[82] Mazu's biography in Song gaoseng zhuan relates an episode that took place during the Jianzhong era (780–783) that sheds light on Mazu's relationship with local officials and the importance of close ties with them.[83] At that time there was an imperial edict stipulating that monks must return to the temples in which they were registered.[84] It is not clear where Mazu was registered, but apparently it was not at Kaiyuan monastery. In order to comply with the edict, he would have had to leave Hongzhou and move to back to his old residence (which might have meant his monastery at Gonggong mountain). At that time, Bao Fang (723–790), who in 780 assumed the post of civil governor of Jiangxi—Lu Sigong had left the post in 778—helped Mazu to evade the order and remain at Kaiyuan monastery.[85]

During his stay at Kaiyuan monastery, which lasted about two decades, Mazu attracted an ever-increasing number of disciples. As his fame spread,

FIGURE I.I.   Entrance gate of Youmin monastery, Nanchang.

monks from all over the empire, not just the South, came to study under him. Noted disciples who joined the community at Kaiyuan monastery included Nanquan, Fenzhou Wuye (761–823), Guizong Zhichang (dates unknown), Xingshan Weikuan (755–817), Zhangjing Huaihui (756–815), Danxia Tianran (739–824), Dongsi Ruhui (744–823), Tianhuang Daowu (748–807), and Furong Taiyu (747–826).

Final Days and Passing Away

In 788, the last year of his life, Mazu was seventy-nine years old. He had been a monk for sixty years and had been teaching and training disciples for over forty years. The final years of his monastic career had been a great success. He was a leader of a large and flourishing monastic community, a successful Chan teacher surrounded by numerous disciples. Locally, he was an important religious figure respected by the local officials and the gentry. On a broader scale, he emerged as a leading Chan teacher and attracted followers from throughout the empire.

One month before he died, in the late winter of 788, Mazu traveled to Shimen mountain in Jianchang (located in the northwest corner of Hongzhou prefecture).[86] This mountain become his resting place, and it continued to be a religious center for the Hongzhou school after his death. It thus seems likely that during his final years Mazu had a connection with the monastery located on the mountain, Letan monastery, which provided a quieter environment than the urban Kaiyuan monastery.[87]

According to Quan's inscription, while walking through the mountain accompanied by his disciples, Mazu "designated a clear and open area at Shimen as his final resting place. All of a sudden he told his close disciples, 'When the second month arrives, I will return [here]. Take note of it.' "[88] Premonitions about imminent death are a frequent motif in the hagiographies of Chan teachers. They serve as testimonials to an individual monk's great spiritual achievements, especially the greatest achievement of all: mastery over the cycle of birth and death (saṃsāra). The early sources indicate that when it was time for him to leave this world, Mazu departed in a calm, controlled, and dignified manner, as one would expect from a saintly and spiritually accomplished monk.

During his final stay at Shimen, Mazu became sick. He told his disciples that he would be leaving them soon "so that he can be buried in the remote mountain [i.e., at Shimen]."[89] During this final period Li Jian (dates unknown), the local governor at the time, was at the bedside of the ailing Mazu. According to Quan's account, Mazu gave the following final teachings to the devout Li:

> [The master taught Li that,] generally speaking, for the sake of the one [vehicle] one should forsake the three [vehicles], and one should renounce the provisional [teaching] in order to approach the true [teaching]. He revealed the unchanging, immaculate nature, and the teaching that is without discrimination and gradualness. Once he said, "The Buddha is not far away from people, and he is to be realized by comprehending the mind. The Dharma does not incorporate anything, and the external objects are all suchness—how could it be divided into many?"[90]

The earliest sources do not give the exact location of Mazu's death, and later sources are ambiguous. A note inserted in the Song edition of *Chuandeng lu* states that he died at Kaiyuan monastery and was then cremated at Shimen mountain.[91] It seems more probable that Mazu did not return to Kaiyuan monastery, but instead passed his final days at Shimen and was subsequently cremated and buried there in accord with his earlier request.[92] However, the early descriptions of his elaborate funeral (described later) cast doubt on this scenario. The large scale of the funerary services and the fact that the provincial governor and most of Mazu's disciples were present make it appear that the funeral took place in the provincial capital rather than at the mountain monastery.

Mazu passed away on the first day of the second month of the fourth year of the Zhenyuan era (March 13, 788).[93] The early sources describe Mazu's final moments in a similar fashion, adhering to a pattern representative of the medieval Buddhist hagiographic tradition. According to the *Song gaoseng zhuan* biography, when the time of his departure from this world approached, Mazu conducted himself in the same manner as usual. On his final day he washed and purified himself in preparation for his death. He then "in a stern and dignified manner" sat cross-legged and "entered extinction" (i.e., Nirvāṇa).[94] In a similar vein, Quan Deyu writes that, "When it was time for him to die, the master set cross-legged and announced his passing away. When he was about to truly die, it was like putting together the two halves of a tally."[95]

Mazu's funeral was a grand and elaborate affair, organized by his senior disciples and Li Jiang, with the help of other local officials. Following "Western" precedents, in deference to traditions transmitted from India, the disciples cremated Mazu's body in the prescribed manner.[96] Zanning compares Mazu's funeral service to the grand ceremonies performed at the burials of two well-known monks who lived during the first half of the Tang era: Shandao (613–681), the great propagator of the faith in Amitābha Buddha's Pure Land, and Huayan (i.e., Puji), one of the leaders of the Northern school of Chan.[97] Quan Deyu describes the funeral procession:

> When [the master's death] did actually occur during the second month,
> it corresponded to the torching [of the Buddha's body] at Kuśinagara.
> Monks and lay people, young and old, lost their voices [from crying
> too much], and approached the road [on which the funeral procession
> was passing]. While [the procession] was crossing a dried up stream,
> there was a torrential splash of Dharma rain, and when they reached
> the monastery gate there appeared varied mists of heavenly fragranc-
> es. On that occasion, when there was such a mystical response, the
> ignorant were unaware of it.[98]

Quan Deyu's comparison of Mazu's funeral with that of the Buddha, while somewhat formulaic, reflects the surviving disciples' belief that the deceased Mazu had achieved religious perfection. The description of auspicious preternatural occurrences during the funeral procession serves as further evidence of Mazu's spiritual attainments.

Following Mazu's wishes, his remains were buried at Shimen, at a site he had previously chosen. Mazu's disciples decided to build a memorial pagoda on the grounds of Letan monastery. The pagoda was finished in 791 and was named Da Zhuangyan (Great Adornment). As was customary, on the opening of the pagoda and the enshrining of Mazu's relics in it, Quan Deyu was asked to write an inscription. During the Yuanhe era (806–820) of Emperor Xianzong's reign, Mazu received the imperially bestowed title Daji Chanshi (Chan Master of Grand Quiescence).[99] The monastery and Mazu's pagoda were damaged during the Huichang-era (841–845) persecution of Buddhism. After the end of the persecution, the next emperor, Xuanzong (r. 846–859), ordered Pei Xiu (787?–860), who at the time was a governor of Jiangxi and a student of Mazu's second-generation disciple Huangbo, to restore them.[100]

NOTES

1. For the primary biographical sources about Mazu's life, see the first section of the appendix. Relevant secondary sources are: Nishiguchi Yoshio, "Baso no denki"; Ui Hakujū, *Zenshū shi kenkyū*, vol. 1, 377–96; Suzuki Tetsuo, *Tō-godai zenshū shi*, 369–88, and *Tō-godai no zenshū*, 114–23; Ishikawa Rikisan, "Baso kyōdan no tenkai to sono shijishatachi" and "Basozen keisei no ichisokumen"; Yanagida Seizan, "Basozen no sho mondai," 33–41, and *Shoki zenshū shisho no kenkyū*, 335–49.

2. For maps of Jiangnan around the time of Mazu's arrival in the area, see Tan Qixiang, *Zhongguo lishi ditu ji*, vol. 5, 55–58.

3. The date of Mazu's birth is extrapolated from information about the date of his death presented in the stone inscription from Baofeng monastery and the information about his age recorded in his stele inscription. With the exception of the QTW edition of his stele inscription, all other sources—including the *Tang wencui* and *Quan zaizhi wenji* editions of the inscription—are in agreement with the Baofeng stone inscription concerning the year of Mazu's death: the second month of the fourth year of the Zhenyuan era (788). All editions of the stele inscription also state that he died when he was eighty years old (according to the Chinese reckoning, which means that he was seventy-nine years old at the time), which places his birth in 709. The QTW edition of the stele inscription, however, states that he died in fourth month of the second year of the Zhenyuan era (786), which would mean that he was born in 707. Suzuki Tetsuo, *Tō-godai zenshūshi*, 369–71, presents a long argument demonstrating that the QTW edition of the stele inscription is mistaken about the year of Mazu's death. Nishiguchi, "Baso no denki," 112, argues that the date in the QTW edition was probably deliberately changed by the QTW editor. Suzuki's and Nishiguchi's lengthy arguments about Mazu's dates are redundant, since the extant stone inscription from Baofeng monastery, the most reliable source, clearly states that Mazu died during the fourth year of the Zhenyuan era. Based on that, it is obvious that the QTW edition of the stele inscription is mistaken.

4. Although various sources give different names to Mazu's birthplace, they all refer to the same place. The discrepancies among the different texts are because the authors refer to the birthplace by names used during different periods. The stele inscription says that Mazu was born in Deyang (present-day Deyang county), while SGSZ 10 (T 50.766a) states that he was born in Hanzhou. The name Hanzhou was used during the 686–742 period and was thus the name that was in vogue at the time of Mazu's birth. The name Deyang was used from 742 until 758, when the area's name once more reverted back to Hanzhou. See Suzuki, *Tō-godai no zenshū*, 114. CDL 6, T 51.245c, states that he was born in Sifang (county) in Hanzhou, while ZTJ 14.304 has 十方 instead of 什方, which is probably a misprint.

5. It is uncertain when the appellation "Mazu" was first used, and it is possible that this usage was not in vogue during Mazu's lifetime. Neither the stele inscription

nor the SGSZ biography refers to him as Mazu. Instead, they both use the appellation Ma dashi (Great Teacher Ma). Moreover, in SGSC 9, T 50.762b, the name Mazu is used to refer to Xuansu (668–752, also known as Masu), a monk of the Niutou school. For Xuansu, see his stele inscription, composed by Li Hua (c. 715–774), in QTW 320.3246b–48b, as well as his biographies in ZTJ 3.64, and CDL 4, T 51.229b–c.

6. *Tang gu hongzhou kaiyuansi shimen daoyi chanshi beiming bingxu*, QTW 501.5106a.

7. Ibid.

8. This conjecture becomes even more plausible when we consider that many of Mazu's disciples and his key lay supporters came from upper-class backgrounds. The notion that Mazu's family belonged to the local gentry in Hanzhou is brought into question only by *Wujia zhengzong zan*. In the first fascicle of this text, written by Shaotan (d.u.) during the Southern Song period, there is a story that suggests Mazu came from a peasant family. According to it, Mazu returned to his native place after obtaining Huairang's teachings at Nanyue mountain. Upon his arrival, the local people greeted him warmly, and this cordial reception supposedly led an old lady to complain about such a fuss being made over the son of the Ma, the "winnow family" (*boji jia*). XZJ 135.454b. The old woman's disdainful statement can be interpreted to mean that the Ma were a family with low social standing. This story was known during the Northern Song period, as can be seen from an allusion to it in Yuanwu Keqin's (1063–1135) *Yuanwu xinyao* (XZJ 120.351b). See also Yanagida, *Shoki zenshū shisho no kenkyū*, 339, and 347 n. 7, where Yanagida accepts the story as true. Nonetheless, the story does not appear in any source written before the twelfth century. There is also no evidence that Mazu returned to Sichuan after his journey to Nanyue. The story represents a popular tradition that tried to depict Mazu as a leader of a Buddhist tradition close to the common people, a mistaken assumption that finds an echo in the work of contemporary scholars. Therefore, it seems prudent to read the *Wujia zhengzong zan* story about Mazu's humble family background as a product of popular Song imagination.

9. QTW 501.5106a.

10. QTW 501.5106b.

11. Following Mazu's biographies in SGSZ and CDL. Though the stele inscription does not give the name of Mazu's first teacher, it states that he became a novice (literally "shaved his head") in Zizhong (i.e., Zizhou), where Chuji resided at that time. On the other hand, ZTJ 14.304 states that he was ordained in Luohan monastery and makes no mention of Chuji at all. This account seems to deserve some credence, as there was indeed a Luohan monastery in Mazu's native county that was built in 709, the year of Mazu's birth. See *Sichuan tongzhi* 38.1558b, which states that Mazu was ordained at Luohan monastery, and Suzuki, *Tō-godai no zenshū*, 114. It is also possible that the monastery tried to establish a connection with Mazu after he became famous by claiming that he was ordained there. There are three versions of Chuji's dates. His biography in *Lidai fabao ji*, T 51.184c, states that he died in 732 when he was sixty-eight years old. The Taishō edition of *Lidai fabao ji* is based on the Pelliot manuscript, but the Stein manuscript gives the year of his death as 736. Moreover, according to his biography in SGSZ 20, T 50.836b, Chuji died in 734 at the age of eighty-seven, which means his dates were 648–734.

Ui Hakujū, *Zenshū shi kenkyū*, vol. 1, 174, accept the SGSZ version, while Yanagida vacillates between the various dates—following the SGSZ dating in *Shoki zenshū shisho no kenkyū*, 278, and the Pelliot manuscript version in *Shoki no zenshi II: Rekidai hōbōki*, 278. Ishikawa Rikisan, "Basozen keisei no ichisokumen," 105, follows the SGSZ version, while Nishiguchi, "Baso no denki," 115, correctly concludes that there is no definitive evidence to support any version of Chuji's dates. Here I follow the SGSZ version.

12. For Chuji, see his brief biographies in SGSZ 20, T 50.836b, and *Lidai fabao ji*, in Yanagida, *Shoki no zenshi II*, 140–42; see also CDL 4, T 51.224b, 226a. The SGSZ biography and a passage in the appendix to Weikuan's biography in SGSZ 10, T 50.768b, state that his lay surname was Zhou. SGSZ is most likely mistaken about the surname, since all other sources—including the stele inscription of his disciple Nanyue Chengyuan (QTW 630.6354b, WYYH 866.4569a)—state that his surname was Tang.

13. For Zhishen, see *Lidai fabao ji*, in Yanagida, *Shoki no zenshi II*, 137–39. He does not have a biography in SGSZ, and in CDL only his name is listed at the beginning of fascicle 4.

14. T 85.1289c; Yanagida, *Shoki no zenshi I*, 273.

15. Here I follow the stele inscription's dating of Mazu's ordination, as it is the oldest and most reliable source. The year 728 also makes the best sense and fits into the overall narrative sequence of Mazu's life. An alternative dating can be established on basis of Mazu's biography in SGSZ 10, T 50.766b, which states that he was a monk for fifty years. That would mean he was ordained in 738, at the age of thirty.

16. During the Kaiyuan era (713–741) there was a county called Baxi in Mianzhou and a county called Ba in Yuzhou, but these were two separate places. See the monograph on geography in XTS 42.1079, 1089, and Nishiguchi, "Baso no denki," 117. See also Suzuki, *Tō-godai no zenshū*, 114, for a somewhat different interpretation. The two accounts cannot be reconciled, unless perhaps we read the stele inscription's Baxi as "the western part of Ba [county]."

17. SGSZ 10, T 50.766a; CDL 6, T 51.245c.

18. XZJ 14.279a. For an English translation of the relevant passages, see Jan Yun-hua, "Tsung-mi: His Analysis of Ch'an Buddhism," 45–47. For Wuxiang's biography, see SGSZ 19, T 50.832b–33a, and *Lidai fabao ji*, in Yanagida, *Shoki no zenshi II*, 142–54. Additional information about Wuxiang can also be found in Shenqing's *Beishan lu* 6, T 52.611b. Ui, *Zenshū shi kenkyū*, vol. 1, 380, disputes Zongmi's claim that Wuxiang was Mazu's teacher, arguing that as Mazu was ordained in 727 [*sic*], he could not be Wuxiang's disciple since Wuxiang arrived in Sichuan in 730, after Mazu's ordination. Ui mistakenly interprets Zongmi's statement that Mazu was Wuxiang's disciple to mean that Wuxiang ordained Mazu as a novice. As Zongmi simply says that Mazu studied with Wuxiang, there is no conflict between his statement and the SGSZ account; that is, Mazu could have been first ordained by Chuji and have subsequently gone to study with Wuxiang. It is also possible that Zongmi confused Mazu with Zhangsong Ma, another monk from Sichuan who was a disciple of Wuxiang (see below).

19. SGSZ 19, T 50.832b.

20. *Lidai fabao ji*, in Yanagida, *Shoki no zenshi II*, 142.

21. Ibid. For the history of Jingzhong monastery, see *Sichuan tongzhi* 38.1534a–b. For the general history of Chengdu during the Sui-Tang period, see Jeannette L. Faurot, *Ancient Chengdu*, 63–92.

22. See JTS 196.5234–35, and XTS 216.6086, as well as Denis Twitchett, "Hsüan-tsung (reign 712–756)," 428.

23. Nishiguchi, "Baso no denki," 115. Most likely Zhangqiu invited Wuxiang to Chengdu soon after he assumed his post in Sichuan, in 740 or 741. *Lidai fabao ji* tells us that Wuxiang (who died in 762) was actively teaching at Jingzhong monastery for over two decades.

24. *Yuanjue jing dashu chao* 3b, XZJ 14.278c, *Lidai fabao ji*, T 51.185a–b, and Yanagida, *Shoki no zenshi II*, 143. See also Peter Gregory, *Tsung-mi and the Sinification of Buddhism*, 41.

25. See Ōbata Hironobu, "*Rekidai hōbōki* to kodai Chibetto no Bukkyō," 325–29.

26. Biography in SGSZ 9, T 50.764a.

27. *Yuanjue jing dashu chao* 3b, XZJ 14.278c. See also the discussion of Wu-xiang's disciples in Yanagida, *Shoki zenshū shisho no kenkyū*, 283. Among them, Shenhui, who became the abbot of Jingzhong monastery after Wuxiang's death, was his generation's best-known representative of the Chan movement in Sichuan. To Zongmi's list of Wuxiang's disciples we can also add Shenqing (d. 806–820), the author of *Beishan lu*.

28. CDL 4, T 51.224c, 226c.

29. Yanagida, *Shoki zenshū shisho no kenkyū*, 283, 338. Suzuki, *Tō-godai no zenshū*, 115, also agrees with Yanagida on this point.

30. See Suzuki, *Tō-godai no zenshū*, 115. Yanagida's assertion that these two monks were one and the same person, for which he does not provide persuasive evidence, seems to be supported by a passage in the section on temples in *Sichuan tongzhi*. There we find the statement that Zhangsong monastery on Zhangsong mountain was built during the Kaiyuan era (713–741) by Chan teacher Mazu. *Sichuan tongzhi* 38.1556b. However, the evidence from *Sichuan tongzhi* is suspect. The gazetteer was written centuries after Mazu's death, and it is likely that its authors wanted to associate their local temple with the famous Mazu rather than with an obscure monk whose name barely merited a footnote in Sichuan's local religious history. In gazetteers from Sichuan and Jiangxi there are many references to monasteries that supposedly had some connection with Mazu. The origin of this kind of information is often open to doubt, and such evidence cannot be taken at face value. For examples of references about monasteries in Sichuan which supposedly had various kinds of connections with Mazu, see *Sichuan tongzhi* 38.1547b, 1551b, 1556c, 1558b.

31. The discussion presented here is based in part on Nishiguchi, "Baso no denki," 119–20, although I disagree with some of his arguments. For more on Mazu's relationship with Sichuan Chan, see Mario Poceski, "Mazu Daoyi (709–788) and Chan in Sichuan."

32. Biography in SGSZ 9, T 50.763b.

33. Biographies in SGSZ 29, T 50.894c, and SGSZ 9, T 50.761b–c, respectively.

34. See CDL 8, T 51.260a, 261a.

35. See Chengyuan's stele inscription, *Nanyue Mituosi Chengyuan heshang bei,* composed by Lü Wen (772–811), in WYYH 866.4568b–70a, and QTW 630.6354b–55a. See also Nishiguchi, "Baso no denki," 120.

36. See discussion in Ui, *Zenshū shi kenkyū,* vol. 1, 381; Ishikawa Rikisan, "Basozen keisei no ichisokumen," 106; and Nishiguchi, "Baso no denki," 120.

37. *Yuanjue jing dashu chao* 3b, XZJ 14.279a. For the location of Mingyue mountain, see *Jingzhou fuzhi* 3.50a and 28.313a.

38. See Aoyama Sadao, *Tō-sō jidai no kōtsū to chishi chizu no kenkyū,* 8, 10, 49 n. 36; and Ishikawa, "Basozen keisei no ichisokumen," 106. There is information about a disciple of Wuxiang who resided at Mingyue mountain, an obscure monk called Chan teacher Rong. See CDL 4, T 51226c, which only lists his name among Wuxiang's disciples.

39. QTW 501.5106a. Hengyue is an alternate name for Nanyue.

40. SGSZ 10, T 50.766. See also the discussion in Ishikawa, "Basozen keisei no ichisokumen," 106.

41. See T 48.343b and Philip B. Yampolsky, *The Platform Sūtra of the Sixth Patriarch,* 170.

42. This has led to questions about whether Huairang really studied with Huineng and suspicions that Mazu's disciples in the capital misconstrued the connection between the two in order to provide Mazu with a proper spiritual pedigree, although they seem to somewhat overstate their case. See Nishiguchi, "Baso no denki," 122–24; McRae, *The Northern School,* 94; and Hu Shi, "Ch'an/Zen Buddhism in China: Its History and Method," 12.

43. Even Huairang's later biographies are completely dominated by Mazu. For example, his biography in CDL 5, T 51.240c–241a, hardly discusses any other aspect of Huairang's life beyond his relationship with Mazu.

44. The oldest source of biographical information about Huairang is his stele inscription, *Hengzhou buoresi guanyin dashi beiming bingxu,* written by Zhang Zhengfu in 815 (QTW 619.6246a–47a). The stele inscription was commissioned by Mazu's disciples in the capital long after Huairang's death (see discussion in "Mazu's Disciples in Chang'an" in chapter 2), so the historical reliability of its contents is open to question. For other sources, see his biographies in ZTJ 3.86–88, SGSZ 9, T 50.761a–b, and CDL 5, T 51.240c–241a. There are also extant fragments of his biography in BLZ (which was part of the lost tenth fascicle), written fourteen years before his stele inscription. See Shiina Kōyū's two articles, "*Hōrinden* makikyū makiju no itsubun," 193, 196, and "*Hōrinden* itsubun no kenkyū," 248.

45. The extant fragment from his biography in BLZ 10 states that he entered monastic life at the age of fifteen, but it gives the year as 687, when he was only ten years old. I am assuming that the information about his age is correct and the year of his ordination is wrong, but it might well be the other way around. See Shiina, "*Hōrinden* makikyū makiju no itsubun," 193, and "*Hōrinden* itsubun no kenkyū," 248.

46. BLZ 10, quoted in Shiina, "*Hōrinden* makikyū makiju no itsubun," 193.

47. See Linda L. Penkower, "T'ian-t'ai During the T'ang Dynasty: Chan-jan and the Sinification of Buddhism," 191–93.

48. See McRae, *The Northern School,* 50–51.

49. Yanagida, "Shinzoku tōshi no keifu, jo no ni," 5–6. For a more detailed discussion, see Tsukamoto Zenryū, *Tō chūki no jōdokyō*, 127, 324–29.

50. BLZ 10, quoted in Shiina, "*Hōrinden* makikyū makiju no itsubun," 196. The same information can also be found in ZJL 97, T 48.940c, and ZTJ 3.87.

51. Lao'an's relationship with Hongren is problematic. Since Lao'an was twenty years Hongren's senior and close in age to Daoxin (580–651), Hongren's teacher and the putative fourth Chan patriarch, it is very unlikely that he would have become a disciple to a monk who was so much younger than he was.

52. For Lao'an's biography, see his stele inscription in QTW 396.4040; his two biographies in SGSZ 18, T 50.823b–c, and SGSZ 19, T 50.829c–30a; and McRae, *The Northern School*, 56–58.

53. ZTJ 3.87. Admittedly this is not the most reliable source, and there is no way to collaborate this version of events.

54. For an extended period, he seems to have stayed in Wudang, Hubei province. See *Hengzhou buoresi guanyin dashi beiming bingxu*, QTW 619.6246b, and Ui, *Zenshū shi kenkyū*, vol. 1, 385.

55. SGSZ 9, T 50.761a; CDL 5, T 51.241a. The noticeable increase in the number of Huairang's disciples presented in later texts is an indication of ongoing efforts to enhance his image as one of Huineng's two main disciples.

56. *Yuanjuejing dashu chao* 3b, XZJ 14.279a. The date of Mazu's departure from Mingyue mountain is not clear. Since he reached Nanyue before 740 (see below), he must have left Mingyue sometime during the 736–740 period; 738, the same year Chengyuan went to Nanyue, seems a reasonable guess.

57. ZTJ 3.87; a similar version of the same story is part of his biography in CDL 5, T 51.240c–241a. The story is also alluded to in Mazu's biography in CDL 6, T 51.245c.

58. T 51.245c has 習禪定 instead of 習定.

59. "Dharma-eye of the mind-ground" *(xindi fayan)* is a peculiar expression that is not attested in canonical literature. It seems to appear first in Mazu's record, although its two constituent parts—"Dharma-eye" and "mind-ground"—are common Chinese Buddhist terms.

60. MY, XZJ 119.405c–d; translation adapted from Cheng-chien, *Sun-Face Buddha*, 59–60. See also the other edition in Huairang's biography in CDL 5, T 51.240c–241a.

61. Tang sources, including Mazu's and Huairang's inscriptions, make no mention of the story. See QTW 619.2767b–c. An earlier version of the CDL story can be found in ZJL 97, T 48.940a–b. Though this version contains Huairang's instructions and transmission verse, it lacks the incident with the polishing of a brick. On the other hand, the story is alluded to in *Zuochan ming* (Inscription on Sitting Meditation), a short text attributed to Dayi (see T 48.1048c). If the authorship attribution is correct, it suggests that the story goes back to the early ninth century at the latest.

62. CDL states that Mazu spend ten years with Huairang, but that is an obvious exaggeration. CDL 5, T 51.241a. There is also a story in which Huairang comments about Mazu's successful teaching, implying that Mazu had left his teacher and started his own teaching career while Huairang was still alive. See CDL 5, T 51.241a.

63. Ui, *Zenshū shi kenkyū*, vol. 1, 387, states that Mazu stayed with Huairang for nine years, while Ishikawa, "Basozen keisei no ichisokumen," 107, argues that Mazu studied with Huairang only for a very short period. Ishikawa's inference is based on his problematic reading of a passage in Mazu's stele inscription that compares his meeting with Huairang to the meeting between Yan Hui and Confucius (see QTW 501.5106a). The whole passage bears no direct relevance on the length of Mazu's stay with Huairang.

64. The biographical sources tell us little about Mazu's activities following his departure from Nanyue, but by putting together various pieces of information, especially brief comments from the biographies of Mazu's disciples, it is possible to trace his major moves during the 740s. For a helpful discussion of Mazu's itinerary during that period, see Suzuki, *Tō-godai zenshū shi*, 371–75.

65. The stele inscription does not mention his stay at Fojiyan, but the biography in CDL 6, T 51.246a, notes that he went to Fojiyan after he left Nanyue.

66. See Suzuki, *Tō-godai zenshū shi*, 371, and Nishiguchi, "Baso no denki," 127. Daotong's biography in SGSZ states that during the first year of the Tianbao era (742) he went to see Mazu, who at that time was teaching a group of disciples at Fojiyan. SGSZ 10, T 50.767c. Similarly, the biography of Zhixian, who was a native of Jianyang, states that during the same year he studied with Chan master Daoyi, who at the time was residing in the area. SGSZ 9, T 50.763b. In Mazu's stele inscription, Zhixian is listed as one of his main disciples. See QTW 501.5106b.

67. Mingjue's study with Mazu at Fojiyan is mentioned in his biography in SGSZ 11, T 50.774b, which says that when he heard that Mazu was cultivating the Chan teachings at Fojiyan, he went there and became a monk. Though there is little reliable information about Dazhu, we do know that he was born in Jianzhou, which was not far from Fojiyan. Moreover, we also know that he was one of Mazu's earliest disciples, and it thus seems likely that he met Mazu at Fojiyan. Xitang's biography in CDL 7, T 51.252a, also states that he joined Mazu at Fojiyan. That is probably a mistake, since he was from Qianhua in Jiangxi, and at the time of Mazu's stay in Fojiyan he was too young to travel to Fujian. See Suzuki Tetsuo, *Tō-godai zenshū shi*, 372–73. Moreover, Xitang's stele inscription states that he joined Mazu at Xili mountain in 750, when he was twelve years old. See Ishii Shūdō, "Kōshūshū ni okeru Seidō Chizō no ichi ni tsuite," which contains the text of Xitang's stele inscription.

68. Following Nishiguchi, "Baso no denki," 127–28; but see also Suzuki, *Tō-godai zenshū shi*, 373, for a discussion of various problems with the dating of Mazu's move from Fujian to Jiangxi.

69. See SGSZ 11, T 50.774b.

70. Following Xitang's stele inscription, reprinted in Ishii, "Kōshūshū ni okeru Seidō Chizō no ichi ni tsuite," 282. It is also probable that during this period Mazu converted Shigong Huizang (d.u.), one of the most colorful characters among his disciples, who worked as a hunter prior to becoming a monk. See CDL 6, T 51.248b.

71. The conclusion that Mazu moved to Gonggong mountain by 757 at the latest is based on the information presented in the biography of Zhaoti Huilang (738–820) in ZTJ 4.102, which states that Huiliao went to Gonggong mountain to study with Mazu during that year. See Nishiguchi, "Baso no denki," 128.

72. QTW 501.5106a.

73. Biography in JTS 126.3567–68, and XTS 130.4490–91. Both Mazu's stele inscription and his SGSZ biography do not give his full name, but in addition to his surname, they also provide information about his title, official positions, and approximate dates of official postings. That has enabled Suzuki and Nishiguchi to identify him as Pei Xu. See Suzuki, *Tō-godai no zenshū*, 119, and Nishiguchi, "Baso no denki," 130–33 (which also has a Japanese translation of Pei's biography in JTS).

74. SGSZ 10, T 50.766b.

75. For Lu's biographies, see JTS 122.3499–3551 and XTS 138.4623–24.

76. Suzuki, *Tō-godai no zenshū*, 115, states that Mazu was invited to Kaiyuan monastery by Lu. The stele inscription, however, does not state that—it only says that Lu invited Mazu to the official residence (*lisuo*) and it does not mention Kaiyuan monastery at all. Most other sources indicate that Mazu was already residing in the monastery when he first met Lu. The SGSZ account of his move to Kaiyuan monastery suggests that Mazu met Lu only after he took up residence at Kaiyuan monastery, which would mean that Lu was not the one who initiated Mazu's move to Hongzhou. However, Xitang's biography in SGSZ 10 (T 50.766c) states that Lu invited Mazu to the prefectural capital (i.e., Hongzhou).

77. For Lu's assumption of the governorship of Jiangxi, see Daizong's basic annals in JTS 11.299. However, while it is stated there that he became a civil governor of Jiangxi in 772, according to Lu's biography in JTS 122.3500, he assumed the post during the seventh month of the previous year (771). See Nishiguchi, "Baso no denki," 137.

78. See Stanley Weinstein, *Buddhism under the T'ang*, 53–54.

79. See Nishiguchi, "Baso no denki," 139.

80. *Jiangxi tongzhi* 121.2519b and Suzuki, *Tō-godai zenshū shi*, 115.

81. Suzuki Tetsuo, *Sekkō kōzei chihō zenshū shiseki hōroku*, 72. Nengren is a Chinese rendering of Śakyamuni. At present the monastery is centrally located in the downtown area of Nanchang. It has a thriving monastic congregation—numbering over thirty when I visited in 2005—and holds regular liturgical services and festivals. The monastery is also a popular place of worship in the local community.

82. Though it is possible that he was recommended by Pei Xu, as suggested by Nishiguchi, there is no evidence to confirm that. See Nishiguchi, "Baso no denki," 139. Nishiguchi also suggests that after Mazu accepted Lu's invitation, he moved to the official government residence. He speculates that Mazu taught from there until the end of his life and did not return to Kaiyuan monastery. Nishiguchi's supposition is based on a dubious interpretation of a passage in Mazu's stele inscription that recounts Lu's invitation to come to reside at his official residence. It is improbable that Mazu would have stayed at Lu's residence for an extended period, using it to train the throngs of disciples who flocked to him. Nishiguchi's hypothesis makes even less sense when we consider that Lu left Hongzhou in 778.

83. SGSZ 10, T 50.766b.

84. It is unclear which edict the text is referring to. During his early reign, Dezong envisioned various measures proposed by his Confucian advisers, aimed at controlling the growth of Buddhism and curbing the activities of Buddhist monks and monasteries. However, most of the proposed measures were not implemented. For Dezong's early policies toward Buddhism, see Weinstein, *Buddhism under the T'ang*, 89–93.

85. For Bao Fang's biographies, see JTS 146.3956 and XTS 159.4949–50.

86. QTW 501.5106b and SGSZ 10, T 50.766b. The visit to Shimen is also recorded in TGDL 8, XZJ 135.327d. For more on Shimen mountain, see *Yudi jisheng* 26.1158.

87. See *Jiangxi tongzhi* 50.1082b, 121.2526a; and Suzuki, *Tō-godai zenshū shi*, 117. Subsequently, the name of Letan monastery was changed to Baofeng monastery. See *Jiangxi tongzhi* 121.2526 and Nishiguchi, "Baso no denki," 142.

88. QTW 501.5106b.

89. SGSZ 10, T 50.766b. A famous story that appears in later sources (and might be of apocryphal origin) describes a conversation between Mazu and the monastery's head monk about his illness: "Not long afterwards the Master become ill. The head monk asked him, 'How is the Venerable feeling these days?' The Master replied, 'Sun-Face Buddha, Moon-Face Buddha.'" MY, XZJ 119.405b; translation from Cheng-chien, *Sun-Face Buddha*, 61. The same story also appears in *Biyan lu* (case no. 3), T 48.142c.

90. QTW 501.5106b.

91. CDL 6, T 51.246c. The information provided in the note is suspect, however, since it mistakenly quotes Quan Deyu's stele inscription as a source for this information.

92. This is the tentative conclusion reached by Nishiguchi, 142. *Yudi jisheng* 26.1157 also states that Mazu died at Baofeng temple in Shimen mountain during the Zhengyuan 正元 era (which is a mistake—it should read Zhenyuan 貞元), and that his relics were preserved at the mountain.

93. Following the stone inscription from Baofeng monastery.

94. SGSZ 10, T 50.766b. 95. QTW 501.5106b.

95. QTW 501.5106b.

96. Ibid.

97. SGSZ 10, T 50.766b. For Shandao's life, see Julian F. Pas, *Visions of Sukhāvatī: Shan-tao's Commentary of the* Kuan Wu-Liang-Shou-Fo Ching, 79–104.

98. QTW 501.5106b. The last sentence is an allusion to the passage in the *Lotus Scripture*, in which the arhats fail to see the preternatural powers displayed by the Buddha, even though they are fully visible to the bodhisattvas.

99. SGSZ 10, T 50.766c.

100. CDL 6, T 51.246c. This information comes in the form of a note attached to the Song edition of the text.

2

Regional Spread of the Hongzhou School

Although Mazu was a central figure within the Hongzhou school, his subsequent standing in Chan history was dependent on the accomplishments and influence of his disciples. As a general rule, the fortunes of their disciples and the longevity of their lineages shaped the long-term stature of Chan teachers.[1] This clearly applies in Mazu's case, as much of his subsequent fame was predicated on his success in teaching a large number of talented disciples. This chapter focuses on Mazu's disciples and traces the regional growth of the Hongzhou school throughout the Tang empire during the late eighth and early ninth centuries. The discussion is organized according to regional boundaries, covering four major geographical areas: Jiangxi and the rest of southern China, central China or the middle Yangtze area (primarily covering Hunan and Hubei), the lower Yangtze area (roughly covering the present-day provinces of Jiangsu, Zhejiang, and Anhui), and the North. Xitang, Baizhang, and the disciples responsible for the spread of the Hongzhou school to the two Tang capitals are accorded separate sections.

Backgrounds of Mazu's Disciples

Mazu had the largest number of close disciples (*rushi dizi*, literally, "disciples who entered the room") among Chan teachers from the Tang period.[2] The earliest source of information about Mazu's disciples is his stele inscription, which identifies eleven prominent disciples, while also indicating that it is not a comprehensive listing of Mazu's students: "The monks [Dazhu] Huihai, [Xitang] Zhizang, Gaoying, [Ganquan] Zhixian, Zhitong, [Tianhuang] Daowu, [Zhangjing] Huaihui, [Xing-shan] Weikuan, Zhiguang, Chongtai, Huiyun, and others, dedicated their bodies to his [i.e., Mazu's] service and their minds penetrated his teaching. They considered our teacher's true nature to be calm and united with empty space, and that only his body would be transformed into relics."[3]

This list resembles analogous listings of disciples that appear in other medieval texts, such as those of the ten main disciples of Hongren and Huineng.[4] Such lists were modeled on the lists of the ten great disciples (shi da dizi) of the Buddha and Confucius.[5] It is worth mentioning that the list does not include some key disciples, most notably Baizhang.

The information about the places of birth and the locations of the monasteries of Mazu's leading disciples (see the second section of the appendix) yields some interesting observations. The diversity of the disciples' regional backgrounds is striking. As one would expect, monks native to the provinces where Mazu taught (Fujian and Jiangxi) and the adjacent provinces (especially Hunan and Zhejiang) are the most numerous. However, Mazu's disciples included monks who came from most parts of China. A similar diversity is evident when we look at the places where Mazu's disciples eventually settled and established their monastic congregations. A considerable number of them settled in Hongzhou and other prefectures in Jiangxi, but a much larger number left Jiangxi for other parts of China, and quite a few ended up in the North. Moreover, after finishing their study with Mazu, only a relatively few disciples returned to their native provinces; most of them chose to settle in new areas.[6] Table 2.1 presents a province-by-province breakdown of the regional spread of the Hongzhou school, giving the number of disciples active in each province.[7]

Among Mazu's disciples active in the South, those with monasteries in Jiangxi form the largest group, comprising roughly 19 percent of the total (21 out of 111 monks), but most disciples settled elsewhere. No fewer than twenty-two of Mazu's disciples settled in two northern provinces, Shaanxi and Shanxi. Not many disciples were active in the northeastern provinces, some of which after the rebellion had semi-independent status and were not fully integrated into the Tang empire; still, five disciples were active in Hebei and one in Shandong. In all, by the early ninth century the Hongzhou school had strongholds in virtually all areas of China.

As a group, Mazu's disciples come across as monks at home in their dealings with powerful officials. They appear conversant with Buddhist texts, doctrines, and practices, and proficient at preaching to monks and literati alike.[8] The popular view of the Hongzhou school as an egalitarian tradition that brought the teachings of Buddhism to the Chinese masses is patently misleading.[9] During the Tang period—and for that matter throughout most of

TABLE 2.1. Regional Spread of Mazu's Disciples

Province	Number of disciples	Number of biographies in CDL
Anhui	6	3
Fujian	4	2
Guangdong	6	1
Hebei	5	5
Henan	4	2
Hubei	11	3
Hunan	13	10
Jiangxi	21	16
Jiangsu	7	1
Shandong	1	0
Shanxi	11	5
Shaanxi	11	6
Zhejiang	11	6
Subtotal	111	60
Unclear/other	28	16
Total	139	76

its history—Chan teachers were leaders of an elitist contemplative tradition, and the majority of Mazu's disciple clearly fit into that pattern.

Xitang Zhizang

Following Mazu's death in 788, Xitang became the leader of the monastic community at Kaiyuan monastery.[10] He taught there for at least the next few years, and Mazu's followers looked to him for guidance more than any other senior disciple.[11] Despite Xitang's prominent role, Chan sources provide little information about him. His biographies in the Chan chronicles, including *Chuandeng lu*, are brief, and he was not accorded a record of sayings. The lack of biographical information about Xitang during the tenth century is evident in *Zutang ji*. There, toward the end of Xitang's brief hagiographic entry, which contains virtually no biographical information, the compilers note: "Besides these [three short stories], we have not seen any other records about his activities, and the dates of his death and birth are not known."[12] Moreover, although Zanning allocated separate biographies to more than thirty of Mazu's disciples in *Song gaoseng zhuan*, he did not provide a full biographical entry for Xitang, possibly because of a lack of sufficient information. The text of Xitang's stele inscription was not widely circulated and was not included in the standard collections of documents from the Tang period. With the exception of a few short stories of questionable provenance, there are also no records of Xitang's teachings.

Xitang's neglect at the hand of later writers and historians reflects a subsequent demotion of his stature. After the Tang period, other monks, in particular Baizhang and Nanquan, supplanted him as leading representatives of the Hongzhou school's second generation. Even so, because his historical position as Mazu's leading disciple was established, he could not be ignored, and Chan chronicles usually mention him as one of Mazu's two main disciples, along with Baizhang.[13]

Xitang's emergence as one of Mazu's principal disciples goes back to the late 760s, when Mazu left him in charge of the monastic community at Gonggong mountain at the time of Mazu's move to Hongzhou. He also appears second, after Dazhu, in the list of senior disciples in Mazu's stele inscription.[14] Another indication of Xitang's prominence comes from an inscription for a monastery in Mazu's native Sichuan that was composed by the famous poet Li Shangyin (812–858).[15] The inscription commemorates Mazu, Xitang, Wuxiang, and Wuzhu. Xitang was presumably included in that illustrious company as a representative of Mazu's disciples, even though he is the only one of the four monks with no connection to Sichuan. Zongmi's *Pei xiu sheyi wen* also mentions Xitang—together with Huaihui, Baizhang, Weikuan, and Daowu—as one of the five main disciples of Mazu.[16]

Predictably, Xitang's stele inscription describes him as Mazu's most influential and capable disciple. It states that Xitang and Weikuan were the two main disciples whose teachings flourished in the South and the North, respectively.[17] That statement suggests an analogy with the famous representation of Shenxiu and Huineng as the Chan school's leaders in the North and the South, respectively. *Song gaoseng zhuan* also states that Xitang received Mazu's robe. Since the transmission of the robe served as a metaphor for the transmission of Chan enlightenment, Mazu's putative bestowal of his robe indicates the selection of Xitang as his spiritual successor.[18]

Xitang was born in 738 in Qianhua prefecture (in present-day Jiangxi).[19] His family name was Liao. He entered monastic life when he was only eight years old. In 750, at the age of twelve, he joined Mazu, who at the time was residing at Xili mountain in Fuzhou.[20] The young novice followed Mazu in the move to Gonggong mountain, located in Xitang's native prefecture.[21] In 761, at the age of twenty-three, Xitang received full monastic ordination.[22] As has been noted, when two decades later Mazu received an invitation to take up residence in Hongzhou, he left Xitang to lead the community at Gonggong mountain.

During the later part of his life, Xitang emerged as a prominent and well-connected Chan teacher. His lay disciples included powerful local officials such as Li Jian and Qi Ying (748–795).[23] Li became Mazu's disciple and supporter after he assumed the position of governor of Jiangxi in 785.[24] Li and Xitang were together involved in the organization of Mazu's funeral. Subsequently, Li remained a supporter of the monastic community and continued his study of Buddhism with Xitang. Qi Ying, a *jinshi* examination graduate, followed Li Jian as a civil governor of Jiangxi after 791.[25] Another official connected to Xitang was Li Bo (773–831), the author of his first stele inscription.[26] Xitang's biography in *Chuandeng lu* also records this conversation between him and the famous Confucian apologist Li Ao (772–841):

> Secretary of State Li Ao once asked a monk, "What was the teaching of Great Master Ma?" The monk replied, "The Great Master sometimes would say that mind is Buddha; sometimes he would say that it is neither mind nor Buddha." Li said, "All pass here." Li then asked the master [i.e., Xitang], "What was the teaching of the great master Ma?" The master called, "Li Ao!" Li responded. The Master said, "The drum and the horn moved."[27]

There is not much information about the last two decades of Xitang's life. Presumably he spent his late years at Gonggong mountain. He died in 817, at the age of seventy-nine. His disciples erected him a stūpa on the grounds of the monastery on Gonggong mountain. According to the stele inscription, at the time of his death Xitang did not suffer from any illness. He simply asked his disciples to assemble and then quietly departed from this world. In 824, Emperor Muzong (r. 820–824) posthumously bestowed on him the title Dajue (Great Awakening), in response to a request made by Li Bo.[28] His memorial pagoda was named Da bao guang (Great Precious Light). Wei Shou (dates of birth and death unknown) compiled a record of Xitang's teachings and life, which is no longer extant.[29]

Xitang did not have disciples who made any notable impact on the subsequent history of Chan in China, which is one reason behind his neglect by later historians.[30] On the other hand, he was a teacher of Korean monks who exerted significant influence on the growth of the Chan (Sŏn) tradition on the Korean peninsula. Three of the reputed founders of the main Sŏn schools that emerged during the Silla dynasty—Toŭi (d. 825), Hongch'ŏk (fl. 826), and Hyech'ŏl (785–861)—were disciples of Xitang. The first of the Korean monks to come to study with Xitang was Toŭi. According to his biography, he met Xitang while the latter was residing at Kaiyuan monastery.[31] This meeting probably happened after Toŭi's arrival in China in 784. After his study with Xitang, Toŭi also visited Baizhang's monastery. The Korean monks presumably went to study with Xitang because at the time he was Mazu's best-known disciple; consequently, he ended up attracting the largest number of Korean disciples among his contemporaries.

Baizhang Huaihai

Notwithstanding Xitang's prominence following Mazu's death, the Chan tradition came to recognize Baizhang as Mazu's main disciple.[32] Baizhang's transformation into one of the greatest Chan teachers was a gradual process that stretched well beyond his lifetime. His relatively modest standing among the monks at Kaiyuan monastery is indicated by the exclusion of his name from the list of disciples presented in Mazu's stele inscription (even though he was at Shimen when the stele was erected). Zhen Xu, the author of Baizhang's stūpa inscription, was aware of the omission and offered this somewhat unconvincing explanation for the absence of Baizhang's name on the list: "[Baizhang's] words were succinct and his reasoning was perspicacious. His appearance was affable and his spirit was lofty. He was respectful to all those he came across, slighted himself wherever he stayed, and being virtuous, he did not seek renown. Thus, in the inscription of his late teacher [i.e., Mazu] only his name [among all main disciples] was obscured."[33]

Baizhang was a scion of the powerful Wang clan of Taiyuan, one of the greatest aristocratic clans of Tang China.[34] He was born in 749 in Changle prefecture in Fuzhou (Fujian), where his ancestors had moved from the North during the Yongjia rebellion of 307–313.[35] Considering his family's background, he probably received a classical education during his early childhood, a conclusion reinforced by the intellectualism and learning evidenced in his record. The *Zutang ji* biography contains a charming story that in a dramatized fashion describes Baizhang's early religious aspiration: "When he was a young boy, his mother took [Baizhang] to a monastery to worship the Buddha. Pointing to a Buddha's image, he asked his mother, 'What is that?' His mother said, 'That is the Buddha.' The child said, 'His appearance resembles that of a man, and is not different from mine. In the future I will also become like that.'"[36]

Baizhang entered monastic life in his youth under Huizhao (dates unknown), a monk from Xishan in Guangdong. The same monk was also the teacher of Yaoshan Weiyan (745–828), who was Baizhang's senior by four years. It is possible that Baizhang and Yaoshan knew each other during their early years, and they might even have studied together under Huizhao.[37] Baizhang received his monastic ordination at Nanyue in 767, with Vinaya teacher Fazhao (dates unknown) serving as his preceptor. After his ordination he moved to Lujiang (Anhui), where he studied the Buddhist scriptures.

Baizhang joined Mazu at Gonggong mountain. He probably moved to southern Jiangxi around 770, while he was still only in his twenties. He then followed Mazu in the move to Hongzhou.[38] After Mazu's death in 788, he took up residence close to Mazu's memorial pagoda at Shimen mountain. There he started to teach a group of disciples. Later he received an invitation to take up residence at the nearby Baizhang mountain, also known as Daxiong mountain.[39] Located southwest of Shimen, the mountain was in a remote area and had no previous association with the Chan tradition.[40] During the two decades he spent at the mountain, Baizhang taught a number of disciples, including Guishan Lingyou (771–853) and Huangbo, who became leading Chan teachers of their generation.

If we compare Mazu's and Baizhang's impacts as teachers, there are notice-able differences in the number and regional background of their disciples. Baizhang had fewer disciples than his teacher, and virtually all of them were active in only a limited geographical region. Baizhang's disciples mostly con-fined their activities to Jiangxi and the adjoining provinces, in contrast to the wide geographical spread of Mazu's disciples. Among the twenty-five disciples for whom we have data, eleven were active in Jiangxi, eight in the adjacent prov-inces, and none in Northern China. Table 2.2 provides a province-by-province breakdown of the location of the monasteries of Baizhang's disciples.[41]

According to his stūpa inscription, Baizhang died seated on his meditation seat on February 10, 814, at the age of sixty-five.[42] His burial took place on May 21 at Baizhang mountain's western peak. The rites used at the occasion of his fu-neral were in accordance with the *Abhidharma-mahāvibhāṣa-śāstra* (*Da piposha lun*).[43] Recalling a similar passage in Mazu's inscription, the note about the or-thodox rites performed at Baizhang's burial reveals a sense of respect for an-cient Buddhist traditions. It also evokes an image of a community for which canonical texts were objects of reverence and sources of religious authority. Af-ter Baizhang's death, his disciple Baizhang Fazheng (d. 819) took over as leader of the monastic community, and after his death five years later he was suc-ceeded by another of Baizhang's disciples, Baizhang Niepan (d. 828?).[44] In 821, the imperial court bestowed on Baizhang the posthumous title Dazhi chanshi (Chan Teacher of Great Wisdom) and the appellation Dabao shenglun (Excel-lent Discourse of the Great Treasure) to his memorial pagoda. The monastery at Baizhang mountain continued to function as an important center of the Chan school throughout the late Tang and into the Five Dynasties period.[45]

The stūpa inscription states that some of Baizhang's sermons were written down by two of his disciples, Shenxing and Fanyun, who compiled a record (*yuben*) of his teachings.[46] Baizhang also left correspondence with a monk from Fujian called Ling'ai, which contained a discussion about the existence of the Buddha-nature (*foxing*).[47] Although Baizhang's records continued to circulate and their descriptions of Chan doctrines are among the most illuminating, they did not contribute greatly to his subsequent fame.[48] The later Chan tradi-tion mostly ignored his sermons, and instead focused on the apocryphal stories

TABLE 2.2. Regional Spread of Baizhang's Disciples

Province	Number of disciples	Province	Number of disciples
Hebei	2	Jiangxi	11
Henan	2	Hunan	2
Jiangsu	2	Fujian	1
Zhejiang	3	Guangdong	2

composed in the encounter dialogue style and on his legendary role as founder of a distinctive system of Chan monasticism. His putative creation of Chan monastic rules—usually referred to as Baizhang's "rules of purity" (*qinggui*)—is traditionally interpreted as an epochal event in Chan history that marked its emergence as an institutionally independent tradition. Because of his supposed role as the originator of Chan monasticism, from the early Song period onward Baizhang was widely perceived as one of the principal figures in the history of Chan, and his stature was compared to that of Bodhidharma, Huineng, and Mazu.[49]

The legend about Baizhang's creation of a unique system of Chan monasticism is beyond the scope of the present volume.[50] Here it will suffice to say that his traditional image as a patron saint of "Chan monasticism" is not in any meaningful way related to him as a historical person. Baizhang did not institute a novel system of Chan monastic rules that was institutionally disengaged from the mainstream tradition of Tang monasticism. The earliest text that makes the connection between Baizhang and the creation of Chan monastic rules is *Song gaoseng zhuan*, compiled in 988, 174 years after Baizhang's death.[51] As Baizhang's legend became an important part of Chan lore only from the Song period onward, it is not directly related to the history of mid-Tang Chan.[52]

During the Song period the ascendancy of the Linji school—which traced its lineage back to Baizhang via Huangbo and Linji, the putative founder of the Linji school—also reinforced Baizhang's status as recipient of Mazu's "orthodox transmission." This genealogical representation established a direct link between Mazu and Linji, which strengthened the Linji school's claim to orthodoxy. Here again, however, we are dealing with an image of Baizhang that was retroactively created during the post-Tang period. Although he was an influential Chan teacher during his lifetime, Baizhang was not Mazu's principal disciple, except perhaps in the eyes of his own disciples. In fact, no disciple took over Mazu's mantle, nor did anyone come to be widely accepted as the "orthodox" recipient of his transmission. Instead, numerous disciples carried their teachings throughout the Tang empire, as discussed in the following pages.

Other Monks Active in Jiangxi and the South

The monastic congregation at Letan monastery on Shimen mountain, the site of Mazu's burial, remained inhabited by Mazu's disciples into the ninth century. In addition to Baizhang, disciples who resided there included Fahui, Weijian, and Changxing.[53] Mazu's disciples also settled at Lushan, the famous scenic mountain celebrated by generations of Chinese poets and writers. Located northwest of the Poyang lake in Jiangzhou prefecture, just north of Hongzhou, Lushan's long history as a center of Buddhist practice went back to the period of disunity. There were a number of monasteries at the mountain, including the famous Donglin (Eastern Grove) monastery where Huiyuan (334–416), the eminent Buddhist leader and propagator of the faith in the pure land of Amitābha Buddha, resided during the Eastern Jin dynasty (317–420). Until the end of the eighth century, no Chan teachers settled there, although according to some sources Daoxin (580–651), the putative fourth Chan patriarch, sojourned to Lushan before moving to Huangmei mountain (in present-day Hubei), where he established a monastic community.[54] Mazu's disciples Guizong Zhichang (dates unknown) and Fazang (dates unknown) were the first monks associated with the Chan school to take up residence at Lushan.

Born in Nan'gang (Jiangxi) in the Zhou family, Fazang received a classical education in his youth.[55] The focus of his early study was historical works. Fazang probably joined Mazu at Gonggong mountain, which was in his native prefecture. After taking leave of his teacher, he traveled to Lushan. According to his biography, while trekking around the mountain he became enchanted by the area around Wulao peak and decided to stay there. He spent the rest of his life at Lushan, leading a reclusive life in a temple built by local supporters.

In contrast to Fazang's solitary lifestyle, Guizong was the active leader of a flourishing monastic community. The initial impetus provided by him and his disciples helped make Lushan one of Chan school's regional centers throughout the ninth century and beyond. Unfortunately, there is little biographical information about him.[56] Guizong moved to Lushan during the Yuanhe period (806–820) and took up residence at Guizong temple, located in the southern part of the mountain.[57] The temple, which was later renamed Guizong Chan monastery, had a long history as a local Buddhist establishment. It was originally founded in 340, during the Eastern Jin dynasty, to house an Indian monk. Guizong was the first monk associated with the Chan school to assume the temple's abbacy.[58] During his stay there, Guizong was called "Red-eyed Guizong" because of an inflammation of his eyes that made them red.[59]

As his monastic community grew and he became a locally prominent religious leader, Guizong came in contact with noted officials and literati who visited Lushan during assignments to provincial posts in the South. Among them were Bo Juyi (772–846), the celebrated poet, and Li Bo, the official who wrote Xitang's stele inscription. It seems that Guizong himself was interested in poetry, as a few of his poems are preserved in Chan collections.[60] Bo Juyi probably met Guizong between 815 and 818, when he served as a marshal in Jiangzhou.[61] At the time, Bo often visited Lushan, where he had a cottage in which he enjoyed a life of solitude and reflection. He immortalized his experience at the cottage in a famous essay composed in 817, titled "Caotang ji" (Record of the Thatched Cottage).[62] Bo also composed a poem for Guizong and asked him questions about Buddhism.[63]

Li Bo—who was also known as Li Wanjuan (Ten-thousand Fascicles Li) because of his extensive learning—was Bo Juyi's close friend. They shared an interest in Buddhism, and at different times they both served as marshals of Jiangzhou.[64] *Zutang ji* records a conversation between him and Guizong about the famous metaphor of a mustard seed containing Sumeru mountain, which appears in a few canonical texts, including the *Vimalakīrti Scripture*:[65]

> Li Wanjuan asked the master, "Among the Buddhist teachings, there is the saying, 'Sumeru mountain receives a mustard seed, and a mustard seed receives Sumeru mountain.' Nobody will doubt that Sumeru can receive a mustard seed, but as for a mustard seed receiving Sumeru, is not that really a false statement?" The master responded by asking, "What kind of qualification do you have for serving the country?" With indignant voice Li replied, "Has not the reverend heard that your disciple has mastered ten thousand fascicles [of classical texts]." The master said, "Why do you try to deceive me?" Li said, "How do I try to deceive you?" The master said, "As your body composed of the four elements can be compared in size to the seed [mentioned in the previous simile], where did you place the ten thousand fascicles [of texts]?" Upon hearing these words, Li showed his respect and thanked the master, and afterwards he served him [as a disciple].[66]

It appears that during the ninth century Guizong was regarded as one of Mazu's leading disciples. In Huangbo's record, we find the following testimony about Guizong's eminent position among Mazu's disciples: "Among the eighty-four disciples of the great teacher Ma who sat at the site of enlightenment, the number of those who obtained teacher Ma's proper eye does not go beyond two or three. Reverend Lushan [i.e., Guizong] was one of them."[67]

The disciples of Mazu who formed monastic congregations in other parts of Jiangxi included Shigong Huizang (dates unknown), Nanyuan Daoming (dates unknown), and Yangqi Zhenshu (d. 820). Shigong, the most colorful character among the three, was a hunter with anti-Buddhist feelings before Mazu converted him during his stay in Linchuan.[68] Later he settled on the nearby Shigong mountain, located within the same prefecture south of Linchuan.[69] Daoming's monastery was located on Nanyuan mountain (Yuanzhou prefecture), in the western part of Jiangxi,[70] near Zhenshu's monastery on Yangqi mountain.[71]

Zhenshu is described as a bright and unconventional child. He became interested in Buddhism during his youth and joined Mazu's community soon after becoming a monk. He moved to Yangqi mountain during the late 770s and remained there for over forty years. He led a quiet contemplative life, mainly concerning himself with the training of his disciples. Yangqi mountain continued to serve as a hub for Chan practice long after his death. It be-

came an especially important Chan site during the early eleventh century under the leadership of Yangqi Fanghui (992–1049), the founder of the Yangqi
lineage of Linji Chan, one of the two main lineages of the Linji school that
flourished during the Song period. In addition to these monks, Dayi (746–
818) taught at Ehu mountain in northeastern Jiangxi, after which he moved to
Chang'an (discussed later, in the section on Mazu's disciples in Chang'an).
Disciples of Mazu who established monastic communities in other parts of the
South included Guiyang Wuliao and Shuitang in Fujian and Shaozhou Ruyuan
and Luofu Xiuguang in Guangdong.

Spread to Central China

Outside of Jiangxi, the bordering province of Hunan was among the regions
with the largest number of monasteries led by Mazu's disciples. The best
known among them were Yaoshan, Ruhui, Tanzang (758–827), Deng Yinfeng (dates unknown), and Zhaoti Huilang (738–820). As Shitou resided in
Nanyue, one of the main pilgrimage sites and practice centers in the region,
most of Mazu's students in Hunan—including Yaoshan, whose monastery
was in the northern part of the province, just west of Dongting lake—also
trained under Shitou.

A native of Guangdong, Ruhui was among the students of Jingshan Faqin
(714–792; also known as Daoqin), the famous Niutou school master, who
came to study with Mazu.[72] After leaving Mazu's monastery, he was invited to
take up residence at Dong (eastern) monastery in Changsha, eastern Hunan.
Zanning writes that when Ruhui moved to Changsha the Hongzhou school
was flourishing and had no equal.[73] At the time, Dong monastery was popu-
larly called the "Chan grotto" (chanku).[74] Ruhui's lay supporters included Cui
Qun (772–832).[75] A scion of the Cui clan from Qingho, one of the seven main
clans of the Shandong aristocracy, Cui Qun served as prime minister during
Xianzong's reign. The two probably met during Ruhui's final years, after Cui's
appointment as civil governor of Huainan at the beginning of 819.[76] After
Ruhui's death in 823 at the age of seventy-nine, he received from the emperor
the posthumous title Chuanming (Transmission of Clarity), and his memorial
stūpa was named Yongji (Everlasting Opportunity). Liu Ke, who wrote epitaphs for other Chan monks, composed his commemorative inscription.[77]

Tanzang, Huilang, and Deng Yinfeng studied with both Mazu and Shitou.[78] Tanzang was a reclusive monk who in 786 settled near a secluded peak in
the Nanyue mountain range.[79] As he grew old, because of poor health—his biography says that he developed a leg ailment—he moved to the Western Garden
hermitage (Xiyuan lanre), where he taught those who came for spiritual guidance. Like Tanzang, after his stay at Shitou's monastery, Yinfeng also took up
residence at Nanyue. Born in Fujian, the young Yinfeng was an awkward child

and a slow learner.[80] After a long stay at Nanyue, during the Yuanhe era (806–820) he moved to Wutai mountain in Shanxi, the famous pilgrimage center dedicated to Bodhisattva Mañjuśri.[81] Although Yinfeng did not settle permanently at the sacred mountain, he did die there. His biography in *Chuandeng lu* states that he spent the summers at Wutai and the winters at Nanyue, and that he undertook pilgrimages to other regions. During his peripatetic phases, he visited various Chan centers, including the monasteries of Nanquan and Guishan. Yinfeng's biographies contain an interesting (if somewhat bizarre) story about his death at Wutai. The *Chuandeng lu* version of the story is as follows:

> When he was about to pass away in front of the Diamond Cave, [Yinfeng] asked his monks, "I have already seen people passing away while sitting or lying. Has there been anyone who has passed away standing?" The monks answered, "Yes, there has been." The Master asked, "And how about anyone passing away while standing on his head?" The monks said, "We have not heard about anyone doing that." The Master then stood on his head and passed away. He looked dignified and his robe stayed properly attired on his body. When the monks decided to lift the body and take it away for cremation, the body was still standing erect and it was impossible to move it. People from near and far came to see this. Everyone greatly marveled at this occurrence.
>
> The Master had a sister who was a nun. When she came to see the body, she bowed, came close, and shouted, "Brother! While alive you didn't comply with the Dharma-Vinaya; even after your death you are still confusing people." She then pushed the body with her hand and the body fell flat on the ground. Soon afterwards, the body was cremated and the relics were placed into a stūpa.[82]

Although this story has a problematic provenance, it is worth noting because it a rare instance in which a nun appears in a record about Tang Chan. Indeed, the story is remarkable because of its portrayal of the nun, who is presented as spiritually superior or at least equal to a noted Chan teacher—yet she remains anonymous and her existence is noted only in reference to her brother's life.

As we move north, Daotong and Wudeng were the main disciples who settled in the area of the present-day province of Hubei.

Growth in the Lower Yangtze Region

After Jiangxi, Zhejiang witnessed the largest influx of disciples of Mazu. The best known among them were Yanguan, Dazhu, and Damei Fachang

(752–839). Yanguan was born in Haiting county, Zhejiang.[83] His surname was Li and he was related to the Tang royal family. Yanguan entered monastic life in his native county during his youth. At the age of twenty he received the monastic precepts at Nanyue, with the Vinaya teacher Zhiyan serving as his preceptor.[84] Soon after his ordination, Yanguan traveled to Jiangxi and joined Mazu's community, probably not long before the move to Hongzhou. He then followed his teacher to Kaiyuan monastery.

There is no information about Yanguan's whereabouts during the three decades following Mazu's death. Toward the end of the Yuanhe era (806–820), when he was over seventy years old, Yanguan settled at Fale monastery in Yuezhou, located just south of Hangzhou (in present-day Zhejiang province). He then received an invitation to move to Yanguan, just north of Yuezhou across the Hangzhou bay. There a new temple, named Haichang-yuan, was built for him. After taking up residence at the temple, Yanguan attracted a large number of disciples and became a prominent Chan teacher. He remained there until his death on January 24, 843.

According to Yanguan's biography in *Song gaoseng zhuan*, before assuming the throne Emperor Xuanzong visited Yanguan's monastery. The elderly abbot greatly impressed the future monarch, who was a generous supporter of Buddhism. After becoming emperor in 846, Xuanzong bestowed on Yanguan the posthumous title Wukong (Awakened to Emptiness).[85] Yanguan's best-known disciple was the Korean monk Pŏmil (810–889), who later became "founder" of the Sagul-san school of Silla Chan/Sŏn.

Dazhu was among Mazu's leading disciples, although unfortunately there is little reliable information about his life.[86] His prominent position among Mazu's disciples is indicated by the inclusion of his name at the top of the list of disciples that appears in Mazu's stele inscription. In addition, his biographies in *Chuandeng lu* and *Zutang ji* come just after Mazu's biographies and ahead of the biographies of all of Mazu's other disciples. He was born in Jianzhou (Fujian), and he probably joined Mazu at Fojiyan, not far from Dazhu's native town, which makes him one of Mazu's earliest disciples.[87] Dazhu primarily played the role of an outsider within the Hongzhou school, perhaps because he left Mazu before the latter became a well-known teacher. He is best known as the author of *Dunwu rudao yaomen lun* (Treatise on the Essentials of Entering the Way through Sudden Awakening), a seminal exposition of Chan doctrine (figure 2.1).[88]

Damei was born in Huaiyang (in present-day Hubei).[89] His family name was Zheng, and he entered monastic life during his youth at Yuquan monastery in Jingzhou (Hubei). According to his biography in *Song gaoseng zhuan*, as a child Damei had a prodigious memory and was able to memorize long passages from the scriptures. Considering his age, he probably met Mazu at Kaiyuan monastery during Mazu's final years. The dramatized account of Damei's study with Mazu is a well-known story in Chan literature. According to it,

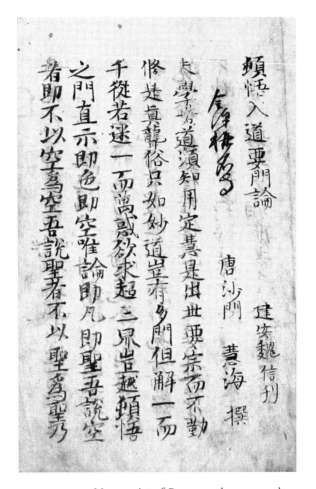

FIGURE 2.1.   Manuscript of *Dunwu rudao yaomen lun*.

Damei became enlightened after hearing Mazu's teaching of "mind is Buddha."[90] After leaving Mazu's monastery, Damei went to Tiantai mountain. He might have developed an interest in Tiantai studies during the early years of his monastic life, since Yuquan monastery, where he was ordained, was a center for the study of Tiantai doctrine.[91] From there, in 796 he moved to Damei mountain in Zhejiang, where he spent the next four decades in seclusion, leading a contemplative life. In 836, when he had reached the ripe old age of eighty-four, his supporters built for him a larger temple at the mountain. There he attracted a number of disciples, but in 839 he suddenly became ill and died. Damei's best-known disciple was Hangzhou Tianlong (dates unknown). He also taught a few Korean monks who came to China to study Chan.[92] Some of Damei's sermons were recorded and later included in a text titled *Mingzhou dameishan chang chanshi yulu*. This text was not included in any Chan collection and seems not to have circulated widely; subsequently it was lost in China. Fortunately, a Kamakura-period copy of the manuscript was preserved in Japan, now kept in the Kanazawa bunko collection in Yokohama.[93]

Other disciples of Mazu active in Zhejiang were Hangzhou Zhizang (741–819), Lühou Ningbi (754–828), Tianmu, and Wuxie Lingmo (747–818). Further north, in the area occupied by the present-day provinces of Anhui and Jiangsu, the main representatives of the Hongzhou school were Nanquan, Shanshan Zhijian (dates unknown), Taiyu, and Qiling Zhitong (dates unknown). From the perspective of later Chan/Zen traditions, Nanquan is by far the best known among them. During his lifetime Nanquan was merely one among the many locally prominent disciples of Mazu, but by the early Song dynasty he became widely recognized as one of Mazu's main disciples; having largely eclipsed Xitang, he emerged as second in fame after Baizhang. The transformation of Nanquan into a leading representative of classical Chan was a result of a prolonged process that included the refashioning of his image in ways that mirrored key developments in post-Tang Chan. The subsequent inclusion of Nanquan into the limited circle of Mazu's elite disciples is evident in later versions of stories that originally featured only Baizhang and Xitang. One such example is the well-known (but probably apocryphal) story about Mazu watching the moon with his disciples, which first appears in Northern Song texts:

> Once, Xitang, Baizhang, and Nanquan accompanied the Patriarch [i.e., Mazu] to watch the moon. The Patriarch asked, "What shall we do now?" Xitang said, "We should make offerings." Baizhang said, "It is best to practice." Nanquan shook his sleeves and went away. The Patriarch said, "The scriptures enter the treasury (*zang*), meditation returns to the sea (*hai*).[94] It is Puyuan [i.e., Nanquan] alone who goes beyond all things."[95]

An earlier version of the story mentions only Xitang and Baizhang. Later editors added Nanquan to their versions of the story, while also implying that he was superior to Mazu's two leading disciples. The reasons for the change in Nanquan's standing within the Hongzhou school (and more broadly within the history of Tang Chan) are not entirely clear, but it is possible to discern two contributing factors: the fame of his disciple Zhaozhou Zongshen (778–897) and, more important, the popularity of numerous iconoclastic stories that feature Nanquan, often together with Zhaozhou (such as the story about Nanquan killing a cat quoted in the introduction). These stories first appeared during the late tenth century, well over a century after Nanquan's death. As some of the stories were included in popular *gongan* collections such as *Biyan lu* (Blue Cliff Record) and became an acclaimed part of Chan lore, they buttressed Nanquan's fame and his position as a seminal Chan teacher.

Expansion to the North

While many of Mazu's disciples established monasteries in Jiangxi and other southern provinces, a large number of them moved north of the Yangtze river. The two northern provinces with the largest number of disciples were Shaanxi and Shanxi. Monks who moved to that area (excluding Chang'an, discussed separately in the next section) included Wuye, Zhixian, and Magu Baoche (dates unknown). Monks who settled in the area of the present-day province of Henan (excluding Luoyang, which is discussed in the last section) included Danxia and Funiu. While not quite as influential as Xitang and Baizhang in the South or Weikuan and Huaihui in the capital, they became leaders of monastic communities and prominent members of the local clergy. Among them, Wuye attained the greatest renown as a Chan teacher.

According to his biography in *Song gaoseng zhuan*, Wuye was a native of Shangluo in Shangzhou province.[96] His family's surname was Du. At the early age of nine he started to study the Mahāyāna scriptures under the guidance of a Chan teacher called Zhiben. Among the texts he studied were the *Diamond, Lotus, Vimalakīrti,* and *Huayan* scriptures. After receiving the full monastic precepts from Vinaya teacher Yu of Xiangzhou in 779, Wuye studied the commentaries of the *Four-Division Vinaya (Sifen lü)*. He was supposedly able to lecture on them as soon as he had finished reading them. His biography also notes that he often lectured on the *Nirvāṇa Scripture*.

Wuye joined Kaiyuan monastery in Hongzhou during the last decade of Mazu's life. After leaving Hongzhou, he went on a long pilgrimage; initially he traveled south to pay respects to the stūpa of the Sixth Patriarch, after which he visited Lushan, Nanyue, Tiantai, and other sacred mountains. During his travels, he also visited Chang'an, where he stayed at Ximing monastery.[97] Situated in the western part of the city, the monastery was built in 656 by Gaozong and was among the leading Buddhist establishments in the capital. The famous monks who resided there included the legendary translator Xuanzang (602–664), the leader of the Vinaya (Lu) tradition Daoxuan (596–667), and the celebrated Huayan exegete Fazang (643–712). During his stay there, Wuye was recommended for the post of "Great Worthy of the Capital" (*liangjie dade*), which he declined.[98]

Eventually Wuye settled at Shangdang (northeast of Luoyang, in the southern part of present-day Shanxi). There the military commissioner of Zhaoyi province, Li Baozhen, held him in high esteem and visited him frequently. As Wuye became a popular teacher, he found the increasing demands on his time to be distractions from his spiritual pursuits. Consequently, he left Shangdang and went to live at Wutai mountain, where he spent eight years reading the whole Buddhist canon. After that he moved to Fenzhou (located in present-day Shanxi, just southwest of Taiyuan), where he was invited by Dong Shuchan, the district magistrate, to stay at Kaiyuan temple. Wuye settled down in Fen-zhou and remained there during the following two decades.

Wuye's biography states that after Xianzong heard about his reputation, the emperor sent two invitations, in 819 and 820, for Wuye to appear at the court in Chang'an. The emperor had already received religious instruction from Mazu's two senior disciples who taught in Chang'an, Weikuan and Huaihui, both of whom died not long before the court issued the first invitation to Wuye. Wuye apparently did not comply with the request, offering illness as an excuse. After the next emperor, Xianzong's son Muzong, succeeded to the throne in 820, he also sent messengers to invite Wuye to come to the capital. Wuye again de-clined to appear at court, and died during the following year.[99] Subsequently, he received the posthumous title National Teacher Dada (Great Penetration), and the stūpa built in his memory was called Chengyuan (Clear Source).

Mazu's Disciples in Chang'an

By the mid-Tang period the economic base of the dynasty's prosperity had largely moved south to the Yangtze valley; nevertheless, Chang'an remained the political and cultural center of the empire. During the second half of the eighth century, on a few occasions the city suffered looting and destruction. In the sixth month of 756, during the early phase of the An Lushan rebellion, the rebel armies sacked the city. They remained in command for three months, to be chased away by government soldiers with the help of Uighur troops. In the tenth month of 763, soon after the end of the rebellion, the Tibetans briefly occupied Chang'an, looting and burning the city. Then in 783, Emperor De-zong had to flee the city after garrison troops mutinied and was able to return only after loyalist troops recaptured the city half a year later.

Notwithstanding the loss of dynastic prestige and the physical damage suf-fered by the city, at the beginning of the ninth century Chang'an was a vast me-tropolis with a population of over a million. An imperial capital of a somewhat weakened but still great empire, the city was a cosmopolitan hub of thriving economic activity and rich cultural life. It had lively literary and scholarly com-munities, as well as a vibrant religious scene marked by pluralism and tolerance of diverse viewpoints and practices. In addition to a substantial Daoist presence, the Tang capital was also home to followers of Zoroastrianism, Manichaeism, and Nestorian Christianity. Buddhism, however, was unmistakably the domi-nant tradition and had the strongest impact on the workings of the government and the lives of the people. The Tang capital had over 150 monasteries and con-vents, among which were the empire's largest and most splendid Buddhist es-tablishments.[100] Chang'an's magnificent monasteries were centers of diverse religious functions and other cultural activities. People from all walks of life, from powerful officials to ordinary townsfolk, frequented these monasteries.

Some of the larger ones housed hundreds of monks, and their residents included eminent ecclesiastics such as the Huayan exegete Chengguan, the Tantric master Huiguo (746–805), and the Vinaya scholar Yuanzhao.

Mazu's disciple Dayi was the first monk associated with the Hongzhou school to enter Chang'an.[101] Born in 749 (the same year as Baizhang), Dayi was a native of Xujiang in Quzhou (present-day Jiangshan in Zhejiang province). His family's surname was Xu; they were of Korean ancestry. Dayi entered monastic life in his native prefecture during his youth, and at the age of twenty he received the monastic precepts. At the time, he was interested in both Chan and the Vinaya. Soon after his ordination, around 770, he joined Mazu's monastery. Dayi's stele inscription states that he moved to Ehu mountain (located in western Jiangxi) during the Dali era (766–779).[102] At the time of this move, Ehu mountain had no previous recorded history as a center of Buddhist activity, and Dayi was the first monk to establish a monastery (*kaishan*, literally, "open the mountain") there.[103] After Dayi settled on the mountain, other monks came to study with him, and eventually a sizable monastic community grew around him.

In the course of his stay at Ehu, Dayi met with various officials and literati who came to the area during their terms of duty in the South. One of those officials was Liu Taizhen, who met Dayi at the beginning of the Zhenyuan era (785–805).[104] Liu invited Dayi to come down from the mountain to teach in the nearby city, where Liu held the office of local prefect.[105] Another famous scholar with whom Dayi met during that time was the Confucian apologist Li Ao.[106] Dayi's supporters and admirers presumably conveyed favorable reports about him to others in the capital, including officials in high places; this eventually led to an official invitation from the imperial court for Dayi to go to teach at Chang'an.

The imperial court summoned Dayi to the capital during Dezong's long reign, which ended with emperor's death in 805.[107] After his arrival, he took up residence at Cien monastery, one of the large government-supported monasteries in the city. One of his early patrons was the eunuch Huo Xianming (d. 798), who after a dream went to the monastery to see Dayi. Huo was impressed by Dayi and submitted a memorial to the throne requesting that Dayi be given the title "great worthy, chaplain of the palace sanctuary" (*neidaochang gongfeng dade*).[108] Dayi lectured to Dezong soon after his arrival in Chang'an. He also attended official ceremonies and functions at the court, including a large public debate held as part of the emperor's birthday celebrations.[109] The debate took place at the Linde Hall in the Daming palace complex, which from 663 served as the main imperial residence.[110] After Dezong's death, Dayi also lectured to the new emperor Shunzong (r. 805), whose short reign lasted less then a year.[111] Shunzong was a devoted student and supporter of Buddhism;[112] he commissioned commentaries from the famous Huayan exegete Chengguan, with whom he studied Buddhist doctrine, and he was interested in Chan.[113] The association between Dayi and Shunzong began while the latter was still a crown prince. In addition to Dayi, Shunzong also attended the lectures of other Chan monks at the court, including Mazu's disciple Ruman and Shitou's disciple Shili (dates unknown).[114]

Dayi's stele inscription states that during his stay in Chang'an he held a debate with a "dharma teacher" (*fashi*) called Zhanran at a public assembly in Shenlong monastery. This might be a mistaken reference to a meeting with the famous Tiantai exegete Zhanran (717–782); such an encounter is not possible, however, as Zhanran died over two decades before the alleged meeting.[115] It is more likely that the note refers to another monk with the same name, probably the Northern school Chan teacher from Shangu monastery who participated in the Chan council held in the capital in 796.[116] The inscription states that Zhanran was critical of southerners (presumably a reference to Chan teachers from the South) and their mistaken teachings. Dayi won the debate, and the crown prince—the future emperor Shunzong, who was officiating at the debate—ordered Zhanran and his followers to be expelled.[117] Chen Jinhua has suggested that this debate was none other than the famous Chan council of 796 described by Zongmi.[118] He argues that Zongmi's account of the council's decision to award Shenhui the title of seventh Chan patriarch is incorrect.[119] Rather, it was Dayi's tradition—namely, the Hongzhou school and more broadly the Southern school it represented—that was recognized as the bearer of Chan orthodoxy.[120] If this interpretation is correct, it means the Hongzhou school was officially recognized as the main tradition of Chan a mere eight years after Mazu's death.

Dayi's stay in the capital did not last very long. According to his inscription, as Shunzong's health was not good, Dayi returned to Ehu in 805. There is virtually no information about Dayi's activities after his return to the old monastery at Ehu mountain, although we can presume that he continued to teach his disciples until his death more than a decade later. According to his inscription, on February 18, 818, Dayi announced to his disciples that seven days later he would make his "last offering." On the specified day, he peacefully left the world in the kind of dignified manner that was deemed fitting for a sagely monk. In *Zimen jingxun* there is a short text about meditation attributed to Dayi, titled *Zuochan ming* (Inscription on Sitting Meditation).[121] If he was the author of this text, that would make it the only text composed by a member of the Hongzhou school that is directly concerned with the practice of meditation.

Despite its relatively short duration, Dayi's visit to the capital was significant because it was the first introduction of the Hongzhou school at the political and cultural center of the Tang empire. During his stay in Chang'an, Dayi had opportunities to interact with people occupying high positions in the central government and propagate the teachings of the Hongzhou school. He thus paved the way for other disciples of Mazu, who soon followed in his footsteps. Among them, Huaihui and Weikuan had the greatest impact on the Hongzhou school's fortunes in Chang'an and beyond.

Born in Xin'an, Quzhou (in present-day Zhejiang, the same prefecture where Dayi was born), Weikuan's family name was Zhu.[122] He entered a monastery when he was twelve and received the monastic precepts in 778, at the age of twenty-three. Weikuan probably joined Mazu around that time and remained in Hongzhou during the last decade of Mazu's life. In 790, soon after Mazu's death, Weikuan moved to the Minyue area (which corresponds to the northern part of Fujian and the southern part of Zhejiang). This was the beginning of an extended period of peripatetic life. He first went to Huiji (Zhejiang) in 791, which was followed by sojourns to Poyang (Jiangxi) in 792, Shaolin monastery on Song mountain in 797, Weiguo monastery in 805,[123] and Tiangong monastery (in Hongzhou) in 806.[124]

In 809 Emperor Xianzong, who had assumed the throne four years earlier, invited Weikuan to come to the capital and preach at the imperial court.[125] Like his father Shunzong, the new emperor was an enthusiastic supporter of Buddhism and had an interest in Chan. The invitation to Weikuan followed a summons addressed to Huaihui, issued during the previous year. After his arrival in Chang'an, Weikuan took up residence at Anguo monastery, one of the capital's most imposing monasteries. In 810, he received invitation to lecture to the emperor at the Linde Hall, where Dayi had lectured earlier. Later Weikuan moved to Xingshan monastery, where he remained until the end of his life. Since its establishment as an official monastery at the beginning of the reign of the emperor Wendi (r. 581–604) of the Sui dynasty, Xingshan—which, like Anguo monastery, was located in the eastern part of the city—was one of the largest monasteries in Chang'an. Weikuan's stay there placed him at the center of the capital's religious life. During his stay in Chang'an, which lasted eight years, Weikuan attracted a large number of monastic and lay disciples and emerged as one of the most influential Chan teachers in the imperial capital. According to Bo Juyi's inscription, he had over a thousand disciples, of whom thirty-nine realized his teachings.[126] Bo was one of Weikuan's lay disciples.

Weikuan was a learned monk who possessed a number of qualities that made him appealing to the religious audiences in Chang'an. In addition to his study of Chan with Mazu, during the early years of his monastic training he studied the Vinaya and the scriptures and doctrines of Mahāyāna Buddhism. He was also proficient in the teachings of the Tiantai school, especially the theory and practice of calming and contemplation (Chinese: *zhiguan*; Sanskrit: *śamatha-vipaśyanā*).[127] Weikuan also had a reputation as a charismatic religious figure with thaumaturgic powers. According to Bo's inscription, during his travels Weikuan performed such extraordinary feats as subduing a tiger, bestowing the eight precepts upon a mountain spirit, and overcoming a group of bandits. Weikuan was also known for his meritorious deeds (the exact nature of which is not spelled out). It seems that Weikuan possessed most of the qualities associated with the image of an eminent and sagely monk: extensive learning, contemplative expertise, exemplary conduct, thaumaturgic power, and a flair for popular meritorious activities.

Bo Juyi and Weikuan first met in 814, after Bo returned to the capital to assume the post of assistant secretary to the crown prince, following a three-year mourning period for his deceased mother. At that time, Bo went to Xingshan monastery to request Weikuan's instructions about the teachings of the Chan school. Bo himself recorded some of the conversations with the aged monk. They consist of four questions posed by Bo, followed by Weikuan's responses. The first question is about the role of a Chan teacher, and the other three are about related aspects of spiritual practice:

Bo's first question: "Since you are called a Chan teacher (*chanshi*), why do you explain the dharma (*fa*)?"

Weikuan's answer: "When the unsurpassed *bodhi* (awakening) is expressed with the body, it is the Vinaya (*lü*, rules of discipline); when it is explained with the mouth, it is the dharma; when it is practiced with the mind, it is Chan. Though there are these three applications, in reality they are the same. It is like different names given to rivers and lakes; though their names are not the same, the nature of the water is the same everywhere. Vinaya is Dharma, and Dharma is not separated from Chan. How could one falsely create any distinctions among the three?"

Bo's second question: "Since there are no distinctions, why should one engage in mental cultivation?"

Weikuan's answer: "The mind is fundamentally without defects, so how can one try to improve it through cultivation? One must not give rise to any thoughts, regardless of their defilement of purity."[128]

Bo's third question: "Since one should not think about defilements, is it that one should [also] not think about purity?"

Weikuan's answer: "There should be nothing inside a man's eye. Though gold dust is precious, it merely becomes a source of trouble when it enters the eye."

Bo's fourth question: "When there is no cultivation and no thought, how does one differ from an ordinary person?"[129]

Weikuan's answer: "Ordinary people are ignorant, while the followers of the two vehicles are prone to attachments. The forsaking of these two defects is called true cultivation. As to true cultivation, one should not move, nor should one forget things. Moving leads to attachment, while forgetting leads to sinking into a state of oblivious ignorance. These are the essential principles of mind [cultivation]."[130]

In these paragraphs, Weikuan comes across as a conservative exponent of Chan doctrine. His answers present doctrinal positions found in other records of the Hongzhou school, including Mazu's sermons. In the first paragraph, Weikuan blurs the distinctions between the three main aspects of Buddhist practice and the types of monks who represent them: specialists in doctrine, monastic discipline, and contemplative practice (i.e., Chan); thus he highlights the essential unity of the various elements that constitute Buddhism. Weikuan's responses to Bo's other queries are expressed in a fairly conventional manner. They deal with standard doctrinal and contemplative issues, such as the mind's innate purity, the perfection of mental detachment, and the safeguarding of a mental state of numinous awareness.

In the course of Weikuan's teaching career in Chang'an, his influence helped to advance the standing of the Hongzhou school and solidify the status of Mazu as a leader of the Chan movement. It is probable that Xianzong's bestowal of an honorary posthumous title upon Mazu during the Yuanhe era (806–821)—when Weikuan's prestige in Chang'an was at its peak—was influenced by Weikuan and the other disciples active in Chang'an. Moreover, in 815 Weikuan and Huaihui commissioned a memorial stūpa and a stele inscription for Mazu's teacher Huairang (who, as discussed in chapter 1, was an obscure figure whose life was not well documented).[131] The inscription, titled *Hengzhou buoresi guanyin dashi beiming bingxu*, was composed by Zhang Zhengfu (dates unknown) and is the earliest extant source about Huairang's life.[132] The commissioning of the inscription and the bestowal of Mazu's official title might appear to be the result of efforts led by Weikuan and Huaihui to ensure official recognition for Mazu and the Hongzhou school. A less cynical interpretation would be to view them as natural consequences of the prominent status and influence attained by the two monks, combined with an increased public recognition of Mazu and his lineage.

Weikuan and Huaihui were themselves recipients of official recognition. The court promptly granted posthumous titles to both of them the same year each of them died. Those disciples of Mazu who remained in the South also acknowledged Weikuan's success in the capital. As was already noted, his name appears in the list of prominent disciples in Mazu's stele inscription, and Xitang's memorial inscription presents Xitang and Weikuan as Mazu's two main disciples, whose teachings flourished in the South and the North, respectively.[133]

There are striking parallels between the lives of Weikuan and Huaihui.[134] They were of approximately the same age (Huaihui was younger by one year), they joined Mazu at roughly the same time, and after Mazu's death they both left Hongzhou and embarked on long periods of peripatetic life. The dates of their entry into Chang'an were also only one year apart, as were the times of their deaths. Huaihui was born in 755 in Quanzhou (in present-day Fujian) as a member of the Xie family.[135] He joined Mazu in 785 and remained with him until Mazu's death three years later. Over the next two decades, Huaihui stayed at a number of locations: first in Jiangsu, then north in Shandong, and finally in Hebei.[136] In Hebei, he took up residence at Baiyan monastery in Dingzhou. There he attracted a larger number of disciples and became a prominent Chan teacher.[137] According to Huaihui's biography in *Song gaoseng zhuan*, the constant requests for instruction from his students, whose numbers continued to swell, eventually became bothersome to him. He finally retired to the solitude of Zhongtiao mountain (located on the border of Shaanxi and Shanxi provinces), where he practiced meditation.

In 808, Emperor Xianzong invited Huaihui, who was fifty-two years old at the time, to come to preach at the capital. After his arrival, Huaihui settled at the Vairocana cloister of Zhangjing monastery, established by Daizong in 767 to commemorate his deceased mother. Before long, Huaihui became a popular Chan teacher in the capital. We are told that he instructed many monastic and lay students about the "essentials of Chan" (*chanyao*) and that numerous "imperial officials and famous scholars came daily to ask for his instructions."[138] Like Dayi and Weikuan, he also lectured and participated in public debates at the Linde Hall, and he attended vegetarian banquets for monks at the court, during which he was a guest of honor.[139]

Huaihui's teaching career in Chang'an ended with his death on January 14, 816, following a short illness he contracted during the cold Chang'an winter. Soon afterward, the emperor bestowed on him the posthumous title Chan teacher Da xuan jiao (Great Propagation of the Teaching),[140] and Quan Deyu and Jia Dao (779–843) wrote his memorial inscriptions. His most influential disciples were Hyŏnuk (787–868) and Hongbian (781–865). Hyŏnuk was a Korean monk who, after returning to his native land, established a thriving monastic community at Pongnim-san and later came to be recognized as the founder of one of the nine schools of Silla Sŏn.[141] Following his teacher, Hongbian taught in the capital. His primary place of residence was Jianfu monastery, located in the center of Chang'an. Hongbian also offered religious instructions to Emperor Xianzong.[142] He was a prominent Chan teacher whose active role in Chang'an ensured the Hongzhou school's continuous presence in the capital following the deaths of Weikuan and Huaihui.

Dayi, Weikuan, and Huaihui were the best-known monks associated with the Hongzhou school to teach in Chang'an, but not the only ones. Other disciples of Mazu active in Chang'an were Huayan Zhizang, Haozhi (who, like Weikuan, resided at Anguo monastery), Caotang, and Xingping.[143] *Chuandeng lu* also lists the names of three more disciples of Mazu who settled in Chang'an without giving any additional information about them: Huaitao, Jueping of Xiantong monastery, and Fuchong.[144]

Ruman and Chan in Luoyang

Like Chang'an, prior to the Tang period Luoyang had a long history as a capital of numerous dynasties. The government designated it as the dynasty's eastern capital in 657; it had already served as a temporary location of the court on a couple of occasions during Taizong's (r. 626–649) reign. The height of Luoyang's prestige and power came under the reign of Empress Wu, who designated it as the primary seat of her government during the 683–701 period. At that time, there was a sizable buildup of palaces, monasteries, and public projects, and Luoyang largely eclipsed Chang'an as the empire's political and cultural center. The reign of Empress Wu was also the high mark of the growth of Buddhism in the city. Under the generous patronage of the pious empress, the monasteries of Luoyang became vibrant hubs of multifarious Buddhist activities. The eminent monks supported by the empress included Fazang, the great systematizer of Huayan doctrine, and Shenxiu, the famous Chan teacher and leader of the Northern school.

Luoyang continued to serve as a seat of government during Xuanzong's early reign, as the emperor was forced to move the court there on a number of occasions due to the problem of transporting supplies to Chang'an, most of which came by water route from the South. After the government devised a new transportation system that enabled it to bring adequate provisions to Chang'an, the court returned there in 736, and Luoyang ceased to be the seat of government until the end of the dynasty. The city and the surrounding area suffered extensive damage during the An Lushan rebellion, when the rebels, the government troops, and their Uighur allies alike pillaged it. By the early ninth century, life in Luoyang was back to normal, although politically and culturally the city occupied a somewhat marginal position in comparison to Chang'an. Perhaps that was why more disciples of Mazu went to Chang'an than Luoyang.

The best-known representative of the Hongzhou school in Luoyang was Foguang Ruman (752–842?),[145] whose family name was Lu. He joined Mazu's monastery in Hongzhou; later he moved north and eventually took up residence at Jinge monastery on Wutai mountain. He visited Chang'an in 805 and offered religious instructions to the ailing emperor Shunzong. A record of a conversation between the emperor and Ruman includes this exchange:

> Shunzong asked, "Whence did the Buddha come? Where did he go after his passing away? As it is said that he constantly dwells in the world, where is the Buddha right now?"
> Ruman said, "The Buddha comes from the unconditioned (wuwei), and after his passing away he goes back to the unconditioned. The dharma body is like empty space—it is constantly

present when there is no mind (*wuxin*). When there is thought, it returns to no-thought (*wunian*), and when there is abode, it returns to no-abode (*wuzhu*). When coming, he comes for the sake of living beings, and when leaving he leaves for the sake of living beings. The pure ocean of suchness (*zhenru*) is transparent and its essence abides forever. The wise ones think about it thoughtfully, and then do not give rise to any doubts about it."[146]

In style and substance Ruman's response resembles Weikuan's passage introduced in the previous section. He comes across as a mainstream exponent of Mahāyāna doctrine. He uses popular Chan terms such as *wunian* (no-thought) and *wuxin* (no-mind), but his ideas reflect widely accepted views about the nature of Buddhahood that are not unique to the Chan school.

It is not clear when Ruman arrived in Luoyang,[147] but there he met his best-known disciple, Bo Juyi. The relationship with Bo is the best-documented part of Ruman's life, which is not surprising since most information about Ruman comes from Bo's writings. Ruman spent his final years at Xiangshan monastery, located in the area of the famous Longmen caves south of Luoyang's city gates. From a record about Bo's donation of a collection of his works to Shengshan monastery in 836, we learn that at an earlier date Bo received religious instructions from Ruman at that monastery.[148] In 842, Ruman and Bo founded a Buddhist association called the "Incense Fellowship." During this period Bo, who in 841 had retired with the title of minister of the Ministry of Justice, was most fervent in his Buddhist practice. He adopted a semi-monastic lifestyle and spent a substantial part of his time in religious practice, including meditation. Bo also wore the white robes of a Buddhist layman and called himself the "Layman from Xiangshan," a reference to the monastery where Ruman resided.[149]

Ruman died and was buried at Xiangshan. The exact date is uncertain, but he probably died in 842. Upon Bo's explicit request, made to his family shortly before his death in 846, he was buried next to Ruman's memorial pagoda.[150] The striking choice of burial site indicates the closeness between the two. Besides Ruman, other disciples of Mazu active in Luoyang were Funiu Zizai, Danxia, and Heijian.[151]

NOTES

1. Early Chan history is filled with monks who during their heyday enjoyed great popularity and had large followings, only to sink into historical oblivion and cede the place of preeminence to some of their less illustrious contemporaries. Probably the best example of such a monk is Shenxiu, the leader of the Northern school. Despite Shenhui's highly successful monastic career and the great influence he exerted during his lifetime, subsequently the relatively little-known Huineng supplanted Shenxiu as the "sixth patriarch" of Chan. For Shenxiu, see Faure, *The Will*

to Orthodoxy, 13–36, and McRae, *The Northern School*, 44–56. In an interesting case of historical irony, the near-oblivion of the Northern school from the Chan tradition's communal remembrance was shared by Shenhui, whose campaign against Shenxiu and his disciples was a consequential (even if sometimes overestimated) factor in the eventual demise of the Northern school. For Shenhui's campaign against the Northern school, see John R. McRae, "Shen-hui and the Teaching of Sudden Enlightenment," 234–35.

2. The number of Mazu's disciples is discussed in the second section of the appendix. The term "entering the room" implies personal closeness and mastery of the teachings learned from one's teacher. It thus conveys a sense of intimacy in the relationship between teacher/master and pupil/apprentice. Its origin goes back to a passage in *Lunyu* (The Analects of Confucius) 11/15: "You have ascended to the hall, but have not yet entered the [inner] room." Cf. D. C. Lau's translation of *The Analects*, 108. The term is used in both Confucianism and Buddhism.

3. QTW 501.2262a. Of the eleven monks listed, we know virtually nothing about five: Gaoying, Chongtai, Zhitong, Zhiguang, and Huiyun. The names of the first three appear at the beginning of fascicle 6 of *Chuandeng lu*, while the names of the last two appear nowhere else. It is probable that the inscription mentions these monks because of their seniority and/or their involvement in the building of the memorial stūpa at Shimen and the commissioning of the inscription.

4. For the list of Hongren's main disciples, see Jingjue's *Lengqie shizi ji*, T 85.1285c; for Huineng's list, see *Liuzu tanjing*, T 48.360a, and Philip B. Yampolsky, *The Platform Sūtra of the Sixth Patriarch*, 170.

5. For a reference to the ten great disciples of the Buddha in the Chinese Buddhist canon, see T 21.517c; for information about them, see Zenno Ishigami, *Disciples of the Buddha*, 17–75.

6. Among the monks listed in the table in "Information about Mazu's Disciples" in the appendix (table A.1) for whom we have information about both their birthplace and the location of their monastery, only five—Taiyu, Wuliao, Fazang, Xitang, and Huilang—returned to their native areas.

7. Table 2.1 is based on a table that appears in Ishii, *Sōdai zenshūshi no kenkyū*, 34, which in turn is based on data from CDL. The second column gives the number of disciples whose names appear CDL and whose primary monastery was located in the province listed in column 1. The third column lists the number of those who, among the monks listed in column 2, have biographical entries in fascicles 6, 7, or 8 of CDL (the other monks have only their name listed at the beginning of one of these three fascicles). The information presented in the table is tentative and should be used as a rough estimate only. There is little information about a number of these monks, and in some cases the connection with Mazu is not well documented. It should also be understood that not all data presented in CDL, which was published in 1004, are reliable. Notwithstanding such caveats, the table gives us a rough outline of the regional spread of the Hongzhou school.

8. It is difficult to assess the socioeconomic background of the families of Mazu's disciples. The biographical sources focus almost exclusively on events and activities that fit into predetermined patterns of religious behavior and only rarely provide data about the family background and social status of individual monks.

However, on the basis of various clues, such as observations about educational backgrounds, networks of association, and patronage, I postulate that for the most part the socioeconomic circumstances of Mazu's disciples were similar to those of Mazu: they came from local gentry families and received at least some classical education during their childhood. Some of them, such as Wuxie and Danxia, spent their youth in intensive study and preparation for the state examinations, an important step toward a career in the imperial bureaucracy. While some monks were from local branches of prestigious aristocratic families—e.g., Baizhang and Yanguan—most of them probably came from gentry families of local prominence.

9. Such a view is often presented in the writings of Japanese scholars and in popular books on Zen. For an example, see Kagamishima, "Hyakujō shingi no seiritsu to sono igi," 130. According to him, the self-supporting monastic lifestyle adopted by Chan monks serves as evidence that they led productive lives very much like the lives of the common people.

10. The earliest biographical source about Xitang's life is his stele inscription, *Gonggongshan xitang chishi dazhue chanshi chongjian dabaoguangda beiming*, which can be found in *Ganzhou fuzhi* 16.14a–15a (published in 1873) and *Ganxian zhi* 50.3a–4b. The same text is also reproduced in Ishii Shūdō, "Kōshūshū ni okeru Seidō Chizō no ichi ni tsuite," 281. Ishii also has a Japanese translation in his *Chūgoku zenshū shiwa*, 199–202. There was an earlier stele inscription composed by Li Bo (773–831) soon after Xitang's death in 817, which was destroyed in 845 during the Huichang-era persecution of Buddhism. The existence of the earlier inscription is confirmed by the extant inscription and by Xitang's brief biography in SGSZ. Furthermore, Xitang's original memorial pagoda is still extant at the site of his monastery in the vicinity of Ganzhou, Jiangxi. For a description of the site and the stone inscription from 820 that records the completion of Xitang's stūpa, which was rediscovered in 1987, see Suzuki Tetsuo, *Chūgoku zenshūshi ronkō*, 155–65, and *Sekkō kōzei chihō zenshū shiseki hōroku*, 113. In addition to the inscription, brief biographical information about Xitang can also be found in CDL 7, T 51.252a–b, SGSZ 10, T 50.766c (where he is not accorded a full biography, but only a brief entry attached at the end of Mazu's biography), and ZTJ 15.327. Xitang's significance is also discussed in Yanagida, "Shinzoku tōshi no keifu: jo no ichi," 26.

11. Mazu had two other disciples named Zhizang. The first one was Wushan Zhizang, a scholarly monk of Indian ancestry who wrote a commentary on the *Huayan Scripture*, whose study with Mazu is recorded in his biography in SGSZ 6, T 50.740c. The other was Huayan Zhizang, who taught at Huayan monastery in the capital; for his biography see SGSZ 11, T 50.775c, and Yanagida, *Shoki zenshū shisho no kenkyū*, 348 n. 10.

12. ZTJ 15.327.

13. In later Chan texts, Nanquan is also added to Xitang and Baizhang, and the three are presented as Mazu's greatest disciples. For examples, see MY, XZJ 118.407a, *Baizhang yulu*, XZJ 119.409b, 410c–d, and CDL 6, T 51.249b–c (translation in Cheng-chien, *Sun-Face Buddha*, 69).

14. See the previous section. Probably Dazhu was listed first because he was Mazu's most senior disciple, having joined Mazu during the early days in Fujian.

15. See *Tang zizhou huiyijingshe nanchanyuan sizhengtang beiming*, QTW 780.3608b–9c.

16. See discussion in Yanagida, "Goroku no rekishi," 464, and Ishii, "Kōshūshū ni okeru Seidō Chizō no ichi ni tsuite," 284. Moreover, in his preface to *Chuanxin fayao*, Pei Xiu states that Huangbo was a "Dharma nephew" of Baizhang and Xitang. Pei's mention of Xitang, who had no direct connection with Huangbo, indicates that around 850 Xitang was still regarded as a leading figure among Mazu's disciples.

17. See the text of the inscription in Ishii, "Kōshūshū ni okeru Seidō Chizō no ichi ni tsuite," 281.

18. SGSZ 10, T 50.766c. The use of the bestowal of a robe as a symbol of the orthodox transmission of the Dharma comes from the apocryphal story of the transmission from Hongren to Huineng. This story was probably invented by Shenhui as part of his campaign to establish Huineng as the sixth patriarch. For a popular version of this legend, see the Dunhuang version of *Liuzu tanjing*, T 48.338a. For Shenhui's argument about the transmission of the robe to Huineng, see Yang Zengwen, *Shenhui heshang chanhua lu*, 27, 202–3, and Tanaka Ryōshō, *Tonkō zenshū bunken no kenkyū*, 485–90.

19. The year of Xitang's birth is based on his stele inscription. The SGSZ biography, however, states that he died in 814, in which case his dates would be 735–814, rather than 738–817. For a further discussion of Xitang's dates, see Ishii, "Kōshūshū ni okeru Seidō Chizō no ichi ni tsuite," 282, and Suzuki, *Tō-Godai no zenshū*, 175–81. The evidence about which set of dates is correct is inconclusive (Ishii is inclined to follow the inscription, while Suzuki favors the SGSZ biography). Here I follow the stele inscription because it is an earlier and presumably more reliable source (even though it is preserved in late texts).

20. I am following the stele inscription. See the original text in Ishii, "Kōshūshū ni okeru Seidō Chizō no ichi ni tsuite," 281. According to CDL 7, T 51.252a, however, Xitang joined Mazu at Fojiyan (Fujian). As was noted in chapter 1, that is improbable. This information about the place of Xitang's first meeting with Mazu might be just a simple mistake, but it is possible that it was invented in order to present Xitang as a member of the first group of disciples who joined Mazu at Fojiyan.

21. SGSZ 10, T 50.766c.

22. The year of his ordination is the same according to both the stele inscription and the SGSZ biography, even though the two texts are in disagreement over the date of his death. For a summary of the differences between the dates for major events in Xitang's life in these two sources, see Suzuki, *Tō-Godai no zenshū*, 176–77.

23. SGSZ also mentions Pei Tong (d.u.) as an official who was among Xitang's supporters. His identity is not clear, although he might have been a member of the Pei clan and a relative of Pei Xu, the official who became Mazu's disciple at Gonggong mountain.

24. See "Training of Disciples in Hongzhou" and "Final Days and Passing Away" in chapter 1.

25. See Suzuki, *Tō-Godai no zenshū*, 177. For Qi's biography, see JTS 136.3750–51.

26. Biographies in JTS 171.4437–42, and XTS 118.4281–86. A supporter of Buddhism, Li was also associated with other Chan monks, including Mazu's disciple Guizong (see "Other Monks Active in Jiangxi and the South," below). He might have visited Xitang's monastery in 821, when he wrote the inscription, during a brief

period of service as a district magistrate (*cishi*) of Qianzhou, the prefecture where Xitang's monastery was located. See Suzuki, *Tō-Godai no zenshū*, 179.

27. CDL 7, T 51.252b; translation from Cheng-chien, *Sun-Face Buddha*, 98. For more information about Li Ao's relationship with Chan monks, see Timothy Hugh Barrett, *Li Ao: Buddhist, Taoist, or Neo-Confucian?* (especially 46–57). While it is conceivable that Xitang and Li Ao met, the story is late and of uncertain provenance, which casts doubt on its reliability. See Barrett, *Li Ao*, 50. In addition to Xitang, there are records about Li Ao's meetings with three other disciples of Mazu: Yaoshan, Dayi, and Daotong. See Tokiwa Daijō, *Shina ni okeru Bukkyō to Jukyō Dōkyo*, 128, and Suzuki, *Tō-Godai no zenshū*, 54–55. The alleged meeting between Li Ao and Yaoshan is memorialized in a painting by Ma Gongxian (thirteenth century), kept in the collection of Nanzenji, Kyoto. See Helmut Brinker and Hiroshi Kanazawa, *Zen: Masters of Meditation in Images and Writings*, 229.

28. SGSZ 10, T 50.766c. See also the text of the inscription in Ishii, "Kōshūshū ni okeru Seidō Chizō no ichi ni tsuite," 281. The CDL biography states that Dajue was his second title, and that he first received the title Daxuan. As Ishii points out (282–83), this mistake probably arose from a mix-up of the names of the posthumous titles and pagodas of Xitang and Huaihui, also evident in the ZTJ biography.

29. I am following the account in SGSZ. For Wei's official biographies, see JTS 162.4244–45 and XTS 160.4976–77.

30. CDL includes a brief entry of only one disciple of Xitang, a little-known monk called Qianzhou Chuwei (d.u.). See CDL 9, T 51.269a. ZTJ 17.373 also records two of Chuwei's dialogues, with Yangshan and an anonymous monk.

31. ZTJ 17.374. For a brief record of his teaching, see *Sŏnmun pojang nok*, XZJ 113.499a–b, translated in Buswell, *The Korean Approach to Zen*, 12–13. For Hyech'ŏl's memorial inscription, which was composed in 872, see *Chōsen kinseki sōran*, vol. 1, 116–19. He and Honch'ŏk are also briefly mentioned in ZTJ 17.374; the same fascicle has a somewhat longer biography of Toǔi (ZTJ 17.373–74). All three monks are also listed as Xitang's disciples at the beginning of fascicle 9 of CDL (T 51.264a), with the note that they are not accorded biographies because the compiler did not have any materials about them. Faure, *The Will to Orthodoxy*, 47, mistakenly identifies them as disciples of Mazu. For further discussion of the Hongzhou school's impact on the development of Chan/Sŏn in Korea, see "Influence on the Spread of Chan in Korea" in chapter 3.

32. The earliest source about Baizhang's life is his stūpa inscription, *Tang hongzhou baizhangshan gu huaihai chanshi taming*, composed by Chen Xu soon after Baizhang's death. According to inscription's colophon, Baizhang's memorial stūpa was unveiled on November 2, 818. In the inscription, Zhen states that he personally received Baizhang's teachings while he was in Jiangxi on an official duty. There are two editions of the text: in QTW 446.2014a–b, and *Chixiu baizhang qinggui*, T 48.1156b–57a. For a Japanese *yomikudashi* rendering of the inscription (accompanied with the original text), see Ishii Shūdō, "Hyakujō shingi no kenkyū," 20–23. Other pertinent sources are Baizhang's biographies in CDL 6, T 51.249b–250c, and ZTJ 14.317–21. His biography in SGSZ 10, T 50.770c–71a, mostly recounts the legend about Baizhang's establishment of a separate Chan monastery and is of little value as a biographical source.

33. QTW 446.2014a.

34. I am following the stūpa inscription. ZTJ 14.317 mistakenly states that his surname was Huang.

35. There is a discrepancy between Baizhang's dates given in his stūpa inscription and the dates in his biographies in CDL and SGSZ. Though all three sources agree on the date of his death, they disagree about his age at the time of his death. The stele inscription states that he died at the age of sixty-five, while the other two texts claim he lived to the age of ninety-four, in which case his dates would be 720–814. I follow the inscription because it is a more reliable source, and because the other dates make little sense in the context of the general chronology of Baizhang's life. For further discussion of Baizhang's dates, see Yanagida, "Goroku no rekishi," 234; Ishii, "Hyakujō shingi no kenkyū," 19–20; and Ui, Zenshū shi kenkyū, vol. 2, 371–72.

36. ZTJ 14.317.

37. See Yaoshan's biography in SGSZ 17, T 50.816a–c (which is included under the category "Dharma protectors," hufa). Ui has suggested that Huizhao is the same monk as Huairang's disciple Shenzhao, whose name is listed at the beginning of fascicle 6 of CDL. See Ui, Zenshūshi kenkyū, vol. 2, 329, and Yinshun, Zhongguo chanzong shi, 321, which makes the same argument. I find this inference, based on circumstantial evidence, to be unconvincing.

38. Following the CDL and SGSZ biographies.

39. For information about the mountain, see Jiangxi tongzhi 3, 1082, and Suzuki Tetsuo, Sekkō kōzei chihō zenshū shiseki hōroku, 67.

40. There is a famous (but also rather late) story that supposedly expresses Baizhang's feelings about the mountain: "A monk asked Baizhang, 'What is [most] unique?' Baizhang said, 'Sitting alone on the summit of Daxiong [Mountain].' The monk bowed, and Baizhang hit him." Baizhang yulu, XZJ 119.409c. The same story forms the core of case 26 in Biyan lu 3, T 48.166c.

41. Based on a table presented in Ishikawa Rikisan, "Baso kyōdan no tenkai to sono shijishatachi," 167–68. The contrast between the regional affiliations of Mazu and Baizhang's disciples becomes evident when we compare this table with table 2.1 in the first section of this chapter.

42. See the text of the inscription in Ishii, "Hyakujō shingi no kenkyū," 22.

43. The Chinese translation of this lengthy Indian treatise can be found in T 27.1–1004.

44. See Ishii, "Hyakujō shingi no kenkyū," 39–40. However, in Tō-Godai no zenshū, 143, Suzuki suggests that Baizhang Fazheng, Baizhang Niepan, and Baizhang Weizheng are all the same person. The confusion started with Fazheng's and Nieban's stele inscriptions (see QTW 713.3246a for a fragment of Fazheng's inscription). The mix-up is also evident in the shifting of Weizheng's biography in CDL from among the biographies of Mazu's disciples to among the biographies of Baizhang's disciples, and vice versa, by the editors of different editions of the text. It seems to me that Mazu's disciple Weizheng should not be mixed with Baizhang's disciple(s). As for the Fazheng, who is mentioned in Baizhang's stūpa inscription, and Niepan, it is still uncertain whether they are the same person (as suggested by Suzuki) or two persons (as implied by Ishii), but to me Ishii's argument seems more convincing. To

add to the confusion, Yanagida has suggested that Fazheng was a disciple of Mazu, not Baizhang. See Yanagida, "Shinzoku tōshi no keifu: jo no ichi," 25.

45. For the later history of Baizhang mountain and the monastery, see Ishii's two articles, "Hyakujō kyōdan to Isan kyōdan (zoku)," 293–95, and "Hyakujō shingi no kenkyū," 38–44.

46. Fanyun's name appears in the list of Baizhang's disciples in CDL 9, but nothing is known about either him or Shenxing.

47. QTW 446.2014a. There is no further information about Ling'ai.

48. The contents of BGL are discussed in part II of this volume, especially in the last chapter.

49. An example of the later tendency to exalt Baizhang's achievements as a monastic legislator can be found in "Baizhangshan dazhi shoushengsi tianxiashi biaogeji," a short text that is appended at the end of *Chixiu Baizhang qinggui*, the influential Chan monastic manual compiled in 1336. There Baizhang is compared to Bodhidharma, the putative founder of Chan. T 48.1157b–c.

50. Writings on the scope and significance of Baizhang's putative rules have been a minor cottage industry in Japanese Buddhist scholarship. Examples of publications that highlight Baizhang's role as a monastic legislator include Ui Hakuju, *Zenshū shi kenkyū*, vol. 2, 375–95; Ōishi Shuyū, "Ko shingi ni tsuite"; Kagamishima Genryū, "Hyakujō shingi no seiritsu to sono igi" and *Zennen shingi*, 1–3; Yanagida Seizan, "Chūgoku zenshū shi," 58–60, and "Goroku no rekishi," 250, 472, 548; Suzuki Tetsuo, *Tō-Godai no zenshū*, 142–43; Sato Tatsugen, *Chūgoku Bukkyō ni okeru kairitsu no kenkyū*, 479–89; Tanaka Ryōshō, *Tonkō zenshū bunken no kenkyū*, 469–76; Ishii, *Chūgoku zenshū shiwa*, 212–26. Similar views can also be found in Kenneth Ch'en, *The Chinese Transformation of Buddhism*, 148–51. For a critique of these views, see Griffith Foulk "The Ch'an School and Its Place in the Buddhist Monastic Tradition."

51. SGSZ 10, T 50.770c. A brief account of Baizhang's establishment of separate Chan monastery can also be found in Zanning's short history of Buddhist monasticism in China, *Da Song sengshi lüe* (c. 978–999), in a section entitled "Bieli chanju" (Establishment of Separate Chan Residence). T 54.240a–b.

52. For the Chan "rules of purity" genre, see Yifa, *The Origins of Buddhist Monastic Codes in China: An Annotated Translation and Study of the* Chanyuan Qinggui, and Theodore Griffith Foulk, "*Chanyuan qinggui* and Other 'Rules of Purity' in Chinese Buddhism."

53. For brief entries for these monks, see CDL 6, T 51.248a (Weijian and Fahui), and CDL 7, T 51.252a (Changxing). Daotong's biography in SGSZ also states that he resided at Shimen for some time, after which he traveled to Nanyue to meet Shitou. SGSZ 10, T 50.767c.

54. See Suzuki, *Tō-Godai no zenshū*, 123.

55. The little information we have about Fazang's life comes from his short biography in SGSZ, which is included in the section named "spiritual resonance" (*gantong*). See SGSZ 20, T 50.840b.

56. We do not know the year of birth and the birthplace of Guishan. The main source about his life is the short biography in SGSZ 17, T 50.817b–c. For some reason, Zanning placed Guizong's biography in the category of "Dharma

protectors," along with Yaoshan's biography. Guizong's biography in CDL 7, T 51.255c–56b, is somewhat longer, but it mostly contains short dialogues and has little relevant information about his life. The biography in ZTJ 15.340–44 adds a couple of poems and a few records of his conversations with noted literati. There are a few stories that suggest he was close to Nanquan, who also joined Mazu in Hongzhou. See SGSZ 17, T 50.817b.

57. SKSZ 17, T 50.817b.

58. See *Lushan ji*, T 51.1032b; *Lushan chengtian guizongchansi zhongxiusi ji*, in *Wuxi ji* 7.4b (*Siku quanshu* ed.); and Suzuki, *Tō-Godai no zenshū*, 148.

59. SGSZ 17, T 50.817c.

60. In addition to the poems included in his biography in ZTJ, another one of his poems is preserved in CDL 29, T 51.251b–c.

61. Bo Juyi's meeting with Guizong is described in SGSZ 17, T 50.817b.

62. *Bo Juyi ji* 43.933–35. For a translation, see Richard E. Strassberg, *Inscribed Landscapes: Travel Writing from Imperial China*, 134–36. For Bo's involvement with Buddhism during this period, see Hirano Kensho, "Haku Kyoi no bungaku to bukkyō," 132–41, and Kenneth Ch'en, *The Chinese Transformation of Buddhism*, 200–205. Bo's relationship with Lushan and its impact on his poetry are discussed in Shimosada Masahiro, *Hakushi bunshō o yomu*, 200–224. For a general overview of Bo's life and literary activities during his posting in Jiangzhou, see Arthur Waley, *The Life and Times of Po Chü-i*, 105–6, 115–28, and Hanafusa Hideki, *Haku Kyoi kenkyū*, 53–61.

63. See *Bo Juyi ji* 16.328–29 (vol. 2) and Sun Changwu, *Tangdai wenxue yu fojiao*, 186, and "Haku Kyoi to bukkyō: zen to jōdo," 187. Most of the information about their encounter comes from Buddhist sources rather than Bo's writings. It appears that their connection was not as strong as the one that Bo developed with Weikuan and Ruman, whom he met in Chang'an and Luoyang (see discussion in "Mazu's Disciples in Chang'an," below).

64. Li's study with Guizong is noted in the following sources: SGSZ 17, T 50.817b–c; CDL 7, T 51.256b; ZTJ 15.340–41; and *Lushan ji*, T 51.1032b. Li also had contacts with other Chan monks.

65. See T 14.546b. The mustard-seed metaphor also appears in the *Huayan jing* and the *Da baoji jing*.

66. ZTJ 15.340; cf. CDL 7, T 51.256b. According to the SGSZ version of the story, Li went to Guizong's monastery at the urging of Bo, and Bo was present when this conversation took place. SGSZ 17, T 50.817b. Such a conversation could have taken place in 822, when Bo visited Lushan again en route to his new post as governor of Hangzhou. The same scriptural passage is quoted in Bo's record of a debate between the three teachings held in 827 at the court in Chang'an, in which he participated. See *Bo Juyi ji* 68.1437 (vol. 4).

67. CDL 9, T 51.266c, and ZTJ 16.364. The ZTJ version and the Song edition of CDL have "eighty-eight" disciples instead of "eighty-four." *Daochang*, translated here as "site of enlightenment," was originally a Chinese rendering of the Sanskrit term *bodhimaṇḍa*; it is also sometimes translated as "sanctuary."

68. See Suzuki, *Tō-Godai no zenshū*, 168. Shigong's biography in CDL contains a well-known story that in a dramatized fashion depicts his first meeting with Mazu.

See CDL 6, T 51.248b, and Cheng-chien, *Sun-Face Buddha*, 71–72. A similar version of the story can also be found in ZTJ 14.314.

69. The traditional account of Shigong's humble origins is not without problems. In ZTJ 14.314–15 there is a poem composed by him that has the same title as, and literary form similar to, a poem composed by the well-educated Danxia (see ZTJ 4.100–101). If the poem's attribution is correct, it implies that Shigong was not an illiterate country person.

70. Daoming's brief biographies in CDL 6, T 51.249a, and ZTJ 14.316, which contain little of great interest, mention that during the early years of his monastic training Dongshan came to study with Daoming.

71. The main sources about Zhenshu are his stele inscription, *Yangqishan zhenshu dashi beiming*, QTW 919.4245a–b, composed by Zhixian, and his biography in SGSZ 10, T 50.770b–c (which for the most part is based on the inscription). There is also his brief biographical entry in CDL 8, T 51.262a–b, which does not add any useful information. The identity of the stele inscription's author is unclear. Suzuki has argued that the name in QTW is mistaken, and that this monk's name should be read as Zhixian; Suzuki, *Tō-Godai no zenshū*, 165–66. If that is the case, he might be the same monk as Zhixian, who is mentioned in Wuxie's biography in SGSZ 10, T 50.769a, as the author of Wuxie's record. See the discussion in Yanagida, "Goroku no rekishi," 531.

72. The main biographical sources about Ruhui are SGSZ 11, T 50.773b, ZTJ 15.338–39, and CDL 7, T 51.255b–c. Ruhui went to Jingshan's monastery in 773, and he later joined Mazu's congregation in Hongzhou. For the study of Mazu's disciples under Niutou school teachers, see "Interactions with Other Chan Lineages" in chapter 3.

73. "After Daji [i.e., Mazu] departed from the world, his teachings flourished without equals." SGSZ 11, T 50.773b.

74. SGSZ 11, T 50.773b.

75. Official biographies in JTS 159.4187–90 and XTS 165.5080–82.

76. Cui's commission to this provincial post came about as a result of his and Chief Minister Pei Du's (765–839) unsuccessful bid in 818 to block an appointment of the finance official Huangfu Bo (c. 755–820) to the position of chief minister. See SGSZ 11, T 50.773b; Suzuki, *Tō-Godai no zenshū*, 27; and Michael T. Dalby, "Court Politics in Late T'ang Times," 632–33.

77. SGSZ 11, T 50.773b. Liu is not accorded a biography in the standard histories. He composed inscriptions for Shitou, Ruhui, Danxia, Huilang,· and Nanquan.

78. For Huilang, see CDL 14, T 51.264, and ZTJ 4.102.

79. The main biographical sources about Tanzang are his entries in SGSZ 11, T 50.774a–b, and CDL 8, T 51.261a–b, which are brief and similar. Large parts of both of them consist of a hagiographic account about Tanzang's mystical dog and his feat of subduing a large malevolent python.

80. The main biographical sources about Deng Yinfeng are his entries in SGSZ 21, T 50.847a, and CDL 8, T 51.259b–c. The headline of the SGSZ biography has Beitai (mountain) instead of Wutai.

81. SGSZ 21, T 50.847a.

82. CDL 8, T 51.259c; translation adapted from Cheng-Chien, *Sun-Face Buddha*, 135–36. There is a different version of the same story in SGSZ 21, T 50.847a.

83. The main source about Yanguan's life is his stūpa inscription, *Hangzhou yanguan-xian haichan-yuan chanmen dashi tabei,* composed by Lu Jianqiu (789–846). The inscription is preserved in QTW 733.3354b–c and WYYH 868.4578a–79a. Lu also wrote another inscription on the back of the original stele, titled *Chanmen dashi beiyin ji,* QTW 733.3354a–b. The second inscription was written during the restoration of Buddhism initiated by emperor Xuanzong after the end of the Huichang persecution. An additional source is the biography in SGSZ 11, T 50.776b–77a, which seems to be based on the stūpa inscription, although there are some discrepancies between the two (mainly differences in the names of persons and places, which might be due to copying errors or misprints). There are also the less useful biographies in CDL 7, T 51.254a–b, and ZTJ 15.332. None of these sources gives the year of his birth, but based on the inscription's statement that he was "over seventy years old" around 820, we can deduce that he lived to be over ninety.

84. Following SGSZ; the stele inscription gives an alternate rendering of the name of this monk as Zhiyan 知嚴.

85. SGSZ 11, T 50.777a. The second stele inscription makes no mention of the title. Suzuki surmises that the source used by Zanning was another inscription, which is no longer extant but whose title is mentioned in *Yudi jisheng.* Suzuki, *Tō-godai zenshū shi,* 135–36.

86. The earliest sources of information about Dazhu are his biographies in ZTJ 14.309–11 and CDL 6, T 51.246c–48a. The earlier of the two was compiled well over a century after his death.

87. The CDL biography, whose reliability is suspect, seemingly contradicts this sequence of events. Instead, it suggests that Dazhu was ordained in Yuezhou (Zhejiang), and then went to Jiangxi, where he studied with Mazu for six years. After that he supposedly returned to Yuezhou to take care of his first teacher, who at the time was old and sick. CDL 6, T 51.246c.

88. The treatise was probably written between 765 and 785. It exhibits traces of influence from Shenhui's writings. According to a story in CDL, Mazu read the treatise and was impressed by it. CDL 6, T 51.246c.

89. The main biographical source about Damei is his short biography in SGSZ 11, T 50.776a–b. This biography was probably based on a stele inscription composed by Jiang Ji, which was written one year after his death. See Suzuki, *Tō-godai zenshū shi,* 148. Other sources are his biographies in CDL 7, T 51.254c–55a, and ZTJ 15.336–37. It is interesting to note that the SGSZ biography makes no mention of his study with Mazu.

90. See XZJ 119.47c–d; and Cheng-chien, *Sun-Face Buddha,* 73–74. The story is translated in the section "It is not a thing" in chapter 5.

91. For Yuquan monastery, see "Study with Huairang" in chapter 1.

92. His Korean disciples are mentioned in CDL 10, T 51.273b, 280a.

93. For an edited copy of this manuscript, see *Kanazawa bunko shiryō zensho: Butten 1, zenseki hen,* 13–18. A copy of the original manuscript can be found in Yanagida Seizan and Shiina Kōyū, *Zengaku tenseki sōkan, betsukan,* 253–63. For a discussion of the text, see Ishikawa Rikisan, "Kanazawabunko-hon 'Minshū Daibai-san Jō zenji goroku' ni tsuite."

94. The phrase "scriptures enter the treasury" refers to Xitang, as the character for "treasury" appears in his religious name, Zhizang. In the same vein, "meditation returns to the sea" refers to Baizhang, whose religious name, Huaihai, means "cherishing the sea."

95. MY, XZJ 118.407a; CDL 6, T 51.249b–c; Cheng-chien, *Sun-Face Buddha*, 69. A note inserted in the CDL edition points out that Nanquan does not appear in the earlier version of the story.

96. See SGSZ 11, T 50.772b–73a.

97. SGSZ 11, T 50.772c.

98. See Victor Cunrui Xiong, *Sui-Tang Chang'an: A Study in the Urban History of Medieval China*, 264. According to Xiong, the position was a leadership post of the Buddhist community in the capital.

99. SGSZ 11, T 51.773a, and *Fozu tongji* 42, T 49.384b.

100. Xiong, *Sui-Tang Chang'an*, 252; and Zou Zongxu, *The Land within the Passes: A History of Xian*, 195. For additional information on Chang'an (and Luoyang), see also Hiraoka Takeo, *Chōan to Rakuyō* (3 vols.).

101. The earliest source about Dayi's life is his stele inscription, *Xingfusi neidaochang gongfeng dade dayi chanshi beiming*, QTW 715.3258a–59a (vol. 4). The scholar-official Wei Chuhou (773–823) composed the inscription soon after Dayi's death. For a Japanese *yomikudashi* rendering of the inscription, see Ishii Shūdō, "Enshū Yōgisan o meguru nanshūzen no dōkō," 199–202. Other relevant sources are his biographies in ZTJ 15.328–29 and CDL 7, T 51.253a, both of which are largely based on the inscription. For Wei Chuhou's official biography, see JTS 159.4182–87.

102. QTW 715.3258c.

103. A wealth of information about Ehu mountain, especially its Buddhist history and the monks who resided on it, can be found in *Ehu fengding zhi*, in *Zhongguo fosi zhi conkan*, vol. 20, 17–270.

104. For Liu's biography, see JTS 137.3762–63.

105. QTW 715.3258c.

106. A conversation between Dayi and Li Ao is recounted in CDL 7, T 51.253a. See also the conversation between Li Ao and Xitang in the section on Xitang, above.

107. Following the inscription and the ZTJ biography. Yanagida Seizan, *Shoki zenshū shisho no kenkyū*, 395, states that he arrived in Changan in the fourth month of 803, without indicating the source of this information. The CDL biography, on the other hand, mistakenly states that he was invited to the capital by emperor Xianzong (r. 805–820). See CDL 7, T 51.253a. The discrepancy between the sources concerning the time of his arrival in Changan is briefly discussed in Suzuki, *Tō-Godai no zenshū*, 169.

108. QTW 715.3258b; Jinhua Chen, "One Name, Three Monks: Two Northern Chan Masters Emerge from the Shadow of Their Contemporary, the Tiantai Master Zhanran (711–782)," 29–31.

109. In ZJL there is a short record of Dayi's answers to questions posed by other monks in the capital. See ZJL 1, T 48.419a. The same record also contains a short question-and-answer exchange between Dayi and the emperor, although it is not clear whether the emperor in question is Dezong or Shunzong.

110. For the palace, see Nancy Shatzman Steinhardt, *Chinese Imperial City Planning*, 101–2, and Xiong, *Sui-Tang Chang'an*, 91–93.

111. A record of a conversation between Dayi, Shunzong, and another monk can be found in ZTJ 15.329. In the version of the same conversation in CDL 7, T 51.253a, the emperor participating in the discussion is Xianzong instead of Shunzong. The CDL biography also contains another record of a different conversation between Shunzong and Dayi.

112. For more information on the short reign of this Tang monarch, see the translation of his veritable record, originally composed by Han Yu, in Bernard S. Solomon, *The Veritable Record of the Tang Emperor Shun-ts'ung*.

113. Chengguan wrote a short piece on the nature of the mind for Shunzong when the latter was still a crown prince. Because of its Chan-like idiom, this composition is included in CDL 30, T 51.459b–c. Shunzong's commissioning of this and other two texts from Chengguan are mentioned in Chengguan's biography in SGSZ 5, T 50.737a–b.

114. For Shunzong's invitation to Shili to teach at the court, see *Fozu tongji*, T 49.380b. Shili's brief biographical entry in ZTJ 4.95 also contains the same brief excerpt from a conversation with the emperor. That is followed by a related conversation between the emperor and Dayi, presented in a manner suggesting that both monks had an audience with the emperor at the same time. Ruman's meeting with Shunzong is discussed later.

115. In her dissertation, Linda L. Penkower suggests that the meeting between the two could have taken place in 775, even though there is no mention in any of the sources about Zhanran's life that he ever visited Changan. See Penkower, "T'ian-t'ai during the T'ang Dynasty: Chan-jan and the Sinification of Buddhism," 111. As that was some three decades before Dayi's sojourn to Changan, the two could not have met at that time.

116. For the different monks with the name Zhanran, see Chen, "One Name, Three Monks."

117. QTW 715.3258b; Chen, "One Name, Three Monks," 32–33.

118. See Zongmi's accounts in XZJ 14.277c, XZJ 15.131c, and XZJ 110.432b. A brief reference to the council also appears in *Fozu tongji*, T 49.380a, but with no mention of Shenhui.

119. Questions about Zongmi's account are also raised in Yanagida, *Shoki zenshū shisho no kenkyū*, 346.

120. Chen, "One Name, Three Monks," 35–37.

121. *Zimen jingxun* 2, T 48.1048b–c.

122. The earliest source about Weikuan's life is his memorial inscription, *Xijing xingshansi chuanfatang bei*, composed by Bo Juyi soon after Weikuan's death in 817. The inscription can be found in the following collections: QTW 678.3069c–70a; *Boshi wenji* 41.11a–14a (*Sibu congkan* ed.); *Bo juyi ji* 41.911–13; and WYYH 866.4570b–71b. Additional sources are his biographies in SGSZ 10, T 50.768a–b, and CDL 7, T 51.255a–b, both of which are based on Bo's inscription.

123. The location of Weiguo monastery is uncertain.

124. *Chuanfatang bei*, in *Boshi wenji*, 12b.

125. In addition to Bo Juyi's inscription, Xianzong's invitation to Weikuan is also recorded in *Fozu tongji*, T 49.380c.

126. CDL 10, T 51.273c, lists the names of six of Weikuan's disciples, all of whom were active in the capital. Two of them—Yichong and Yuanjing—are mentioned in Bo's inscription as Weikuan's main disciples. CDL has different spellings of the two names.

127. *Chuanfatang bei*, in *Boshi wenji*, 12a.

128. The same idea is expressed in one of Mazu's sermons. See Cheng-chien, *Sun-Face Buddha*, 63.

129. Some versions have *qin* 勤 (diligent) instead of *dong* 動 (movement, to move) in this and the following sentence.

130. *Bo Juyi ji* 41.912; cf. *Boshi changqing ji*, 24.13a–b; translation adapted in part from Cheng-chien, *Sun-Face Buddha*, 36–37, and Kenneth Ch'en, *The Chinese Transformation of Buddhism*, 199–200. A similar version of the conversation appears in CTL 7, T 51.255a–b. See also Arthur Waley, *The Life and Times of Po Chü-i*, 99. In addition to Bo's record of his conversation with Weikuan, the only other extant account of Weikuan's teachings is a sermon recorded in ZJL 98, T 48.942b–c.

131. There is a slight confusion about the dating of the inscription. The QTW edition states that the inscription was composed in the eighteenth year of the Yuanhe era (806–820), which is probably a misprint as that era did not last eighteen years. The *Fozu lidai tongzai* edition of the inscription has the "tenth year of the Yuanhe era" instead, which is probably the correct reading, as suggested in Suzuki, *Tō-Godai no zenshū*, 11. The commissioning of the inscription by Weikuan and Huiahui is clearly stated at the beginning of the text.

132. QTW 619.2767b–c, *Tang wenzui* 62.5b–6b, and *Fozu lidai tongzai*, T 49.595c–96a (the last version omits the closing verse section). Weikuan and Huaihui figure prominently in Huairang's biography in SGSZ 9, T 50.761a–b, but the account presented there is somewhat confused and makes no mention of their commissioning of the inscription, which is mistakenly attributed to Guideng.

133. See the inscription in Ishii, "Kōshūshū ni okeru Seidō Chizō no ichi ni tsuite," 281, and the section on Xitang in this chapter.

134. The main biographical source about Huaihui's life is his stele inscription, *Tang zhangjingsi baiyan dashi beiming bingxu*, composed by Quan Deyu, who also wrote Mazu's inscription. The inscription is preserved in QTW 501.2260b–c and WYYH 866.4568a–b. Additional sources are his biographies in SGSZ 10, T 50.767c–68a, CDL 7, T 51.252b–c, and ZTJ 14.325–26. There was also another inscription composed by the poet Jia Dao (779–843). That inscription is no longer extant, but it is mentioned in the SGSZ and ZTJ biographies. On basis of a reference in *Minzhong jinshi zhi* 1, which states that Jia Dao wrote down the inscription composed by Quan, Suzuki, *Tō-godai zenshū shi*, 374–75, suggests that it is probable that there was only one inscription. However, the differences between the SGSZ biography and Quan's inscription, together with the fact that the SGSZ biography mentions only Jia's inscription, suggests that there were two different inscriptions; Zanning probably only used the one composed by Jia when he wrote Huaihui's biography in SGSZ.

135. There is a discrepancy between his dates as presented in the stele inscription and the SGSZ biography on one side, and in the CDL and ZTJ biographies on the other. According to the last two texts, the year of his death was 818 instead of 816. That is probably a mistake. See the discussion in Ishii, "Kōshūshū ni okeru Seidō Chizō no ichi ni tsuite," 282–83. However, note that Ishii gives the year of Huaihui's death as 815, probably erring in the conversion of the date of his death—in January 816—from the Chinese into the Western calendar.

136. See SGSZ 10, T 50.767c–68a, and Du Jiwen and Wei Daoru, *Zhongguo chanzong tongshi*, 236.

137. Throughout his life, Huaihui remained closely associated with Baiyan monastery. In the title of his inscription he is referred as the "the great teacher of Baiyan [monastery]." Quan Deyu also notes that during his life Huaihui was commonly referred to as Baiyan.

138. SGSZ 10, T 50.768a.

139. WYYH 866.4568a and SGSZ 10, T 50.768a.

140. SGSZ 10, T 50.768a.

141. For Hyŏnuk's brief biography, see ZTJ 17.374–75.

142. A series of questions posed by Xianzong accompanied by Hongbian's answers are recorded in his biography in CDL 9, T 51.269a–c. It is interesting to note that in response to the first question about the Northern and Southern schools of Chan, Hongbian presents a summary of Chan's early genealogical history that is in tune with the "orthodox" view presented in later Chan chronicles such as CDL and ZTJ.

143. For Huayan, see his biography in SGSZ 11, T 50.775c; for Haozhi, see his biography in SGSZ 30, T 50.894c–95a; for Caotang, see his brief entry in CDL 8, T 51.262a; and for Xingping, see CDL 8, T 51.262b, and ZTJ 20.453–54.

144. See CDL 6, T 51.245c; and CDL 7, T 51.251c.

145. The earliest biographical source about Ruman is a brief inscription titled *Foguang heshang zhenzan bingxu*, QTW 677.3054c and *Bo Juyi ji* 71. 1503 (vol. 4), composed by Bo Juyi shortly after Ruman's death. I suspect that the extant text in QTW is only a fragment of the whole composition. An additional source is his short biography in CDL 6, T 51.249a, which consists almost entirely of a record of a conversation between him and Emperor Shunzong. The rest of the information about Ruman comes from scattered references in the writings of Bo Juyi.

146. CDL 6, T 51.249a. The late date of the text in which this conversation is recorded raises doubts about its authenticity. However, its contents and style resemble those of similar records composed around that time, which suggests that it might be a record of conversation between Shunzong and Ruman.

147. According to "Henglongsi ji" (Record of Henglong monastery) in *Hunan tongzhi* 239, Ruman established Henglong monastery, located in Hengzhou (Hunan) during the Zhenyuan era (785–805). This record was composed in 1075, and because of its late date the reliability of this information is questionable, although it is possible that Ruman established this monastery. See the discussion in Suzuki, *Tō-Godai no zenshū*, 45.

148. *Boshi changqing ji* 61.22a–b.

149. JTS 166.4356 and Eugene Feifel, "Biography of Po Chü-i—Annotated translation from *chüan* 166 of the *Chiu T'ang-shu*," 305.

150. JTS 166.4358 and Feifel, "Biography of Po Chü-i," 310. It is also interesting to note that Bo Juyi is accorded a short biography in CDL 10, T 51.279c–80a, where he is presented as the only disciple of Ruman.

151. For Funiu, see SGSZ 11, T 50.771c–72a, CDL 7, T 51.253a–b, and ZTJ 15.329–30. Regarding Heijian, there are only the two very brief references in CDL 8, T 51.262b, and ZTJ 15.347.

3

The Hongzhou School and Mid-Tang Chan

The Hongzhou school is usually described as an essentially local or provincial movement based in the South.[1] The provincial character is suggested by its name, which comes from a prefecture in Jiangxi, located far away from the two capitals in the North. The Hongzhou school is also singled out for its putative lack of interest in engaging and seeking support from the imperial court and the aristocratic elites, especially those based in the capitals. This attitude is said to stand in contrast to the court-oriented outlook of early Chan, especially the Northern school, and of Tang Buddhism as a whole. These characterizations of the Hongzhou school's growth are closely related to the general view of it as the vanguard of a new Chan movement that initiated a sharp break with past traditions. The survey of the Hongzhou school's regional growth presented in the previous chapter, which traced the forming of monastic communities by Mazu's disciples in various parts of the Tang empire, challenges the interpretations of the school's local character and its refusal to obtain imperial and aristocratic patronage. As we saw, the establishment of monastic centers by Mazu's disciples was not restricted to the South, but rather extended to virtually all reaches of the vast empire, with significant ramifications for the development of the whole Chan tradition.

This chapter concludes the study of the Hongzhou school's history by integrating and interpreting the data about its growth pattern and the patronage networks that facilitated it. It also situates the rise of the Hongzhou school in relation to the broader historical context of Tang Chan, explores its interactions with other Chan schools, and elaborates on its conception of spiritual lineage. In addition, it briefly notes the Hongzhou school's direct role in the transmission of Chan beyond China and assesses its overall impact on the evolution of the Chan movement.

Pattern of Growth

The emergence of the Hongzhou school goes back to Mazu's monasteries at Gonggong mountain and Hongzhou. Mazu's move to Kaiyuan monastery around 770 serves as a convenient turning point in his rise to preeminence as a Chan teacher. As we have seen, during the final decades of his life Mazu attracted a large number of students, many of whom became leading Chan teachers of their generation. These monks formed the nucleus of the Hongzhou school. At this early stage, for a brief period it was possible to characterize the nascent Hongzhou school as a local tradition, based in the capital of a southern province.

Although after Mazu's death in 788 some disciples stayed at the monasteries associated with him in Hongzhou, Gonggong mountain, and Shimen, most went their own ways. In fact, even before Mazu's death, some of his disciples went on to establish monastic communities in other parts of China. A large number, including Baizhang and Xitang, settled in Jiangxi and other southern provinces. If we were to look only at this information, it might be tempting to accept the conventional viewpoint of the Hongzhou school's identity as a regional movement whose geographical center was in Jiangxi, or more broadly the South.

However, the activities of monks in the South form only a part of a more complex story about the Hongzhou school's early growth. If we stop there, we are leaving out some of the story's main protagonists and skipping key events in which they were involved. Fixation on the monastic centers in the South— notwithstanding the South's great importance in the subsequent history of Chan—obscures the true character of the Hongzhou school's development by failing to discern the scope of its success in becoming the main representative of the Chan tradition throughout the Tang empire.

As we saw in the preceding chapter, numerous disciples of Mazu settled in central China and the lower Yangtze area, especially Zhejiang, and a considerable number moved to the North. Many of these monks became leaders of monastic communities and prominent members of the local clergy. Among them, there were variations in the institutional settings in which they taught.[2] Some—including Baizhang and Dayi in Jiangxi, and Yanguan and Damei in Zhejiang—became founders of new monasteries. Others—such as Guizong at Lushan and Wuye in Fenzhou—took over as abbots of established monasteries. These were the prevalent types of institutional arrangements among Mazu's leading disciples. In both cases, they had control over their monasteries, although it is a mistake to assume that their establishments were "Chan mon-asteries" in the sense that this institutional designation was used during the Song period.

Other disciples did not establish new congregations, and their residence in different monasteries does not imply their control of those monasteries. Among this group, a few monks, such as Deng Yinfeng, assumed peripatetic lifestyles. Then there are the monks who took up residence in the large monas-teries in the capitals. Although we have no clear picture of the exact status of Chan teachers such as Dayi and Weikuan when they resided in official monas-teries in Chang'an, it is unlikely that they exerted control over those monastic establishments and congregations; rather, they probably enjoyed privileged status as prominent clerics, able to teach and have their own disciples and sup-porters, without necessarily exerting broad control over the running of the monasteries in which they resided.

Among Mazu's disciples active in the North, the monks who taught in the capitals were especially influential. Dayi, Weikuan, and Huaihui were promi-nent Chan teachers who introduced the Hongzhou school to key audiences in the cultural and political center of the Tang empire, which included three em-perors and numerous high-ranking officials and noted literati. Their influence in Chang'an was crucial in the procurement of official recognition for the Hongzhou school and its rise to prominence, as is evident in the bestowal of a posthumous title on Mazu and the commissioning of Huairang's stūpa and memorial inscription.[3]

The Hongzhou school's move from the province to the capital invites com-parison with the combined historical trajectory of the Northern school and its immediate predecessor, the East Mountain tradition. For a period of five decades—from Daoxin's move to Huangmei in 624 until Hongren's death in 674—the East Mountain tradition developed at a remote mountain monastery in Hubei. The provincial character of Daoxin's and Hongren's communities was replicated in the next phase of early Chan history, which corresponds to Shenxiu's stay at Yuquan monastery in Jingzhou (also in Hubei).[4] The shift away from the Northern school's initial regional character and its appearance on the national scene was marked by Shenxiu's move to Luoyang in 701.[5] A court-oriented outlook is evident among Shenxiu's leading disciples; Yifu (661–736) and Puji both served as imperial teachers, the first focusing on Chang'an and the second on the Luoyang area, although they each taught in both capitals.[6]

The main difference in the case of the Hongzhou school was that the move to the capitals did not come at the expense of its provincial base. Unlike Shenxiu, Mazu never made a trip to the capitals. Even as some of his disciples settled in Chang'an, many more remained at regional centers in Jiangxi and elsewhere. In that sense, unlike the Northern school, the move to Chang'an did not imply the adoption of a court-centered outlook by the Hongzhou school as a whole. With its larger numbers, the Hongzhou school was able to simultaneously maintain strongholds in numerous locations, both at the imperial center in the capital and in the provinces.

Accordingly, the prevalent but dated notion that the Hongzhou school was a regional tradition, formed in part as a response to the court-oriented outlook of the elite segments of the Buddhist church (which included noted Chan teachers of the previous generations), is not tenable. Instead of normative views that underscore the Hongzhou school's Southern or regional character, it is more accurate to interpret its growth as the first emergence of a truly empire-wide Chan tradition. As Mazu's disciples established monastic communities or a teaching presence in various parts of China, they transformed the Hongzhou school into a broad movement with strongholds throughout the large empire. By the early ninth century, the Hongzhou school had become the main representative of the Chan movement, the end result of a process that unfolded over a short span of only a few decades and involved several related developments. The Hongzhou school's geographical expansion initially involved the creation of a strong regional base in Jiangxi and the nearby southern provinces. That was accompanied by the setting up of monastic centers in other parts of the empire. Before long, this was followed by the establishment of a solid presence in the two capitals. This pattern of the Hongzhou school's growth and its spread throughout the empire was not the result of a planned and coordinated strategy. Rather, its momentous growth was largely due to the efforts and religious activities of the individual monks recounted in the preceding chapter and was also helped by a confluence of exterior conditions that favored the Hongzhou school's rise to preeminence, including the demise of the earlier schools of Chan.

There are interesting parallels between the geographical spread of the Hongzhou school, on the one hand, and the changing relationship between the center and the provinces in the Tang political landscape on the other. The Hongzhou school's initial creation of a regional basis in and around Jiangxi coincided with Daizong's reign and the early part of Dezong's reign. During this period, following the end of the An Lushan rebellion, the weakened imperial government had only limited ability to assert central control. Because of the devolution of direct control from the capital, regional power centers formed, and the influence of local civil and military officials, like the ones who supported Mazu's community in Hongzhou, increased. The tension between the customary center denoted by the Tang imperium and the aristocratic elites, on the one hand, and the new centrifugal forces represented by the military and civil officials in the provinces, on the other, to some extent paralleled the contrast between the Buddhist establishment in the capitals and the emerging provincial Chan represented by Mazu's community in Hongzhou.

Following its initial spread beyond the South during the latter part of Dezong's reign, the Hongzhou school's true emergence on the national scene as a major Buddhist tradition took place during Xianzong's reign, a period of resurgence of the Tang state's power and restoration of the dynasty's prestige. As the institutions of the central government were renewed and the emperor was able to project his power to most of the independent-minded provinces, Chang'an and, to a smaller extent, Luoyang enjoyed an extended lease on life as cultural and political centers of a large and powerful empire. The entry of Mazu's disciples into the capital took place precisely during the period when the foundations for Xianzong's restoration of Tang rule were laid down, and their rise to prominence coincided with the rejuvenation of the imperial state. In that sense, the spread of the Hongzhou school was symbolic of the ongoing reconfiguration of the relationship between the center and the provinces. The Hongzhou school ended up encompassing the two, the capital-centered and the provincial, drawing on the advantages provided by both.

Literati Associations and Networks of Patronage

Related to the Hongzhou school's conventional depiction as a regional Southern movement is the aforementioned notion that Mazu and his disciples refused to seek official support and patronage from those with political and economic power in Tang society. As in the case of the assertion of its local character, traditionalist Chan historiography contrasts the Hongzhou school's independent spirit with the heavy reliance on imperial and aristocratic patronage that were characteristic of early Chan and the rest of elite Chinese Buddhism. An examination of the patterns of economic support and political patronage that were behind the Hongzhou school's emergence on the Tang religious landscape and its supplanting of the earlier Chan traditions—largely introduced in the previous two chapters—reveals a different picture. Far from shunning involvement with the ruling elites, from its very inception the Hongzhou school was a recipient of support from a number of powerful officials, and before long it received governmental sanction and imperial patronage.

In contrast to Mazu's traditional image as a revolutionary figure and an iconoclast par excellence, in chapter 1 we found him to be the well-connected leader of a fairly conventional monastic community. His Kaiyuan monastery was a large official establishment that was part of the network of state-sponsored monasteries instituted by Emperor Xuanzong in 739. During his long tenure as a prominent Chan teacher and leader of large monastic community, Mazu encountered a number of noted literati and government officials. The support of such high-placed individuals was a significant factor in the growth of his monastic community.

The first of Mazu's lay patrons for whom we have information is Pei Xu.[7] Pei was born in Wenxi, Hedong province (in present-day Shanxi), as a scion of the powerful Pei clan, which was closely associated with the Tang ruling house and produced a number of prominent officials. His father, Pei Kuan (681–755), held a number of important posts, including military governor of Youzhou (in Hebei) from 742 to 744, which was followed by an appointment as a president of the Board of Finance.[8] As a child, Pei Xu received a classical education, and he passed the *mingjing* (classical studies) examination while still young. His first official appointment was as a military staff officer in Henan. His career was interrupted when he moved to Luoyang to mourn the death of his mother. He was still in Luoyang when the An Lushan rebellion broke out and had to go into hiding when the rebellious armies entered the city. After the end of the rebellion, Pei Xu held a number of official posts, including commissioner for salt and iron in Hedong. In 766 he was appointed prefect of Qianzhou, the prefecture where Gonggong mountain was located. During his posting there, he met Mazu. After serving as prefect at three other locations in Jiangxi and Huainan, Pei returned to the capital and assumed a military post. In his late years, during the reign of Dezong, he held a series of increasingly important posts, including governor of Henan and deputy viceroy of the Eastern capital (Luoyang).

Pei Xu was from a family that had strong ties with Buddhism. According to the official biography of his father, the elder Pei had a deep interest in Buddhism throughout his life. He frequented Buddhist monasteries, associated with monks, and often read Buddhist scriptures. Pei Kuan's fascination with Buddhism became even stronger as he grew older.[9] He studied Chan with Puji, Shenxiu's great disciple and the most prominent Chan teacher in the two capitals in the period between 725 and 739.[10] On his mother's side, Pei Xu's grandfather Wei Xian was associated with Xuansu of the Niutou school of Chan.[11] In an interesting passage that juxtaposes elements of spiritual cultivation from the Buddhist and Confucian traditions, Mazu's stele inscription describes Pei as follows: "Provincial Governor Pei, now a vice-prefect of Henan, was a follower [of Buddhism] for a long time. He had a lot of faith and respect [for the Buddhist teaching]. Using [the Buddhist practices] of concentration (*ding*) and wisdom (*hui*), he perfected [the Confucian] virtues of clarity (*ming*) and sincerity (*cheng*)."[12] When Pei Xu first met Mazu in 766, he was already a devout follower of Buddhism. During his tenure as an official in the area, Pei occasionally returned to Mazu's monastery to ask for spiritual teachings.

All the other officials about whom we have information met Mazu during his years at Kaiyuan monastery in Hongzhou. Lu Sigong and Bao Fang started their official careers during the latter half of Xuanzong's reign. Lu's original name was Jianke; Xuanzong gave him the name Sigong (literally "successor of Gong") after Lu Gong of the Later Han dynasty (25–220).[13] During his official career, Lu held a number of provincial posts and an appointment at the Department of State Affairs. In the course of his tenure as a civil governor of Jiangxi from 772 to 778—at the beginning of which he met Mazu—Lu proved to be a capable administrator. He later received enfeoffment as the Duke of Ji.

Bao Fang, who met Mazu in 780 when he assumed the post of civil governor of Jiangxi previously occupied by Lu Sigong, was a native of Xiangyang in Xiangzhou (in present-day Hubei province). He lost his parents while still young, but despite the ensuing poverty he applied himself to his studies and developed good writing skills. He obtained a *jinshi* degree in 756. During his early official career, he served in a number of junior posts in the capital and the provinces. After the end of the rebellion, he received successive appointments as a civil governor of Fujian and Jiangxi. He was subsequently appointed a vice minister (*shilang*) in the Board of Rites, and was enfeoffed as the Duke of Tonghai commandery.[14]

During the final years of Mazu's life, one of his closest lay disciples was Li Jian, who also held the post of civil governor of Jiangxi.[15] Li became a governor in 785, three years before Mazu's death.[16] Mazu's stele inscription says of Li: "He was diligent and sincere in his protection of the dharma, and he received the master's last teaching."[17] Li was also involved in organizing Mazu's funeral and constructing his memorial pagoda. He continued to support the monastic community after Mazu's death and developed a close relationship with Xitang, with whom he continued his study of Buddhism.[18]

Other noted officials with whom Mazu was associated were the writers of his two inscriptions, Quan Deyu and Bao Ji (418–514). In addition to his highly successful bureaucratic career, Quan Deyu also achieved fame as a writer.[19] He came from a provincial family that produced a number of officials, although it did not belong to the top echelons of the aristocratic elite. He showed literary talent from a young age, and by the age of fifteen he had already written several hundred literary pieces. Quan probably first met Mazu in 785, when at the age of twenty-six he received a junior post as an executive officer in the provincial administration of Li Jian, who at the time was the governor of Jiangxi and a lay follower of Mazu. In 792, Pei Zhou (729–803), who succeeded Li as a governor of Jiangxi in 791, recommended Quan to Emperor Dezong.[20] Pei Zhou was a cousin of Mazu's disciple Pei Xu (see above), and after Mazu's death he became a supporter of Mazu's monastic community, developing especially close ties with Xitang.[21] With the help of Pei's recommendation, in 792 Quan received the post of scholar at the Court of Imperial Sacrifices. Subsequently Quan had a distinguished official career, rapidly rising in the ranks of the central bureaucracy without encountering any significant setbacks. During the reign of emperor Xianzong, he rose to the position of grand councilor and was among the empire's most prominent officials.

Throughout his life, Quan associated with numerous Buddhist monks, including the famous Huayan exegete Chengguan (738–839) and Mazu's disciple Huaihui, who, as we saw in the previous chapter, was active in the capital during the 810s.[22] In 791, Quan visited Mazu's newly completed memorial stūpa. According to his account, "As I paid my respects I was able to briefly dispel my ignorance."[23] On that occasion, Mazu's disciples asked him to write

Mazu's memorial inscription. Quan also wrote memorial inscriptions for other monks, including Huaihui.[24]

Bao Ji, the author of Mazu's other memorial inscription (which is no longer extant), was an associate of Quan Deyu and Li Jian.[25] He was a native of Yanling in Ruzhou (present-day Jiangsu), and his father, Bao Rong, was a scholar in the Jixian academy. Bao Ji had a *jinshi* degree and was a man of literary ability. His official career suffered a setback in 777, when he was exiled to Lingnan (present-day Guangdong province) during the purges that followed the removal from power and execution of Yuan Zai (d. 777), the powerful chief minister who from 762 to 777 exerted great influence on state policy. Bao was soon pardoned and appointed as a tax commissioner responsible for implementing the new dual-tax system (*liangshui fa*, first introduced in 780, the second year of Dezong's reign) in the eastern part of Biansong province (present-day Henan). He eventually received enfeoffment as the Duke of Danyang. Bao probably met Mazu around 780, when he was a prefect of Jiangzhou, which bordered Hongzhou.[26]

In their biographical sketches of Mazu's life, both Quan Deyu and Zanning (919–1001), the author of *Song gaoseng zhuan*, emphasize his connections with powerful government officials. This is indicative of the importance of such ties for the early growth of the Hongzhou school. Mazu's dealings with local officials should not come as much of a surprise, considering his role as leader of an official monastery and key member of the local religious establishment. Presumably, such a role involved the adoption of conservative attitudes and adherence to conventional mores representative of the ecclesiastical hierarchy. The fact that he could count on the support of at least three provincial governors—Lu Sigong, Li Jian, and Bao Fang—and other officials such as Pei Xu and Quan Deyu, points to a set of favorable socioeconomic circumstances that fostered the growth of his monastic community.

There is an interesting difference between the economic sponsorship received by Mazu's communities at Gonggong mountain and Kaiyuan monastery and that received by the communities of other famous Chan teachers of the preceding generations. Earlier important Chan monks in the North, such as Shenxiu, Puji, and Shenhui, had prominent officials of the central government and members of the aristocracy, including the royal family, as their supporters. In contrast, Mazu's supporters were for the most part provincial administrators who gradually came to power after the end of the rebellion. They were powerful local officials who, though nominated by the central government, wielded considerable regional power and were able to act independently.[27]

The shift of economic sponsorship away from the central government and aristocracy, and toward increased reliance on support from local officials, coincided with a shift of the geographical center of the Chan school's activities from the North to the South. Both of them reflected an ongoing transfer of political and economic power to the provinces that was a result of the weakening of central governmental institutions in the aftermath of the An Lushan rebellion. The growth of Mazu's community reflected these developments, as it benefited from the economic and political patronage of local officials and from the increased importance of the South in the political, economic, and cultural life of the Tang empire.

Similar links with literati/officials and comparable patterns of patronage can also be found when we look at the monasteries led by Mazu's senior disciples in Jiangxi and the other provinces, both south and north of the Yangtze. Although the data are limited, it is apparent that many of Mazu's disciples received support from local government officials in the areas where their monasteries were located. For example, after Mazu's death Xitang continued to receive support from Li Jian during the remainder of Li's posting as governor of Jiangxi. Xitang's other lay disciples included Qi Ying, who followed Li Jian as a governor of Jiangxi. Additional examples of monks who had prominent lay patrons are Ruhui and Guizong. During his abbotship at a monastery in Changsha, Ruhui had as his lay disciple and benefactor Cui Qun, who served as a prime minister during Xianzong's reign. Guizong's contacts among noted officials and literati included Li Bo and Bo Juyi, both of whom came to visit his monastery at Lushan when they served as marshals of Jiangzhou, the prefectural capital.

The same pattern of patronage continued during the Hongzhou school's next generation. For example, one of the lay supporters of Guishan, Baizhang's leading disciple, was the noted official and lay Buddhist Pei Xiu (787?–860).[28] Guishan's funeral inscription, composed by Zheng Yu of Fanyu (present-day Guangzhou), states that Pei Xiu met Guishan in 846, after the end of the anti-Buddhist persecution initiated by emperor Wuzong (r. 840–846). During the persecution, Guishan had to flee his monastery, which was seriously damaged, and disguise himself as a layman. In the early stages of the restoration of Buddhism initiated soon after the next emperor Xuanzong ascended to the throne, Pei Xiu (who at the time served as civil governor of Hunan) offered support to Guishan's Tongqing monastery. Pei even donated a landed estate to Guishan's monastic community to supply the monks with provisions.[29] At the time, Pei received religious instructions from Guishan;[30] later he became a lay disciple of Huangbo, also a leading pupil of Baizhang, and compiled a record of Huangbo's teachings.

Other noted officials who were Guishan's lay disciples and supporters included Li Jingrang (dates unknown), who probably met Guishan while he was serving as a civil governor of Shannan-dao during the Dazhong era (847–860),[31] and Cui Shenyou (dates of birth and death unknown), who during the same period was a civil governor of Hunan.[32] Furthermore, the author of Guishan's first stele inscription—which was probably composed two or three year after his death and was subsequently lost—was Lu Jianqiu (789–846),[33] and the calligraphy for the inscription was done by the famous poet Li Shang-yin.[34] Apparently, even at his remote provincial monastery in Hunan, Guishan came in contact with and received patronage from a broad array of leading political and literary figures.

Mazu's disciples active in the capitals—especially Dayi, Weikuan, and Huaihui—were supported by those at the apex of the Tang power structure, including three emperors: Dezong, Shunzong, and Xianzong. During their stay in the capital, they resided in some of the main official monasteries that were closely associated with the imperial family and the Tang state. For example, after his arrival in Chang'an, Dayi took up residence at Dacien (also called Cien) monastery. Located in the southeast part of the city, Dacien was among the large imperial monasteries founded during the first few decades of the Tang dynasty;[35] it was established in 648 by Taizong in memory of his deceased mother. The monastery halls were decorated with pearl, jade, and gold. It also housed the famous Dayan (Great Wild Goose) pagoda, which remains one of the few surviving structures in Xi'an from the Tang period. Dacien was also the monastery where the famous translator Xuanzang wrote many of his translations of Buddhist scriptures after his return from India. In addition to its religious functions, the monastery served as a popular venue for entertainment and was frequented by high-ranking officials and eminent literati.

When Huaihui arrived in Chang'an, a few years after Dayi's stay at Dacien, he settled at Zhangjing Monastery. Established in 767 to commemorate the deceased mother of Emperor Daizong, Zhangjing was located outside of the eastern city walls and close to the Tonghua gate on land that was previously occupied by the mansion of the eunuch official Yu Chaoen (d. 770).[36] With its forty-eight courtyards, it was the largest urban monastery in the empire and was among the capital's leading Buddhist establishments. In a similar vein, Weikuan, after his arrival in Chang'an, took up residence at Da'anguo Monastery (also called Anguo), another of the most imposing monasteries in the capital. Da'anguo had a long-established connection with the imperial family, as it was originally built by the first Tang emperor, Gaozu (r. 618–626), in 583, while he was still an official of the Sui dynasty.[37] Later Weikuan moved to Xingshan Monastery (also called Daxingshan), where he remained until the end of his life. Originally built by Emperor Wendi after the reunification of China under his Sui dynasty, Xingshan—which, like Anguo, was located in the eastern part of the city—was another of Chang'an's premier Buddhist establishments.[38] Another important monastery in Chang'an that was associated with the Hongzhou school was Ximing Monastery, where Wuye stayed when he visited the capital.

Their stays at these leading monastic institutions placed Dayi, Huaihui, and Weikuan at the center of the capital's religious life. Thus, as early as the first decade of the ninth century, barely two decades after Mazu's death, the Hongzhou school had established its presence at the center of the empire's social, political, and cultural life and was a direct recipient of imperial patronage. That is as far removed from the popular image of a provincial movement, wary of dealings of any kind with those in power, as it is possible to imagine. Reliance on imperial support, however, did not replace dependence on the patronage of local officials in the provinces. Rather, they both became fixtures in the institutional arrangements and networks of patronage that were behind the growth and flourishing of the Hongzhou school.

The pertinent evidence about the support received by Mazu and his leading disciples undermines the popular notion of an independent Chan movement that refused to seek economic and political patronage from officialdom and the aristocracy. Consequently, there is little historical basis for the normative view of Chan's putative search for institutional autonomy that was supposedly initiated by the Hongzhou school. There is also no indication that at the time there was a move toward a system of economic self-sufficiency that relied on the agricultural labor of Chan monks.

Romantic images of Chan monks living in self-sustaining communities that followed the agrarian ethos of the Chinese countryside and stayed away from the usual networks of wealth and political patronage—epitomized by the legend about Baizhang's establishment of a unique form of Chan monastic life—are a standard fixture in popular and scholarly writings about Tang Chan. But such images are little more than products of scholarly and religious imagination—often a curious combination of both. They are based on false readings of Chan history and lack of knowledge about the practical realities of religious life in Tang China. It is clear that from its very inception and throughout its later history, the Hongzhou school relied on the support of the social and political elites of the medieval Chinese state. A similar situation also obtained during the subsequent eras and culminated with the establishment of a network of official Chan monasteries during the Song period.

Endorsement and backing from the imperial government and the sociopolitical elites offered the Hongzhou school a formal veneer of legitimacy at a time when the Tang state reestablished most of the authority it had lost in the course of the An Lushan rebellion and its aftermath. This in turn enhanced both the secular and religious fortunes of the Hongzhou school and facilitated its further integration into the mainstream of Tang Buddhism. The result of these events was the establishment of a Chan orthodoxy centered on Mazu and his followers, as the Hongzhou school eclipsed the diverse traditions of early Chan.

Interactions with Other Chan Lineages

At the onset of the An Lushan rebellion, the Chan school's main centers were predominantly located in the North, including the two capitals, where monks associated with the Northern school had established a dominant presence. After the rebellion, the Chan school's geographical center shifted with the rise to prominence of Mazu and other teachers in the South. Mazu was apparently aware of other contemporaneous Chan teachers and maintained cordial relations with some of them. Moreover, some of Mazu's disciples started their training under other Chan teachers active in the South, especially monks associated with the Niutou school. There are also records of Mazu's disciples visiting other teachers, sometimes on Mazu's advice. After their return to Mazu's monastery, they brought information about the Chan teachers they met and the monastic communities they visited.

Mazu's teaching career coincided with the ascendancy of the Niutou school, which received its name from Niutou mountain (located south of present-day Nanjing), where its putative founder Farong (594–657) resided during the initial decades of the Tang dynasty.[39] Under the leadership of Niutou Huizhong (683–769) and Jingshan, the Niutou school reached the pinnacle of its influence during the same period when Mazu was teaching at Gonggong mountain and Hongzhou.[40] Jing mountain, where Faqin's monastery was located, was in the vicinity of Hangzhou. Faqin entered the mountain around 742 and remained there until the Dali era (766–780), when he went to the capital at the invitation of emperor Daizong.[41] Faqin had a long and distinguished monastic career, and his disciples included many noted officials and monks. There are records of at least three of Mazu's disciples visiting his monastery: Xitang, Daowu, and Danxia (the last two were also students of Shitou). Xitang went to see the Niutou teacher—under Mazu's instructions, according to some sources—prior to Faqin's departure for the capital.[42] Moreover, some of Mazu's early disciples were Faqin's students before they joined the community at Gonggong mountain. They include Funiu Zizai, Chaoan (who was born in Danyang, Jiangsu, not far from Jingshan), and Ruhui of Dong (Eastern) monastery. Faqin's disciples were not the only ones to join Mazu's congregation. Chaoan was originally a student of Xuansu (668–752), another major Niutou figure; another of Xuansu's students, Longan Ruhai (dates unknown), also trained under Mazu.[43] Furong Taiyu, who entered monastic life under Huizhong in 758, also went to study with Mazu after Huizhong's death in 769.[44]

The connection with the Niutou school sheds light on the broader religious milieu that shaped the Hongzhou school's formation. As we will see in part II of this study, in addition to the personal interactions noted earlier, there are interesting parallels between the attitudes toward meditation in the two schools. It is also possible to draw connections between the centrality of Madhyamaka themes in Niutou teachings and the doctrinal formulations presented in the Hongzhou school's records, especially Baizhang's sermons. However, while there was considerable movement of monks between Mazu's monastery and the monasteries of Niutou teachers, the sources indicate that the exchanges were not reciprocal. While some of Mazu's disciples went to study with Jingshan and other Niutou masters, they all returned to Mazu's monastery and remained his disciples (or at least the later Chan tradition remembered them as such). In contrast, there are numerous examples of monks who were originally students of Niutou teachers, but who eventually became Mazu's disciples.

All the movement, then, was in one direction, with monks leaving the Niutou school's milieu, in which they started their Chan training, and ending up as Mazu's disciples, a turn of events that correlates with the decline of the Niutou school and the concurrent ascendancy of the Hongzhou school. But it is also possible that with the Niutou school's demise and the Hongzhou school's rise to prominence, monks who studied with both Mazu and Niutou teachers were labeled as members of Mazu's lineage. This trend is especially evident in the early transmission of the lamp chronicles written during the Five Dynasties and Song periods. Unfortunately, from the present vantage point it is virtually impossible to untangle the dynamics by which such collective memories were produced, transmitted, adapted, and recorded.

In addition to the Niutou teachers, there are also examples of monks who studied with both Mazu and Shitou, who led a small community at Nanyue mountain in Hunan. Shitou's teacher Xingsi was, like Mazu's teacher Huairang, an obscure disciple of Huineng.[45] Although the later Chan tradition elevated Shitou—together with Mazu—to the status of progenitor of one of the two main Chan lines of transmission, during his lifetime Shitou was far less famous and influential than Faqin, Huizhong, or Mazu.[46] His relatively marginal position is largely responsible for the lack of reliable biographical information. Born in Gaoyao county in Guangdong province, Shitou was nine years Mazu's senior. According to his biographies, he met Huineng in 713 when he was only thirteen years old.[47] As Huineng soon died, Shitou could have spent only a short period with him (if indeed he met Huineng at all). Later Shitou studied with Xingsi, who resided at Qingyuan mountain in Jiangxi. After Xingsi's death in 740, Shitou moved to Nanyue. *Zutang ji* states that Shitou had already visited Nanyue on an earlier occasion, when Xingsi sent him there to deliver a letter to Huairang, although that story is of doubtful provenance.[48] After he moved to Nanyue, Shitou met with Huairang. The connection with Huairang was helpful to Shitou as he was settling at the mountain, as Huairang arranged the building of a small temple for him.[49]

Shitou reached Nanyue around 741, probably shortly before Mazu's departure for Fujian. It is thus possible, perhaps even likely, that the two met there. They might also have met during Shitou's earlier visit to Nanyue (if the story in *Zutang ji* is correct). Such a meeting is an intriguing possibility, even though there is no conclusive evidence to prove it. There are several stories in Mazu's later biographies that imply a close connection between the two. They all suggest that Mazu was aware of Shitou's activities at Nanyue and had a high opinion of him. In some instances, post-Tang sources even report that Mazu directed some of his disciples to go to Shitou in order to receive religious instruction. The list of disciples that Mazu supposedly sent (or recommended) to visit Shitou's monastery includes Danxia, Daotong, Daowu, Lingmo, Zhaoti, and Deng Yinfeng.[50] Just as in the case of the movement of monks between Mazu's monastery and the monasteries of Niutou teachers, this exchange was one-sided, but in the opposite direction: the sources describe Mazu encouraging his disciples to call on Shitou, but there is no record of Shitou sending his students to Mazu's monastery.[51] It almost seems as if Shitou did not reciprocate Mazu's admiration for him.

The lack of information about Shitou reflects the fact that he was a little-known teacher who led a reclusive life and had relatively few disciples. For decades after Shitou's death, his lineage remained an obscure provincial tradition, notwithstanding attempts to elevate his stature and present him as Mazu's equal. To that end, his disciples commissioned Liu Ke during the 821–824 period to compose Shitou's stele inscription, which is no longer extant. The famous saying that describes Mazu and Shitou as the main Chan teachers of their time first appeared in this inscription. The biography of Shitou in *Song gaoseng zhuan* quotes Liu's inscription as stating: "Daji [i.e., Mazu] was the master in Jiangxi; Shitou was the master in Hunan. Those who were wavering and did not go to see these two great teachers were considered completely ignorant."[52]

The ongoing perception of Shitou as a marginal figure as late as the 830s is evident in Zongmi's writings, which barely mention him. The same is true of epigraphic sources from the early ninth century that identify the main Chan lineages, including the inscriptions composed for Mazu's disciples in Chang'an.[53] As they found themselves playing catch-up with the Hongzhou school, Shitou's disciples were probably eager to elevate their teacher's status and bring it to the same level with that of Mazu, and for that purpose they created or reworked existing stories to suggest that Mazu considered Shitou to be his equal.

Most of Shitou's main disciples, including Daowu, Danxia, and Yaoshan, also studied with Mazu, which perhaps indicates an absence of obsession with lineage among some monks at the time. However, that changed from the mid-ninth century onward, as Shitou's lineage became increasingly influential, largely due to the prominence of Dongshan Liangjie (807–869) and his disciples. With the recognition of Shitou, together with Mazu, as one of the two ancestors of the whole Chan movement, the lineage affiliation of monks who studied with both of them became a contested issue. Two prime examples are Yaoshan and Daowu. Yaoshan was a student of both Mazu and Shitou, and as he came to figure prominently in the genealogical charts of later Chan groups, the decision to list him as a disciple of either Mazu or Shitou became a point of debate, since the rigid genealogical schema necessitated the artificial drawing of singular lines of transmission.[54] Similarly, Daowu first studied with Jingshan and then became a pupil of Mazu and Shitou.[55] Daowu's lineage affiliation became increasingly important, and thus more complicated, during the Song period, because the last two of the five main lineages recognized by Song Chan—those of Yunmen Wenyan (864–949) and Fayan Wenyi (885–958)—traced their lineage back to him.[56] While this demonstrates how the principle of dharma inheritance (*si*) framed the ideological constructs and historical narratives of the later Chan tradition, it has no direct relevance to the construction of religious identities and the institutional arrangements in place during the mid-Tang period. For our present purposes, the main points to note are that it was not uncommon for monks to study under different teachers, and that Mazu and his disciples were on friendly terms with monks associated with other Chan lineages. These points will be useful to keep in mind as in the next section we delve into the broader milieu of Tang Chan and look into the Hongzhou school's amicable and by-and-large ecumenical attitudes toward other lineages and traditions.

Contours of the Chan Movement

The Hongzhou school's growth took place against the backdrop of broader developments within the Chan movement. Early sources that discuss the main Chan traditions recognized during the early ninth century help situate the Hongzhou school within the broader milieu of mid-Tang Chan. Especially useful in that respect is Dayi's stele inscription. Composed by the official and scholar Wei Chuhou (773–823) soon after Dayi's death in 818, the inscription contains an outline of the main Chan lineages recognized at the time.[57] Even though the inscription takes for granted the status of Huineng as the sixth Chan patriarch, it displays a sense of ecumenism in that it includes a number of lineages in its delineation of the parameters of Chan orthodoxy. The author lists four main Chan lineages: those of Shenxiu (the Northern school) and Shenhui in the North, and of Farong (the Niutou school) and Mazu (the Hongzhou school) in the South.

The same four lineages appear in other sources composed in the capitals during roughly the same period, such as Zongmi's *Chanyuan zhuquanji duxu* (Preface to the Collected Texts on the Source of Chan) and Weikuan's inscription.[58] Zongmi's text identifies three principal Chan schools that correspond to the three main types of Mahāyāna doctrine: the Northern school, the Niutou school, and the Southern school.[59] He further subdivides the Southern school into two groups, the Heze lineage of Shenhui and the Hongzhou lineage of Mazu,[60] thus yielding the same four lineages as those listed in Dayi's inscription. The fact that these diverse sources agree on this point suggests that during the early ninth century these four groups were recognized as the main branches of the Chan school.

Dayi's inscription starts with a brief summary of early Chan "history," formulated in terms of the familiar narrative about the six Chinese patriarchs:

> The "transformation bodies" (Chinese: *yingshen*; Sanskrit: *sambhogakāya*) [of the Buddha] are limitless in number, and one of them descended in India. There were six Chan patriarchs [in China], three of whom lived during the sagely reign of the Tang dynasty. During the reign of emperor Gaozu, there was Daoxin under whose leadership the Chan school prospered. During the reign of emperor Taizong, there was Hongren, who revealed the original pearl [of awakening?]. During the reign of Gaozong there was Huineng, whose fish trap was like a finger pointing to the moon [i.e., he propounded expedient teachings that led to enlightenment].[61]

By the mid-Tang period, the notion of six patriarchs was already an established fixture of Chan belief. It is evident in *Baolin zhuan,* composed in 801, the first text to provide the patriarchal list of twenty-eight Indian and six Chinese patriarchs, with Bodhidharma as the last Indian and first Chinese patriarch. In time, that list became normative and was incorporated in seminal Chan chronicles such as *Chuandeng lu.* Comparable (but shorter) lists of patriarchs had already appeared in early Chan texts composed during the eighth century, such as Jingjue's (683–750?) *Lengqie shizi ji* and the Baotang school's *Lidai fabao ji.* The differences among them are mostly at the sixth and subsequent generations and reflect the sectarian affiliations of their authors.

Dayi's inscription identifies the main Chan lineages that emerged after the singular transmission of Chan, from a single teacher to a single disciple, purportedly ended with the sixth Chinese patriarch. From then on, singular transmission was replaced by transmission to multiple disciples:

> After that, the main [Chan] lineage was divided into various branches: some retired to Qin [the area of present-day Shaanxi province, where the Tang capital Chang'an was located], some settled in Luo [the area around Tang's secondary capital Luoyang], some moved on to Wu [the area around present-day Shanghai in the lower Yangtze delta], and some went to reside in Chu [the area of present-day Hunan and Hubei provinces]. The [monk active in] Qin was called [Shen] xiu. By means of expedient means (*fangbian*), he revealed [the truth of Buddhism?]. Puji was his faithful follower. The [monk active in] Luo was called [Shen] hui; he attained the seal of *dhāranī* (*zongchi*) and singularly glimmered on the bright pearl. His disciples were confused about the truth, and thus they mixed things up. Somewhat unexpectedly, they construed the transmission of the Chan teaching as presented in the *Platform Scripture*, which [purports to] explicate

the good and bad [Chan lineages and teachings]. The [monk active in] Wu was called [Fa] rong, who was also known as Niutou [from the name of the mountain where he resided]. Jingshan was his spiritual descendant. The [monk active in] Chu was called Daoyi [i.e., Mazu]. He absorbed [all] by means of the Great Vehicle (Mahāyāna). The great teacher [i.e., Dayi] belonged to his faction.[62]

Although the inscription recognizes Huineng as the main disciple of Hongren, it also affirms that the two main Chan lineages that were independent of him, those of Farong and Shenxiu, were authentic branches of the Chan tradition. There is an implicit contradiction between the affirmation of Huineng's status as the sixth patriarch and the acknowledgment of the Northern school's and Niutou school's orthodoxy. The text suggests that the division into various lineages occurred after Huineng, as the singular line of transmission ended, even though the "founders" of two of those lineages, Farong and Shenxiu, were Huineng's seniors. Notwithstanding such discrepancies, this description of the main Chan lineages reveals an attitude of inclusiveness and a sense of broad-mindedness. In the passage just cited, there is no explicit assertion that Dayi's lineage, which went back to Mazu (and by extension to Huineng), was superior to or more authentic than the other Chan lineages. The same kind of ecumenical attitude is evident in other records from the same period, including *Baolin zhuan*, which highlights Mazu as the leading Chan teacher of his generation but also includes information about other prominent contemporary figures. This inclusiveness and pluralistic outlook were characteristic of the Hongzhou school, although they were not necessarily limited to it.

Not everybody adopted an ecumenical perspective, however. The inscription is critical of sectarian divisions within the Chan movement, the prime instance of which was the factional infighting between the Northern and Southern schools. This clash, epitomized by the alleged verse competition between Shenxiu and Huineng, is among the best-known elements of traditional Chan lore. While normative Chan historiography caricatures Shenxiu and underscores the inferiority of the Northern school, modern scholarship has suggested a rather different set of circumstances.[63] Instead of a conflict between two opposing factions, there was a one-sided attack on the part of Shenhui, directed toward those whom he considered his main competitors for the position of "orthodox" representative of Chan. Apparently, the author of Dayi's inscription was aware of that, although for some reason he placed the blame for the misguided sectarian infighting on the disciples of Shenhui rather than on Shenhui himself. The inscription is critical of efforts on the part of Shenhui's disciples to judge the "good and bad" (i.e., orthodox and heterodox) lineages. This in turn apparently led to the inclusion of biased sectarian statements in the *Platform Scripture*, a popular text that propounded the orthodoxy of Huineng's Southern school and the superiority of its teachings vis-à-vis those of the Northern school. These critical comments echo Nanyang Hui-zhong's remarks about the unwarranted altering of the text of the *Platform Scripture*.[64] The inscription continues by presenting an explicit criticism of Shenhui and his cohorts' attempts to engender sectarian divisions within the Chan school:

> From that time onward, they [i.e., the followers of Shenhui] were confused about their direction and impeded in their tracks. [Views about] right and wrong arose one after another, and there was no end to [their attachment to] things and self. They asserted that the South-ern school is orthodox and the Northern school is heterodox, and that the Northern school [holds on to] existence, while the Southern school [follows the doctrine] of emptiness. Yet, they do not know that when the [true] mind is engendered [as taught by] the Southern school, that itself is the same as the Northern school, and when views are extinguished [as taught by] the Northern school, then that intersects with [the teachings of] the Southern school.[65]

The inscription rejects the sharp distinctions between the Northern and Southern schools propounded by Shenhui and his followers and instead ar-gues for a rapprochement between the two. Its take on things is not necessar-ily unique, as it echoes statements found in other sources. For instance, Shi-tou's poem *Cantongqi* contains these two lines: "Though people's faculties might be sharp or dull, in the Way [to Buddhahood] there are no Southern or Northern patriarchs."[66] By condemning the Shenhui faction's sectarian cru-sade, the inscription implies that Mazu's disciples adopted a tolerant attitude toward other Chan schools/lineages and eschewed the pursuit of narrow sec-tarian agendas (or at least were more subtle about it).

A similarly accommodating attitude is also evident in Weikuan's inscrip-tion, composed by Bo Juyi soon after Weikuan's death in 817, around the same time as Dayi's inscription.[67] In it, Bo identifies the main branches of Chan and lists the same four lineages found in Dayi's inscription and Zongmi's *Chanyuan zhuquanji duxu*.[68] Weikuan's inscription accepts the principle of inclusiveness and asserts that the various Chan lineages that arose after the fourth patriarch, Daoxin, "inherited the true teaching" (*si zhengfa*). Bo explains the relationship among the different lineages in terms of the kinship ties that existed among the elite aristocratic families of Tang China. For instance, a fellow disciple of Mazu, such as Xitang, is described as Weikuan's brother born of the same fa-ther (namely, Mazu), while the relationship with Jingshan (of the Niutou school) is described as that between sons of paternal uncles, and that with Puji (of the Northern school) as cousins born of the same grandfather. Although Bo is mix-ing up the different generations a bit, the principle he tries to establish is quite clear—the various Chan lineages belong to the same extended family.

It is tempting to interpret the description of the main Chan lineages presented in Dayi's and Weikuan's inscriptions and Zongmi's text as describing the contours of the Chan movement at the time they were written (namely the early ninth century), but it would be a mistake to read them that way. Although they all write about four major Chan lineages that emerged at various points during the eighth century, if we look at the situation that obtained at the beginning of the early ninth century, only one of the four lineages was still flourishing. While at the time the Hongzhou school was in ascendancy, all monks mentioned as representatives of the other lineages have been dead for quite a while. By the early ninth century the Niutou, Northern, and Heze lineages were for all practical purposes defunct. In reality, only the Hongzhou school was still flourishing at the time, and most leading Chan teachers were disciples of Mazu.

The inclusive attitude evidenced in Dayi and Weikuan's inscriptions probably reflects sentiments prevalent within the Hongzhou school. Then again, they could afford to be generous toward schools/lineages that were already defunct. By accepting the orthodoxy of earlier schools/lineages, Mazu's disciples were perhaps implying that the Hongzhou school inherited their mantle of authority and was the bearer of Chan orthodoxy. That seems to be the meaning of the somewhat ambiguous statement in Dayi's inscription quoted earlier, according to which Mazu "absorbed [all Chan traditions?] by means of the Great Vehicle (Mahāyāna) (yi dasheng she)." It is interesting to note that the text describes the absorption of the schools of Chan—assuming that is what is implied—by invoking the Great Vehicle, thereby adopting a traditional perspective.

Lineage and Religious Identities

By the mid-Tang period, the Chan school had established its identity as a distinct tradition within Chinese Buddhism, even if the contours of that identity were not rigid and its key elements were still evolving. The precise connotations of the term "Chan school" and the lines of demarcation between it and the rest of Buddhism were not without ambiguities.[69] "Chan school" was an umbrella designation that included a number of groups, sometimes with tenuous connections among them as members of a single movement. Nonetheless, texts from the Tang period, especially epigraphic sources, reveal a clearly identifiable awareness among a segment of the monastic order of belonging to a distinctive Chan movement. The formation of this religious identity was anchored by a common acceptance of the notion of dharma inheritance—in which Bodhidharma was recognized as a key patriarchal figure—and the loose adoption of common frames of reference, including shared religious attitudes, doctrinal tenets, and terminology.[70] At the same time, the Chan school was subsumed within the larger Buddhist tradition, and its evolution as a discrete subset of Chinese Buddhism did not imply institutional independence.[71]

Stele inscriptions from the mid-Tang period, including those of Dayi, Baizhang, Huaihui, and Weikuan (and to a lesser degree Mazu), reveal a concern with spiritual lineage (*pai*) that helps us understand the manner in which monks associated with the Hongzhou school constructed their identity as a distinct religious group.[72] Such a concern is not surprising, since the notion of lineage—already evident in early Chan texts such as *Lengqie shizi ji* and *Lidai fabao ji*—was a centerpiece of the Chan school's emerging ideology and a potent tool in the construction of its identity. At the time, the manufacture of spiritual genealogies also took place in other Buddhist schools, such as Tiantai, in part as a response to developments in the Chan school and perhaps indicative of increased emphasis on the teacher-disciple relationship within Chinese Buddhism.[73]

The notion of dharma transmission was thus evolving as a principle of religious affiliation and identity that mapped the parameters of orthodoxy. Even so, it is worth noting that the terse statements found in Tang texts do not give a complete picture of the full range of meanings and sentiments associated with the notion of spiritual lineage. The term doubtless implied real (or in some cases forged or imagined) connections between individuals, related to each other as teachers and students, conveying a sense of membership in a larger tradition. Nevertheless, we should be wary of reading into it the full-blown Song conception of lineage. The Song construct was part of a complex ideology that encompassed a pseudo-historical vision of the Chan school's past and determined the allocation of prestige and distribution of power in Buddhist ecclesiastical structures and Song society. It might be best to read statements about lineage affiliation during the mid-Tang period primarily as indicative of personal connections that highlighted an individual monk's spiritual pedigree. In that sense they are somewhat analogous to contemporary statements that, for example, Professor X was a student of Professor Y from Z University, a founder of the U school of social anthropology, which establishes Professor X's personal connection with his mentor and situates him within the larger intellectual and institutional contexts.

It is not clear whether Mazu's disciples employed the term "Hongzhou school," but since it appears in the writings of Zongmi, we know it was in vogue during the early ninth century.[74] Regardless of whether they used the exact name, early texts, such as the stele inscriptions mentioned above, indicate that Mazu's disciples were aware of being members of a distinctive group that was part of the larger Chan movement. The term "Hongzhou school" is simply a convenient way to refer to Mazu and his disciples as a confraternity of monks with a shared vision of the Buddhist path. The notion of Dharma lineage, in which Mazu was a key patriarchal figure, buttressed their group identity.

Monks associated with the Hongzhou school thus shared several overlapping identities. They were followers of Mazu and members of his lineage, which also made them members of the broader Chan tradition. (We can also insert an intermediate layer between these two identities, that of representatives of the Southern school of Chan.) At the same time, they were monks whose religious identities were shaped by the cumulative wisdom and lore of Buddhism. As such, they accepted the core tenets, mores, and institutions of the larger Buddhist tradition. The boundaries between these identities—members of Mazu's lineage, the Chan tradition, and the Buddhist saṅgha—were porous, overlapping, and flexible. The Buddhist notion that all identities are provisional reinforced the manner in which such open-ended, adaptable, and context-sensitive attitudes and identities were constructed. The weight placed on specific identities was thus contextual, and they were not antithetical to each other.

Explicit mention of lineage affiliation and membership in the Chan school appears in a number of inscriptions for monks associated with the Hongzhou school. For example, Baizhang's inscription presents his spiritual genealogy, stating that he was a ninth-generation representative of the Chan school in China. The inscription starts by introducing Chan as a singular tradition or school of Buddhism (*channa yi zong*) that leads to salvation from the cycle of birth and death. It then traces Baizhang's lineage back to Huineng via Huairang and Mazu, without implying that his connection with Mazu was unique in relation to other prominent disciples.[75]

Weikuan's inscription also highlights his lineage affiliation. It includes a genealogical outline of the Chan lineage in India and China up to and including Weikuan.[76] This lineage is unusual because it is based on a genealogical chart that is at variance with the prevalent scheme of twenty-eight Indian and six Chinese patriarchs, formulated by the authors of *Baolin zhuan* just over a decade earlier. Bo's inscription presents a different line of transmission, according to which Bodhidharma was the fifty-first patriarch and Weikuan the fifty-ninth,[77] based on a transmission lineage found in a text composed some three centuries earlier by Sengyou (445–518).[78] The reasons for Bo's choice of this lineage is not clear, but its existence indicates that at the time the account of the transmission of Chan formulated in *Baolin zhuan* was not unanimously accepted as the orthodox version. Bo's inscription suggests that during the early ninth century the situation was quite fluid. There were still competing accounts about the exact contours of the early Chan lineage, even if the notion of lineage transmission was established as an organizing principle in the construction of the Chan school's religious identity.

An important development evident in the Hongzhou school's records is the multilinear conception of lineage. While the earlier part of Chan's genealogical schema was a singular line of transmission, from the mid-Tang period onward the Chan lineage after the sixth patriarch was depicted as multitude of branches stemming out from a single trunk. This pluralistic view of the Chan lineage is evident in *Baolin zhuan*: although the text ends with Mazu as the main figure of his generation, it also acknowledges Shitou and other Chan teachers of the preceding generation, including Xingsi, Huizhong, and Shenhui.[79] Such an ecumenical stance was a reflection of the Hongzhou school's previously noted tolerant attitude toward other schools and lineages, which contrasts with Shenhui's sectarian stance and his insistence on the notion of unilinear transmission. While this open and inclusive outlook may not have been unique to the Hongzhou school and may reflect wider changes in mid-Tang Chan, its adoption by Mazu and his disciples greatly contributed to its becoming an article of faith in the Chan movement from that point onward.

Reconfiguration of Chan Orthodoxy

The early part of the story of Tang Chan is customarily told with reference to the supposed rift between the Northern and Southern schools, epitomized by the verse competition between Shenxiu and Huineng. The victory of the Southern school, traditionally ascribed to the inherent superiority of its sudden awakening paradigm, is interpreted as an epoch-making event that changed the course of Buddhist history. Modern scholarship has deconstructed that normative account and exposed the problematic origin of its sources, especially the *Platform Scripture*. Instead, the Southern school's rise to preeminence has come to be perceived largely as a consequence of the campaigns against the Northern school instigated by Shenhui, who secured Huineng's status as the sixth Chan patriarch, even though his role was largely overlooked by the later Chan tradition.[80]

Shenhui introduced the designation "Southern school" during his attacks on Shenxiu's disciples, whom he pejoratively called the "Northern school," a label that was not in vogue among them. He employed this designation in order to draw a sharp distinction between the "orthodox" tradition of Chan that he claimed to have received from Huineng and the "heterodox" teachings of Shenxiu's followers. In a general sense, the two terms, Northern and Southern, denoted geographical locations, as Huineng's monastery was located in the South while Shenxiu and his key disciples, Puji and Yifu, were active in the North. Nevertheless, the terms were primarily employed as convenient slogans and symbols for real or imagined fractures within the Chan movement rather than as designations that denoted the geographic areas where the two schools were based. After all, Shenhui staged his anti–Northern school campaign in the North, which remained his main base of operation until the end of his life.

While Shenhui undoubtedly played a central role in instigating the Southern/Northern divide, it is possible to overstate the success of his campaigns and his broader impact on Chan history. During Shenhui's lifetime, the Southern school's supremacy was not yet established, and it did not go uncontested until the end of the eighth century. The Northern and Niutou schools continued to flourish after Shenhui's death in 758, and their disappearance from the Chan scene coincided with the rise of the Hongzhou school. The same applies to the Jingzhong and Baotang schools in Sichuan. When Wuzhu's disciples compiled *Lidai fabao ji*, they did not present their Baotang tradition as a mere alternative to the Northern and Southern schools, but as the orthodox Chan lineage.[81]

Moreover, the Niutou school reached the apogee of its influence, under the leadership of Huizhong and Jingshan, during the final years of Shenhui's life and the following two decades. Members of the Niutou school did not consider either the Northern or the Southern school to be superior, and a number of texts composed during this period include critical comments directed against the sectarianism exemplified by Shenhui.[82] Other Chan teachers criticized Shenhui's campaign and the biased contents of the *Platform Scripture* (as previously discussed). Even the *Platform Scripture*, written in order to further the cause of the Southern school, presents a largely negative image of Shenhui. Apparently, the divisiveness and sectarianism epitomized by Shenhui's campaigns were not representative of much of the Chan movement.

While Shenhui's championing of the Southern school's orthodoxy served as catalyst for subsequent developments, his failure at training disciples, along with a backlash against his acrimonious campaigns, precluded the long-term success of his lineage. There are indications that even when his influence was at its peak during the last few years of his life, he was not commonly recognized as a representative of the Southern school. This is evident in an inscription composed by the famous writer Li Hua (c. 715–774) for Xuanlang (673–754), which includes a discussion of the main traditions of meditation (which includes Chan but is not limited to it). In this text written just before Shenhui's death, Li Hua lists four traditions as representative of the Chan school: two belonging to the Northern school, the Southern school of Huineng, and the Niutou school.[83] Although Li provides the names of Chan teachers who at the time were leaders of two Northern school factions and the Niutou school (represented by Xuansu's faction), he makes no mention of Shenhui as a representative of the Southern school. Li's inscription also indicates that at the time the Northern school was still perceived as the main representative of Chan.

Furthermore, if we accept Chen Jinhua's interpretation of the Chan council of 796, Zongmi's statement about the decision to award Shenhui the title of seventh Chan patriarch is inaccurate. Instead, the hero of the council was Dayi, the Hongzhou school's representative, whose tradition was recognized as the carrier of Chan orthodoxy.[84] In retrospect, we can surmise that if it were only up to Shenhui, the Southern school would have been a short-lived phenomenon. The Southern school's eclipsing of the other schools of early Chan and its emergence as uncontested orthodoxy came about only after the rise to prominence of the Hongzhou school, which coincided with the decline of the Northern and Niutou schools. By the early ninth century, for all practical purposes the Hongzhou school became almost synonymous with the Southern school, being widely accepted as the bearer of Chan orthodoxy. In that sense, it played a key role in the consolidation and continuance of the Chan movement, as well as in its spread beyond the geographical confines of China, especially the Korean peninsula.

Influence on the Spread of Chan in Korea

The Hongzhou school's influence was not limited to China. Mazu's disciples were also heavily involved in the initial transmission of Chan (or Sŏn in Korean) on the Korean peninsula. According to traditional accounts, the first monk to bring Chan to Korea was Pŏmnang (fl. 632–646), a presumed disciple of the fourth Chan patriarch, Daoxin. However, the main transmission of Chan to the Korean peninsula took place during the first half of the ninth century and coincided with the Hongzhou school's rise to dominance.[85] Virtually all the Korean monks who transmitted Chan to their native land during this period were students of Mazu's disciples (and thus Mazu's second-generation disciples). The records of their travels to China thus offer further testimony to the Hongzhou school's ascendancy.

After returning to their native land, the Korean monks established monastic communities at various mountain sites throughout the peninsula. Before long, they came to be recognized as founders of the so-called mountain schools that came to dominate the Sŏn tradition during the later part of the Unified Silla dynasty (668–935). By the Koryŏ dynasty (937–1392), they were known collectively as the "Nine mountain schools of Sŏn" (kusan sŏnmun) and were perceived as representing the early Sŏn tradition of the Silla period. Silla monks who during the early ninth century studied under Mazu's first-generation disciples founded seven of these schools. The other two schools were the Hŭiyang-san, which traced its lineage back to Pŏmnang, and the Sumi-san, the last school to become established during the early tenth century. These two schools, then, originated before and after the heyday of the Hongzhou school's influence. Even the Hŭiyang-san school, considered the earliest of the Sŏn schools, eventually came to present its lineage as going back to Mazu, thus leaving the Sumi-san school as the only one that was not an offshoot of the Hongzhou school.[86]

Thus, the main transmission of Chan to the Korean peninsula took place during the first half of the ninth century, and the monks regarded as founders of the Korean Sŏn tradition were disciples of Chan teachers affiliated with the Hongzhou school. In that sense, early Korean Sŏn was a direct offshoot of the Hongzhou school. Table 3.1 lists the Korean monks who are regarded as "found-

TABLE 3.1. Mazu's Second-Generation Korean Disciples

Name	Dates	Teacher	Study in China	Monastery location	Biographical sources
Hongch'ŏk	unknown	Xitang	809–826?	Silsang-san	CKS 1.90
Hyech'ŏl	785–861	Xitang	814–839	Tongni-san	CKS 1.116–19
Hyŏnuk	787–868	Huaihui	824–837	Pongnim-san	ZTJ 17
Muyŏm	799–888	Magu	821–845	Sŏngju-san	CKS 1.72–83, ZTJ 17
Pŏmil	810–889	Yanguan	831–846	Sagul-san	ZTJ 17, Samguk yusa 3
Toŭi	d. 825	Xitang	784–821	Kaji-san	CKS 1.62–63, ZTJ 17
Toyun	797–868	Nanquan	825–847	Saja-san	ZTJ 17

ers" of the mountain school of Silla Sŏn and who were Mazu's second-generation disciples.[87]

These were not the only Korean monks who went to study Chan in China during this period. The designation "Nine Mountain schools" was retroactively introduced during the Koryŏ period as a convenient designation for the main streams of Silla Sŏn. The term is somewhat problematic, as it obscures the greater diversity of Sŏn communities that were formed during that period, and should best be understood as a schematization of a complex historical process. There were other Korean monks not associated with the nine mountain schools who went to China to study with noted Chan teachers and established monasteries after their return to Korea. Among them, again, disciples of Hongzhou school figures are dominant. For example, there are records of Korean monks who studied with Damei, Guizong, and Yangshan Huiji (807–883), who was Mazu's third-generation disciple.[88]

When Korean monks sojourned to China with the intention of bringing back to their native land the newest teachings of Buddhism, they presumably sought out opportunities to study under the most prominent Chinese teachers. Becoming students of leading Chinese teachers added to the Korean monks' prestige and allowed them to address their compatriots with greater authority after their return to Korea. This was especially the case with the Chan school, at the time a newcomer that occupied a relatively marginal position within the world of Silla Buddhism, which was largely dominated by the Huayan (or Hwaŏm in Korean) school. As they faced tough competition from the better-established scholastic schools, it was important for the Korean Sŏn monks to be seen as bringing back with them the best that Chinese Chan had to offer. The fact that virtually all Korean monks who went to study Chan in China during the ninth century became disciples of Hongzhou school teachers, even though doing that in most cases involved long travel to the South, confirms that at the time the Hongzhou school was widely perceived as the main tradition of Chan. It seems that for the Korean monks, finding a suitable Chan teacher meant choosing one of Mazu's leading disciples.

Transitions in Tang Chan

The Hongzhou school's growth occurred in the wake of the Chan school's initial emergence as a major tradition of Chinese Buddhism. Early Tang was a formative period in Chan history, marked by intense and varied activity involving experimentation in the areas of doctrine and practice, and the establishment of novel forms of spiritual genealogies, idioms, and literary genres. During the early eighth century, many of those activities centered on the metropolitan areas in the North. Chan teachers such as Shenxiu and Puji of the Northern school, and later Jingshan of the Niutou school, became leading monks in the capitals and the recipients of imperial patronage and public reverence. There were also regional Chan movements, such as the Jingzhong and Baotang schools in Sichuan, with their own claims to religious legitimacy. The Hongzhou school thus emerged on the Tang religious landscape as part of a movement that was at the vanguard of new developments in Chinese Buddhism.

The mid-Tang period was a turning point in the evolution of Chan marked by a changing of the guard, as the Hongzhou school's rise to preeminence coincided with the disappearance of the previously dominant groups. The Northern school, which enjoyed its heyday under Shenxiu, Yifu, and Puji, died out by the early ninth century (and probably earlier).[89] Similarly, the Niutou school also disappeared from the Chinese religious scene soon after the deaths of Mazu's contemporaries Jingshan and Huizhong, its last leaders. Analogous fates befell other regional traditions, such as the Jingzhong and Baotang schools in Sichuan. Other noted Chan teachers who lived during the eighth century, such as Nanyang Huizhong and Shenhui, were not successful in attracting and training capable disciples, which doomed their lineages to oblivion. The only other lineage that survived past the early ninth century was the one that traced its spiritual ancestry back to Shitou. But as has already been noted, during the mid-Tang period this was a marginal lineage with only limited local influence.

It is difficult to establish a direct causal relationship between the Hongzhou school's ascendancy and the demise of the schools of early Chan. It is evident that Mazu and his disciples had more success in attracting followers; for example, we have seen that the sudden demise of the Niutou school can be traced to Mazu's lifetime, when a number of monks who started their Chan training with Niutou teachers ended up becoming Mazu's disciples. On the other hand, the downfall of other schools often appears to have been a result of a natural course of events unrelated to the Hongzhou school's growth. A main factor was probably their failure to produce new generations of strong leaders, along with the shift of interest and support in the direction of the Hongzhou school.

As the other schools of Chan fell by the wayside, the Hongzhou school emerged as the most influential Chan tradition. Its success depended in part on its ability to transform itself from a regional southern tradition into a broad movement with a presence throughout the vast empire. As Mazu's disciples formed monastic congregations and became well-known Chan teachers, the Hongzhou school emerged as an empire-wide tradition that dominated the Chan movement, as is evidenced by the number of disciples who flocked to the monasteries of Mazu, Baizhang, and other key figures. As we have seen, these also included virtually all of the Korean monks who came to China to study Chan. Moreover, monks associated with the Hongzhou school received wide public acclaim and became the spiritual teachers of many important public figures, including a few Tang emperors. The Hongzhou school's dominance is also reflected in the support and recognition (both official and unofficial) it received from the state and its elites, as is evident in diverse Tang sources.

By superseding the diverse traditions of early Chan, the Hongzhou school performed a unifying role within the Chan movement. Instead of repudiating the earlier traditions, the Hongzhou school emerged as their successor and the bearer of Chan orthodoxy (although there were still individuals, like Zongmi, who unsuccessfully tried to push forward alternative visions of Chan orthodoxy). In that role, Mazu's disciples further strengthened the Chan school's position as an integral part of the Buddhist mainstream, even as they reinforced its distinct identity. They adopted a vision of Chan as an inclusive tradition that embodied the quintessence of Buddhism, steering it along a middle course, away from the antinomian excesses of the Baotang school and the sectarianism epitomized by Shenhui. This led to the establishment of a Chan orthodoxy that remained normative during the succeeding centuries throughout China and the rest of East Asia, even if by the Song period the images of Mazu and his disciples had undergone a radical transformation that reflected far-reaching changes in the Chan movement itself.

Later Developments

The Hongzhou school's dominant position within the Chan movement continued throughout most of the ninth century. Its influence also extended to other parts of East Asia; in addition to its role in the transmission of Chan to Korea, there are records that attest to missionary activities in Japan and Vietnam undertaken by monks associated with the Hongzhou school.[90] During the early ninth century, a few texts connected with the Hongzhou school were taken back to Japan by the Tendai monks Ennin (799–852) and Enchin (814–891), who went to study Buddhism in China. Those texts included *Baolin zhuan*, an early edition of Baizhang's record, and Bo Juyi's memorial inscription for Weikuan.[91] One of the first Chan monks to travel to Japan was Yikong (dates unknown), a student of Yanguan (and thus Mazu's second-generation disciple), who was welcomed at the Japanese court by Danrin, the consort of Emperor Saga (r. 809–823).[92] Yikong spent a few years at the Japanese capital, after which he returned to China.

After the end of the Huichang-era persecution of Buddhism, other Chan groups that traced their lineages back to Shitou gained in popularity, in particular a group that later became known as the Caodong school, whose leader, Dongshan, was among the leading Chan teachers of the late Tang period.[93] Dongshan's monastery was in the Hongzhou area, not far from the monasteries of Mazu, Baizhang, Huangbo, and Yangshan. He enjoyed cordial relationships with Mazu's second- and third-generation disciples. With the increased renown of monks who traced their spiritual ancestry back to Shitou, there was adjustment of the contours of the "orthodox" Chan tradition, as Shitou joined Mazu as key second-generation successor of Huineng. Because of those changes, Shitou retroactively became known as a major Chan patriarch, and his stature came to approach (even if not quite equal) that of Mazu. From then onward, all Chan lineages traced their ancestry back to either Mazu or Shitou, while recognizing the orthodoxy of each other's transmission (figure 3.1).

By the end of the Tang dynasty, the Hongzhou school's existence as a loosely organized movement was gradually superseded by the emergence of various regional traditions. The first of these groups to be perceived as a distinct tradition was the Guiyang school/lineage, whose putative founders, Guishan and his disciple Yangshan, were Mazu's second- and third-generation disciples, respectively. The Guiyang lineage was among the most influential Chan groups—perhaps the dominant one—during the final decades of the Tang period. However, as it did not continue past the fall of the dynasty, in the eyes of later Chan writers and practitioners the main heir of Mazu and the Hongzhou school was the Linji school, whose "founder," Linji, was recognized as Mazu's third-generation disciple. After a slow start during the late Tang period,

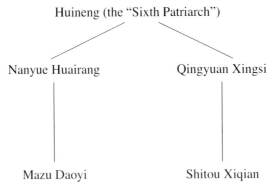

FIGURE 3.1. The two main lines of "orthodox" Chan.

by the Northern Song period the Linji school established itself as the main Chan tradition.

Recognition of separate Chan lineages is evident in Fayan's *Zongmen shigui lun* (Discourse on the Ten Rules of the Chan School).[94] There he lists the Guiyang, Deshan, Linji, Caodong, Xuefeng, and Yunmen lineages as main representatives of the Chan school. By the early Song period, four of these— Guiyang, Linji, Caodong, and Yunmen—together with the Fayan lineage, became known as the five schools/lineages of Chan. Within this new configuration, several narrower lineages replaced the broader movement once dominated by the Hongzhou school. All of these lineages emerged as regional traditions during the political fragmentation of the late Tang and the Five Dynasties eras. It is probable that the sociopolitical realities of the period of division shaped the broader contours of the Chan movement, as political fragmentation fostered the growth of regional traditions.

The unification of the empire (in 960) under the Song dynasty coincided with a further realignment within the Chan movement. At that time, the Linji school emerged as the main Chan tradition within the unified empire. The other lineages simply died out or merged into the Linji school. The only exception was the Caodong school, which resurfaced during the late Song period. From the thirteenth century onward, it also established a distinct institutional identity in Japan, where it is known as the Sōtō school.

From the Song era onward, the Linji school occupied the dominant position as the main bearer of Chan orthodoxy, not only in China but also throughout East Asia (including Korea, Vietnam, and Japan). Since the Linji school was regarded as a direct successor of the Hongzhou school, Mazu and his prominent disciples continued to occupy a central place in normative narratives about Chan history, which glorified the Tang period as the "golden age" of Chan. Various stories that feature key Hongzhou-school figures became prominent fixtures in traditional Chan lore, and their study and exegesis continued to occupy a central place in the monastic curriculum of Chan/Zen monks.[95] Mazu and his disciples thus continued to be celebrated as seminal figures whose words and actions defined Chan orthodoxy, even if the image of the Hongzhou school celebrated by later traditions was the stuff of legend, a mythical creation disjoined from the historical realities of mid-Tang Chan.

The continuing appeal of leading Hongzhou school figures is evident in the construction of Vietnamese Buddhist history, undertaken after the Vietnamese freed themselves from long-standing Chinese political hegemony. During the Lý dynasty (1010–1225), the Buddhist elites attempted to establish a Chan-centered version of Buddhist orthodoxy by linking the native tradition with the Chan school in China. As part of that strategy, Vô Ngôn Thông (dates unknown), the putative founder of the Vietnamese Chan school that bears his name, was represented as a disciple of Baizhang. According to his biography in *Thiền Uyển Tập Anh*, a fourteenth-century text that chronicles the history of Zen in medieval Vietnam, Vô Ngôn Thông originally went to see Mazu. As Mazu had already passed away by the time he arrived in Hongzhou, he became a student of Baizhang.[96] The Vô Ngôn Thông was considered the main school of Vietnamese Chan; the compiler of *Thiền Uyển Tập Anh* asserts that "the Chan school in our country [Vietnam] began with Vô Ngôn Thông."[97] While the historical accuracy of this text is open to doubt, it is evident that medieval Vietnamese Chan writers were eager to link their tradition with Mazu and Baizhang because it would serve as a powerful legitimizing tool.

With the passage of time, some of the luster of Mazu's religious personality was transferred to Linji, and the image of the Hongzhou school was altered in ways that reflected the ideological stances of subsequent Chan/Zen traditions. This process is reflected in later mythologized constructions of the Hongzhou school's teachings and character. The mystique ascribed to Mazu and his disciples was accompanied with assorted obscurations of the Hongzhou school's history, doctrines, practices, and institutions. The second part of this volume is an attempt to go beyond conventional explanations based on layers of interpretations that reflect the religious beliefs and ideological orientations of later generations of Chan/Zen writers and adherents. Its primary aim is to ascertain the doctrinal stances and approaches to spiritual cultivation that comprised the Hongzhou school's vision of the Buddhist path—as preserved in a few extant textual sources—and map out their relations to the broader religious and intellectual milieus of the mid-Tang period.

NOTES

1. Examples of highlighting of the Southern and provincial character of the Hongzhou school can be found in the works of Suzuki Tetsuo, especially his *Tō-godai no zenshū* and (to a somewhat lesser degree) *Tō-godai zenshū shi*. Both works provide detailed data about monasteries established by Chan teachers during the Tang and Five Dynasties periods in various prefectures. Suzuki provides considerable information about Mazu's disciples in the southern provinces, but he ignores the activities of disciples such as Weikuan and Huaihai, who were popular Chan teachers in Chang'an.

2. The lack of data for the status of many minor disciples and the monasteries where they resided precludes a comprehensive assessment. Often the only information we have is that Chan teacher X resided at Y monastery in Z region, with the implicit assertion that he was in charge of the monastic congregation.

3. See "Mazu's Disciples in Chang'an" in chapter 2.

4. See McRae, *The Northern School*, 30.

5. Ibid., 51–54.

6. Ibid., 61–67.

7. Biographies in JTS 126.3567–68 and XTS 130.4490–91. See also "Initial Teaching in Fujian and Jiangxi" in chapter 1.

8. Biographies in JTS 100.3129 and XTS 130.4488–90.

9. XTS 130.4490. After a brief demotion to a provincial post, in 747 Pei Kuan retired in order to devote himself to religious life (although there are also indications that his retirement was forced).

10. See Puji's biography in SGSZ 9, T 50.760c–61a. For Puji's life, see also his stele inscription in QTW 262.2657b–61a, and McRae, *The Northern School*, 65–67.

11. See Xuansu's stele inscription, written by Li Hua, in QTW 320.3246b–48b; his biography in SGSZ 9, T 50.761c–62b; and Nishiguchi, "Baso no denki," 134.

12. QTW 501.5106a.

13. XTS 138.4623.

14. JTS 146.3956, XTS 159.4949–50; Suzuki Tetsuo, *Tō-godai zenshū shi*, 121.

15. The stele inscription refers to him as Li of Chengji, while SGSZ gives his name as Li of Longxi. His identification as Li Jian is based on the extant stone inscription from Mazu's memorial pagoda unearthed in Baofeng monastery, which gives his complete name Li Jian. Suzuki Tetsuo, *Tō-godai zenshū shi*, 121, and Nishiguchi, "Baso no denki," 142, also identify him as Li Jian on the basis of inferential evidence.

16. See JTS 12.348 and Nishiguchi, "Baso no denki," 144 n. 49.

17. QTW 501.5106b.

18. See Xitang's biography in SGSZ 10, T 50.766c.

19. For his biographies, see JTS 148.4001–5 and XTS 165.5076–80. For the text of his funeral inscription (accompanied by a Japanese translation), which was composed by the famous writer and Confucian apologist Han Yu, see Ogawa Tamaki, *Tōdai no shijin: sono denki*, 321–34. For a study of his life and thought, see Anthony Augustine DeBlasi, " 'To Transform the World': A Study of Four Mid-Tang Intellectuals," 27–77.

20. For Pei Zhou's biographies, see JTS 122.3507–8 and XTS 130.4491–92.

21. See Nishiguchi, "Baso no denki," 135.

22. In Chengguan's biography in SGSZ 5, T 50.737a–c, Quan is mentioned as one of the ten noted officials who associated with him. For a study of Chengguan's life, see Imre Hamar, *A Religious Leader in the Tang: Changguan's Biography*.

23. QTW 501.5106b–7a.

24. See *Tang gu zhangjingsi baiyan dashi beiming bingxu*, by Quan Deyu, QTW 501.5103b–4a, and WYYH 866.4568a–b.

25. He only has a brief biography in XTS 149.4798–99.

26. Jia Jinhua, "The Hongzhou School of Chan Buddhism and the Tang Literati," 162–63. Suzuki Tetsuo, *Tō-godai zenshū shi*, 122, speculates that he might have met Mazu when he was exiled to Lingnan in 777. Bao might have passed though Hongzhou on the way to or from Lingnan, but there is no evidence to prove that he actually did so. Suzuki also speculates that the stele inscriptions of Quan Deyu and Bao Ji mentioned in Mazu's biography in SGSZ might refer to the same original stele inscription, but I believe his contention is based on a mistaken reading of the relevant SGSZ passage.

27. Ishikawa Rikisan, "Basokyodan no tenkai to sono shijishatachi," 162–63.

28. Pei's official biographies are in JTS 177.4592–93 and XTS 182.5371–72. For a study of his life, which places substantial emphasis on his Buddhist activities, see Yoshikawa Tadao, "Hai Kyū den: Tōdai no ichi shidaifu to bukkyō."

29. *Tanzhou daguishan zhongxing ji*, included in *Shimen wenzi chan* 21 (a Song period text), in *Zenshū zensho* 95, 282a. Relevant passages from this text are quoted in Yoshikawa, "Hai Kyū den," 165.

30. *Tangwen cui* 63, vol. 2, 12; QTW 820.3832c; CTL 9, T 51.264c. See also Jeffrey Broughton, "Kuei-feng Tsung-mi: Convergence of Ch'an and the Teaching," 35.

31. See SGSZ 11, T 50.777c, and Suzuki, *Tō-Godai no zenshū*, 29–30. For Li's biographies, see JTS 187b.4891–92, and XTS 177.5290–91. In response to Li's petition, the court granted to Guishan's monastery the name Tongqing. See SGSZ 11, T 50.777c, and Yoshikawa, "Hai Kyū den," 164.

32. For Cui, see JTS 177.4577–80.

33. Biographies in JTS 163.4271–73 and XTS 177.5284–85. Lu was also the author of the stele inscription for Mazu's disciple Yanguan Qi'an, titled *Hangzhou yanguanxian haichangyuan chanmen dashi tabei*, in QTW 733.3354b–c and WYYH 868.4578a–79a. Moreover, QTW 733 also contains another short inscription by Lu, similarly titled *Chanmen dashi beiyin ji*, which immediately precedes this inscription.

34. Li's biographies are in JTS 190c.5077–78 and XTS 203.5792–93. For an annotated Japanese translation of the JTS biography, see Ogawa, *Tōdai no shijin*, 527–33. Li was also the author of *Tang zizhou huiyijingshe nanchanyuan sizhengtang beiming*, QTW 780.3608b–9c, an inscription that commemorates Mazu, Xitang, Wuxiang, and Wuzhu. Lu's composition of Guishan's inscription and Li's writing of its calligraphy are also mentioned in Guishan's biography in SGSZ 11, T 50.777c.

35. For more information about Dacien Monastery, see Ono Katsutoshi, *Chūgoku Zui Tō Chōan jiin shiryō shōsei: shiryō hen*, 84–115, and *Chūgoku Zui Tō Chōan jiin shiryō shūsei: kaisetsu hen*, 55–69; Xiong, *Sui-Tang Chang'an*, 260–62; and Stanley Weinstein, *Buddhism under the T'ang*, 26–28.

36. For the establishment of Zhangjing Monastery, see *Zizhi tongjian* 224.7195–96 and the biography of Yu Chaoen (d. 770), the influential eunuch who donated the estate on which the monastery was built, in JTS 184.4764. For further references and information, see also Ono, *Chōan jiin shiryō shūsei: shiryō hen*, 327–32, and *Chōan jiin shiryō shūsei: kaisetsu hen*, 112–14; Xiong, *Sui-Tang Chang'an*, 270; and Weinstein, *Buddhism under the T'ang*, 83–84.

37. For more information about Anguo monastery, see Ono, *Chōan jiin shiryō shūsei: shiryō hen*, 118–28, and *Chōan jiin shiryō shūsei: kaisetsu hen*, 69–77.

38. For the historical sources about Xingshan monastery, see Ono, *Chōan jiin shiryō shūsei: shiryō hen*, 118–28, and *Chōan jiin shiryō shūsei: kaisetsu hen*, 8–20. For the establishment of the monastery during the Sui dynasty, see Yamazaki Hiroshi, *Zui-tō bukkyō shi no kenkyū*, 45–47.

39. For Farong's stele inscription, see QTW 606.6117b–18a.

40. For biographical information about Jingshan, see his stele inscription in QTW 512.5206a–8a, as well as his biographies in SGSZ 9, T 50.764b–65a, and CDL 4, T 51.230a–b. For Huizhong's biography, see CDL 4, T 51.229a–b. See also John R. McRae, "The Ox-head School of Chinese Ch'an Buddhism: From Early Ch'an to the Golden Age," 180–82, 191–95. Huizhong is not to be confused with National Teacher Huizhong (675–775, also known as Nanyang Huizhong), an influential

monk who is often identified as a disciple of Huineng (biography in CDL 5, T 51.244a–c).

41. ZTJ 3.65.

42. CDL 7, T 51.252b; SGSZ 10, T 50.766c. Faqin's short biography in ZTJ includes a story in which Mazu sends Xitang to visit Jingshan and instructs him to ask a few questions; ZTJ 3.65. In CDL there is a similar story in which Mazu sends Xitang to Jingshan in order to deliver a letter; CDL 4, T 51.230a. In CDL there is also a story according to which Mazu asked Xitang to go to the capital to deliver a letter to National Teacher Huizhong.

43. See McRae, "The Ox-head School," 188. CDL lists the Niutou monk Longya Yuanchang (d.u.), who, like Faqin, was a disciple of Xuansu, as a disciple of Mazu; see CDL 7, T 51.251c. This, however, seems to be a mistake, perhaps caused by the fact that Xuansu was also known as Mazu.

44. CDL 7, T 51.253c, and SGSZ 11, T 50.773. See also Suzuki, *Tō-godai zenshū shi*, 373.

45. For Xingsi's biography, see ZTJ 3.70 (where his name is listed as Reverend Jingju), and CDL 5, T 51.240a–c.

46. For Shitou's biography, see SGSZ 9, T 50.736c; ZTJ 4.88–93; and CDL 14, T 51.309b–c. For studies of his life, see Ishii, *Sōdai zenshūshi no kenkyū*, 123–46, and Ui, *Zenshū shi kenkyū*, vol. 1, 396–411.

47. ZTJ 4.89; CDL 14, T 51.309b. Shitou's disciples or biographers could have invented the meeting with Huineng in order to enhance his religious authority. At the same time, Shitou's native place was close to Caoxi, where Huineng resided, and it is possible that the two were acquainted, even if only for a short time.

48. ZTJ 4.90.

49. Ibid.

50. For Danxia, Lingmo, and Zhaoti, see ZTJ 4.96, ZTJ 15.333, and ZTJ 4.102, respectively; for Deng Yinfeng see CDL 6, T 51.246b; and for Daotong and Daowu, see SGSZ 10, T 50.777c, and T 50.769a–70a, respectively.

51. Pang Yun might be an exception, but the sources are at odds about the sequence of his meetings with Mazu and Shitou. While his record of sayings and biography in CDL 8, T 51.263b, state that he met Shitou first, according to ZTJ he initially went together with Danxia to see Mazu. See Danxia's biography in ZTJ 4.95. In Shitou's biography in ZTJ 4.92, there is also a story in which an anonymous monk from Mazu's community comes to visit him. The monk returns to Mazu after taking leave of Shitou, but there is no indication that he acted on Shitou's advice.

52. SGSZ 9, T 50.764a; English translation from Cheng-chien, *Sun-Face Buddha*, 19.

53. See the discussion in the next section.

54. Later Chan texts that use lineage affiliation as a key organizing principle define Yaoshan's relationship with Mazu and Shitou according to the sectarian predilections of their authors or the sources they used. The later (i.e., post-Tang) Chan tradition came to regard Yaoshan, together with Daowu, as one of Shitou's two main disciples. Accordingly, Chan texts composed from the late tenth century and after—such as SGSZ, CDL, and ZTJ—list Yaoshan as a disciple of Shitou.

However, the text of his stele inscription (which is of questionable authenticity) states that he was disciple of Mazu and makes no mention of Shitou. See QTW 536.5443b–45a.

55. See his biography in SGSZ 10, T 50.769a–b. Early records—including Mazu's and Huairang's stele inscriptions and Zongmi's writings—present Daowu as a disciple of Mazu, and he seems to have been predominantly perceived as such during the mid-Tang period. Conversely, in later texts, beginning with ZTJ and CDL, he is listed as a disciple of Shitou.

56. The compilers of both ZTJ and CDL classified Daowu as a successor of Shitou, but some early Song Linji monks rejected this genealogy and argued that Daowu was Mazu's disciple. They contended, based on the evidence provided by a stele inscription written for Daowu of Tianwang monastery (regarded by some to be a forgery), that during the mid-Tang period there were two monks called Daowu: one the ancestor of the Yunmen and Fayan traditions who was a disciple of Mazu, the other one a disciple of Shitou.

57. *Xingfusi neidaochang gongfeng dade dayi chanshi beiming,* QTW 715.3258a–59a.

58. For more on Zongmi's text, see Jeffrey L. Broughton, "Tsung-mi's *Zen Prolegomenon:* Introduction to an Exemplary Zen Canon."

59. The Northern, Southern, and Niutou schools are also treated as the main branches of Chan in an inscription composed by Li Hua composed some half a century earlier (discussed in the section "Reconfiguration of Chan Orthodoxy").

60. See Gregory, *Tsung-mi,* 224–25.

61. QTW 715.3258a.

62. Ibid..

63. See McRae, "Shen-hui and the Teaching of Sudden Enlightenment," and *The Northern School,* 1–8.

64. See CDL 28, T 51.437c. For Huizhong's criticisms, see Ishii's "Nanyō Echū no nanpō shūshi no hihan ni tsuite," as well as the discussion in the section "Some Critiques" in chapter 5.

65. QTW 715.3258a.

66. CDL 30, T 51.459b.

67. *Xijing xingshansi chuanfatang bei,* QTW 678.3069c–70a.

68. QTW 678.3069c.

69. The historical study of Chinese Buddhism is often approached in terms of distinct "schools" (*zong*). The Chinese term *zong* is a source of confusion—evident, for example, when *zong* is mistranslated as "sect" in discussions of Tang Buddhism—largely stemming from its multivalent connotations and the different historical contexts in which it was employed. In the medieval context, *zong* covers a broad semantic field. It can mean a specific religious doctrine or interpretation; an essential purport or teaching, especially of a canonical text; an exegetical tradition; or a religious group formed on the basis of shared religious ideals and/or adherence to a set of principles. The last sense is applicable to the Hongzhou school, but even there it does not denote a separate sect, as defined by sociologists of religion. The distinct schools of Buddhism that emerged during the late medieval period lacked institutional independence. Some of them, such as Dilun, Shelun, Faxiang, Sanlun, and even Huayan, primarily represented doctrinal or exegetical traditions. Others, such

as Chan and Tiantai, evolved into distinct, loosely organized religious groups, but they were also subsumed *within* the mainstream monastic order.

70. The central role of Bodhidharma is evident in early Chan texts such as *Lengqie shizi ji* and *Baolin zhuan* and in epigraphic sources such as Huaihui's stele inscription (see QTW 501.2260b).

71. Griffith Foulk and others have raised questions about the identity of Tang Chan as a distinct tradition. For example, in the conclusion of his dissertation Foulk writes, "I doubt that the members of the Chan school ever . . . made a break with the Buddhist monastic tradition that resulted in the establishment of separate, independent, uniquely 'Chan' institutions"; Foulk, "The Ch'an School and Its Place in the Buddhist Monastic Tradition," 389. I partially agree with Foulk's statement as far as the institutional history of Tang Chan is concerned. However, that does not preclude the existence of a distinct identity as a religious tradition, even if institutionally the Chan school was integrated into the monastic order. There are numerous mentions in Tang sources, including the inscriptions introduced above, of the Chan school as a distinct tradition. There are also statements to the effect that the various Chan schools/ lineages were subsumed within a single tradition. For an example, see Baizhang's inscription in QTW 446.2014a. We also find similar statements in non-Buddhist texts, including the poems of Bo Juyi. In a number of poems Bo explicitly mentions the "Chan of the Southern school" (*Nanzong chan*), and he makes mention of "Bodhidharma's mind transmission." For examples of the first, see *Bo Juyi ji* 6.125, 45.968; for the second, see *Bo Juyi ji* 31.711. For references to sitting meditation (*zuochan*)— which need not necessarily be tied to a distinctive Chan school, although that is often implied—see *Bo Juyi ji* 6.120, 25.558, 29.662, 31.712, 35.802, 35.804, and 36.827.

72. Both normative and modern historiography blur the distinction between the categories of "school" and "lineage," both of which are feasible translations of *zong*. Foulk has drawn attention to the need to distinguish between "lineage" as a semimythological creation, a spiritual clan in which individuals are linked by Dharma inheritance, and "school" as a historical one, made up of real persons united by common sets of beliefs and practices; Foulk "The Ch'an *Tsung* in Medieval China: School, Lineage, or What?" 19–20. While this distinction has its usefulness, it is not without problems as both meanings overlap and intersect, and they are both applicable in the case of the Hongzhou school. The notion of "lineage" has a narrower range of connotation and is one of the elements that made Mazu and his disciples function as a "school," albeit one without distinctive institutional moorings, which would imply separate ordinations, monasteries, and so forth. In other words, the notion of linear descendants implied by the genealogical model was part of a group identity that also included common beliefs, teachings, and practices, which are subsumed under the category of "school." Since the early sources collapse the distinction between lineage and school, at the risk of introducing some vagueness I have reflected that ambiguity by using both terms as appropriate.

73. For the Tiantai school's efforts to construct its own religious genealogy, which to a substantial degree were a response to developments within the Chan school, see Penkower, "T'ian-t'ai during the T'ang Dynasty," 220–299.

74. See *Zhonghua chuan xindi chanmen shizi chengxi tu*, XZJ 110.434b, 438a.

75. QTW 446.2014a. Inscriptions from the same period often invoke Huineng as a source of authority and an exemplar of orthodoxy, which suggests that by that time his position as the sixth Chan patriarch was firmly established.

76. *Bo juyi ji* 41.911 (vol. 3).

77. Hu Shi first pointed out this idiosyncrasy in 1928; see his "Bo Juyi shidaide chanzong shixi," reprinted in Huang Xianian, *Hu Shi ji*, 36–39. It is also discussed in Yanagida, *Shoki zenshū shisho no kenkyū*, 396.

78. *Chu sanzang jiji* 12, T 55.90a.

79. See Shiina Kōyū, "*Hōrinden* makikyū makiju no itsubun," 195, and Yanagida, *Shoki zenshū shisho no kenkyū*, 357–61.

80. See McRae, *The Northern School*, 240. This modern reinterpretation was made possible by the discovery of a few significant texts attributed to Shenhui among the Dunhuang manuscripts. Hu Shih first noted the significance of Shenhui's anti–Northern school campaigns in the 1930s, and other Chan/Zen scholars, including Yanagida, subsequently explored it. Shenhui is the subject of a manuscript by John R. McRae, *Zen Evangelist: Shenhui (684–758), the Sudden Teaching, and the Southern School of Chinese Chan Buddhism*.

81. Hirai Shunei, "The School of Mount Niu-t'ou and the School of Pao-T'ang Monastery," 359. According to the author of *Lidai fabao ji*, their tradition was older than the division between the Northern and Southern schools, as it went back to Zhishen, a disciple of the fifth patriarch Hongren. In support of these claims, he recounts a peculiar version of the fictional story about the transmission of the patriarchal robe, which was supposedly handed down to Wuzhu. See Yanagida, "The *Li-Tai Fa-Pao Chi*," 21–22.

82. See McRae, "The Ox-head School," 201–2.

83. See *Gu zouxi dashi bei*, QTW 320.1433a, and Yampolsky, *The Platform Sutra*, 38–39.

84. See the discussion of Dayi in "Mazu's Disciples in Chang'an" in chapter 2.

85. See Robert Buswell, *The Korean Approach to Zen: The Collected Works of Chinul*, 9, and *The Formation of Ch'an Ideology in China and Korea:* The Vajrasamādhi-Sūtra, *A Buddhist Apocryphon*, 166–68.

86. See Chōsen Sōtokufu, *Chōsen kinseki sōran*, 90–91, and Faure, *The Will to Orthodoxy*, 47.

87. This table is based on tables that appear in Chŏng Sŏng-bon, *Silla sŏnjong ŭi yŏn'gu*, 51–52, and Robert Buswell, *The Korean Approach to Zen*, 10–11. In the last column, CKS is an abbreviation for *Chōsen kinseki sōran*. Some of the dates are problematic; for example, Hyŏnuk could not have studied with Huaihui after 824, since Huaihui died in 816.

88. Damei's Korean disciples are mentioned in CDL 10, T 51.273b, 280a. For the names of other Korean monks mentioned in CDL who were students of Mazu's first-through third-generation disciples, see the chart in Han Kidu, "Keitoku Dentōroku ni miru Shiragi zen," 131.

89. See McRae, *The Northern School*, 67–69, 242–44, and Faure, *The Will to Orthodoxy*, 91–93.

90. For the connection with Vietnam, see below.

91. Ibuki Atsushi, *Zen no rekishi*, 182.

92. Ibid., 184.

93. For studies of the Caodong school, both of which focus on the Song period, see Ishii Shūdō, *Sōdai zenshūshi no kenkyū: Chūgoku sōtōshū to dōgen zen*, and Morten Schlütter, "Chan Buddhism in Song-Dynasty China (960–1279): The Rise of the Caodong Tradition and the Formation of the Chan School."

94. XZJ 110.439d

95. The standing of Mazu and his disciples within the world of Song Chan is evident in the famous *gongan* collections, which exemplify the Chan school's literary production during that period. For example, Mazu and his first- and second-generation disciples appear in almost a third of the hundred cases included in *Biyan lu*. Mazu appears in two cases, his first-generation disciples in fourteen cases, second-generation disciples in fifteen cases, and an additional six cases feature third-generation disciples.

96. Cuong Tu Nguyen, *Zen in Medieval Vietnam: A Study and Translation of the Thiền Uyển Tập Anh*, 44.

97. Quoted in Nguyen, *Zen in Medieval Vietnam*, 43.

PART II

Doctrine and Practice

4

Doctrinal Contexts and Religious Attitudes

The early growth of Chan coincided with one of the most creative phases in the history of Chinese Buddhism. Having assimilated the canonical texts, tenets, and ideals of Mahāyāna that slowly filtered into China from the beginning of the Common Era, by the Sui-Tang period Chinese Buddhism encompassed distinctive worldviews, systems of philosophical analysis, styles of religious discourse, modes of ritual expression, and methods of praxis. Some of the traditions that evolved during this period, such as Huayan and Tiantai, introduced doctrinal systems of remarkable conceptual coherence and intellectual sophistication. Others focused on formulating new beliefs or approaches to spiritual praxis, as was the case with Chan and the Pure Land movement. The new traditions absorbed and creatively reconfigured received doctrines. They also introduced new models of theory and praxis that reflected native religious predilections, ethical values, and intellectual perspectives. As the Chan school was part of these developments, the evolution of its doctrinal outlooks and soteriological approaches occurred against the larger backdrop of Sui-Tang Buddhism, and thus its teachings reflected viewpoints and values shared by the medieval Buddhist traditions.

This chapter begins with brief surveys of the religious and intellectual milieus of Tang Buddhism. The subsequent sections elaborate on the Hongzhou school's attitudes in four key areas: monastic mores and ideals, meditative praxis, canonicity and religious authority, and the use of scriptures.

The Traditions and Doctrines of Tang Buddhism

In the eighth century, Chinese monks such as those who joined Mazu's congregation in Jiangxi had access to a broad range of Buddhist doctrines and practices. This was a time of great intellectual ferment and ingenuity, headed by some of the brightest minds to appear in the history of Chinese Buddhism. At the time of Mazu's birth (709), Fazang had just finished formulating—on foundations laid down by his teacher Zhiyan (602–668)—the grand doctrinal system that came to be identified with the Huayan school. Mazu was a contemporary of Zhanran, who revived the sagging fortunes of the Tiantai school and systematized its doctrines. Xitang and Baizhang were contemporaries of Chengguan, the brilliant exegete who was posthumously recognized as the fourth patriarch of the Huayan school.

In addition to canonical and exegetical works, the textual sources available at the time included numerous works that propounded innovative doctrines and interpretations. These included systematic expositions of Buddhist theory and praxis formulated by the new schools of the Sui-Tang period: Tiantai, Sanlun, Faxiang, and Huayan. Devotional forms of religious piety were echoed in the development of Pure Land beliefs and practices and other popular movements. There was also the Tantric or Esoteric (Mijiao or Zhenyan) tradition, whose focus on thaumaturgy and elaborate rituals captured the imagination of key religious audiences, including a few Tang emperors. In addition, much of the Buddhist fervor during this epoch was channeled outside of the recognized schools, finding manifold forms of religious, intellectual, social, and artistic expressions among the clergy and the laity.

Late medieval Chinese Buddhism exhibited a grasp of the range of Mahāyāna doctrines. Each of the main systems of Mahāyāna philosophy—Madhyamaka, Yogācāra, and tathāgatagarbha—were significant within the context of Tang Buddhism, and their continued influence is discernible in the records of the various schools of Chan, including the Hongzhou school. In terms of chronology, the first doctrinal system of Indian Mahāyāna appropriated by Chinese scholiasts was the Madhyamaka or Middle Way (Zhongguan) tradition. The Madhyamaka teachings of emptiness (Sanskrit: *śūnyatā*; Chinese: *kong*), conditioned origination (Sanskrit: *pratītyasamutpāda*; Chinese: *yuanqi*), and two levels of truth (*erdi*) were introduced to China by the famous translator Kumārajīva (c. 350–409) and popularized by his disciples, such as Sengzhao (374?–414). During the sixth century, there was a shift in interest toward the teachings of the Yogācāra (Yuqiexing) school. The sophisticated analyses of different types of consciousness and elaborate explanations of the stages of meditative practice presented in Yogācāra texts attracted the attention of leading Buddhist scholars, whose creative intellectual and religious responses were evident in the production of learned treatises and elaborate exegetical works, such as those written by the monks associated with the Shelun and Dilun schools.

Chinese appropriations of Yogācāra thought were accompanied by astute interest in the related doctrines of the tathāgatagarbha (*rulaizang*, variously interpreted as womb or embryo of Buddhahood) and Buddha-nature (*foxing*).[1] These doctrines stressed mind's essential purity, the immanence of enlightenment, and the universality of Buddhahood. The assimilation of the tathāgatagarbha and Buddha-nature theories was an event with profound ramifications for the history of Buddhism in East Asia. The Chinese embrace of the notion that Buddhahood is immanent in each person—which came to be especially associated with the Chan and Huayan traditions—represented a recognition of the soteriological value of kataphatic (positive/affirmative) modes of religious discourse. This contrasted with the seemingly relentless apophatic (negative use of language) approach associated with orthodox Madhyamaka doctrine.[2] In the Buddha-nature doctrine's optimistic outlook on human perfectibility, Chinese Buddhists found a compelling theory that validated the phenomenal world as the arena where spiritual practice and realization took place. Its influence is evident in the records of the various schools of Chan, including those of the East Mountain tradition and the Northern school, as well as the Hongzhou school.

As understood by Tang Buddhists, the tathāgatagarbha doctrine postulated that everybody is endowed with a luminous, true mind of suchness, which is primordially enlightened and pure. Although the pure mind is originally present in each person, because of the inveterate force of ignorance—whose origin is not explained in a satisfactory manner—it is covered with defilements.[3] As a result, ordinary people are ignorant of their true nature and are unable to experience spiritual liberation, although through the practice of Buddhism they can start redressing that predicament.

Notwithstanding its broad-based appeal, the Buddha-nature theory was not without problems and ambiguities. A key sticking point was the ontological status of the Buddha-nature. When canonical texts proclaim the universality of Buddha-nature, what exactly is meant by the term "Buddha-nature"? Furthermore, in what sense can we assert that sentient beings "possess" Buddha-nature? These are important issues because one of the criticisms leveled against the Buddha-nature doctrine is that it goes against the basic Buddhist teaching of "no-self" (Sanskrit: *anātman*; Chinese: *wuwo*).

In Indian texts such as the *Śrīmālādevī* and the *Ratnagotravibhāga*, the tathāgatagarbha represents the true conception of emptiness, and the authors of these texts presumably saw themselves as heirs of the orthodox Madhyamaka tradition.[4] In the *Mahāparinirvāna Scripture* (*Da niepan jing*), the notion of having Buddha-nature is used in the sense of human ability to attain the nature of the Buddha in the future. The text rejects the idea that human beings are at present endowed with the sublime qualities of Buddhahood or that they have already achieved enlightenment.[5] The scripture's teaching about the eventual attainment of Buddhahood by all beings is primarily a soteriological doctrine, not an attempt to postulate an ultimate reality that entails pure essence.[6] The writings of Jizang (549–623), the great Sanlun scholar, express similar sentiments. Jizang equates the Buddha-nature with the middle way, which transcends all dualistic views. He interprets the Buddha-nature in a way that was consistent with the Madhyamaka doctrine, taking a clue from Madhyamaka tradition's aversion to ontological speculations.[7]

Other Buddhist thinkers, in addition to explicating the Buddha-nature as *śūnya* (empty of self-nature), also described it in opposite terms, as *aśūnya* (non-empty). In this second sense, Buddha-nature was conceived of as a kind of essentialized substratum of being that involves the notion of permanent self (*ātman*). This reification of the Buddha-nature reflected a broader Chinese reaction against the teaching of emptiness, which was perceived as being open to nihilistic interpretations that potentially inhibited religious aspirations and created obstacles to praxis. Examples of this point of view appear in the writings of Zongmi, whose interpretations reflect a doctrinal stance prevalent at the time.[8] According to this perspective, since the mind of an ordinary person is essentially the same as the mind of the Buddha, the purpose of the teachings of Buddhism is to lead the spiritual seeker to see through the misguided attachment to illusory "false thoughts" and realize his or her true nature, which is none other than the pure luminous mind of suchness. At the moment of awakening, the latent potency of the Buddha wisdom inherent in each person's mind is transformed into the actuality of an enlightened vision of reality, accompanied by manifestations of the overabundance of wisdom and compassion that characterize the Buddha's presence in the world.

The Southern school of Chan is sometimes described as promoting a substantialist interpretation of the tathāgatagarbha/Buddha-nature doctrine, an interpretation evident, for example, in the *Platform Scripture's* famous injunction to "realize the [Buddha] nature directly."[9] Because of the unsystematic presentation of the Hongzhou school's records, it is difficult to assess precisely the conception of the Buddha-nature among Mazu and his disciples. Some passages identify the Buddha-nature with emptiness, but others seem to be pointing to some sort of substratum with the characteristics of self. Nevertheless, overall there is a disposition to avoid imputing explicit ontological status to the Buddha-nature. As we will see in the next two chapters, this is accompanied by a Madhyamaka-like stress on nonattachment and elimination of one-sided views—especially evident in Baizhang's record—that are based on the notion that ultimate reality cannot be predicated.

Doctrinal Taxonomies

The various schools of Tang Chan adopted the notion of Buddha-nature and explored its ramifications for spiritual cultivation, integrating it into larger conceptual frameworks that incorporated other doctrinal tenets and ideas. Although the Buddha-nature theory served as a doctrinal foundation for diverse Chan teachings and practices, it was employed alongside other Mahāyāna doctrines. It is not uncommon in Chan texts to find the Madhyamaka teaching of emptiness and the Yogācāra's affirmation of mind's pivotal role in the construction of phenomenal reality presented alongside varied assertions of inherent enlightenment. Occasionally, permutations of Buddhist doctrines are also mixed with Daoist ideas. A case in point is the use of the concept "guarding the one" (shouyi)—derived from Daoist meditation practice—by the East Mountain tradition and the author(s) of the apocryphal Vajrasamādhi Scripture (Jin'gang sanmei jing). Such borrowings exemplify a tendency to formulate the practice of Chan meditation by recourse to concepts and categories derived from native religious traditions, especially Daoism.[10]

When Robert Sharf describes the rhetorical strategy of a group of early Chan texts—a group that includes Xinxin ming (Inscription on Faith in Mind) and Jueguan lun (Treatise on the Transcendence of Cognition)—as a "synthesis of Madhyamaka-style deconstruction, with more kataphatic prose drawing loosely from Yogācāra and Daoist works," he underscores a prevalent tendency to mix doctrinal themes and concepts derived from diverse sources.[11] A similar propensity is evident in the records of the Hongzhou School. This eclectic approach reflects an expansive outlook and an accommodating stance vis-à-vis the canonical teachings and other doctrinal traditions. It also accentuates the fact that the Chan school did not formulate comprehensive and carefully constructed systems of doctrine along the lines of those produced by the Tiantai and Huayan schools.

Zongmi made a noteworthy effort at unraveling the complex connections between the various Chan teachings and the main Mahāyāna doctrines. As the centerpiece of his self-proclaimed agenda of healing perceived splits between Chan and the doctrinal schools on one hand, and among the various schools of Chan on the other, Zongmi formulated a taxonomic model that highlighted correspondences among the three major doctrinal traditions and the three main schools of Chan. One of the operative principles behind Zongmi's analysis was the notion of unity between Chan and doctrinal (or canonical) Buddhism (jiaochan yizhi). In Zongmi's theoretical model, the teachings of the Northern school are paired with those of Faxiang Yogācāra and those of the Niutou school with the Madhyamaka teaching of emptiness, while the Southern school (which includes the Hongzhou and the Heze schools) is matched up with the tathāgatagarbha doctrine.[12]

Zongmi's classification scheme exemplifies a concern for harmony, order, and conceptual clarity typical of medieval doctrinal taxonomies (*panjiao*). But his analysis also exemplifies the polemical character of such classificatory models. Medieval doctrinal taxonomies posited organic relationships among diverse doctrines, based on a premise that they comprise an all-inclusive whole. However, they also functioned as control mechanisms, instituting hierarchies of validity that supported specific truth-claims, thus ascribing fixed ranks of authenticity and legitimacy. In that sense, they promoted particular points of view and justified sectarian agendas. The authors of such doctrinal hierarchies typically placed whatever teachings they advocated at the top and relegated competing teachings to lower levels. This is evident in Zongmi's taxonomy, in which he reserved the top spot for the Heze school, the one he associated himself with.

The classificatory scheme introduced by Zongmi represents a significant attempt to draw connections between the schools of Chan and the Mahāyāna doctrines. Nonetheless, his analysis obfuscates as much as it clarifies those connections, and the actual links and correlations are more complex than he suggests. For example, his assertion of direct correspondence between the teachings of the Northern school and Faxiang Yogācāra is simplistic at best, misleading at worst.[13] The forced pairing of the two seems to reflect a desire to assign the Northern school a position in a fixed conceptual grid, thereby relegating it to a marginal position. That agenda supersedes concerns about providing a balanced account of the broad range of doctrinal positions adopted by Shenxiu and his followers, which included the Buddha-nature doctrine. In a way, the whole intellectual exercise resembles an effort to place square pegs into round holes. The drawing of clear-cut linkages and correspondences between specific Chan teachings and Mahāyāna doctrines is problematic because, among other things, the various Chan schools were eclectic in their usage of canonical texts and tenets and did not rigidly confine themselves to a specific doctrinal position.

Reflecting the Chan movement's early origins in the meditative traditions of sixth- and seventh-century China, Chan teachers used various doctrines in ways that fitted into their ideas about spiritual cultivation. The same applies to the Hongzhou school: Its use of canonical sources was accompanied by an aversion to dogmatic assertions of indelible truths and an awareness of the provisional nature of conceptual constructs. As we will see in the next chapter, various teachings were introduced in order to deal with issues that arose in the course of spiritual cultivation. They were not to be attached to as unassailable representations of reality; in the final analysis, ultimate reality was deemed indescribable and unobtainable, beyond words and concepts. Therefore, Mazu and his followers made free use of various doctrines—Madhyamaka, tathāgatagarbha, and to a lesser degree Yogācāra—without adopting a narrow point of view or a fixed theoretical perspective.

Having briefly surveyed the doctrinal contexts that informed the teachings of Mazu and his disciples, let us turn to their religious attitudes in a few key areas, beginning with the ideals and practices of monasticism.

Monastic Mores and Ideals

The Chan tradition adopted an elitist attitude from early on, and its main audiences were monks committed to the pursuit of arcane truths. Thus Chan doctrines and practices cannot be divorced from the religious mores and institutional ethos of Tang monasticism. Among the traditions of early Chan, the stress on monastic discipline is especially evident in the Northern school. Important monks associated with it were noted for their expertise in the Vinaya, and in Northern school texts emphasis is placed on the importance of strict observance of the precepts.[14] Moreover, many Northern school monks resided at monasteries that were well known as centers for the study and observance of the monastic precepts. These tendencies can be observed in the life of Shenxiu, who after his ordination studied the Vinaya and for over two decades resided at Yuquan monastery in Jingzhou, which (as already noted) was an important center of Vinaya—as well as Tiantai and Pure Land—studies.[15] Puji, Shenxiu's best-known disciple who joined the community in Jingzhou, was also a student of the Vinaya. There was also a considerable overlap between some Vinaya lineages and the spiritual genealogy of the Northern school.[16]

Overall, the records of Mazu and his disciples only rarely directly address monastic ideals and institutions. In comparison to the Northern school, there is less explicit stress on linking Chan with the Vinaya. The monastic context is simply assumed, thus needing no special elaboration. Even so, there are passages scattered throughout the extant records that shed light on the conceptions of sanctity and the monastic ideals current within the Hongzhou school. For example, the following passage from Baizhang's record briefly describes the monastic vocation:

When a person who studies the Way [i.e., a monk] encounters all kinds of painful or pleasant, agreeable or disagreeable situations, his mind does not recoil. Not thinking about fame and profit, robes and food, and not being greedy for any merit and blessings, he is not obstructed by anything in the world. With nothing dear, free from love, he can equally accept pain and pleasure. He uses a coarse robe to protect himself from the cold and simple food to support his body. Letting go, he is like a fool, like a deaf man, like a dumb man. It is only then that one gains some understanding. If one uses one's mind to engage broadly in intellectual study, seeking merit and wisdom, then all of that is just birth and death, and it does not serve

any purpose as far as reality is concerned. Blown by the wind of
knowledge, such a person is drowned in the ocean of birth and
death.[17]

The image of religious ascetics conveyed by this passage underscores
themes and ideas familiar to students of Buddhist monasticism. It resonates
with deeply cherished—even if in actual practice often neglected—ideals that
are at the core of Buddhist conceptions of sanctity. The monastic paradigm
expressed by Baizhang evokes hallowed traditions of long standing in the history of Buddhism. Its values and sentiments are echoed in a broad range of
monastic literature of South Asian and Chinese provenance. The general tenor
resonates with ideals espoused by monks belonging to traditions that stress
ascetic and contemplative practices. As such, Baizhang's image of the exemplary monk epitomizes a religious calling grounded in core monastic virtues
and practices.

The monastic ethos Baizhang describes involves the renunciation of fame,
profit, and material things. It also calls for detachment from ordinary human
emotions, including love, and the development of mental equanimity. The
adoption of a simple ascetic lifestyle, symbolized by the coarse robe and plain
food, reinforced appropriate spiritual qualities, thereby indicating monks' renunciation of worldly pleasures and dedication to the cultivation of religious
perfection. Baizhang's description of the monastic ideal continues:

> If one could only for a lifetime keep a mind that is like a wood or
> stone, without being moved by the aggregates, the realms of sense,
> the entrances, the five desires,[18] and the eight winds,[19] then one cuts
> off the cause of birth and death, and is free to go or stay. Then such a
> person is not bound by any phenomenal causes and results, and is
> not hindered by any of the afflictions. At that time, because of himself
> being free, he can help others by adapting to them and acting in
> beneficial ways.[20] With an unattached mind he responds to all things;
> with unobstructed wisdom he unties all bonds. This is what has been
> called "giving medicine according to illness."[21]

By cultivating mental detachment, the exemplary monk eventually transcends the realm of saṃsāra and realizes genuine freedom. In accord with the
Bodhisattva ideal, the attainment of this liberated state is not an end of the
spiritual path; rather, it serves as a prelude to a monk's selfless activity, moti-
vated by compassion and dedicated to the benefit of others. A similar emphasis
on the monastic ideal, which valorizes the image of an otherworldly ascetic
unconcerned with mundane affairs, is also evident in Wuye's sermons. There
he urges his disciples to follow the principles and examples set by the monks
of yore, who led austere eremitic lives. According to Wuye, authentic monks
immerse themselves in spiritual practice, completely unwilling to bend their

lofty religious principles and aspirations in order to accommodate the demands and pressures of the secular world:

> The way of our Chan school (*chanzong*) is different. After the ancient worthy people of the Way [i.e., monks] attained realization, they went to live in thatched huts and stone houses. They used old cauldrons with broken legs to cook their food, and passed twenty or thirty years in that way. Unconcerned about fame and wealth, they never thought of money and riches. Completely forgetting about human affairs, they concealed their traces among rocks and thickets. When summoned by the monarch, they would not respond; when invited by the princes, they would not go. How can they be same as those who, greedy for fame and desirous for wealth, sink into the worldly ways? That is like a peddler who by seeking small profit loses great gain. If the sages of the ten stages have not realized the principle of the Buddhas, then are they not like ordinary people of the broad earth? There is no such thing really.[22]

The spiritual exemplar invoked by Wuye is the recluse who has realized perfect detachment. Notwithstanding these passages, in the records of the Hongzhou school there is a general lack of attention to the daily exigencies of monastic life. The scarcity of information about the monks' actual practices, including meditation (see next section), probably reflects a disinclination or indifference to recording commonplace instruction and everyday practices that were part of a common Buddhist heritage. *Guishan jingce* (Guishan's Admonitions) is a notable exception to this lack of detailed coverage of monastic ideals and practices.[23]

Composed by Guishan around the time of the Huichang-era persecution of Buddhism (845), *Guishan jingce* is the main source for study of the Hongzhou school's attitudes toward monasticism and morality. The text displays a fairly conventional approach to monastic life and practice, and if it were not for a brief section on Chan practice, there would be little in it to identify it as a product of the Hongzhou school. Its descriptions of monastic ideals and aspirations revolve around the renunciation of secular values and a single-minded devotion to the pursuit of religious perfection. Much of the text consists of reiteration of mainstream notions about the monastic ethos. Guishan's exhortations to follow a disciplined way of life, dedicated to the study, practice, and realization of the teachings of Buddhism, reveal a religious leader who conceived monastic life in traditional terms. Such a stance is evident throughout the text, including this representative passage:

> [Monks] do not supply their parents with tasty foods, and they steadfastly leave behind the six relations.[24] They cannot pacify their country and govern the state. They promptly give up their family's

property and do not continue the family line [by their failure to produce a male heir]. They leave far away their local communities, and they shave their hair and follow [religious] teachers. Inwardly they strive to conquer their thoughts, while outwardly they spread the virtue of noncontention. Abandoning the defiled world, they endeavor to transcend [the mundane realm of birth and death].[25]

In Buddhism, just as in other religious traditions, the monastic regulations fulfill two basic functions. First, they serve as communal rules that regulate monks' daily life and ensure the orderly functioning of the monastery. They form a communal charter that organizes monastic life in a way that reflects core religious values and beliefs, and they codify institutional structures that aim at creating an environment favorable to monks' pursuit of their vocation. Second, the monastic rules also serve as guides for proper individual conduct. They mold each monk's internal and external attitudes and reinforce his commitment to a religious way of life.[26] In that sense, the monastic rules provide a broad contextual framework for disciplined conduct and foster mores conducive to cultivation of the Buddhist path. *Guishan jingce* affirms both of these functions.

Guishan's text reveals a concern for both the communal and personal facets of monastic life. While it places emphasis on the harmonious functioning of the monastic community, it also addresses individual religious aspirations and lays stress on each monk's commitment to a genuine pursuit of the monastic calling. The communal and personal aspects are not separable, because the smooth operation of monastic life depends on individual monks' espousal of common values and commitment to a collective pursuit of shared objectives. However, the text indicates that such unity of purpose was difficult to achieve, in large part because the monastic order attracted people with dubious motives, many of them uncommitted to spiritual practice. Consequently, much of Guishan's discussion consists of critiques of transgressions of monastic ideals and decorum, accompanied by stern warnings about the unwholesomeness of such actions and the negative karmic effects they bring about:

Their words and actions are absurd and coarse, and they falsely receive alms from the faithful. Their present actions do not differ at all from those of the past [i.e., before becoming monks]. As they absent-mindedly pass their whole lifetime [without achieving anything], what is there that they can rely on? Furthermore, there are some with the impressive appearance of monks and handsome countenances. [That is the case because] they have all already planted wholesome roots in previous lives, because of which they receive such a fortuitous recompense. That being so, they are like someone who only stands tidily with his hands folded, unconcerned about the value of time. Without being diligent in their undertaking [of religious life], such people will not be able to receive any further merits or [spiritual] rewards. How can they pass their whole life in vain? There will be no one at all to help them with their future karma.[27]

Guishan jingce vindicates the role of monastic precepts and conventional morality in Chan's soteriological program by postulating a two-tiered path of practice and realization. The Chan ideal of transcendence of the realm of delusion and defilement, which leads to a nonconceptual realization of reality, represents the higher level. The experience of sudden awakening constitutes the apex of the Buddhist path, as diverse virtues and practices integrate into a holistic state, from which ensues a balance between insight and activity. Nonetheless, from a conventional standpoint traditional monastic practices and observances still form the basis of authentic spirituality and serve as a stepping-stone for the realization of reality. *Guishan jingce* thus shows how the Hongzhou school's conception of Chan practice incorporated traditional Buddhist morality, and how age-old models of monastic discipline served as its ethical foundations. In light of that, we must keep the monastic context in mind when interpreting the Hongzhou school's doctrines and practices.[28]

Attitudes toward Meditation

As its name indicates, the Chan school grew out of earlier meditative traditions that went back to the period of disunion prior to the Sui and Tang dynasties. Accordingly, throughout its history it was perceived as a school of Buddhism that specializes in the practice of meditation. Bodhidharma, the putative founder of Chan in China, was an itinerant meditation teacher. The East Mountain tradition of early Chan also stressed formal meditation practice. The contemplative practices taught by Daoxin and Hongren reflected the influence of earlier types of Mahāyāna meditation. A text attributed to Daoxin describes the "one practice samādhi" (*yixing sanmei*), which was based on the *Wenshu shuo jing* (Scripture Spoken by Mañjuśrī). It was similar to Zhiyi's "constantly sitting samādhi," also based on the same scripture.[29] Similarly, Hongren's practice of "guarding the mind" (*shouxin*) was derived from native meditation techniques and showed Daoist influences. Comparable stress on the practice of sitting meditation was also characteristic of the Northern school.[30]

With the Niutou school, we have the emergence of a critical attitude toward the conventional practice of meditation. The extant sources indicate that, beginning with the school's putative founder, Farong, Niutou teachers tried to distance themselves from the kinds of meditative practices taught by their contemporaries. At the same time, the biographical records of Niutou teachers show a predilection for the contemplative lifestyle that seemingly contradicts the outward rejection of formal meditation conveyed in some texts. As Shiina has suggested, the Niutou school's critique of meditative practice was meant to highlight qualitative differences between its contemplative praxis and the practices of the Northern school.[31] The drawing of such distinctions was related to the Niutou school's efforts to establish its religious identity as a viable alternative to the Northern and Southern schools. This need not be construed as a repudiation of the formal practice of meditation per se, but rather as adoption of a different approach or modus operandi in regard to contemplative practice.

With Shenhui, we have a clear rejection of traditional conceptions of meditative practice. However, one cannot help but wonder how much that rejection was determined by his sectarian agenda of discrediting the Northern school, which openly advocated meditation practice, instead of reflecting thoughtful consideration and sincerely held beliefs about the actual practice of Chan.[32] A similar tendency to reinterpret the meaning of meditation in abstract terms is also found in the *Platform Scripture*. Because of the difficulty of tracing the authorship of this text, it is unclear whether the views of Huineng affected Shenhui's thinking, or whether Shenhui's ideas influenced the *Platform Scripture*.[33]

The Hongzhou school's attitudes toward formal meditation show similarities to those of the Niutou school. The lack of sustained discussion of the topic gives an impression that the practice of formal meditation was not high on the Hongzhou school's agenda. Occasional explicit criticisms of meditative practice reinforce that impression, although most of them appear in later and generally unreliable sources. A famous example of such a criticism is the story in which Huairang compares Mazu's sitting in meditation with the intention of becoming a Buddha to polishing a brick in order to make a mirror.[34] Another example is this passage from one of Mazu's sermons: "If one comprehends the mind and objects, then false thinking is not created again. When there is no more false thinking, that is acceptance of the non-arising of all dharmas.[35] Originally it exists and it is present now, irrespective of cultivation of the Way and sitting in meditation. Not cultivating and not sitting is the Tathāgata's pure meditation."[36]

For Yanagida, this passage indicates that Mazu repudiated the practice of formal meditation,[37] a reading that reflects Yanagida's acceptance of popular views about classical Chan's rejection of formal meditation, which go back to Hu Shi's pioneering studies of Shenhui and early Chan history. In fact, the passage simply asserts that the originally existing Buddha-nature does not depend on the practice of meditation or any other spiritual exercise[38]—in itself, little more than a sound doctrinal statement. Mazu's position is echoed in canonical texts, most notably the *Vimalakīrti Scripture*, where the main hero,

Vimalakīrti, criticizes Śāriputra for sitting at the foot of a tree in the forest absorbed in contemplation.[39]

The reference to "not cultivating and not sitting" in the passage from Mazu's sermon can be interpreted as a cautionary remark about the correct practice of meditation, directed to monks who were engaged in it. The same applies to the story about Huairang polishing a brick in front of Mazu. Instead of interpreting the story as evidence for their rejection of meditation, it seems better to read it as a warning against misguided contemplative practice and advice about the proper approach to spiritual cultivation. This interpretation is reinforced by *Guishan jingce*, which indicates that the monks at Guishan's monastery (and presumably monks at other monasteries associated with the Hongzhou school) engaged in a regimen of traditional monastic practices, of which meditation was an integral part.

Furthermore, the only text associated with the Hongzhou school that directly deals with meditation, the brief *Zuochan ming* (Inscription on Sitting Meditation) attributed to Dayi, presents the practice in fairly conventional terms.[40] The text advises practitioners to "sit straight and proper like Tai mountain" (*zhengzuo duanran ru taishan*) and advocates "sitting and probing the source" (*zuo jiutan yuanyuan*). It also talks about "sitting quietly without exertion" (*jingzuo buyong gong*) and makes mention of Mazu's story about the brick polishing.

We do not have enough evidence to judge the extent to which Mazu and his followers practiced sitting meditation (*zuochan*), but it seems that the lack of attention to meditation in their records had less to do with an anticontemplative stance and more with the fact that they had little new to say on the subject. Probably the meditative practices they engaged in were not that different from those of other contemplative traditions, such as early Chan and Tiantai. This does not preclude the possibility that they interpreted them somewhat differently and integrated them into a soteriological scheme that was specific to their tradition. The following passage from *Baizhang guanglu* (Baizhang's Extensive Record) supports such an interpretation:

> If one were to speak to deaf worldly persons, then they should be told to leave home, keep the precepts, practice meditation, and study wisdom. To worldly people who are beyond ordinary measures—such as Vimalakīrti and Bodhisattva Fu—one should not speak in that way. If one is speaking to śramaṇas [monks], they have already committed themselves to religious life,[41] and the power of their śīla, samādhi, and prajñā is already complete. If one still speaks to them in that way, that is called untimely speech, because it is not appropriate to the situation; it is also called improper talk.[42] To śramaṇas, one should explain the defilement of purity. They should be taught to leave all things, whether existent or nonexistent, to forsake cultivation

and attainment, and let go of the very notion of forsaking. If among śramaṇas, in the abandonment of defiling habitual tendencies, they cannot let go of the diseases of greed and hatred, they are also to be called deaf worldly persons. In such a case, they should also be told to practice meditation and study wisdom.[43]

According to Baizhang, ethical conduct and meditation practice are basic aspects of religious life. Since they are widely recognized as such and their practice is familiar, they need not be emphasized. For monks and advanced laymen, Baizhang offers the subtler Chan teaching that points to the realm beyond assertion and denial, cultivation and attainment. However, he adds that those who do not have a strong foundation in the observance of precepts and meditative praxis should first focus on perfecting them, since without them they are bound to go astray. A similar perspective is evident in *Guishan jingce*. Guishan's text presents a brief exposition of Chan practice as a spiritual path that leads to direct realization of reality:

> If you want to practice Chan and study the Way, then you should suddenly go beyond the expedient teachings. You should harmonize your mind with the arcane path [that leads to spiritual liberation], explore the sublime wonders,[44] make final resolution of the recondite [meaning], and awaken to the source of truth. You should also extensively ask for instructions from those who have foresight, and should get close to virtuous friends. The sublime wonder of this teaching (*zong*) is difficult to grasp—one must pay attention very carefully. If someone can suddenly awaken to the correct cause, then that is the stage of leaving defilement behind. He then shatters the three worlds and twenty-five forms of existence.[45] Such a person knows that no phenomena, internal or external, are real. Arising from mind's transformations, they are all provisional designations. There is no need to anchor the mind anywhere. When feelings merely do not attach to things, then how can things hinder anyone? Let the nature of other things flow freely, without [interfering by] trying to break apart or extend anything. The sounds that one hears and the forms that one sees are all ordinary. Whether being here or there, one freely responds to circumstances without any fault.[46]

This passage speaks of the wonders of Chan practice and realization, but with the caveat that they are difficult to perfect and attain. Guishan then goes on to advise the monks who did not belong to the highest-ranking category of spiritual virtuosi, namely, all those who cannot readily make the sudden leap into the recondite realm of enlightenment. The text also makes it clear that most monks belonged to this second group of less gifted practitioners:

In the case of those of average abilities, who have not been able suddenly to go beyond [the expedient teachings], they should pay attention to the doctrinal teachings (*jiaofa*). They should review and rummage in the palm leaves of the scriptures, and thoroughly inquire into their principles. [Furthermore, they should also] hand them down to others from mouth to mouth, and should expound and make them known, thus guiding the younger generations and repaying the Buddha's benevolence. Moreover, they should not waste their time in vain, but they must uphold [the teachings of Buddhism] in this manner. When someone has dignified conduct in all postures and activities, then he is a monk who is worthy and able to receive the teachings.[47]

In this passage Guishan is mainly talking about scriptural study and transmission (after which he goes back to his main theme, the observance of monastic precepts), but he is basically pointing out that for most monks the expedient practices of traditional Buddhism are the proper approach to spiritual cultivation. That leads back to the earlier point, that the lack of emphasis on basic Buddhist practices and observances in the Hongzhou school's records need not be interpreted as evidence that they were not part of the religious training at the monasteries led by Mazu's disciples. Rather, they were the backdrop against which the teachings specific to their tradition were developed and disseminated. As their teachings were directed toward monks already familiar with basic Buddhist doctrines and practices, the emphasis was on recording their tradition's distinctive ideas and perspectives.

Canonicity and Attitudes toward Scriptural Authority

In medieval Chinese Buddhism, the scriptures functioned as chief sources of religious authority. They provided standards for adjudicating the authenticity and orthodoxy of different doctrines and practices. Throughout the period of division and into the Tang era, the translation and exegesis of Indian scriptures and treatises were major concerns of Chinese Buddhists, and leading translators and exegetes were among the most esteemed members of the clergy. Canonically sanctioned traditions shaped virtually all aspects of Buddhist life and praxis, including rituals, ethical observances, monastic mores, and institutions.

The exalted status of canonical texts did not preclude their creative use (and misuse) by thinkers eager to lend scriptural support to the new forms of religious and philosophical discourses they were creating as participants in the ongoing Sinification of Buddhism.[48] As they were formulating tenets that reflected native intellectual concerns and ways of thinking, leading Chinese monks such as Zhiyi (of the Tiantai school) and Fazang (of the Huayan school) bolstered their interpretations with copious quotations from canonical texts. They made considerable efforts to find scriptural support for their creative philosophical formulations, even when they were moving in directions not envisaged by the canonical texts.

In the case of the Huayan school, its complex doctrinal system was supposedly meant to elucidate the essential meaning of the *Huayan Scripture*, while the Tiantai school made similar claims concerning the *Lotus Scripture* (*Miaofa lianhua jing*). Starting with Zhiyi, the emphasis in scriptural exegesis shifted from literal interpretation toward an exploration of the texts' "profound meaning" (*xuanyi*). An example of this tendency is Zhiyi's *Fahua xuanyi* (Profound Meaning of the Lotus Scripture), which supposedly provides exegesis of the *Lotus Scripture*. In fact, much of Zhiyi's lengthy discussion consists of exhaustive interpretation of the five characters that constitute the title of the Chinese translation of the *Lotus Scripture*. In his explanation of the scripture's subtle meaning, Zhiyi enters into all sorts of philosophical speculations that—although of great significance in the intellectual history of Chinese Buddhism—have little connection with the original text of the scripture.[49] Similarly, when he developed his ingenious scheme of interpreting the four noble truths in four different ways, Zhiyi claimed that he was following the *Mahāparinirvāṇa Scripture*.[50]

The same reverential attitude toward the Buddhist canon was characteristic of early Chan, even if scriptural exegesis was not a major concern of Chan teachers.[51] The tradition's early history was marked by a tendency to legitimize Chan practice by recourse to the canonical tradition. An eagerness to co-opt scriptural authority can be seen in the appropriation of the *Laṅkāvatāra Scripture* (*Lengqie jing*) as a symbol for the transmission of Chan, initially advanced by the followers of Hongren and retroactively imputed back to Bodhidharma.[52] The choice of the scripture as a symbol for the Chan transmission was a logical step in the Chan school's search for legitimacy. As Faure has suggested, the *Laṅkāvatāra* was probably transmitted in the early Chan school more as a talismanic text than as a doctrinal scripture, as there is little evidence that its doctrines were of great interest to Chan monks.[53] *Lengqie shizi ji*, the earliest text that makes the connection, goes as far as to recognize Guṇabhadra (394–460), the Indian monk who produced the first Chinese translation of the scripture, as a Chan patriarch who directly preceded Bodhidharma, even though he had no connection with the Chan school, which in any event did not exist at the time.[54]

Another example of the symbolic use of a canonical text is Shenhui's employment of the *Diamond Scripture* (*Jin'gang jing*) to buttress his claims to orthodoxy and authority. His recourse to the *Diamond Scripture* as a symbol for the Chan transmission was a response to the Northern school's appropriation of the *Laṅkāvatāra*. Shenhui claimed that all Chan patriarchs, from

Bodhidharma until Huineng, advocated and transmitted the *Diamond Scripture*, not the *Laṅkāvatāra*.[55] A similar emphasis on the *Diamond Scripture* is evident in the *Platform Scripture*, which might point to Shenhui's influence on this text. There Huineng is recorded as saying: "With only the one volume of the *Diamond Scripture* you may see into your own nature and enter the samādhi of prajñā."[56] In these instances, we can see how scriptures were used as tokens of authority in conflicts over orthodoxy. In effect, the scriptures became symbols of authenticity and tools of legitimization appropriated by different monks and factions within the early Chan movement.

Comparable attitudes toward canonical texts and traditions are discernble in the records of the Niutou school, whose teachings were influenced by the philosophical tenets of the Madhyamaka tradition, mediated by the doctrinal formulations of the Tiantai and Sanlun schools.[57] A penchant for invoking canonical authority is also evident in *Lidai fabao ji*, the main record of the Baotang school. Notwithstanding the image of its leader, Wuzhu, as an iconoclast who repudiated traditional doctrines and practices, the text starts with a list of Buddhist works popular at the time (thirty-seven titles in total). The list includes canonical texts such as the *Nirvāṇa*, *Lotus*, and *Diamond* scriptures, as well as apocryphal works such as *Faju jing* and *Chanmen jing*. These works are also quoted in the main body of the text, along with other Buddhist and non-Buddhist works.[58] Early Chan also took the additional step of creating apocryphal scriptures. One such example, probably originating in Korea, was the *Vajrasāmadhi Scripture* (*Jin'gang sanmei jing*), composed during the seventh century in order to lend scriptural support to the doctrines of the nascent Chan school.[59]

The method of "symbolic exegesis" is yet another example of the tendency to legitimize Chan practice by recourse to concepts and passages from canonical texts.[60] Examples of it can be found in the *Platform Scripture*, the Northern school manuscripts, the records of Shenhui, the *Lidai fabao ji*, and Dazhu's *Dunwu yaomen*.[61] Its employment as an exegetical strategy involved redefining traditional Buddhist practices and rubrics, which were reinterpreted as metaphors in a manner peculiar to the Chan school. One of the key objectives of this procedure was to establish a close connection between Chan meditation and ideas found in the scriptures. Here is an example from the *Lidai fabao ji*, in which Wuzhu correlates the three propositions taught by Wuxiang (no remembering, no thought, and no forgetting) with the traditional Buddhist rubric of the three trainings (observance of the precepts, concentration, and wisdom) and then collapses them all into the Chan formula of "no thought":

The Minister [Du Hongjian (709–796)] asked: "Did Reverend Kim [Wuxiang] talk about no remembering, no thought, and no forgetting?" The Reverend [Wuzhu] relied: "Yes." The Minister also asked: "Are these three propositions one or three?" The Reverend relied:

"They are one, not three. No remembering is [the observance of]
precepts, no thought is concentration, and no forgetting is wisdom."
He also said: "Not giving rise to thoughts is the precepts, not giving
rise to thoughts is concentration, and not giving rise to thoughts is
wisdom. No thought is the complete perfection of the precepts,
meditation, and wisdom."[62]

The employment of symbolic exegesis as a kind of "expedient means" reflects early Chan's efforts to trace its doctrines back to the scriptures. This
strategy developed as the Chan school was moving from the margins into the
mainstream and aimed at demonstrating that its teachings were genuine expressions of the Buddhadharma.[63] If bizarre metaphors and forced interpretations could help achieve that, Chan teachers apparently were quite willing to
use them.

In the records of the Hongzhou school, there is little evidence of symbolic
exegesis or the other strategies for bridging the gap between Chan and the
canonical tradition noted previously. In fact, there are hardly any instances of
explicit invocation of canonical authority. A rare exception is a passage that
opens one of Mazu's sermons:

The Patriarch [Mazu] said to the assembly, "All of you should believe
that your mind is Buddha, that this mind is identical with Buddha. The
Great Master Bodhidharma came from India to China and transmitted the One Mind teaching of Mahāyāna so that it can lead you all to
awakening. Fearing that you will be too confused and will not
believe that this One Mind is inherent in all of you, he used the
Laṅkāvatāra Scripture to seal the sentient beings' mind-ground.
Therefore, in the Laṅkāvatāra Scripture, the Buddha stated that
mind is the essential teaching, and the gate of nonbeing is the
Dharma-gate."[64]

This passage is remarkable because it indicates that Mazu accepted the
connection between Chan and the Laṅkāvatāra Scripture. It can also be read as
implying his rejection of the link between the Southern school and the Diamond Scripture promoted by Shenhui and his followers—which, in regard to
this particular issue at least, places Mazu closer to the position of the Northern school.[65] While this kind of explicit invoking of scriptural authority is
atypical of the Hongzhou school's records, that does not mean Mazu and his
disciples rejected the canon or were immune to its influences. In fact, scriptural quotations and allusions fill their records, even though the full extent of
their usage of canonical sources is not immediately obvious, as an example
from one of Mazu's sermons shows:

Those who seek the Dharma should not seek for anything. Outside
of mind, there is no other Buddha; outside of Buddha, there is no

other mind. Not attaching to good and not rejecting evil, without reliance on either purity or defilement, one realizes that the nature of offense is empty: it cannot be found in each thought because it is without self-nature. Therefore, the three realms are mind-only and all phenomena in the universe are marked by a single Dharma. Whenever we see form, it is just seeing the mind. The mind does not exist by itself; its existence is due to form. Whatever you are saying, it is just a phenomenon that is identical with the principle. They are all without obstruction, and the fruit of the way to awakening is also like that.

If not familiar with classical Buddhist literature, one might at first assume that this passage expresses a viewpoint unique to the Chan school. After all, we are often led to believe that Chan teachings are unique expressions of sublime wisdom, unlike the teachings of other Buddhist traditions. Let us now present the same passage, but this time interpolating information about the canonical quotations and allusions in the text:

> [The *Vimalakīrti Scripture* says] "Those who seek the Dharma should not seek for anything." [As it is taught in the *Huayan Scripture*,] Outside of mind, there is no other Buddha; outside of Buddha, there is no other mind. [As taught in the *Mahāsamnipata-sūtra* and the *Huayan Scripture*,] Not attaching to good and not rejecting evil, without reliance on either purity or defilement, one realizes that [as explained in *Foshuo Foming Scripture* and other Buddhist texts,] "the nature of offense is empty": it cannot be found in each thought because it is without self-nature. Therefore, [as explained in the *Huayan* and *Laṅkāvatāra* scriptures] "the three realms are mind-only," and [as stated in the *Faju jing*] "all phenomena in the universe are marked by a single Dharma." Whenever we see form, it is just seeing the mind. The mind does not exist by itself; its existence is due to form. Whatever you are saying, it is just [what Dushun's *Fajie guanmen* refers to as] "a phenomenon which is identical with the principle." [As it is said in Huayan texts,] they are "all without obstruction," and the fruit of the way to awakening is also like that.[66]

What at first sight appeared to be a paragraph of distinctively Chan teachings turns out to be a collection of canonical quotations, accompanied by comments that explicate or draw connections between the scriptural passages. This passage is by no means unique in that regard. Here is another example from Mazu's sermons:

> [The *Vimalakīrti Scripture* says,] "Not obliterating the conditioned and not dwelling in the unconditioned." The conditioned is the function of the unconditioned, while the unconditioned is the

essence of the conditioned. Because of not dwelling on support, it has been said [in the *Huayan Scripture* that it is] "like space which rests on nothing." [According to *Dasheng qixin lun,*] the mind can be spoken of [in terms of its two aspects,] "birth and death, and suchness." [As pointed out in early Chan texts,] The mind as suchness is like a clear mirror that can reflect images.[67] The mirror symbolizes the mind, while the images symbolize the dharmas. If the mind grasps at dharmas, then it gets involved in external causes and conditions, which is the meaning of birth and death. If the mind does not grasp at dharmas, that is suchness.[68]

Rather than repudiating the scriptures or rejecting their authority, the records of Mazu and his disciples are full of quotations and allusions to a range of canonical texts. While this stands in contrast to traditional images of the Hongzhou school, their reliance on the canon should not come as a surprise when we take into account the religious milieu of Tang Buddhism. As we saw in part I of this volume, as members of the monastic elite the leaders of the Hongzhou school were well-read monks conversant with canonical texts and traditions. A number of them came from gentry families, received classical Confucian education in their youth, and dedicated their formative monastic years to scriptural study. A good example of such a monk is Baizhang. Born in the Wang clan of Taiyuan, one of the greatest aristocratic clans, after his ordination in 767 Baizhang dedicated himself to study of the scriptures.[69] The records of Baizhang's teachings reveal that the knowledge of the canonical tradition he acquired informed his religious outlook until the end of his life. The transcripts of Baizhang's sermons and conversations with disciples are full of scriptural quotations and allusions and reveal a monk at ease with both the contemplative and doctrinal aspects of Buddhism.

Use of Scriptures

If Mazu and his disciples made free use of canonical sources, what texts did they cite? Table 4.1 lists some of the main scriptures quoted or alluded to—both with and without attribution—in three important records from the Hongzhou school's literary output: Mazu's sermons,[70] Dazhu's *Dunwu rudao yaomen lun,*[71] and Baizhang's *Baizhang guanglu.*[72] The list is not exhaustive; the two longer texts, Dazhu's treatise and Baizhang's record, quote a wider range of canonical sources.

The texts listed in table 4.1 include major Mahāyāna scriptures. There is considerable overlap in the choice of scriptural texts among the three records; sometimes they are even quoting or alluding to the same scriptural passages. Among the canonical texts, the *Vimalakīrti Scripture* emerges as a clear favorite, which reflects its general popularity during the Tang period, but, more important, indicates that it was a canonical text whose teachings had the closest affinities with those of the Hongzhou school. In that sense, the *Vimalakīrti Scripture* was best suited to illustrate the Hongzhou school's canonical background. Each of the three monks also seems to have felt an affinity with other text(s). Mazu appears inclined to invoke the *Laṅkāvatāra Scripture*, while Dazhu (and to a lesser extend Baizhang) had an affinity with the Prajñāpāramitā scriptures, among which the popular *Diamond Scripture* is quoted most often.

The three records also contain quotations from apocryphal scriptures and other Chinese texts, although they are not as numerous as the scriptural quotations. The most important Chinese sources are listed in table 4.2.

The inclusion of *Dasheng qixin lun* (Treatise on the Awakening of Faith in Mahāyāna) is not surprising, considering its impact on the doctrinal development of Tang Buddhism, including Chan.[73] The records of Kumārajīva's disciple Sengzhao (374?–414) and the lay sage Fu Dashi are also included, and their popularity within Chan circles is attested in other texts from the Tang period.

TABLE 4.1. Scriptural Quotations and Allusions in the Hongzhou School's Records

Scripture	Mazu's sermons	Dunwu Yaomen	Baizhang Guanglu
Lotus Scripture	1	1	4
Huayan Scripture	3		3
Nirvāṇa Scripture	1	5	3
Laṅkāvatāra Scripture	6	1	
Prajñāpāramitā scriptures		12	4
Mahāratnakūṭa Scripture			2
Mahāsaṃnipāta Scripture		1	1
Vimalakīrti Scripture	7	14	4
Foming Scripture	1	1	

TABLE 4.2. Chinese Texts Quoted or Alluded to in the Hongzhou School's Records

Text title	Mazu's sermons	Dunwu Yaomen	Baizhang Guanglu
Chanmen jing		2	
Faju jing	1	3	
Fanwang jing		3	
Shoulengyan jing	1	1	1
Dasheng qixin lun	2	2	
Zhao lun	2		4
Fu dashi's records	1		1

The texts contained in the two tables are pretty much the same as those quoted in earlier Chan texts, such as the records of Shenhui,[74] the Northern school, and those of Mahāyāna (Moheyan), the Chan teacher who was the Chinese representative at the Buddhist council in Lhasa (all of which were discovered in Dunhuang).[75] This is not that surprising, since most texts on the list were popular and widely read during the Tang period (and, for that matter, throughout the history of Chinese Buddhism). But in the Hongzhou school's records there is a subtle difference in usage, which helps us appreciate the manner in which canonical texts were employed in its production of knowledge and creation of a religious identity.

In the passages from Mazu's record introduced in the previous section, we saw how he seamlessly wove into his sermons scriptural quotations and allusions, usually without identifying the sources. The same propensity to embed canonical passages into Chan sermons—which was not without precedent in Chinese Buddhism—is characteristic of other texts, including Baizhang's *Guanglu* and Huangbo's *Chuanxin fayao* (Essential Teachings on the Mind Transmission).[76] The Chan sermons integrate scriptural citations and metaphors into their overall narrative structure, without explicit boundaries or markings that set the canonical excerpts apart from the teachings of the Chan teacher in question. To complicate matters, occasionally a scriptural quotation is marked as such, usually by prefacing it with the phrase "a scripture says" (*jing yun*). In rare instances, the text provides the title of the canonical source quoted, or it indicates that an idea or passage comes from another source by using a phrase such as "it has been said," but without identifying the original source. The following passage from *Baizhang guanglu* (with references to original sources and quotation marks supplied by me) exemplifies some of the ambiguities that surround such use of quotations and allusions:

> As is stated [in the *Vimalakīrti Scripture,*] "The Dharma has nothing it can be equated with," because it cannot be compared [to anything].[77] [Jizang's commentary of the *Lotus Scripture* says,] "The Dharma-body is unconditioned, and it does not fall into all categories."[78] Therefore, it is said [in a commentary on the *Vimalakīrti Scripture* and/or the *Zhaolun?*] that the essence of the sage is nameless and cannot be expressed in words.[79] It is like the simile [from the *Dazhidu lun*] about insects that can settle anywhere except that they are unable to settle on the top of burning flames. Sentient beings are also thus: they can form connections anywhere, except that they cannot form connections with the perfection of wisdom.[80]

This short passage (and many other akin to it) highlights some of the problems we encounter when trying to unravel the web of canonical quotations and allusions embedded in Baizhang's record and similar texts. The difficulty largely arises from the peculiar ways in which Baizhang is using canonical texts, which probably reflects the fact that he was quoting from memory. It appears as if Baizhang and others had internalized sections of the Buddhist canon, spontaneously using scriptural quotations as part of their natural speech, typically without concern for academic pedantry and accuracy. Unfortunately, we cannot ascertain how conscious they were that they were quoting or precisely how well versed they were in the canonical literature. We also have no precise information about which texts or passages were committed to memory and recited liturgically. Do the citations and allusions reflect thorough knowledge of canonical texts, or were they drawn from a standard repertoire of popular passages? My guess is that it was a combination of both. For example, in Baizhang's record we find citations of popular scriptural expressions and passages, but also obscure references and the use of a technical vocabulary that point to a mastery of canonical texts and doctrines.

That brings us to the question of their audience. Did the audiences that received these teachings recognize the infusion of scriptural imagery and exegesis in the sermons of Chan teachers? We can presume that rudimentary knowledge of key scriptures and doctrines was taken for granted within the monastic congregations where the sermons were delivered. Other important audiences were the literati and officials, a good number of whom were conversant with Buddhist tenets and literature. Familiarity with canonical texts is evident in questions from the audience addressed to Chan teachers—especially in the records of Baizhang and Huangbo—although caveats about the level of knowledge of the canon on part of those who asked the questions still apply. Numerous questions contain quotations from scriptures or extracanonical works, and some of them simply ask for explanations of well-known scriptural passages. Here are a couple of examples from Baizhang's record; the first question also appears in an identical form in the records of Huangbo and Linji, as well as the records of many other Chan teachers (including Caoshan and Dahui):

A monk asked: "How is it that Excellence of Great Universal Wisdom Buddha sat at the site of awakening for ten eons without the Buddha-dharma appearing to him, and without him achieving Buddhahood [as described in the famous passage from the *Lotus Scripture*]?"[81]

Question: "What is the meaning of [the well-known saying from the *Śūraṅgama Scripture*], 'Empty space is born within great awareness, like a bubble formed in the ocean.'?"[82]

The presence of questions and answers such as these in the Hongzhou school's records indicate a sense of rapprochement between Chan and canonical

Buddhism. The integration of the two was symbolically enacted by the dissolution of boundaries between the words of the Buddha and the words of Chan teachers. This blurring of distinctions between scriptural authority and the authority of Chan teachers conveys a sense of confidence on part of the Hongzhou school, which stands in contrast to early Chan's appropriations of canonical authority and efforts to show that Chan teachings are in harmony with the scriptures. The confident attitude probably reflected the religious personalities and communal ethos of Mazu and his followers, although it also echoed changes that marked a key transition in Tang Chan, occasioned by the Hongzhou school's rise to preeminence and its eclipsing of the schools of early Chan.

The Hongzhou school's usage of scriptural tropes and images signifies an evolution in the Chan school's attitudes toward the canon and doctrines of Mahāyāna Buddhism. In contrast to the artifice evident in symbolic exegesis and the other strategies noted above, Mazu and his disciples adopted a stance of active yet low-key engagement with the canonical tradition. Rather than rejecting the scriptures and canonical authority, they appropriated them and presented their own teachings as the essence of Buddhism. In doing so, they struck a balance: acknowledging the authority and charisma of hallowed canonical texts and traditions, while also adopting an independent stance and presenting their teachings as expressions of genuine insight. This balancing act involved responses to two contrasting requirements: on the one hand, Mazu and his disciples demonstrated a mastery of the canon and fidelity to the principles and values enshrined in it; but at the same time, they were able to construct a distinct religious identity by reformulating aspects of those traditions and expressing them in innovative ways. The success of the Hongzhou school was partly dependent on its capacity to meet both challenges better than their predecessors within the Chan movement.

It is interesting to note parallel developments outside of Buddhism. The Hongzhou school's appearance on the Tang religious landscape during the postrebellion period coincided with momentous changes in Tang intellectual life.[83] The subtle shift in the Hongzhou school's attitude toward the Buddhist canon paralleled changes in the attitudes toward Confucian canonical scholarship evidenced among scholars active during the postrebellion period. Unofficial Confucian scholarship flourished in the more decentralized scholarly world of the mid-Tang period, which was no longer dominated by the kinds of imperial commissions of large scholarly works that were prevalent during the early Tang. In their writings, Confucian scholars moved away from interpreting the canon in ways consistent with the state's concern with its legitimacy, and instead they presented new ideas in which the classics were primarily utilized to justify their views about a wide range of issues with which they were concerned, including questions of belief.[84] The development of this independent critical tradition in Confucian canonical learning led to what David McMullen has called the "deep interiorization" of the postrebellion Confucian tradition.[85]

The *guwen* ("old-style writing") movement, whose best-known representatives were Han Yu (768–824), Li Ao (772–841), and Liu Zongyuan (773–819), represented an attempt to relate traditional intellectual concerns to the actualities of life in mid-Tang China. *Guwen* proponents were attempting new ways of reading the Confucian classics without recourse to established commentarial traditions, but rather in light of the issues and problems that were relevant to their own time. They adopted an activist tone and a self-conscious reflectiveness that was similar to the attitudes of Chan monks.[86] For them, the appropriate course of action was based on personal acquisition of proper ideas, rather than on knowledge and imitation of normative cultural forms.[87] Yet, while cultivated men were supposed to be able to think by themselves, values had to be grounded in "the way of the [ancient] sages" (*shengren zhi dao*).[88]

Just as in the case of the Hongzhou school, the new Confucian attitude toward canonicity involved the formulation of new responses to received traditions. At their core, these responses involved personal insights into the essential principles revealed by the scriptures and classics, which implied bringing a new life into hallowed traditions by recapturing their substance and making them relevant to contemporary concerns and issues of vital import. Obviously, more research needs to be done before we can draw any conclusions about possible connections between Chan and Confucian scholarship during this period. At present, we can simply note that although internal developments within Chan and Tang Buddhism shaped the Hongzhou school's attitudes toward canonical authority, to some extent they reflected broader changes in the intellectual and social climates that defined the postrebellion period.

Returning to the Buddhist context, I will conclude by reiterating that even as Mazu and Baizhang propounded innovative ideas about the path to awakening, they conveyed insights about the nature of religious practice and experience that were at the core of Sinitic expressions of Mahāyāna Buddhism. They framed their teachings with recourse to canonical texts, while blurring the boundaries between their ideas and those expressed by the canonical tradition. This stance implied an acknowledgment of the legitimacy of canonical authority, but the dissolution of boundaries also suggested a new source of authority: the awakened Chan teacher whose words and deeds supposedly embody the truths of Buddhism.

NOTES

1. The two terms, tathāgatagarbha and Buddha-nature, are often used as synonyms; hereafter, for practical purposes they will be used interchangeably.

2. See Robert Gimello, "Apophatic and Kataphatic Discourse in Mahāyāna: A Chinese View," 119.

3. The problem of the origins of ignorance is discussed in Peter N. Gregory, "The Problem of Theodicy in the *Awakening of Faith*."

4. Brian Edward Brown, *The Buddha Nature: A Study of the Tathāgatagarbha and Ālayavijñāna*, 31–35, 135–41.

5. Liu Ming-Wood "The Doctrine of the Buddha-Nature in the Mahāyāna *Mahāparinirvāṇa-Sūtra*," 70–71.

6. Ibid., 88. A similar position is evident in *Foxing lun* (Buddha-nature Treatise), which stresses the heuristic value of the concept of Buddha-nature. This seminal text, which was either authored or translated by Paramārtha (499–569) in the sixth century, states that "Buddha-nature is the thusness revealed by the dual emptiness of person and things." T 31.787b; quoted in Sallie B. King, *Buddha Nature*, 17. According to it, the Buddha spoke this doctrine in order to help people overcome their shortcomings and develop virtues, so that they might forsake ignorance and realize enlightenment. The Buddha was not trying to postulate something that truly exists, since there is no substantive self or mind. King, *Buddha Nature*, 29–30, 84. The introduction of the concept of Buddha-nature is therefore primarily driven by soteriological concerns, not by a desire to articulate a specific ontology. Ibid., 32.

7. Liu Ming-Wood, *Madhyamaka Thought in China*, 171–73.

8. See *Chanyuan zhuquanji duxu*, T 48.404b–c, also quoted in Cheng-chien, *Manifestation of the Tathāgata: Buddhahood According to the Avatamsaka Sūtra*, 33, and Gregory, *Tsung-mi*, 206. Zongmi's interpretation is based on the famous passage from the *Huayan Scripture* about the presence of the wisdom of the Buddha in every person. See T 10.272c–73a and Cheng-chien, *Manifestation of the Tathāgata*, 105–6.

9. See Yinshun, *Zhongguo chanzong shi*, 381–85. For a critique of the Chan school's teaching of an *ātman* doctrine, see Matsumoto Shiryō, *Zen shisō no hihanteki kenkyū*.

10. See Robert Buswell, *The Formation of Ch'an Ideology in China and Korea: The Vajrasamādhi-Sūtra, A Buddhist Apocryphon*, 137–57, and McRae, *The Northern School*, 138–40.

11. Robert H. Sharf, *Coming to Terms with Chinese Buddhism: A Reading of the Treasure Store Treatise*, 48.

12. For details, see Gregory, *Tsung-mi*, 224–30.

13. For a summary of Zongmi's analysis and critique of the Northern school, see Gregory, *Tsung-mi*, 231–34.

14. For a study of the relationship between the Northern School and the Vinaya, see Shiina, "Hakushūzen ni okeru kairitsu no mondai."

15. See McRae, *The Northern School*, 47, 50–51, and Shiina, "Hakushūzen ni okeru kairitsu no mondai," 145, 148–49.

16. Shiina, "Hakushūzen ni okeru kairitsu no mondai," 144. The view articulated by Shiina, that there is a sharp contrast between the Northern school's conservative stance toward the Vinaya and the Hongzhou School's putative rejection of it, reflects the influence of normative notions of Chan orthodoxy on contemporary scholarship, which creep into otherwise solid research that on the whole is sympathetic toward the "heterodox" Northern School; see 139. This kind of comparison between the two traditions goes hand in hand with other scholars' view that distinctive Chan monastic life had already begun to emerge at Daoxin's and Hongren's monastic communities and that the Hongzhou School was the orthodox successor to that tradition. The idea that the Hongzhou School appropriated and further developed the independent spirit

of Chan monasticism that first emerged at the time of Daoxin and Hongren, while the Northern School deviated from it by aligning itself with mainstream monastic institutions, in effect perpetuates and expands on biased and historically groundless views presented in early Song era texts.

17. BGL (*Sijia yulu* ed.), XZJ 119.411b; translation adapted from Cheng-chien, *Sun-Face Buddha*, 103–4.

18. The desires for wealth, sex, food and drink, fame, and sleep.

19. The eight winds (or influences) consist of four pairs: gain and loss, scorn and praise, fame and ridicule, and suffering and joy.

20. Adaptation to others and beneficial action are two of the four all-embracing Bodhisattva virtues; the other two are giving and kind speech.

21. BGL (*Sijia yulu* ed.), XZJ 119.411c; translation adapted from Cheng-chien, *Sun-Face Buddha*, 104.

22. CDL 28, T 51.444c; Cheng-chien, *Sun-Face Buddha*, 128–29.

23. The oldest version of *Guishan jingce* was among the manuscripts recovered in Dunhuang. The text is part of a manuscript titled *Yan heshang ji* (Reverend Yan's Collection), preserved in Paris as part of the Peliot collection of Dunhuang materials (catalogued as no. 4638). For a photographic reproduction of the original manuscript, see *Dunhuang baozang* 134.91–92. There are three other versions of *Guishan jingce*: QTW 919.4243b–44b, T 48.1042b–43c, and XZJ 111.142c–48d. The *Taishō* version is part of *Zimen jingxun*, a collection of mostly Chan texts, compiled during the Ming dynasty. A Japanese translation of *Guishan jingce* can be found in Kajitani Sōnin, "Isan kyōsaku," in Nishitani Keiji and Yanagida Seizan, *Zenka goroku*, vol. 2, 141–51. Kajitani has another Japanese rendition with the same title in Nishitani Keiji, *Zen no koten: Chūgoku*, 151–74. There is also an earlier rendition in Tomitani Ryūkei, "Butsuso sankyō kōgi," in *Sōtō-shū kōgi*, vol. 3, 175–243. Neither Kajitani nor Tomitani offer proper Japanese translations of the text. Instead, they both present *yomikudashi* readings of the original, followed by notes and running commentaries, both of which are more extensive in Tomitani's work. For a study of the text, see Poceski, "*Guishan jingce* and the Ethical Foundations of Chan Practice," parts of which overlap with the discussion presented here. There are also English translations in Mario Poceski, "The Hongzhou School during the Mid-Tang Period," 456–85, and Melvin M. Takemoto, "The Kuei-shan ching-ts'e: Morality in the Hung-chou School of Ch'an," 79–90.

24. The six relations are mother, father, elder brothers (siblings), younger brothers (siblings), wife, and children.

25. T 48.1042b–c; XZJ 111.143b.

26. For parallels within Christian monasticism, see Talal Asad, *Genealogies of Religion: Discipline and Reasoning Power in Christianity and Islam*, 137.

27. T 48.1043a; XZJ 111.145d.

28. For additional information on the relationship between Chan and monasticism within the context of Tang Buddhism, see Mario Poceski, "Xuefeng's Code and the Chan School's Participation in the Development of Monastic Regulations."

29. For this samādhi and its place in early Chan, see Bernard Faure, "The Concept of One-Practice Samādhi in Early Ch'an," 105–9.

30. See Shiina, "Nanshū no zazenkan to sono tokushoku," 135–36.

31. Ibid., 136–37.

32. As is suggested by McRae in his manuscript on Shenhui, *Zen Evangelist*, he should not be regarded as a "Chan teacher" in the conventional/stereotypical sense, which helps account for his dismissal of meditative praxis.

33. See Shiina, "Nanshū no zazenkan to sono tokushoku," 137.

34. See "Study with Huairang" in chapter 1.

35. "Acceptance of the non-arising of all dharmas" (Chinese: *wusheng faren*; Sanskrit: *anutpattika-dharma-kṣānti*) is a technical term that implies cognition of the unproduced nature of all phenomena, the realization that all things are beyond birth and death. For an example of canonical usage, see *Miaofa lianhua jing* 5, T 9.44a.

36. MY, XZJ 119.407a; Cheng-chien, *Sun-Face Buddha*, 68.

37. Yanagida, *Shoki zenshū shisho no kenkyū*, 452.

38. Foulk, "The Ch'an School and Its Place in the Buddhist Monastic Tradition," 127.

39. T 14.539c; Robert A. F. Thurman, *The Holy Teaching of Vimalakīrti: A Mahāyāna Scripture*, 24; and Burton Watson, *The Vimalakīrti Sūtra*, 37. The *Platform Scripture* and the records of Shenhui both invoke this episode in their critiques of conventional meditation. See Yampolsky, *The Platform Sutra*, 137, and Luis O. Gómez, "Purifying Gold: The Metaphor of Effort and Intuition in Buddhist Thought and Practice," 80–81.

40. See *Zimen jingxun* 2, T 48.1048b–c.

41. In its literal sense, the text refers to the procedure used to receive the Sangha's consent at its formal meeting (*jñapticaturtha-karman*). This is the monastic practice of requesting the whole community's agreement on certain issues, such as confession or ordination, by first making an announcement and then passing a motion three times.

42. "Untimely speech" and "improper talk" are technical terms derived from canonical literature. The first refers to a defeat in disputes, while the second is one of the ten evils. For usage examples in Chinese translations of Indian texts, see T 32.305b and T 30.318c.

43. BGL, XZJ 118.82d; cf. Cleary, *Sayings and Doings of Pai-chang*, 29–30.

44. The three Japanese versions of the text read *jingyao* 精要 (essentials) instead of *jingmiao* 精妙 (sublime wonders). See Kajitani's renderings in *Zen no koten*, 166, and *Zenka goroku*, 147, and Tomitani, "Butsuso sankyō kōgi," 214.

45. The twenty-five forms of existence represent the totality of all forms of existence in the three realms, from the deepest hells to the highest heavens.

46. T 48.1043a–b; XZJ 111.146c–47a. The passage appears in the context of a discussion about the close relationship between Chan soteriology and the monastic precepts.

47. T 48.1043b; XZJ 111.147b.

48. See Stanley Weinstein, "Imperial Patronage in the Formation of T'ang Buddhism," 272.

49. For example, see Paul L. Swanson, *Foundations of T'ien-t'ai Philosophy: The Flowering of the Two Truths Theory in Chinese Buddhism*, 123–56.

50. Swanson, *Foundations of T'ien-t'ai Philosophy*, 9.

51. The popular image of Chan teachers as iconoclasts who repudiated the canonical tradition and whose teachings harbored bibliophobic tendencies is

conveyed by the painting of the Sixth Patriarch destroying a sūtra by Liang Kai (Southern Song), in the collection of the Tokyo National Museum. Anticanonical sentiments are also evident in the famous verse definition of Chan created during the Song period: "A special transmission outside of the teachings that does not institute words and letters, but directly points to the human mind and [leads to] perceiving the nature and becoming a Buddha." The statement first appears in *Zuting shiyuan*, XZJ 113.66c; for the origins of the individual lines, see Yanagida, *Shoki zenshū shiso no kenkyū*, 461–62, 470–77. While this popular motto became a linchpin of the Chan school's identity during the Song era, it is problematic to read its sentiments back into the Tang period.

52. The historical connection between Bodhidharma and the *Laṅkāvatāra* might have some reality, as can be seen from the biography of his main disciple Huike (487–593). There, Bodhidharma singles out this scripture and hands it to his charge with the instruction that he should "practice in accord with [its teachings] (*yixing*)." *Gaoseng zhuan* 16, T 50.552b.

53. Faure, *Chan Insights and Oversights*, 148. For more on the role of the *Laṅkāvatāra Scripture* in early Chan, see Yanagida, "Goroku no rekishi," 285–89, and McRae, *Northern School*, 90–91.

54. T 85.1283c–84c.

55. See Philip B. Yampolsky, *The Platform Sūtra of the Sixth Patriarch*, 34. In one of his sermons, Shenhui proclaims the cultivation of the perfection of wisdom, the central theme of the *Diamond Scripture*, to be the fundamental source (*genben*) of all practices. Yang Zengwen, *Shenhui heshang chanhua lu*, 34. He also states, "If you wish to attain comprehension of the most profound *dharmadhātu* and enter directly into the Samādhi of Single Practice, you must first recite the *Diamond Scripture* and cultivate the Dharma of the perfection of wisdom." Ibid., 35; translation from John R. McRae, *Zen Evangelist*. Although Shenhui was favorably inclined toward the use of the scriptures and promoted the unity of Chan and the canonical teachings, he was prone to misquoting scriptural passages and to using them merely as props for justifying ideas that were not present in them. For a discussion of Shenhui's (mis)use of scriptural quotations, see Suzuki Tetsuo, *Chūgoku zenshūshi ronkō*, 132–34.

56. T 48.340a; Yampolsky, *The Platform Sūtra*, 149.

57. The teachers of Farong, the putative founding patriarch of the Niutou school, were all associated with the Sanlun school (which at the time was the main Chinese representative of the Madhyamaka tradition). See Hirai Shunei, "The School of Mount Niu-t'ou and the School of Pao-T'ang Monastery." Early Niutou figures can be understood as meditation teachers steeped in Madhyamaka doctrines, whose primary concern was to bring theoretical knowledge of the middle-way teachings to bear on contemplative praxis, rather than as members of the nascent Chan school. For the connections between early Chan and Sanlun, see Suzuki Tetsuo, *Chūgoku zenshūshi ronkō*, 93–116; for the influence of Mādhyamaka on the Niutou school, see Liu, *Madhyamaka Thought in China*, 242–57.

58. Yanagida Seizan, *Shoki no zenshi II: Rekidai hōbōki*, 39. The non-Buddhist works include *Laozi*, *Zhuangzi*, other Daoist texts, and various historical works. See Yanagida, "The *Li-tai fa-pao chi* and the Ch'an Doctrine of Sudden Awakening," 36.

59. For a study and translation of this text, see Buswell, *The Formation of Ch'an Ideology in China and Korea*.

60. The origin of symbolic exegesis goes back to Zhiyi's commentary of the *Lotus Scripture*. The expression "symbolic exegesis" comes from the work of Bernard Faure; see Faure, *The Will to Orthodoxy*, 41. McRae uses the term "contemplative analysis," which is a translation of *guanxin shi*; see McRae, *The Northern School*, 201–2.

61. For the presence of symbolic exegesis in Dazhu's *Dunwu yaomen*, see Scott Dennis Peterman, "The Legend of Huihai," 100–102.

62. T 51.189a and Yanagida, *Shoki no zenshi II*, 200. A similar idea can be found in the records of Shenhui. See Hirai Shunei, "The School of Mount Niu-t'ou and the School of Pao-T'ang Monastery," 360–61, and Yanagida, "The *Li-tai fa-pao chi* and the Ch'an Doctrine of Sudden Awakening," 29–30. For an example from the *Platform Scripture*, which involves redefinition of meditation, see T 48.339a, and Yampolsky, *The Platform Sūtra*, 140.

63. See McRae, *The Northern School*, 198.

64. MY, XZJ 119.405d–6a; Cheng-chien, *Sun-Face Buddha*, 62. The last clause can also be translated as "no gate is the Dharma-gate." The two phrases in the last sentence do not appear in the extant Chinese translations of the *Laṅkāvatāra Scripture*, although the saying "mind is the essential teaching" appears in Fazang's commentary on the scripture, *Ru lengqie xin xuanyi* 1, T 39.428c. However, later texts often quote the two phrases as canonical excerpts, especially "mind is the essential teaching" (which appears no fewer than twenty-three times in ZJL). For examples, see ZJL 1, T 48.415a, 417b; ZJL 56, T 48.742c; ZJL 83, T 48.875b; ZJL 100, T 48.953a; *Fozu lidai tongzai* 14, T 49.608c; and *Wumen guan* 1, T 48.292b.

65. The *Laṅkāvatāra Scripture*'s continuing appeal into the early ninth century is evident in the poetry of Bo Juyi, who in a number of poems explicitly mentions its title. See Burton Watson, "Buddhism in the Poetry of Po Chü-I," 10–11.

66. MY, XZJ 119.406a; translation adapted from Cheng-chien, *Sun-Face Buddha*, 62.

67. For a discussion of the mirror metaphor, see McRae, *The Northern School*, 144–46. The metaphor was connected to the Yogācāra doctrine of the "great perfect mirror wisdom," one of the four wisdoms that emerge when *ālaya* is transformed at its basis with the realization of enlightenment. Baizhang seems to have been aware of this connection, as in a number of passages in BGL he refers to the mirror wisdom.

68. MY, XZJ 119.406d; translation adapted from Cheng-chien, *Sun-Face Buddha*, 67.

69. See the discussion of his life in the section on Baizhang Huaihai in chapter 2.

70. This includes the five extant sermons of Mazu, which do not appear together as a single text. For a useful presentation of the Chinese texts of the extant versions of each sermon that facilitates comparison, see Yanagida, "Goroku no rekishi," 484–89, 496–98, 504–7, 512.

71. Here I am dealing only with Dazhu's treatise, not the Song-period collection of stories and dialogues that is traditionally appended to it. Because of the large number of quotations from diverse sources that appear in *Dunwu yaomen*, in this

and the following table I have not included a number of less well-known texts that are only quoted once or twice by Dazhu. Examples of such texts include *Fangkuang jing* and *Fo shuo jiuzhi jing*. For a listing of the texts quoted by Dazhu, see Peterman, "The Legend of Huihai," 369–71.

72. In both Dazhu's and Baizhang's texts, most of the quotations from the Prajñāpāramitā scriptures are from the *Diamond Scripture*, but there are also quotations from other scriptures belonging to the Prajñāpāramitā corpus. For the sake of convenience, here all of these closely related texts are assigned to the same category. Because of the lack of critical editions of Baizhang's text and the way in which it quotes canonical sources (see below), it is likely that I have not been able to identify all quotations from the sources listed in the table; the actual number of quotations/allusions that appear in BGL is probably higher than indicated there.

73. See Kamata Shigeo, "Chūgoku zen shisō keisei no kyōgakuteki haikei: Daijō kishinron o chūshin to shite," *Tōyō bunka kenkyūjo kiyō* 49 (1969), 98–109.

74. For a useful summary of the canonical sources quoted in Shenhui's records, see the table in Suzuki, *Chūgoku zenshūshi ronkō*, 128.

75. See Paul Demiéville, *Le concile de Lhasa: une controverse sur le quiétisme entre bouddhistes de l'Inde et de la Chine au VIIIe siècle de l'ère chrétienne*, 160. For more information about Mahāyāna, see Luis O. Gómez, "The Direct and Gradual Approaches of Zen Master Mahāyāna: Fragments of the Teachings of Mo-ho-yen," and Yamaguchi Zuihō, "Makaen no zen."

76. A tendency to quote scriptures without identifying the sources—often without indicating that a certain passage is a quotation—can also be found in the writings of earlier Buddhist scholiasts, such as Zhiyi. See Paul Swanson's discussion in his "Apocryphal Texts in Chinese Buddhism: T'ien-t'ai Chih-i's use of Apocryphal Scriptures," 249.

77. *Weimojie suoshuo jing*, T 14.0540a; Burton Watson, *The Vimalakīrti Sūtra*, 38.

78. *Fahua youyi*, T 34.640b. The first part of the sentence, "The Dharma-body is unconditioned," also appears in Sengzhao's commentary of the *Vimalakīrti Scripture*; see *Zhu weimojie jing*, T 38. 355a, 360a, 412a. I suspect Baizhang is conflating (or confusing) the two commentaries.

79. An alternative translation could read "the sagely essence . . ." I have been unable to find any text where the exact sentence appears; the closest is a sentence from a fragmentary commentary of the *Vimalakīrti Scripture*: "the essence of the true nature of reality is nameless and cannot be expressed in words." *Weimojie jing shu* 3, T85.381c. Similar ideas are also expressed in the "Nirvana Is Nameless Treatise" in *Zhaolun* (see T 45.157a–58b), which is probably the text Baizhang is referring to. In addition, a similar statement, "the self-essence is nameless" (*ziti wuming*), appears in *Baozang lun* (Treasure Store Treatise), T 45.144b.

80. BGL, XZJ 118.83c–d; cf. Cleary, *Sayings and Doings of Pai-chang*, 35 (note the unidentified quotations and misplaced quotation marks). The last two sentences allude to a passage in *Dazhidu lun* 94, T 25.717a.

81. BGL, XZJ 118.86b; Cleary, *Sayings and Doings of Pai-chang*, 52. For the original passage in the *Lotus Scripture*, see *Miaofa lianhua jing* 3, T 9.22b, and Watson, *The Lotus Sutra*, 119. For the reference in Linji's record, see T 47.502a.

82. BGL, XZJ 118.86c; Cleary, *Sayings and Doings of Pai-chang*, 53.

83. The intellectual changes that occurred during this period have been studied by a number of scholars, starting with Pulleyblank's seminal article, and more recently by McMullen, Bol, Hartman, and others. See Edwin Pulleyblank, "Neo-Confucianism and Neo-Legalism in T'ang Intellectual Life, 755–805"; David McMullen, *State and Scholars in T'ang China*; and Peter Kees Bol, *"This Culture of Ours": Intellectual Transitions in T'ang and Sung China*, 108–47.

84. David McMullen, *State and Scholars in T'ang China*, 69–70.

85. Ibid., 70.

86. See Charles Hartman, *Han Yü and the T'ang Search for Unity*, 5–8.

87. Bol, *"This Culture of Ours,"* 109.

88. Bol, *"This Culture of Ours,"* 125.

5

Mind, Buddha, and the Way

The teachings of Mazu and his disciples, as presented in the extant records, reveal a multifaceted engagement with diverse concepts and a range of doctrinal frames of reference. While individual Chan teachers adopted or responded to tenets and issues that were integral parts of a shared religious milieu—which included the broader Chan tradition and the rest of Tang Buddhism—they also introduced personal points of view and propounded novel doctrinal formulations. Examples of ingenious developments include Mazu's conception of ordinary mind, surveyed in this chapter—which focuses primarily on Mazu's record (although I also draw on other pertinent sources)—and Baizhang's three propositions, discussed in the next chapter. But although the Hongzhou school's records contain many expressions of individual viewpoints and creative impulses, they also point to a common religious outlook and a shared vision of the path of practice and realization. The chapter therefore begins with an outline of some of these central themes and ideas.

The Buddhist tradition teaches that all human beings experience suffering and imperfection. This shared predicament is not imposed by an external divine agency, and it encapsulates a profound sense of dissonance with the true nature of reality. Because of their mental defilements and fallacies, at the core of which is a fundamental ignorance of reality, human beings give rise to desires, form attachments, and misconstrue the world they live in. Yet, despite the power of deep-seated afflictions, attachments, and illusions, human beings have an innate ability and potential to know reality and to be genuinely free. Ultimate reality transcends the realm of ignorance and defilements, yet it is the basis of everything. All things and creatures partake in that reality—a condition of original completeness and perfection, expressed by recourse to a number of terms, such as "One Mind" and "suchness"—which permeates and encompasses all phenomena in the universe.

Since reality is everywhere and in everything—or to put it another way, it is the true nature of all things—including the mind and body of each individual, the prospect of spiritual awakening and liberation is open to all, at all times. In essence, all one needs to do is let go of all false views and attachments, emptying the mind and intuitively apprehending the ubiquitous truth, without any mediation or distortion. But because attachments and ignorance are deep-seated and difficult to dislodge, one usually needs spiritual practices. Although the methods might vary because of peculiar circumstances and individual predilections, at their core these practices involve emptying the mind of all thoughts, images, attachments, and views. This paves the way for the arising of wisdom and the transcendence of dualism, although the adept must also not become trapped in nondualism.

Because of an inveterate human propensity for self-deception, the application of specific teachings and methods needs to be flexible, contextual, and nuanced. Moreover, the teachings themselves must not turn into religious dogmas and sources of attachment; thus all teachings and methods of practice are provisional, functioning as tools for freeing the mind of views, fixations, and clinging. Hence, they must be employed wisely and abandoned when they are no longer needed. When used with sophistication and sensibility, ideally under the guidance of a qualified teacher, the teachings finally dissolve into a totalizing vision of the absolute, as the adept directly realizes the nature of reality and becomes able to act in accord with it.

What this summary shows is that most facets of the Hongzhou school's teachings intersect with key insights and tenets of Mahāyāna Buddhism. They also overlap with the doctrinal stances and soteriological schemes of other Buddhist traditions, including those of early Chan. These similarities, although they stand in contrast to traditional images of the Hongzhou school as the vanguard of a new iconoclastic ethos, should not surprise us when we consider the Hongzhou school's position within the world of Tang Buddhism. Nonetheless, Mazu and his disciples appropriated received doctrinal elements and juxtaposed them with new concepts, thereby reconfiguring and expressing them in a manner unique to their tradition. As a result, their teachings incorporate both old and new elements, bringing them together into a reasoned series of doctrinal propositions, expressed in a distinctive idiom. Thus the teachings of Mazu and his disciples preserve a sense of continuity with earlier traditions, while also putting a distinct imprint on the ongoing evolution of Chan doctrine and expressing distinctive perspectives and insights.

Detachment

The key elements that underscore the conception of a progressive path of practice and realization expounded in the Hongzhou school's records begin with the twin notions of detachment and transcendence, which together serve as a common thread that binds together other concepts and ideas. According to the records of Mazu, Dazhu, Baizhang, Nanquan, and Huangbo, at its core Chan practice involves the cultivation of nonattachment. Spiritual cultivation entails an ascent into increasingly rarefied states of detachment and transcendence, in which the vestiges of dualistic thought are eliminated. This implies not clinging to any doctrine, practice, or experience, including the notions of detachment and nonduality.[1] The perfection of a liberated state of mind that is free from attachment and ignorance, explains Baizhang, is predicated on the realization of the twofold emptiness of person and things, a core Mahāyāna tenet:

> Right now, if someone wishes to attain immediately awakening and realization, then he should just let both person and things disappear, let both person and things be obliterated, let both person and things be empty. Then, passing through the three stages, that is called a person who does not fall within any categorization. That is having faith in the Dharma. It is ethical observance, generosity, learning, wisdom, and so on.[2]

The realization of emptiness implies the sublation of all concepts and views. Baizhang points out that even the views of the Buddha and the Dharma, and of course even more so everything else, hinder the arising of true insight.[3] The realization of sudden awakening, according to Dazhu, consists of the instantaneous giving up of all deluded thoughts (wangnian), while also realizing that awakening does not involve the attainment of anything (wusuode).[4] Therefore, the mind of the Chan adept should not abide (wuzhu) anywhere, including in existence and nonexistence, good and evil, concentration and disturbance.[5] The Buddha mind, explains Dazhu, is simply the mind that abides nowhere.[6] He defines the non-abiding mind (wuzhu xin):

> Not abiding anywhere [means that] one does not abide in good and evil, existence and nothingness, inside, outside, or in-between. Not abiding in emptiness and not abiding in non-emptiness, not abiding in concentration and not abiding in the absence of concentration, that is not abiding anywhere. Only this not abiding anywhere is the [true] abode. When one attains this, it is called the non-abiding mind. The non-abiding mind is the Buddha mind.[7]

Freed from attachments and fixations, the non-abiding mind is without a center or locus, able to perceive reality without mediation or distortion based on preconceived concepts and ideas. But ultimate reality is not simply transcendent and dissociated from conventional reality; there is only one realm of reality (Sanskrit: *dharmadhātu*; Chinese: *fajie*), which encompasses and pervades everything. Adopting a perspective that echoes the Huayan analysis of reality in terms of the relationship between principle (*li*) and phenomena (*shi*), Mazu affirms the mutual identity and inclusion of the two realms:

> If one attains the teaching, then one is always free. If *dharmadhātu* is established, then everything is *dharmadhātu*. If suchness is established, then everything is suchness. If principle is established, then all dharmas are principle. If phenomena are established, then all dharmas are phenomena. When one is raised, a thousand follow. The principle and phenomena are not different, and everything is sublime function. There is no other principle. They all come from the mind.[8]

According to this point of view, everything partakes of the character of reality, except that ordinary people are unaware of it because of their ignorance and defilements. With awakening, one simply realizes the all-pervasiveness of reality, seeing things as they truly are, without adding or subtracting anything. Mazu elaborates on that point in a passage that comes immediately after the previous one:

> For instance, though the reflections of the moon are many, the real moon is only one. Though there are many springs of water, water has only one nature. There are myriad phenomena in the universe, but empty space is only one. There are many principles that are spoken of, but "unobstructed wisdom is only one."[9] Whatever is established, it all comes from One Mind. Whether constructing or sweeping away, all is sublime function, all is oneself.[10]

Here Mazu strikes a positive note, pointing to a state of original perfection—expressed by terms like "suchness," "truth," and "One Mind"—that is manifest in all things, events, and activities.[11] Ultimate reality, the true Buddha, is everywhere and pervades everything, regardless of humans' ability to recognize it. In contrast, the discord, imperfection, and confusion that characterize the human predicament arise from inveterate ignorance and a fundamental misconception of reality, an idea that is not unique to the Hongzhou school or the Chan tradition. In that sense, they are not intrinsic or essential aspects of reality. In the following passage, Mazu contrasts ignorance and awakening and relates both to the immutable actuality of the original mind/nature:

The realization of nonduality is called equal nature. Although the nature is free from differentiation, its function is not the same. When ignorant, it is called consciousness; when awakened, it is called wisdom. Following the principle is awakening, while following phenomena is ignorance. Ignorance is to be ignorant of one's original mind. Awakening is to awake to one's original nature. Once awakened, one is awakened forever, there being no more ignorance. It is like when the sun comes, and then all darkness disappears. When the sun of *prajñā* (wisdom) emerges, it does not coexist with the darkness of defilements.[12]

According to Mazu, the apprehension of nonduality perfects the faculty of wisdom, bringing about an insight into reality. Within this conceptual scheme, the process of freeing the mind entails its divestiture from misguided notions, discriminating thoughts, self-centered feelings, and dualistic views. Deluded thoughts are behind the misapprehension of the way things are, giving rise to arbitrary attachments and desires, facile emotions and fears, and the like. While individuals experience these as being real, they all lack inherent self-nature. Consequently, Mazu argues that the ending of all mental conceptions and the transcendence of duality serve as catalysts for the realization of reality, which is the same regardless of whether the individual is unaware of or awakened to it. In the following passage, he describes what kind of understanding is needed in order to "attain the universal Way":

The self-nature is originally complete. If only either good or evil things do not hinder one, then that is a person who cultivates the Way. Grasping good and rejecting evil, contemplating emptiness and entering samādhi, all of these belong to activity. If one seeks outside, one goes away from it. Just put an end to all mental conceptions in the three realms. If there is not a single thought, then one eliminates the root of birth and death, and obtains the unexcelled treasury of the Dharma king.[13]

A similar emphasis on putting an end to conceptual thought and attachment is evident in other texts. For example, in Huangbo's records he advises his disciples to spend all their time learning how to perfect the state of no-mind (*wuxin*), which implies putting an end to mental activities that give rise to dualistic thoughts. He then goes on to assure them that even though they might not be able to transcend saṃsāra immediately, they will make good progress if they apply themselves to the practice for the next five or ten years.[14] Elsewhere, after critiquing the seeking of truth outside of oneself and the unreflective reliance on conventional practices, Huangbo exhorts his disciples to perfect the state of no-mind. He explains no-mind in terms of definitive knowledge of the fundamental nonexistence (i.e., emptiness) of all

phenomena, non-attainment (*wusuode*), non-abiding (*wuzhu*), absence of subjectivity and objectivity (*wuneng wusuo*), and the non-arising of false thoughts
(*wangnian*).[15] According to Huangbo (as well as Mazu and Baizhang), Chan
practice largely functions as a process of subtraction or elimination; the
practitioner learns how to let go of views and attachments that bind him to
the realm of birth and death. Another passage from Huangbo's record illustrates this point:

> There is not a single Dharma to obtain, not a single practice to
> cultivate. That is the supreme Way. That is the true Buddha. Stu-
> dents of the Way should only worry about giving rise to a single
> thought, in which case they distance themselves from the Way.
> When in each instant there are no forms/signs, when in each
> instant there is no activity, that is the Buddha. If students of the
> Way wish to attain Buddhahood, they need not study all Buddha-
> dharmas. They only need to study "non-seeking" and "non-
> attachment" . . . Just transcend all afflictions, and then there is no
> Dharma that can be obtained.[16]

The Hongzhou school's records present Chan practice as an open-ended
process, in which the adept arrests the flow of habitual thoughts and comes to
perceive reality directly, without superimpositions or self-centered distortions.
In Baizhang's record, we encounter a use of the images of wood and stone as
metaphors for the mind of the Chan sage, which is firm and unmoved when
encountering all kinds of circumstances:

> All things never proclaim themselves empty, nor do they declare that
> they are form. They also do not say that they are right or wrong, pure
> or impure. Neither is there any mind to bind anyone. It is only that
> people themselves create false attachments, thereby giving rise to all
> kinds of understanding, creating various views, desires, and fears. Just
> realize that all things are not created by themselves. They all come into
> existence only because of a single false thought that wrongly attaches
> to appearances. If one perceives that mind and phenomena do not
> mutually reach each other, then one is liberated at that very spot. All
> things are calm and extinct as they are, and that very spot is the
> sanctuary of awakening.[17]

According to Baizhang, people bind themselves by giving rise to false
views and attachments. The perfection of a mind that is like wood or stone
involves the ending of the habitual patterns of thinking and emptying the
mind of thoughts and images. He expands on this theme:

> You should first put an end to all involvements and bring to rest the
> myriad concerns. Whether wholesome or unwholesome, mundane or

supramundane, let go of all things. Do not remember, recollect, get caught up, or think. Let go of both body and mind, affecting them to be free. With a mind that is like wood or stone, a mouth that does not engage in arguments, with a mind that has no activity, the mind-ground becomes like empty space and the sun of wisdom manifests itself. It is like when the clouds open up and the sun emerges.[18]

When the mind is freed from mental defilements, it opens the way for the experience of awakening. Then, the sun of wisdom finally emerges from behind the clouds of ignorance and illuminates the world, declares Baizhang. When he finally lets go of everything, the practitioner enters a recondite realm of awakening, without abandoning the everyday world of people and events, mountains and rivers, secluded monasteries and busy marketplaces.

Expedient Means

The formulation of the Hongzhou school's teachings was predicated on an understanding of Buddhist doctrines and practices as *upāya* (*fangbian*, "expedient means" or "skillful means"). The notion of *upāya* occupies a central position within the Mahāyāna tradition, its influence extending to the areas of ethics, hermeneutics, and soteriology. The idea appears in early scriptures, which describe the skilled means and strategies used by the Buddha in the instruction and guidance of his disciples. The Prajñāpāramitā scriptures use *upāya* in reference to the various methods and techniques used by the Buddha and the bodhisattvas in their work of universal salvation. With the subsequent development of Mahāyāna doctrine, the idea became more complex and was deployed differently in various canonical and exegetical texts.

The notion of *upāya* was often employed as a hermeneutical tool, for the purpose of explaining differences among the various Buddhist teachings and traditions. Within this context, specific teachings were accorded different levels of profundity, thereby creating a hierarchy of teachings that were supposedly formulated by the Buddha in response to the needs and abilities of his followers. By tailoring the message to specific audiences—taking into account their spiritual needs and stages of spiritual development—the Buddha purportedly enabled them to persevere with their practice, gradually leading them toward the ultimate goal. The interpretation of discrete teachings as *upāya*, providing apposite guidance for particular audiences, was thus used to explain the panoply of doctrines attributed to the Buddha (albeit in an ahistorical fashion). This perspective was embraced by Buddhist scholars in medieval China, as they had to deal with hermeneutical quandaries posed by the need to reconcile contradistinctions and disparities evidenced in various canonical texts and teachings. That remained a pressing issue for a long time, because the canon continued to expand as increasing number of scriptures were translated from Indic languages and new apocryphal texts were composed in China.

The concept of *upāya* plays a prominent role in the *Lotus Scripture*. There it performs a polemical function, being used to relegate all earlier Buddhist teachings to an inferior status and facilitate the Buddha's revelation of the final truth, which is supposedly contained in its completeness and full resplendent glory only in the *Lotus Scripture*. In the text, the Buddha uses an array of *upāya* for the purpose of highlighting the provisional nature of earlier teachings and divulging the supremacy and universality of the One Vehicle, the ultimate truth unique to the *Lotus Scripture*. Importantly, throughout most of the text the use of *upāya* is the exclusive province of the Buddha.

In contrast, the *Vimalakīrti Scripture* eulogizes the bodhisattvas for their adept use of *upāya*. This text depicts its main hero, Vimalakīrti, as entering all sorts of places and situations, including gambling houses and brothels, in order to lead wayward persons toward the Buddha's path. The truthfulness of a given teaching is thereby correlated to its efficacy in liberating others; whether a given teaching will work depends on the context and the audience. The text adopts the standpoint of nonduality, symbolized by Vimalakīrti's silence, and communicates the idea that the nature of ultimate reality defies all attempts to conceptualize or verbalize it.[19] Accordingly, even the conception of ultimate truth is an *upāya*, used for the sake of leading individuals to a liberating insight. Therefore, no teaching should be grasped as conclusive formulation of the ultimate truth (a perspective that, as we will see, was also adopted by the Hongzhou school).[20] A similar assault against doctrinaire rigidity and religious dogmatism is also a feature of scriptures belonging to the Prajñāpāramitā corpus and Madhyamaka texts, which warn against attaching even to the most cherished Buddhist notions and ideals.[21]

In keeping with its contemplative character, the Chan tradition adopted a pragmatic orientation that incorporated the concept of *upāya*, regarding Buddhist doctrines as theoretical models that guide actual religious behavior. The notion of *upāya* is found in a number of early Chan texts, starting with *Erru sixing lun* (Treatise on Two Entrances and Four Practices), attributed to Bodhidharma. It also appears in the meditation instructions of *Xiuxin yaolun* (Treatise on the Essentials of Mind Cultivation), attributed to Hongren, and plays an important role in the Northern school's *Wu fangbian* (Five Expedient Means), which, as its title suggests, elucidates five forms of *upāya*.[22] Generally speaking, within Tang Chan there was a tendency to interpret practices or methods of spiritual cultivation, including meditation, as *upāya*.

As the conception of religious teachings as *upāya* was embedded in the weltanschauung of medieval Chinese Buddhism, the Hongzhou school drew on common frames of reference. At the same time, as it integrated the notion of *upāya* into its basic religious perspective, its employment as a central pedagogical principle assumed a distinctive character. The determined refusal on the part of Mazu and his disciples to commit to a narrow doctrinal perspective, while not without parallels in the annals of medieval Buddhism, represented a fresh attempt to rearrange the priorities of religious life. That underscored the Hongzhou school's essential character as an elite contemplative tradition, grounded in the religious ethos of medieval monasticism.

The implicit objective of the Hongzhou school's teachings, as presented in the extant sources, is to explicate a path of practice that leads to the realization of awakening and liberation. Accordingly, they stress the performative aspects of Chan teachings and underscore that religious doctrines are not intended to be simply accepted as faithful descriptions of reality. Adopting a classic Mahāyāna perspective, the records of Mazu and his disciples deem ultimate reality to be "inconceivable" (*buke siyi*), transcending conceptual constructs and verbal expressions. Such an understanding is closely related to the already-noted emphasis on detachment and transcendence. Taken together, they underscore the danger of reifying religious doctrines, practices, and experiences.

If the perfection of detachment is a key facet of spiritual cultivation, then it is necessary to establish safeguards to counteract the natural tendency to become attached to religious texts, teachings, practices, and experiences, which leads to misconstruing their nature and function. When that happens, various elements and aspects of the religious path become parts of the problem, instead of salvific solutions to the perennial quandaries of human existence. The adoption of this perspective, which straddles both the theoretical and practical spheres, explains the centrality of *upāya* with the Hongzhou school's records, which repeatedly emphasize that the truthfulness of specific doctrines depends on their potency in bringing about spiritual transformation and realization. Such an outlook is especially evident in Baizhang's record:

> However, all verbal teachings are just like cures for diseases. Because
> the diseases are not the same, the medicines are also not the same.
> That is why sometimes it is said that there is Buddha, and some-
> times that there is no Buddha. True words cure sickness. If the cure
> manages to bring about healing, then all are true words. [On the
> other hand,] if they cannot effectively cure sickness, all are false
> words. True words are false words, insofar as they give rise to views.
> False words are true words, insofar as they cut off the delusions of
> sentient beings. Because the diseases are unreal, there are only
> unreal medicines to cure them.[23]

The conception of religious teachings as cures for spiritual ailments, suggested by this passage, recalls canonical depictions of the Buddha as a skilled physician who dispenses the proper medicines to cure the assorted spiritual diseases that befall humanity. From this perspective, different doctrines, including explanations of the nature of Buddhahood, are to be understood primarily in terms of their function as guideposts or signs that map various twists and turns on the spiritual path. They are not to be grasped as unassailable dogmas, nor are they to be equated with what is ultimately true and real. Baizhang points out that the teachings themselves are devoid of absolute reality, being like unreal medicines used to cure illusory afflictions. In a way, the medicines by themselves cannot bring about perfect spiritual well-being. A state of authentic spiritual health implies not becoming ill in the first place; the medicines/teachings facilitate the return to an original state of well-being, dissolving after they remove the symptoms of ignorance and afflictions.

"Greed, anger, folly, and the like are poisons, and the twelve divisions of teachings [in the Buddhist canon] are medicines [that cure the poisons of spiritual afflictions]," explains Baizhang. He adds, however, that, "If a person takes a medicine when he does not have [a particular] illness, then the medicine becomes the [cause of] illness."[24] The plethora of Buddhist doctrines exist because the spiritual diseases they are supposed to cure are numerous; as stated in the passage cited above, "since the diseases are not the same, the medicines are also not the same." Therefore, doctrinal rigidity is counterproductive, given that the effectiveness of religious teachings depends on specific contexts and must be responsive to the needs and abilities of actual people.

According to Baizhang (and more broadly the Hongzhou school), a doctrine or theory can be considered as being true if it leads to letting go of mistaken views and attachments, thus performing a constructive role in the process of spiritual cultivation. Conversely, even the most profound doctrine can be deemed false if it becomes an object of intellectual fixation or emotional attachment, thereby fostering dogmatism and giving rise to dualistic views that prevent intuitive insight into the wholeness of reality. Thus the principles for establishing truth and falsehood are flexible and are embedded in concrete situations and actual human experiences. In essence, it boils down to a simple and clear standard of truth: the ability of words to catalyze liberating insight (a position similar to that of the *Vimalakīrti Scripture* and other canonical texts). Therefore, genuine practice and realization imply the cessation of views, including the relinquishment of various doctrinaire assertions, even those expressed in the scriptures or propounded by Chan teachers such as Mazu and Baizhang.

Like all phenomena, religious doctrines and the mental afflictions they are meant to counterbalance are both devoid of inherent reality or intrinsic existence. For Mazu and his followers, all doctrines are provisional. While no doctrine, no matter how profound, can capture the true nature of reality—which, after all, is beyond thoughts and theoretical constructs—that does not mean that all doctrines are equivalent, or that there is no gradation in their capacity to illuminate profound truths and facilitate the comprehension of reality. That brings us to the Hongzhou school's understanding of the function of religious language. In its opening paragraph, Baizhang's record highlights this issue by introducing the standard Mahāyāna division of the teachings of Buddhism into those of the complete (or definitive) teaching (Chinese: *liaoyi jiao*; Sanskrit: *nītārtha*) and the incomplete (or interpretable) teaching (Chinese: *buliaoyi jiao*; Sanskrit: *neyārtha*). The two categories imply a hierarchy of doctrines, and in many instances they were employed to establish the superiority of one teaching over others:

> When [using] language, you must distinguish between [verbal communications addressed to] monks and layman (literally "black and white"). You must discern [the differences between] general and particular language. You must discern [the differences between] the languages of the complete and incomplete teachings. The complete teaching reasons [in terms of] purity. The incomplete teaching reasons [in terms of] impurity. Talking about the defilement of vile things picks out the mundane, while talking about the defilement of pure things picks out the sacred.[25]

Baizhang goes on to clarify the distinction between words or expressions that evoke either purity or impurity. The category of impurity covers things such as greed, hatred, (sensual) love, and attachment, while the category of purity includes awakening (*bodhi*), Nirvāṇa, liberation, and so on.[26] In his discussion of religious language, he also introduces other pairings of related terms, including "live and dead words" (*shengsi yu*), words of "negative and positive metaphors" (*nishun yu*), and "host and guest words" (*zhuke yu*).[27] Dead words, guest words, and positive metaphors correspond to the category of the incomplete teaching. Examples of such teachings, which according to Baizhang are addressed to ordinary (ignorant) people, include the assertions that "one can attain Buddhahood by means of spiritual cultivation," that "there is practice and realization," and that "mind is Buddha." Conversely, live words, host words, and negative metaphors correspond to the category of the complete teaching. They are intended for advanced practitioners who traverse the stages of the bodhisattva path, and are exemplified by statements such as "one cannot attain Buddhahood by means of spiritual cultivation," "there is no practice and realization," and "there is neither mind nor Buddha."[28]

Baizhang first highlights the distinction between the two general categories of teachings. He then asserts the superiority of teachings that employ apophatic expressions over those that rely on kataphatic language. However, he concludes that in the end all of them need to be abandoned. Similarly, Dazhu's treatise comments, "Words are used to reveal the [ultimate] meaning, but when the meaning is realized, words are discarded."[29] Just as in the story about a traveler who abandons the raft he has used to cross the raging river of saṃsāra, Baizhang points out that the Chan practitioner eventually needs to abandon all concepts, verbal formulations, and doctrines, including those of the incomplete and complete teachings:

From entering the stream all the way up to the tenth stage of the bodhisattva path, as long as there are verbal formulations, all belong to the defilement of the dust of teaching. As long as there are verbal formulations, all are contained in the realm of affliction and trouble. As long as there are verbal formulations, all belong to the incomplete teaching. The complete teaching is observance, while the incomplete teaching is transgression. At the stage of Buddhahood, there is neither observance nor transgression, and neither the complete nor the incomplete teachings are admissible.[30]

This passage points to a familiar dilemma. On the one hand, religious doctrines are indispensable templates that provide guidance along the path to awakening. Yet all too often they become reified and turn into objects of attachment. When that happens, they bind the mind and turn into obstacles to genuine insight, hindering spiritual progress and realization. Because of that, Chan teachers such as Mazu and Baizhang continually faced the challenge of reformulating and adjusting their teachings in response to their disciples' tendency to become attached to specific notions or points of view. The debates about Mazu's teaching regarding the purported identity of the mind and the Buddha are a good example of this.

Mind and Buddha

One of the best-known sayings associated with Mazu is "Mind is Buddha" (*jixin jifo* or *jixin shi fo*).[31] This statement appears in Mazu's record and is discussed in the records of his disciples (where it is explicitly attributed to Mazu). Despite the long-established connection with Mazu, the adage "Mind is Buddha" was not his creation. The same expression appears in the records of earlier figures: outside the Chan school, it is found in two poems attributed to Baozhi (418–514) and Fu dashi (497–569);[32] within early Chan literature, the statement or variations on it appear in the records of Huike, Daoxin, Huineng, and Nanyang Huizhong.[33] Similar ideas can also be traced in the records of Shenhui, and they seem to have been current within the Chan school during the eighth century. Regardless of its provenance, "Mind is Buddha" was a central tenet discussed among Mazu and his disciples, and its usage provides clues about their doctrinal stances, exegetical strategies, and soteriological attitudes.

The idea of an essential identity between the mind of the Buddha and the minds of ordinary people was based on the tathāgatagarbha doctrine and the associated belief that everybody possesses Buddha-nature. It was also influenced by the notion of identity or equivalence between saṃsāra and Nirvāṇa, propounded in scriptures such as the *Prajñāpāramitā*, *Vimalakīrti*, and *Huayan*, as well as Madhyamaka texts. As noted in the previous chapter, such beliefs and doctrines had a high currency in medieval Chinese Buddhism and were not peculiar to the Chan school. The idea of an essential identity between the minds of the Buddha and ordinary people (or, in canonical parlance, living/ sentient beings) is illustrated by this famous verse from the *Huayan Scripture*:

> As mind is, so is the Buddha;
> As the Buddha is, so are living beings.
> One should know that the Buddha's and mind's
> Essential nature is boundless.[34]

In Tang Buddhism, the conception of a fundamental identity between the minds of Buddhas and ordinary persons often went beyond a belief in the Buddha-nature as a potential for the realization of Buddhahood. This identity was sometimes premised on belief in the existence of "true mind" (*zhenxin*) inherent in each person. Although the precise ontological status of the true mind was usually glossed over, in some instances it was understood as a substratum of pure awareness residing within every person, which is behind all thoughts and actions, as can be seen in this passage from Zongmi's *Chanyuan zhuquanji duxu*:

> This teaching propounds that all sentient beings without exception have the empty, tranquil, true mind. From time without beginning, it is the intrinsically pure, effulgent, unobstructed, clear, and bright ever-present awareness. It abides forever and will never perish on into the infinite future. It is termed Buddha-nature; it is also termed tathāgatagarbha and mind-ground.[35]

Ordinary people are supposedly unaware of the true mind's sublime actuality because they are caught up in webs of attachments, desires, and views. Accordingly, they fail to see that the deluded thoughts that obscure the true mind are little more than adventitious defilements. Regardless of that fundamental ignorance, according to Zongmi and others, all activities performed in the course of everyday life are functions (*yong*) of the Buddha-nature, which constitutes the real nature or essence of each person.

The association of the adage "mind is Buddha" with Mazu reflects a common perception that it played an important role in his thought. This is mirrored in Mazu's record, which includes such statements as "All of you should believe that your mind is Buddha, that this mind is identical with Buddha. . . . Outside of mind there is no other Buddha, outside of Buddha there is no other mind."[36] In addition, as we will see shortly, in the records of Mazu's disciples there are discussions of the meaning and ramifications of Mazu's adage. But before going there, let us explore a bit more of Mazu's teachings on this subject. In one of his sermons, he compares the tathāgatagarbha with the *dharmakāya* (*fashen*), the essential body of the Buddha:

> In bondage it is called tathāgatagarbha; when liberated it is called the
> pure *dharmakāya*. The *dharmakāya* is boundless; its essence is
> neither increasing nor decreasing. In order to respond to beings, it
> can manifest as big or small, square or round. It is like a reflection of
> the moon in water. It functions smoothly without establishing
> roots.[37]

Mazu's sermon then goes on to introduce the two aspects of the "mind of
sentient beings" described in the *Awakening of Faith*: the mind in terms of
"birth and death" and "suchness." This formulation conveys a sense of intimate correlation and continuity between the phenomenal realm and ultimate
reality, which intersect in the human mind, a key idea in the *Awakening of
Faith*, a text that exerted far-reaching influence on the doctrinal development
of Chinese Buddhism.

> The mind can be spoken of [in terms of its two aspects]: birth and
> death, and suchness. The mind as suchness is like a clear mirror,
> which can reflect images. The mirror symbolizes the mind; the
> images symbolize phenomena (dharmas). If the mind attaches to
> phenomena, then it gets involved in external causes and conditions,
> which is the meaning of birth and death. If the mind does not attach
> to phenomena, that is the meaning of suchness.[38]

Here Mazu alludes to the familiar metaphor of the mind as a clear mirror
that reflects phenomenal reality, which has several parallels in medieval Buddhist literature. The mind's fundamental nature remains the same, but when
there is attachment one experiences saṃsāra, while when attachment is obliterated there is a return to suchness. In another sermon, Mazu adds, "If you
want to know the mind, that which is talking right now is nothing else but
your mind. This mind is called Buddha. It is also the Buddha of the true
Dharma-body (*dharmakāya*), and it is also called the Way."[39]

Among Mazu's disciples, Baizhang's record mostly shies away from the
teaching of "mind is Buddha" and avoids adopting doctrinal stances derived
from it,[40] as does Dazhu's treatise.[41] This probably reflects the backlash against
the unreflective and one-sided appropriations of the adage discussed later, a
trend that is evident among Mazu's first-generation disciples. In contrast,
Mazu's saying is frequently invoked in Huangbo's two records, which overall
are more inclined to bring into play the concepts of the tathāgatagarbha and
Buddha-nature and often employ essentialist expressions.[42] A few examples:

> Mind is Buddha; no-mind is the Way. Simply do not give rise to
> conceptual thoughts, thinking in terms of existence and nothing-
> ness, long and short, others and self, subject and object. Mind is
> originally Buddha; Buddha is originally mind. The mind is like

empty space. Therefore, it has been said, "The Buddha's true Dharma-body is like empty space."[43] There is no use seeking else-where, for when there is seeking it all [leads to] suffering.[44]

Your mind is Buddha. The Buddha is mind, and mind and Buddha are not different. Therefore, it is said [by Mazu], "Mind is Buddha." If you leave the mind, there is no other Buddha.[45]

Mind is Buddha. From the various Buddhas at the top, all the way down to squirming and crawling creatures, all have Buddha-nature and share the same mind essence. Therefore, when Bodhi-dharma came from India, he only transmitted the teaching of One Mind, directly pointing out that all living beings are originally Buddhas. It is not something [to be attained] by means of practice. Right now, only come to know your mind and perceive your original nature, and do not seek anything else.[46]

The teaching of "mind is Buddha" conveyed an optimistic view of the hu-man predicament, laying emphasis on a source of spiritual perfection that is within the mind of each individual. According to it, since ultimate reality is, in a way, present within oneself—in fact, it constitutes one's true nature—all one needs to do is let go of false thoughts and attachments, which hinder the spon-taneous manifestation and unhindered functioning of the true mind. How-ever, notwithstanding the appeal of the premise of universal Buddhahood, the teaching of "mind is Buddha" inherited the problems associated with the tathāgatagarbha doctrine, whose basic message was fraught with ambiguities that had significant ontological, epistemic, and soteriological ramifications. When the "mind" of ordinary people is equated with Buddhahood, what kind of mind is meant? Is the deluded and impure mind of everyday experience, with all its thoughts and feelings, included in it? Alternatively, is the term pointing to a primordially pure mind, a numinous essence that is separate from ordinary mental activities? Or perhaps the two orders—pure and im-pure, deluded and enlightened—can be brought together, so that common mental states such as greed, hatred, and ignorance are seen as manifestation of the Buddha-nature? In his account of the Hongzhou school's teachings as radical nondualism, Zongmi suggests the last possibility:

Hongzhou school teaches that the arising of mental activity, the movement of thought, snapping the fingers, or moving the eyes, all actions and activities are the functioning of the entire essence of the Buddha-nature. Since there is no other kind of functioning, greed, anger, and folly, the performance of good and bad actions, and the experiencing of their pleasurable and painful consequences are all, in their entirety, Buddha-nature.[47]

When delusion and enlightenment, good and evil, are collapsed in a manner suggested by Zongmi, a host of issues are raised, not least in the ethical sphere, where such views can lead to antinomianism. It is possible to take issue with the completeness and accuracy of Zongmi's depiction of the Hongzhou school's teaching, but putting that aside for the moment, it is important to note that he presents a plausible interpretation that ensues from a facile assertion of an essential unity between the minds of ordinary people and the Buddha. As we will see, others both outside and within the Hongzhou school expressed concern about possible misinterpretations of Mazu's adage and took issue with doctrinal and soteriological ramifications arising from the teaching concerning the identity of mind and Buddha.

Some Critiques

As has already been noted, the tathāgatagarbha doctrine was open to critiques, especially for its propensity to reify the "true mind" and construe it as an *ātman*-like essence.[48] This led to the postulation of an intrinsically pure and permanent substratum of ontic subjectivity, which allegedly resides in each person and constitutes the basis of phenomenal existence. Moreover, in the sphere of practical application, there was the lurking danger: the idea that defilements are illusory and everyone is fundamentally enlightened might foster a sense of complacency or be used to justify lax attitudes toward ethical observances and religious practices. Because of such concerns, the teaching about the identity of mind and Buddha prompted warnings and criticism from various quarters.

One of the prominent Chan monks to voice such a criticism was Huizhong, who branded this doctrine as heretical.[49] Huizhong's criticisms—directed toward unnamed "teachers from the South" (*nanfang zhishi*)—are presented alongside his disapproving remarks about unwarranted altering of the text of the *Platform Scripture*, and the two might be connected. Huizhong's comments touch upon key issues debated within the Chan movement during the mid-eighth century and draw attention to significant implications arising from an unqualified affirmation of basic identity between the minds of ordinary people and the Buddha. Huizhong's text begins with a newly arrived monk telling Huizhong about his study in the South. The monk says that there he learned the doctrine of "mind is Buddha," which apparently was taught by a number of teachers. According to them, the mind's nature transcends birth and death and is everlasting; it is behind all physical and mental acts and forms the basis of all seeing, hearing, attentiveness, and knowing.

In his response, Huizhong dismisses this teaching as misguided, comparing the Southern teachers to heretics who teach the *ātman* doctrine, which postulates a permanent soul that is reborn when the body dies. Huizhong chides them for presenting such nonsense as the essential teaching of the Southern school and laments the unwarranted revising of the text of the *Platform Scripture*.[50] In another passage, Huizhong clarifies that he is not against the notion of Buddha-nature per se; he only takes issue with Southern teachers' ill-advised confusion of the deluded mind (*wangxin*) with the true mind (*zhenxin*), and worldly wisdom (*shizhi*) with Buddha wisdom (*fozhi*).[51] That is to say, it is wrong to equate the everyday, deluded mind of an ordinary person, filled with desires and attachments, with the enlightened mind of the Buddha.

The identity of the anonymous teachers from the South is not clear, and there are uncertainties about the historical context behind Huizhong's criticisms. Huizhong died thirteen years before Mazu, and it seems that Mazu and his disciples were not the main objects of Huizhong's censure.[52] In light of the comments about the rewriting of the *Platform Scripture*, it seems probable that Huizhong's critique was directed toward Shenhui or monks connected with him, although there is no conclusive evidence to prove this hypothesis.

Chan teachers associated with the Hongzhou school voiced similar concerns. For example, strongly worded criticisms along similar lines appear in Baizhang's record. There, he reproaches as heretics those who attach to "original purity" and "fundamental liberation" and consider themselves Buddhas or "their own self to be the path."[53] As has been noted, Baizhang also assigns the statement "mind is Buddha" to the category of incomplete teaching, deeming it "dead words" used for teaching ordinary people.[54] An explicit critique of one-sided interpretations of "mind is Buddha" also appears in the record of Mazu's disciple Ruhui, who complains that after Mazu's death the compilers of his record (*yuben*) emphasized that tenet exclusively. By doing so, he argues, they presented a misleading account of Mazu's teachings.[55] Similarly, Baoji, another disciple of Mazu, is recorded as saying, "If you say that 'mind is Buddha,' right now, you have not yet entered the arcane and subtle," while Funiu is quoted as asserting, "Mind is Buddha is a statement [that is like] looking for illness where there is no illness."[56]

An instructive case in point of a critique of substantialist interpretations of "mind is Buddha" comes in the form of a conversation between Nanquan and an anonymous monk. The conversation appears in post-Tang texts, and it might be an edited summary of Nanquan's discussions on the subject presented in a dialogue format, rather than a verbatim record of an actual conversation.[57] At any rate, the conversation recapitulates Nanquan's responses to misapprehensions of Mazu's teaching about "mind is Buddha," which evidently were prevalent at the time. The conversation starts with a question posed by the anonymous monk, who is puzzled by a seeming discrepancy between Mazu's and Nanquan's teachings. He wonders why Nanquan rejects Mazu's teaching of "mind is Buddha":

At the time, a monk asked, "All past patriarchs, including the great teacher from Jiangxi [i.e., Mazu], have taught that 'mind is Buddha' and 'ordinary mind is the Way.' Now, the Reverend [i.e., Nanquan] says that 'mind is not Buddha' and 'wisdom is not the Way.' I have doubts about it. Can the Reverend be compassionate enough to explain this to me?"

Nanquan replied in a loud voice, "If you are a Buddha, how can it be that you still have doubts and have to ask this old monk? Where is there a Buddha who falls by the wayside, harboring doubts like that? I am not a Buddha, and I have not seen the patriarchs. Since it is you who is speaking like that, you can go to seek the patriarchs by yourself."[58]

In his rejoinder, Nanquan points to an apparent discrepancy between theory and reality, which underlines the questioner's basic assumptions. If the monk accepts the premise that he is already a Buddha, how does it happen that he is still harboring doubts and cannot know reality by himself, but instead goes around asking questions about it? Nanquan's response indicates that he is weary of literalist interpretations of Mazu's statements. He denies that he himself is a Buddha, which by extension implies that it is mistaken to assert that ordinary people are Buddhas. Thus he steers the discussion toward the domain of experienced, everyday reality and away from the abstract perspective of a putative absolute truth. The monk appears to go along with that and asks for further instructions:

The monk asked, "Since your reverence explains it in that way, what kind of support [i.e., practical instruction] can you offer to a student [like me]?"

Nanquan said, "Quickly lift empty space with your palm."

The monk asked, "Empty space has no movable form. How can I lift it?"

Nanquan said, "When you say that it is without movable form, that is already a movement. How could empty space say 'I have no movable form?' These are all just your manifest sentiments."

The monk asked, "Since [to say that] space is without movable form is just a manifest sentiment, then what did you asked me to lift?"

Nanquan said, "Since you already know that one cannot speak about lifting it, how are you going to help it?"[59]

In this section, Nanquan shifts the conversation's flow by evoking the image of empty space, which symbolizes the formlessness and ungraspability of reality. He implicitly suggests that the mind and Buddha referred to in

Mazu's statement are both devoid of self-nature. Like empty space, they cannot be grasped or apprehended. That causes the student to reformulate his question:

> The monk asked, "Since 'mind is Buddha' is not correct, is it that 'mind becomes Buddha?'"
>
> Nanquan said, "'Mind is Buddha' and 'mind becomes Buddha' are just ideas created by your thinking. The Buddha is a person who has wisdom; the mind is a host that collects things. When confronted with things, they perform subtle functions. Do not conceive of mind, and do not conceive of Buddha. Whatever you conceive of, it becomes an object [of attachment]. This is the so-called 'delusion of knowing.' Because of that, the great teacher from Jiangxi said, 'It is not mind, it is not Buddha,' and 'it is not a thing.' He wanted to teach you, people of later generations, how to act. Nowadays, students put on their robes and walk around doubting things that are of no concern to them. Have you attained anything that way?"[60]

Nanquan goes on to point out that "mind" and "Buddha" are both just conceptual constructs. They are insubstantial and lack inherent reality. Consequently, he warns against reifying and becoming attached to them. He then introduces into the discussion two different statements taught by Mazu: "it is neither mind nor Buddha" and "it is not a thing." These two statements imply a critical reassessment of the doctrine of "mind is Buddha," pretty much along the lines of Nanquan's critique. In effect, throughout the whole discussion Nanquan is engaged in exegesis of Mazu's earlier statements and teachings. The monk continues his questioning by going back to Nanquan's two statements that appeared at the beginning of the dialogue:

> The monk asked, "Since 'it is not mind, it is not Buddha, and 'it is not a thing' are not correct, what does the Reverend mean when he says 'mind is not Buddha,' and 'wisdom is not the Way?'"
>
> Nanquan said, "Don't consider that mind is [not?] Buddha and that wisdom is not the Way.[61] I have no mind to bring up. What are you going to attach to?"
>
> The monk asked, "If there is nothing at all, then in which way it is different from empty space?"
>
> Nanquan said, "Since it is not a thing, how can you compare it to empty space? Also, who spoke of sameness and difference?"
>
> The monk said, "It cannot be that now 'it is not mind, it is not Buddha,' and 'it is not a thing' are not right!"
>
> Nanquan said, "If you understand it that way, it just becomes 'mind is Buddha' again."[62]

Nanquan extends his critique to the new set of negating statements that replaced the first pair. While "it is neither mind nor Buddha" and "it is not a thing" were introduced in order to counteract attachments and one-sided views arising from the first pair of statements, they are also not to be grasped as unassailable expressions of reality or absolute truths. Nanquan suggests that the true nature of either the mind or the Buddha cannot be predicated in a meaningful way. Attempts to impute substantial existence, or to construe an intrinsically enlightened "true mind" that has an ontological basis, create delusory objects of discriminating knowledge.

Nanquan's reluctance to provide direct answers to the monk's questions suggests that the underlying assumptions the questioner brings into the discussion function as obstacles to genuine understanding. Accordingly, Nanquan's answers try to lead the monk to question and eventually let go of such assumptions, thus opening his mind to viewing reality in a new way. The dialogue represents an engaging way of instruction, in which a Chan teacher instructs his student to abandon preconceived notions and fixed views about the nature of mind and objective reality. Only when dualistic views are obliterated and discrimination ends, according to Nanquan's thinking, is there a possibility for authentic realization.

Nanquan's conversation concurs with Baizhang's counsel to "go beyond the four propositions" (Chinese: *siju fenbie*; Sanskrit: *catuṣkoṭi*) and "realize emptiness," ideas originally propounded by the Madhyamaka school.[63] Any interpretation of the relationship between the mind and the Buddha—such as that the mind is intrinsically enlightened or that it can be transformed into the Buddha-mind through methods of spiritual cultivation—can become a source of attachment. When that happens, even the most profound doctrine turns into a hindrance that prevents the arising of genuine wisdom (as was noted in the preceding discussion of *upāya*). This point of view is especially evident in Baizhang's record, which contains such statements as "There has never been such a thing as Buddha—do not understand it as Buddha. 'Buddha' is a medicine for living beings. When there is no illness, one should not take medicine. When medicine and illness are both dissolved, it is like pure water."[64] Similarly, in the following passage Baizhang again calls for the relinquishment of all views:

> Just have no doctrines of existence, non-existence, and so on. Also, have no views of existence, non-existence, and so on. One by one, pass through and beyond the three propositions. . . . [65] If you create a view about the Buddha or a view about the Dharma, or view about anything at all—existent, non-existent, or whatever—these are all called erroneous visions of those with eye disease. Because of what is seen, they are also called the enclosure of views, the lid of views, and the affliction of views.[66]

This passage constitutes a forceful refutation of all reifications and conceptual attachments, including, as was the case with previous excerpts from the same text, interpretations of the tathāgatagarbha doctrine that postulate the existence of a substance or essence that inheres in each person. This critical assessment seems to be generic rather than directed toward a specific group or individual. It implies a conception of Buddha-nature that is stripped of sticky ontological and epistemic connotations and is in accord with the doctrine of emptiness. That brings us back to the conception of religious teachings as *upāya*, a strategy that could be (and was) used to gloss over problems of interpretation such as those identified here. If a teaching such as "mind is Buddha" is simply an *upāya*, intended to offer practical spiritual guidance to a specific audience, rather than a definitive philosophical formulation of the nature of reality, then some of the criticisms arising from its doctrinal and soteriological implications are deflected. To illustrate that, let us go back to Mazu's record.

"It Is Not a Thing"

It appears that some disciples made efforts to counteract views and interpretations derived from Mazu's teaching regarding "mind is Buddha," which they found problematic. On the other hand, critical reassessments of "mind is Buddha" along the same lines also appear in Mazu's record. Presumably, Mazu's disciples were not taking their teacher to task; rather, they were critical of what they perceived as misunderstandings and ill-advised readings of his teachings. In fact, their critiques take a clue from some of Mazu's comments. Mazu's refutation—or rather qualification—of his adage "mind is Buddha" comes in the form of a discussion between him and an anonymous monk:[67]

> A monk asked, "Why does the Reverend say that mind is Buddha?"
> Mazu said, "To stop small children's crying."
> The monk asked, "What do you say when they have stopped crying?"
> Mazu said, "[I say that] it is neither mind nor Buddha (*feixin feifo*)."
> The monk asked, "And when you have someone who does not belong to either of these two categories, how do you instruct him?"
> Mazu said, "I tell him that it is not a thing (*bushi wu*)."
> The monk asked, "And how about when you suddenly meet someone who is there?"
> Mazu said, "I teach him to intuitively realize the great Way."[68]

In this revealing passage, Mazu underscores the pragmatic function of religious teachings as heuristic devices geared toward specific audiences, in accord with the understanding of *upāya* discussed previously. Teachings and doctrines are not to be interpreted literally or grasped as definitive statements about the nature of mind or reality. Declarations such as "mind is Buddha" and "neither mind nor Buddha" are to be construed as codes embedded in larger theoretical templates that chart a path of practice and realization.[69] Different teachings are applicable to particular points on the path and are directed toward individuals at specific stages of spiritual development.

Within Mazu's scheme, "mind is Buddha" functions as an elementary teaching aimed toward beginning students ("small children") with limited spiritual aptitude and comprehension (which, as noted above, is also the way Baizhang puts it). That teaching is meant to inspire faith and confidence in one's abilities, inducing the practitioner to direct his or her mental energies inwardly, instead of seeking outside or relying on an external salvific agency.

In due course, facile belief in the basic identity of one's mind and the Buddha mind becomes a source of attachment and needs to be negated. Hence the second adage, "it is neither mind nor Buddha." Such negation is eventually superseded by a more refined understanding of reality as something that cannot be reduced to an essence or a basic principle. Since at that point there is no concrete object of knowledge, and there is a realization that reality cannot be predicated by means of signs or concepts, Mazu simply states, "it is not a thing." This negation invites comparison with the third line of the famous verse attributed to Huineng, found in later editions of the *Platform Scripture*: "originally there is not a thing" (*benlai wu yi wu*).[70] Similar phrases appear in other early Chan texts, such as the Northern school's *Wu fangbian*.[71] Eventually, even that subtle knowledge or realization is given up. Having forsaken all views and attachments, the Chan adept simply experiences reality ("the Way") as it truly is.

We can conceivably interpret (or perhaps over-interpret) the above dialogue as implying a *panjiao* type of doctrinal taxonomy, with each of Mazu's statements representing a different doctrinal position. Like other doctrinal taxonomies, this one would be hierarchical and have a cumulative effect. The first and most elementary level, represented by the statement "mind is Buddha," would correspond to an essentialist interpretation of the tathāgatagarbha doctrine. At the second level, there is an apophatic turn, an epistemic shift that involves a Madhyamaka type of deconstruction that negates the validity of the previous conceptualization of mind and Buddha, expressed by the statement "it is neither mind nor Buddha." The third level takes that a step further: as all views are abandoned, there is a realization that reality is not something that possesses an identifiable essence or substance (hence "it is not a thing"); therefore, it is misleading to impute any quality or characteristic to it. Finally,

at the fourth level, we have an unqualified transcendence and a direct apprehension of ultimate reality. Predictably, the text provides no clues about the
nature of the culminating realization or the structure of the realm of reality,
which by definition are beyond words and concepts.

If we decode the suggested doctrinal taxonomy in terms of the main doctrinal systems of Mahāyāna, we have the tathāgatagarbha doctrine placed at
the bottom, below the Madhyamaka doctrine that correspond to levels two and
three. The third level can also be read as a Chinese synthesis of Madhyamaka
and Buddha-nature doctrines, one that shies away from imputing specific ontological underpinnings to the Buddha-nature by rejecting the notion of an
essence or substance—"not a thing"—but accepts a moderate version of the
Buddha-nature doctrine that does not contradict the teaching of emptiness.
The highest level can be interpreted as being analogous to the Chan experience of enlightenment or, in a more ecumenical sense, as the final perfection
of the Buddhist path. When compared with the five-fold doctrinal classification formulated by Zongmi (which is based on Fazang's famous classification
but diverges from it in significant aspects), it is striking that Mazu's placement
of the tathāgatagarbha and Madhyamaka doctrines is exactly the opposite of
the one introduced in Zongmi's scheme.[72]

It seems unlikely that Mazu intended to articulate an explicit doctrinal
taxonomy or engage in doctrinal polemics. The dialogue suggests a progressive
conception of the Path, but the hierarchical ordering of various teachings in
terms of their profundity does not necessary mean that Mazu postulates a series of stages that each person must go through in a specific order. The main
point is that different people are at different stages of spiritual development,
and different teachings are appropriate for different people. At the same time,
reality can be entered at any point because, as indicated by a phrase Mazu
quotes from Sengzhao, "the place one stands is the truth" (*lichu ji zhen*).[73] This
interpretation, which resonates with the Hongzhou school's understanding of
upāya and concurs with Mazu's assertion that the realization of reality does not
depend on cultivation, is illustrated by Damei's story:

> When Chan Teacher Fachang of Damei mountain went to see
> Mazu for the first time, he asked, "What is Buddha?" Mazu replied,
> "Mind is Buddha." [On hearing this,] Fachang had a great awakening.
>
> Later, he went to live on Damei mountain. When Mazu heard
> that he was residing on the mountain, he sent one of his monks to
> go there and ask Fachang, "What did the Reverend obtain when he
> saw Mazu, so that he has come to live on this mountain?" Fachang
> said, "Mazu told me that mind is Buddha, so I came to live here."
> The monk said, "Mazu's teaching has changed recently." Fachang
> asked, "What is the difference?" The monk said, "Nowadays he also

says, 'Neither mind nor Buddha.'" Fachang said, "That old man still hasn't stopped confusing people. You can have 'neither mind nor Buddha,' [but] I only care for 'mind is Buddha.'"

The monk returned to Mazu and reported what has happened. "The plum is ripe," said Mazu.[74]

The story implies that after Mazu's teaching about the identity of mind and Buddha precipitated Damei's enlightenment, he was comfortable enough with his realization that even after being told about Mazu's new teaching of "neither mind nor Buddha," he still affirmed the salvific value of the original teaching he received from Mazu. Damei's record of sayings (see figure 5.1, first page of the only extant edition of the manuscript) provides further discussion of Mazu's adages:

> When you simply do not place highest value on your bodies and lives, are not greedy for wealth and in love with others, do not follow various external conditions, do not give rise to lewdness, anger, and stupidity, [but instead] benefit all living beings—then that is "mind is Buddha." Have you seen the way of the Buddha? [As the *Vimalakīrti Scripture* says,] "Pure mind is the same as the Buddha mind, [even though] the body is the same as that of an ordinary person." Though the Buddha is different [from ordinary people], his nature is not different. Moreover, the saying "neither mind nor Buddha" is also intended to break your attachment. If you talk about the mind, what kind of form does it have? If you talk about the mind/heart inside the body, it can be seen and it is subject to decay, so how can we speak about it being beyond birth and death? It is for the sake of destroying your attachments that [Mazu] spoke of "neither mind nor Buddha."[75]

According to Damei, the fulfillment of "mind is Buddha" involves the perfection of detachment, mental purity, and compassion. Purity is defined in traditional terms, by the absence of defilements such as greed, sensual love (or sexual desire), anger, and stupidity, and by the presence of positive mental states. On the other hand, the negation of both mind and Buddha is introduced in order to break attachments to those mental states and challenge the conception of mind implied by the first statement. Here Damei adopts the familiar perspective that reality should not be reified or conceptualized.

The notion that teachings such as "mind is Buddha" are expedient devices is echoed in the records of other disciples. Another statement attributed to Nanquan makes the same point even more explicitly than the dialogue presented in the last section:

> Therefore, the old worthy from Jiangxi [i.e., Mazu] said, "neither mind nor Buddha" and "it is not a thing." Even though the late

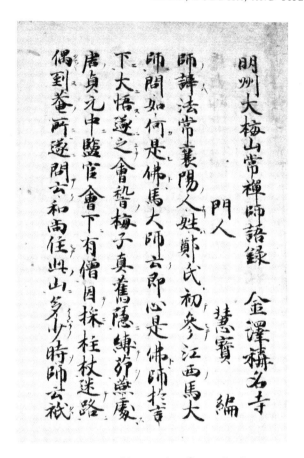

FIGURE 5.1. Manuscript of *Damei yulu*.

Patriarch [also] said, "mind is Buddha," that was just a statement for a particular occasion. That kind of speech is like an empty fist full of yellow leaves used to stop [children's] crying. Nowadays, many people say, "mind becomes Buddha" and "wisdom is the Way." They also consider all seeing, hearing, feeling, and knowing to be the Way. Isn't that being like Yajñadatta who sought his head after seeing his reflection in a mirror?[76] Even if he could find something that way, that would still not be his original head. That is why bodhisattva [Vimalakīrti] scolded Kātyāyana for trying to speak the true Dharma with the mind of birth and death.[77] These are all manifest sentiments. If one says, "mind is Buddha," that is like a hare or a horse with horns. If one says, "it is neither mind nor Buddha," that is like a cow or a goat without horns. If it is your mind, then what need is there of a Buddha? If it is not without form, then how can it be the Way?[78]

While Nanquan is especially critical of "mind is Buddha," in the end he relegates all three of Mazu's adages to the category of *upāya*. Baizhang's sermons express a similar point of view, albeit without directly citing Mazu's adages. In the following excerpt, Baizhang contends that any attempt to construe an image or description of reality is as futile as trying to carve a Buddha image out of empty space:

> Fundamentally, this principle is present in everyone. All the Buddhas and Bodhisattvas are called persons who point out a jewel. Originally, it is not a thing. You need not know or understand it; you need not affirm or deny it. Just cut off dualism. Cut off the supposition that it exists and the supposition that it does not exist. Cut off the supposition that it is non-existent and the supposition that it is not non-existent, so that there are no traces of either side. Then, when the two sides are brought up, you are unattached to them, and no measures can control you. [In reality,] there is neither deficiency nor sufficiency, neither profanity nor holiness, neither light nor darkness. That is not having knowledge, yet not lacking knowledge. It is neither bondage nor liberation. It is not any name or category at all. Why is this true speech? How can you carve and polish empty space to make a Buddha image? How can you say that emptiness is blue, yellow, red, or white?[79]

Baizhang reminds his audience that the true body of the Buddha is nothing other than emptiness. It transcends all forms and concepts and eludes all attempts to categorize or define it. One can realize its true nature only by abandoning dualism and letting go of all views and attachments.[80] Taking a clue from Mazu, Baizhang reiterates that one can obtain a glimpse of the realm of reality only by going beyond all concepts and verbal explanations. Consequently, doctrinal formulations such as "mind is Buddha" and "neither mind nor Buddha" are useful only insofar as they counteract mental fixations and facilitate the experience of nonduality, but in effect they are provisional and eventually have to be given up.

Ordinary Mind

Besides "mind is Buddha," the best-known adage attributed to Mazu is "ordinary mind is the Way" (*pingchang xin shi dao*).[81] Unlike "mind is Buddha," the expression "ordinary mind is the Way" was originally coined by Mazu. The two statements are closely related: the second adage expands on the first, pointing out that the realization of truth is to be found within the context of everyday life, in the mind of each person. The notion of "ordinary mind" points out the proximity and all-pervasiveness of reality. In one of his sermons, Mazu defines "ordinary mind":

> The Way needs no cultivation; just prevent defilement. What is defilement? When with a mind of birth and death one acts in a contrived manner, then everything is defilement. If one wants to know the Way directly: ordinary mind is the Way! What do I mean by "ordinary mind?" [It is a mind] that is devoid of [contrived] activity, and is without [notions of] right and wrong, grasping and rejecting, terminable and permanent, worldly and holy. The [*Vimalakīrti*] scripture says, "Neither the practice of ordinary people, nor the practice of sages, that is the Bodhisattva's practice."[82] Just now, whether walking, standing, sitting, or reclining, responding to situations and dealing with people as they come: everything is the Way.[83]

Presumably Mazu directs these instructions to monks engaged in contemplative practice. In that context, they serve as instruction about the cultivation of a holistic state of awareness, in which the mind abandons all defilements and is unattached to dualistic concepts such as worldliness and holiness, permanence and impermanence. One of Mazu's key points is that such a mental state can be perfected within the context of everyday life. Since all things and events partake of the character of reality, they provide avenues for the cultivation of detachment and transcendence. The passage can also be read as a caution against quietist withdrawal from the world and the cultivation of refined states of meditative absorption, symbolized by the sages who follow the Hīnayāna path.

From Mazu's perspective, the state of "ordinary mind" is the goal of practice. It also denotes a method of cultivation, which involves single-minded endeavor to maintain a detached state of nondual awareness. In that context, religious practice involves a constant effort to abstain from giving rise to discriminating thoughts, which bifurcate reality into dualistic opposites and obscure the essential nature of the "ordinary mind." When the practitioner perfects such a mental state, his or her mind becomes freed from fixations and grasping, as the unobstructed function of the ordinary mind manifests in ordinary acts. As affirmed in one of the poems of Pang Yun (d. 808?), Mazu's famous lay disciple, when someone is liberated, the "supernatural powers (*abhijñā*) and sublime activity" traditionally associated with Mahāyāna notions of spiritual perfection are manifested in such prosaic acts as fetching water and carrying firewood:

> My daily activity is not different,
> It is only that I am spontaneously in harmony with it;
> Not grasping or rejecting anything,
> Everywhere there is nothing to assert or oppose.

Whose are the titles of [those who wear] vermilion and purple?[84]
The mountain is without a speck of dust.
Supernatural powers and wonderful activity:
Fetching water and carrying firewood.[85]

The sublime ordinariness described in Pang Yun's poem presupposes that ultimate reality permeates everything. Suchness, reality, truth, and so forth, are purportedly manifest in all things and events, and infuse all aspects of human life. Since everything partakes of the character of reality, according to Mazu and Pang Yun, authentic practice and realization do not presuppose leaving the ordinary world. In fact, they both insinuate that there is no other place to go. For better or worse, human beings exist in this world and create their own reality. Therefore, spiritual liberation is pursued and realized within the human world, which is not apart from the realm of reality. Mazu describes the all-pervasiveness of truth/reality:

"There is no place to stand where one leaves the Truth."[86] The very place one stands on is the Truth; it is all one's being. If that is not so, then who is that? All dharmas [things] are Buddhadharmas and all dharmas are liberation. Liberation is identical with suchness. All dharmas never leave suchness. Whether walking, standing, sitting, or reclining, everything is always the inconceivable function [of suchness]. The scriptures say that the Buddha is everywhere.[87]

Mazu's explication of ordinary mind, accompanied by a declaration of the ubiquitous presence of reality, evokes a sense of spontaneity and freedom. Such sentiments are made more explicit in the records of later generations of disciples. Here are a few excerpts that expand on Mazu's idea of ordinary mind, the first from the biography of Changsha Jingcen (d. 868), a leading disciple of Nanquan, in *Chuandeng lu*, and the next two from Linji's record of sayings:

A monk asked, "What is [the meaning of Mazu's saying] 'ordinary mind is the Way?'" Changsha replied, "When I want to sleep, I sleep. When I want to sit down, I sit." The monk said, "I do not understand." Changsha replied, "When it is hot, I cool myself. When it is cold, I get close to the fire."[88]

Within the Buddhadharma, there is no room for an [exceptional] exertion of effort. It is only [a matter of being] ordinary, without concerns. Defecate, urinate, wear your clothes, and eat your food. When tired, lay down [to rest]. Fools laugh at me, but the wise understand me.[89]

From the point of view of this mountain monk, there are not that many things [you need to be anxious about]. Only be ordinary, wearing your clothes and eating your food, passing your time without any concerns. [All of] you, coming from various directions, you all have minds [set on something]. You seek the Buddha, seek the Dharma, and seek liberation and transcendence of the three realms. Fools! If you want to leave the three realms, where are you going to go?[90]

This kind of exultation of ordinariness raises some of the concerns noted earlier, including Zongmi's charge that the Hongzhou school taught that "greed, anger, and folly, the performance of good and bad actions, and the experiencing of their pleasurable and painful consequences are all, in their entirety, Buddha-nature."[91] Taking that as a clue, some commentators have suggested that Mazu's ordinary mind corresponds to the everyday mind of ordinary people, which encompasses both purity and defilement, good and evil, awakening and ignorance.[92] Although Mazu's comments are pithy and open to interpretation, such an analysis does not hold. Besides all the evidence about the Hongzhou school's conception of mind and reality introduced in the last three sections, the cited passage in which Mazu defines the ordinary mind makes it clear that he does not include the impure mind and its unwholesome mental states. In the first sentence of the cited passage, he calls for an end of mental defilements. He then explains that the ordinary mind "is devoid of [contrived] activity and without [the notions of] right or wrong, grasping or rejecting, terminable or permanent, worldly or holy." Evidently, he is not collapsing the pure and impure mind or identifying the Buddha-nature with the deluded mind of ordinary people. Instead, he is talking about the nondual mind, which is divested of impurities and transcends all views and attachments.

In that sense, ordinary mind is compatible with the notion of no-mind, which implies a state of mind that maintains numinous awareness but is free from discrimination and attachment. No-mind and the related concept of no-thought appear in a number of early Chan texts, such as *Erru sixing lun*, *Wuxin lun* (Treatise on No-mind; attributed, probably falsely, to Bodhidharma), the *Platform Scripture*, and *Lidai fabao ji*. The two terms are absent from Mazu's sermons and rarely appear in the records of his direct disciples, although, as already noted, no-mind plays a central role in Huangbo's records. The idea of ordinary mind has unique connotations and exemplifies attempts to point to an ideal state of mind by means of positive expressions, in contrast to negative terms such as no-mind and no-thought. Nevertheless, in essence both "ordinary mind" and "no-mind" imply negation of the deluded, discriminating mind of everyday experience, as is evident when we compare Mazu's explanation of ordinary mind with Huangbo's depictions of no-mind. In addition to the passages from Huangbo's records cited earlier in this chapter, there is this explanation of no-mind: "No-mind is the absence of all kinds of [discriminating] mind. Its original essence is inwardly like wood and stone, unmoving and unshakable, and outwardly like empty space, unblocked and unobstructed. It is without subject and object, without locus, without form, and beyond gain and loss."[93] Both ordinary mind and no-mind clearly imply the cessation of conceptual attachments and transcendence of the discriminating mind.

When taken out of context, however, the teaching of ordinary mind can be interpreted in ways that raise the specter of Chan antinomianism. If truth is to be found in everything and can be realized in the context of everyday life, does that not imply that religious practices and institutions are superfluous? Such a line of reasoning seemingly undermines the rationale behind monastic life.[94] Concerns such as this, along with the problems of interpretation raised in the preceding section, bring us back to the need to place the statements of Mazu and his disciples within their pertinent historical and institutional contexts. Teachings such as "ordinary mind" evolved within a medieval monastic framework. When instructing his monastic disciples to cultivate an "ordinary mind," it is safe to presume that Mazu was not advocating a rejection of traditional regimens of monastic discipline or glorifying a secular lifestyle. As has already been noted, disciplined monastic life was the backdrop against which Mazu and his followers framed and implemented their teachings and practices.[95] Accordingly, the naturalness and spontaneity evoked by the idea of "ordinary mind" was to be realized within the context of well-ordered monastic life.

In practical terms, within the medieval monastic milieu notions such as ordinary mind could be understood as attempts to bridge the gap between everyday actions and experiences on one hand and religious acts and functions on another. This implies expansion of the domain of practice, so that it encompasses even such routine acts as eating and putting on the robes. Yet, the spontaneity of ordinary mind was to be realized within the confines of established monastic mores and institutions. Theoretically, this enabled the individual to function in specific socioreligious surroundings without being defined or imprisoned by them. If this analysis holds, then as a religious ideal "ordinary mind" denotes a liberated state of mind, in which the Chan adept may transcend discriminating thought and dualism, even while he freely responds to things and engages in everyday events, without hindrance or confusion.

NOTES

1. There are parallels here with the Madhyamaka tradition. See Liu, *Madhyamaka Thought in China*, 103.

2. BGL, XZJ 118.88a; Cleary, *Pai-chang*, 62. The three stages are discussed in "Stages of the Path" in chapter 6.

3. BGL, XZJ 118.87a; Cleary, *Pai-chang*, 56. Similar ideas can be found in canonical texts, especially the *Huayan Scripture*.

4. Hirano Sōjō, *Tongo yōmon*, 7, 24; Blofeld, *The Zen Teaching of Instantaneous Awakening*, 43, 49–50.

5. Hirano, *Tongo yōmon*, 14; Blofeld, *The Zen Teaching of Instantaneous Awakening*, 45. See also MY, XZJ 119.406c; Cheng-chien, *Sun-Face Buddha*, 65.

6. Hirano, *Tongo yōmon*, 38; Blofeld, *The Zen Teaching of Instantaneous Awakening*, 56.

7. *Dunwu rudao yaomen lun*, XZJ 110.421a; Hirano, *Tongo yōmon*, 14–15; Blofeld, *The Zen Teaching of Instantaneous Awakening*, 45–46.

8. MY, XZJ 119.406c; Cheng-chien, *Sun-Face Buddha*, 66.

9. Quotation from the *Vimalakīrti Scripture;* T 14.554a. The same expression also appears in *Baozang lun* 1, T 45.149a.

10. MY, XZJ 119.406c–d; Cheng-chien, *Sun-Face Buddha*, 66. See also Dazhu's similar statement in Hirano, *Tongo yōmon*, 91–92; and Blofeld, *The Zen Teaching of Instantaneous Awakening*, 76.

11. The notion of One Mind is emphasized in Huangbo's records. It appears in the first sentence of the first record, which reads: "All the Buddhas and all living beings are only One Mind, and there is nothing else." T 48.379c; cf. Blofeld, *The Zen Teaching of Huang-po*, 29.

12. MY, XZJ 119.406d–407a; Cheng-chien, *Sun-Face Buddha*, 67–68.

13. MY, XZJ 119.406a–b; Cheng-chien, *Sun-Face Buddha*, 63. The quoted passage is part of a response to a question posed by an anonymous monk.

14. *Huangboshan duanji chanshi chuanxin fayao*, T 48.379c–380a; Iriya Yoshitaka, *Denshin hōyō, Enryō roku*, 77–80; Blofeld, *The Zen Teaching of Huang-po*, 63.

15. *Chuanxin fayao*, T 48.380c; Iriya, *Denshin hōyō, Enryō roku*, 20–23; Blofeld, *The Zen Teaching of Huang-po*, 38.

16. *Chuanxin fayao*, T 48.381a; Iriya, *Denshin hōyō, Enryō roku*, 25–27; cf. Blofeld, *The Zen Teaching of Huang-po*, 40.

17. BGL (*Sijia yulu* ed.), XZJ 119.411a–b; Cheng-chien, *Sun-Face Buddha*, 103; cf. Cleary, *Pai-chang*, 79.

18. BGL (*Sijia yulu* ed.), XZJ 119.411a; Cleary, *Pai-chang*, 78.

19. For Vimalakīrti's famous silence, see T 14.551c, and Burton Watson, *The Vimalakīrti Sūtra*, 110. The silence represents Vimalakīrti's reply to a question about the teaching of nonduality. His silent response comes after a series of rejoinders made by various bodhisattvas, each of whom introduces a pair of well-known dualistic opposites—such as saṃsāra and Nirvāṇa, purity and impurity, good and evil—to explain how ultimate reality transcends them. The last speaker is Mañjuśrī, the bodhisattva of wisdom, who points out that one enters the teaching of nonduality when all words and speech are abandoned, when there is no knowledge, no questions, and no answers. While Mañjuśrī points out that ultimate reality is ineffable, he still relies on words in order to communicate his understanding. Vimalakīrti's silence is construed as a superior response because it represents a concrete expression of the true meaning of nonduality, without falling into the web of conceptual constructs and verbal explanations.

20. Analogous perspectives are presented in other canonical texts, as well as the works of Chinese scholiasts. Among non-Mahāyāna texts, similar perspectives are expressed in passages in the *Sutta-nipāta* that describe the Buddha's perfected disciples; for example: "Abandoning what has been taken up, and not taking it up [again], he would not depend even upon knowledge. He indeed does not follow any

faction among those who hold different views. He does not believe any view at all." K. R. Norman, *The Rhinoceros Horn and Other Early Buddhist Poems (Sutta-nipāta)*, 135. A similar idea is expressed by the famous simile of the raft, which is alluded to in Baizhang's record.

21. For example, in the *Perfection of Wisdom in Eight Thousand Lines*, after telling the gods that the various classes of beings, including the Buddha, are like a magical illusion, Subhuti goes on to proclaim that even Nirvāṇa is like a magical illusion, and that even if there were something that surpassed Nirvāṇa, that would still be like a magical illusion. He then goes on to add that no (fixed) Dharma has been communicated or indicated by his presentation of the perfection of wisdom. See Edward Conze, *The Perfection of Wisdom in Eight Thousand Lines and Its Verse Summary*, 88–89.

22. For *Erru sixing lun*, see McRae, *The Northern School*, 102–3; for *Xiuxin yaolun*, see p. 130; and for *Wu fangbian*, see pp. 171–96 and 218–30. The five *upāya* discussed in *Wu fangbian* are: (1) comprehensive explanation of the essence of Buddhahood, (2) opening the gates of wisdom and sagacity, (3) manifesting the inconceivable Dharma, (4) elucidation of the true nature of the dharmas, and (5) the naturally unobstructed path of emancipation.

23. BGL, XZJ 118.89b–c; Cleary, *Pai-chang*, 71.

24. BGL, XZJ 118.87d; Cleary, *Pai-chang*, 60.

25. BGL, XZJ 118.82d; cf. Cleary, *Pai-chang*, 29.

26. BGL, XZJ 118.82d; Cleary, *Pai-chang*, 30.

27. BGL, XZJ 118.84a, 84b; Cleary, *Pai-chang*, 37, 39.

28. BGL, XZJ 118.84a–b; Cleary, *Pai-chang*, 37–38. The statements "Mind is Buddha" and "neither mind nor Buddha" are discussed in the next three sections.

29. Hirano, *Tongo yōmon*, 56–57; Blofeld, *The Zen Teaching of Instantaneous Awakening*, 62.

30. BGL, XZJ 118.84b; Cleary, *Pai-chang*, 38.

31. See MY, XZJ 119.405d, 408b; Cheng-chien, *Sun-Face Buddha*, 62, 73, 78.

32. CDL 29, T 51.449b, and CDL 30, T 51.457a, respectively.

33. See Ishikawa Rikizan, "Basozen ni okeru sokushin sokubutsu no rekishiteki kadai," 153, and Suzuki, *Tō-godai zenshū shi*, 376–77.

34. T 10.102a; Thomas Cleary, *The Flower Ornament Scripture*, vol. 1, 452.

35. T 48.404b–c and Gregory, *Tsung-mi*, 217.

36. MY, XZJ 119.405d; Cheng-chien, *Sun-Face Buddha*, 62. Similar versions of the sermon in which this statement appears can also be found in CDL 6, T 51.246a; ZJL 1, T 48.418b; ZTJ 14.304; TGDL 8, XZJ 135.326b–c.

37. MY, XZJ 119.406c; Cheng-chien, *Sun-Face Buddha*, 67.

38. MY, XZJ 119.406c; Cheng-chien, *Sun-Face Buddha*, 67. This paragraph is a paraphrase from a section at the beginning of the *Awakening of Faith*. For the relevant passage, see *Dasheng qixin lun* 1, T 32.575c; and Yoshito S. Hakeda, *The Awakening of Faith*, 28.

39. ZJL 14, T 48.492a.

40. The adage "Mind is Buddha" appears only at two places in BGL; in the first instance, cited above, it is critiqued as an example of the incomplete teaching.

41. The adage "Mind is Buddha" is not cited in Dazhu's treatise; it only appears a couple of times in the record of Dazhu's discussions with various students, a Song-

period compilation of questionable provenance that is traditionally attached to his treatise.

42. The exact adage appears thirteen times in Huangbo's two records; there are even more instances of variations on the same theme, as can be seen in the quotations that follow. It seems as if after questionings of the adage's implications among the first-generation disciples, within the second generation there was a renewed interest in adopting its perspective and exploring its spiritual potency as a teaching tool. Such differences can of course also be explained in terms of the personal points of view and intellectual predilections of the monks in question.

43. Quotation from a verse in *Jin guangming jing* 2, T 16.344b.

44. *Wanling lu*, T 48.384b; Iriya, *Denshin hōyō, Enryō roku*, 94; cf. Blofeld, *The Zen Teaching of Huang-po*, 67–68.

45. *Wanling lu*, T 48.385b; Iriya, *Denshin hōyō, Enryō roku*, 117–23; Blofeld, *The Zen Teaching of Huang-po*, 78.

46. *Wanling lu*, T 48.386b; Iriya, *Denshin hōyō, Enryō roku*, 134–38; cf. Blofeld, *The Zen Teaching of Huang-po*, 87. For additional examples of discussions of "mind is Buddha" in Huangbo's records, see T 48.379c, 383a.

47. XZJ 110.435d; Gregory, *Tsung-mi*, 237.

48. See "The Traditions and Doctrines of Tang Buddhism" in chapter 4.

49. For a discussion of Huizhong's criticisms, see Ishii, "Nanyō Echū no nanpō shūshi no hihan ni tsuite."

50. CDL 28, T 51.437c–38a.

51. CDL 28, T 51.438c.

52. See Ishii, "Nanyō Echū no nanpō shūshi no hihan ni tsuite," 326–27.

53. BGL, XZJ 118.87b; Cleary, *Pai-chang*, 58.

54. See the discussion of the incomplete teaching in the section "Expedient Means" in this chapter.

55. ZTJ 15.338.

56. For Baoji, see CDL 7, T 51.253b, and ZTJ 15.330; for Funiu, see CDL 7, T 51.253b. In both instances, they go on to comment on Mazu's second adage, "neither mind nor Buddha" (discussed in the next section).

57. Then again, its inclusion in Nanquan's record in fascicle 28 of CDL suggests that it is a fairly reliable record of his teachings. That fascicle reproduces records of famous Tang-period Chan teachers, which presumably circulated as independent texts during the mid-tenth century at the latest.

58. CDL 28, T 51.445b; cf. *Gu zunsu yulu* 12, XZJ 118.146b; Cheng-chien, *Sun-Face Buddha*, 109–10.

59. CDL 28, T 51.445b; cf. *Gu zunsu yulu* 12, XZJ 118.146b–c; Cheng-chien, *Sun-Face Buddha*, 110.

60. CDL 28, T 51.445b; cf. *Gu zunsu yulu* 12, XZJ 118.146c; Cheng-chien, *Sun-Face Buddha*, 110.

61. It seems that the primary text has a misprint and omits a negating particle.

62. CDL 28, T 51.445b; cf. *Gu zunsu yulu* 12, XZJ 118.146c; Cheng-chien, *Sun-Face Buddha*, 110–11.

63. BGL, XZJ 118.85c; Cleary, *Pai-chang*, 48. The four propositions or logical possibilities are: empty, existent, both empty and existent, neither empty nor existent.

64. BGL, XZJ 118.83c; Cleary, *Pai-chang*, 34.

65. The three propositions are discussed in "Stages of the Path" in chapter 6.

66. BGL, XZJ 118.87a; Cleary, *Pai-chang*, 56.

67. Like Nanquan's discussion presented in the previous section, this dialogue appears in later sources. Although it is uncertain whether it is a record of an actual conversation, in light of the other pertinent sources introduced here, there are no compelling reasons to doubt that it presents a summary of Mazu's views on the subject. The excerpts from the records of disciples such as Ruhui, Nanquan, and Damei cited in these pages clearly attribute the adages "it is not mind, it is not Buddha" and "it is not a thing" to Mazu.

68. MY, XZJ 119.408b; Cheng-chien, *Sun-Face Buddha*, 78.

69. Suzuki Tetsuo has argued that throughout his stay at Gonggong mountain Mazu taught only "mind is Buddha" and that he developed the teaching of "neither mind nor Buddha" only after his move to Kaiyuan monastery in Hongzhou, during the final years of his teaching career. Suzuki, *Tō-godai zenshū shi*, 379–81. There is no way to establish a chronology of Mazu's teaching, so Suzuki's argument is hypothetical and not supported by pertinent evidence. See also Jia, "Doctrinal Reformation of the Hongzhou School of Chan Buddhism," 8–9.

70. For this and other versions of the verse, see Yampolsky, *The Platform Sūtra*, 94, 132.

71. See McRae, *The Northern School*, 237–38.

72. For Zongmi's classification scheme, see Kimura Kiyotaka, *Chūgoku kegon shisōshi*, 229–32, and Gregory, *Tsung-mi*, 134–35.

73. See MY, XZJ 119.406d; Cheng-chien, *Sun-Face Buddha*, 66. The paragraph where this phrase appears is translated in the final section of this chapter.

74. XZJ 119.47c–d; translation adapted from Cheng-chien, *Sun-Face Buddha*, 73–74. In the SGSZ biography, it is Yanguan who says, "The plum is ripe." The same applies to a longer version of the story in ZTJ 15.335–36. To make matters more complicated, in the CDL version of the story (T 51.254c), which for the most part is similar to the ZTJ version, Yanguan also plays a part in the story line, but the final part is the same as in the MY version. It goes without saying that, in light of the differing version, the provenance and historicity of the story are open to doubt.

75. *Mingzhou dameishan chang chanshi yulu*, in *Kanazawa bunko shiryō zensho: Butten 1, zenseki hen*, 16. This text was lost and is not mentioned in any of the standard Chan chronicles and histories; it is extant only as an ancient manuscript, preserved in the Kanazawa bunko collection in Yokohama. See the discussion in the section on Damei in "Growth in the Lower Yangtze Region" in chapter 2.

76. The story of Yajñadatta comes from the *Śūragama Scripture*. See T 19.121b. According to the story, one day Yajñadatta looked into a mirror and saw his eyebrows and eyes; however, not seeing them on his head, he became crazy and went around looking for his head.

77. In the "Disciples" chapter of the *Vimalakīrti Scripture*, Kātyāyana—one of the Buddha's ten great disciples, regarded as foremost in the expounding of doctrine—is reproved by Vimalakīrti for speaking the true Dharma with a mind of birth and death. See T 14.541a.

78. *Gu zunsu yulu* 12, XZJ 118.148a; Cheng-chien, *Sun-Face Buddha*, 109. There are a number of other references to Mazu's adages in Nanquan's record. Here is another example: "When the reverend from Jiangxi (i.e., Mazu) taught 'mind is Buddha,' that was only speech that was appropriate for a given occasion, meant to cure the illness of busily seeking [the truth outside of oneself]. It was an expression that served as yellow leaves in an empty fist, used to stop [small child's] crying. Therefore, he [also] said, 'it is neither mind nor Buddha,' and 'it is not a thing.'" ZTJ 16.351. See also *Gu zunsu yulu* 12, XZJ 118.150a.

79. BGL, XZJ 118.83c; Cleary, *Pai-chang*, 34–35. Note that Cleary's translation omits twelve characters of the Chinese text, which correspond to the sentence: "Then, when the two sides are brought up, you are unattached to them, and no measures can control you." In a passage that comes just after the last one, Baizhang expands on the notion that ultimate reality cannot be predicated or conceptualized. According to him, "Reality has no comparison, because there is nothing to which it may be likened. The dharmakāya is not conditioned and does not fall within the scope of any classification."

80. BGL, XZJ 118.83c; Cleary, *Pai-chang*, 35.

81. "The Way," a term that appears a number of times in this volume, is a literal and commonly used rendering of the Chinese *dao*, which has a long history and covers a broad semantic field. In Chinese Buddhist literature, it was used to translate a number of Indian terms, such as *bodhi* (awakening), *mārga* (path), and Nirvāṇa. Dao is also a central concept in traditional Chinese thought, including Confucianism and Daoism. Its varied meanings include the impersonal creative force of the universe, which is constant and engenders *yin, yang,* and the myriad things, as well as the proper patterns of human behavior—encompassing both ritual and everyday activities—that accord with the principles of Heaven. The use of the term in the Hongzhou school's texts is often ambiguous, encompassing both Buddhist and traditional Chinese connotations. Accordingly, I have rendered it literally, thus preserving some of its multivalence and ambiguity.

82. T 14.545b.

83. MY, XZJ 119.406c; Cheng-chien, *Sun-Face Buddha*, 65.

84. Vermilion and purple were the colors of the robes worn by high officials during the Tang dynasty.

85. CDL 8, T 51.263b; XZJ 120.28a; Cheng-chien, *Sun-Face Buddha*, 138; Sasaki et al., *The Recorded Sayings of Layman P'ang*, 46.

86. Quotation from *Zhao lun* 1, T 45.153a.

87. MY, XZJ 119.406d; Cheng-chien, *Sun-Face Buddha*, 66. The last sentence can also be translated as: "The scriptures say that there are Buddhas everywhere."

88. CDL 10, T 51.275a. See also the discussion of Mazu's adage between Nanquan and Zhaozhou in CDL 10, T 51.276c; translated in Cheng-chien, *Sun-Face Buddha*, 23.

89. *Linji yulu*, T 47.498a; cf. Burton Watson, *The Zen Teaching of Master Lin-chi*, 31.

90. *Linji yulu*, T 47.500c; cf. Watson, *The Zen Teaching of Master Lin-chi*, 53–54. See also Linji's direct quote of Mazu's adage "ordinary mind is the Way" in T 47.499c.

91. See Zongmi's citation at the end of the section "Mind and Buddha" in this chapter.

92. For this argument, see Jia "Doctrinal Reformation of the Hongzhou School of Chan Buddhism," 12–15. Jia sees it as a significant doctrinal reformation in Tang Chan.

93. T 48.380a; Iriya, *Denshin hōyō, Enryō roku*, 12–14; cf. Blofeld, *The Zen Teaching of Huang-po*, 31–32. See also T 48.380b.

94. See Bernard Faure, *The Rhetoric of Immediacy: A Cultural Critique of Chan/Zen Buddhism*, 59–62.

95. See "Monastic Mores and Ideals" in chapter 4.

6

Path of Practice
and Realization

The development of Chan doctrine during the Tang period is traditionally associated with the ideas of immediacy and suddenness (*dun*). This entails conceptualization of the realization of sudden enlightenment (*dunwu*) as a definitive religious experience; however, in some instances the notion of suddenness is also ascribed to the sphere of practical application (in other words, the process of spiritual cultivation is interpreted as a sudden rather than a gradual process). The sudden approach is typically contrasted with its opposite, the gradual (*jian*) approach. The idea of suddenness became widely recognized as a centerpiece of the Chan school's soteriological paradigm, and within the context of interpreting Tang Chan, it came to be closely linked with the Hongzhou school.

Because of the perceived historical importance of the concept of suddenness in the evolution of Chan doctrine, in this final chapter the study of the Hongzhou school's conception of a path of practice and realization begins with a reexamination of the place of subitism in the records of Mazu and his disciples. In the first two sections, I raise questions about conventional interpretations of the Hongzhou school's alleged advocacy of a radical subitist position. Next, I point to the presence of gradualist motifs in its records, which sets the stage for the concluding discussion of the Hongzhou school's doctrines and practices, centered on the theme of spiritual progress.

The analysis of a progressive path of practice and realization presented in the final three sections of this chapter is based primarily on Baizhang's record and revolves around the "three propositions" (*sanju*) explicated in it.[1] This soteriological model implies the sequential unfolding of increasingly subtle stages of insight, correlated to progressively deeper levels of detachment and transcendence. The three propositions embody an ingenious Chan model of practice, but they also point to parallels with other doctrinal traditions. Accordingly, they exemplify the Hongzhou school's endeavor to formulate direct soteriological approaches—devoid of complex conceptual embellishments and warmhearted devotional sentiments—that highlight the transformative power of Chan practice and point to the expansive vision of enlightenment.

The "Sudden" and "Gradual" Paradigms

From early on, Chan teachers and writers employed the notions of subitism and gradualism as constitutive elements of a polarity that anchors interpretative analyses of Chan doctrine and practice. Traditionally, the subitist perspective is regarded as orthodoxy and is linked with the Southern school, while the gradual approach is associated with the Northern school. From this perspective, the sudden approach represents a superior soteriological model, while the label of gradualism carries pejorative connotations. The distinction between sudden and gradual thus serves as a bipolar modality that underscores two contrasting approaches to Chan practice and realization.

The *locus classicus* frequently cited to illustrate the purported conflict between the sudden and gradual perspectives is the verse competition recounted in the *Platform Scripture*.[2] This contest, which pitted the learned Shenxiu against the illiterate Huineng, is probably the best-known story in Chan literature, and it enjoyed enduring popularity and influence on later Chan/Zen traditions. Modern scholarship, however, has revealed the story's apocryphal origins: the verse competition never took place, and the verses ascribed to Huineng and Shenxiu were composed in the context of polemical discourse aimed at establishing the parameters of Chan orthodoxy. We now know that stereotypical depictions of the Northern school as advocating an inferior brand of gradualism are simplistic and largely inaccurate. In fact, both verses were based on Northern school ideas, and they can be read together as a set of doctrinal formulations that explicate subtle discernment of the perfect teaching.[3] Therefore, what at first sight appears to be a dichotomy constituted by two diametrically opposed elements can be interpreted as a dynamic polarity that encompasses two complementary viewpoints.

The sudden/gradual polarity was a distinctly Chinese development that predated the emergence of Chan.[4] Its philosophical framework was informed by other Buddhist polarities, such as the theory of two truths, which explained reality in term of conventional truth (Sanskrit: *saṃvṛtisatya*; Chinese: *sudi*) and ultimate or absolute truth (Sanskrit: *paramārthasatya*; Chinese: *zhendi*).

Chinese scholiasts sometimes explicated the sudden/gradual paradigm by recourse to other polarities derived from Chinese intellectual traditions, such as the essence/function (*tiyong*) paradigm. They were probably also influenced by other native frames of reference, such as the contrast between intuition and cultivation in the Daoist and Confucian traditions. Daosheng (c. 360–434) was the first Chinese monk to propound the notion of sudden enlightenment, and he initiated the first debate between proponents of subitism and gradualism.[5] Subsequently, the sudden teaching became a fixture in doctrinal taxonomies, including those created by various Huayan and Tiantai patriarchs. In that context, gradual teachings were generally those regarded as expedients, while the sudden teaching was presented as an unmediated and total revelation of ultimate truth/reality.

Within early Chan, a clear-cut distinction between the sudden and gradual approaches emerged during Shenhui's campaigns against the Northern school, echoes of which are discernible in the *Platform Scripture*. Shenhui's polemical invocation of subitism was aimed at driving a wedge between competing Chan factions and "demonstrating" the superiority of the Southern school he championed. For that purpose, he created an impression (or perhaps an illusion) of irreconcilable differences between the two opposing soteriological models. This polemical use of the sudden/gradual dichotomy set a precedent and served as a reference point for subsequent discussions on the subject, and subsequent Chan teachers and writers often used the idea of subitism and its related terms as identifying slogans, rather than as coherent doctrinal positions with explicit contents. The appeal of the notion of suddenness was enhanced by the fact that its meaning was flexible and its applications were adaptable to a wide range of interpretations.[6]

The introduction of the notion of suddenness in early Chan represented an attempt to impose conceptual structure to the experience of awakening. The Chinese term *dun* occupies a broad semantic field, and in diverse contexts it assumes different overlapping and sometimes conflicting meanings. Bernard Faure has identified three main orders of meaning: First, *dun* implies rapidity in the realization of awakening. While the experience of awakening is still understood in terms of temporality, in this sense it entails a denial of sequence, including the stages of the Bodhisattva path. Second, it denotes the absolute nature of realization, which is predicated on the presence of inherent or original awakening (*benjue*) within each person. Third, *dun* also conveys a sense of immediacy, implying that the experience of awakening is not mediated by anything, and thus there is no need for *upāya*.[7]

The imposition of conceptual strictures on the occurrence of awakening was a problematic proposition, since such experience is supposed to be ineffable and beyond theoretical formulations. Consequently, the sudden/gradual paradigm was an unstable construct, and its instability was reinforced by the ambiguity of the notion of suddenness. The superimposition of theoretical models derived from it on the process of practice and the experience of awakening proved to be an unwieldy intellectual enterprise. At a basic level, the idea of suddenness counteracts the view that there is a direct correlation between the methods of cultivation and the realization of awakening. In this view, unmediated insight into the ineffable realm of reality occurs suddenly—all at once instead of in stages—and is not a direct result of practice. In contrast, the traditional understanding of the Bodhisattva path involves a step-by-step perfection of spiritual disciplines and a gradual deepening of insight. While the gradualist perspective is concerned with methods and processes that effect mental purification and removal of the hindrances, from the subitist viewpoint all one needs is a direct realization of reality, which makes all practices superfluous.

The subitist perspective involves a paradox. Unadulterated subitism implies a transcendence of conceptual structures and an absence of any point of view, as all concepts dissolve into a totalizing vision of the absolute. Accordingly, authentic subitism cannot be articulated, defying attempts to superimpose theoretical structures and unsettling linguistic conventions. For that reason, endeavors to express the subitist perspective by recourse to language end up being another form of gradualism.[8] As Fayan stated in response to a question about the ultimate truth posed by one of his students, "If I were to tell you, it would become the secondary truth."[9] As soon as one tries to articulate or conceptualize the absolute truth, it is not the absolute truth anymore.

The problem of articulation inherent in the subitist stance especially comes to the fore when the focus shifts away from abstract doctrinal discussions about the nature of reality and moves into the domain of spiritual cultivation. In the medieval context, when applied in reference to meditation and other forms of practice, subitism undermines the prospect of formulating coherent propositions about the exigencies of spiritual training undertaken by actual people. Therefore, the apophatic rhetorical posture of subitism runs the risk of being interpreted in ways that undercut religious practices and ethical observances.[10]

For those reasons, the rhetorical bravado of subitism is best suited to polemical discourse. Within the medieval Chinese context (as well as in other times and places), its radical rhetoric scored points on the ideological battlefields by advancing the superiority of a given teaching, which enhanced the religious and social standing of those who upheld it. As can be seen from the records of Shenhui's anti–Northern school campaigns, the advocacy of subitism was also a potent tool in fund-raising, attracting disciples, and acquiring the image or pose of a Chan teacher. The rhetoric of subitism might have also involved an appeal to the spiritual egotism of the audience, which was told that this supreme teaching was for select people with superior spiritual aptitudes. In reality, such an audience of individuals with the highest spiritual capacity was largely nonexistent, since the vast majority of monks and laymen engaged in Chan practice did not belong to the lofty group of spiritual virtuosi repeatedly invoked in Chan literature. For that reason, the idea of suddenness fitted well with the evangelical character of Shenhui's mission, in which the focus was on the conversion of others to his vision of Chan orthodoxy, rather than on offering coherent guidance about the spiritual cultivation that was to follow the initial conversion experience.[11] Because of the incongruity between the radical rhetoric of subitism and the exigencies of monastic training, the overt presence of subitism is less evident in texts concerned with practice instead of sectarian polemics (including the records of Mazu and his disciples). For example, in contrast to Shenhui's adoption of a narrow polemical framework and his lack of concern with the exigencies of practice, "Northern Chan masters recognized the unavoidable contradiction between their theoretical 'subitism' and the concrete necessities of spiritual guidance."[12] As we will see, the same statement can be applied to the Hongzhou school, although they resolved those tensions in a somewhat different manner.

The sudden/gradual polarity becomes more complex when the subitist and gradualist perspectives are applied separately to the dynamics of spiritual praxis and the experience of realization or awakening. In his writings, when Zongmi combines these two pairs—sudden and gradual, and practice (*xiu*) and awakening (*wu*)—he comes up with five different approaches to practice and realization. He based these combinations on accounts of different doctrinal positions briefly introduced in the writings of his teacher Chengguan, where they are buried in a mass of scholastic detail.[13] Among them, Zongmi advocated the "sudden enlightenment followed by gradual cultivation" (*dunwu jianxiu*) paradigm as the best and most authentic model of Chan practice, which he (somewhat misleadingly) identified with Shenhui. The five approaches are: (1) gradual cultivation followed by sudden awakening; (2) sudden cultivation followed by gradual awakening; (3) gradual cultivation and gradual awakening; (4) sudden awakening followed by gradual cultivation; (5) sudden awakening and sudden cultivation.[14]

Zongmi's conceptual framework represents an attempt to impose doctrinal coherence and to tackle confusions arising from arbitrary uses of the terms "sudden" and "gradual." A problem arises, however, when he applies these abstract models to an analysis of the teachings and practices of specific Chan traditions, without sufficient attention to the subtle nuances and tensions in their doctrinal positions and soteriological approaches. Zongmi's push for conceptual clarity fosters reductionist tendencies, as the complexities of living traditions are subsumed within rigid schematic representations, which are also clouded by his partisan subjectivity.

In his *Chanyuan zhuquanji duxu*, Zongmi places the Hongzhou school—together with Shenhui—at the top of his threefold taxonomy of Chan teachings. He identifies it with the teaching that directly reveals mind and nature (*zhixian xinxing zong*), which corresponds to the tathāgatagarbha doctrine. The only text in which Zongmi presents a harsh critique of the Hongzhou school is *Pei Xiu shiyi wen* (otherwise known as *Zhonghua chuan xindi chan-men shizi chengxi tu*), perhaps reflecting the fact that this text was composed in order to determine the relative superiority and inferiority among the various schools of Chan. Accordingly, its main concern was to establish the supremacy of the Heze lineage, and by extension of Zongmi himself as the self-proclaimed representative of that lineage.[15] Zongmi's analysis employs the essence/function paradigm; his basic critique is that the Hongzhou school advocates radical nondualism by collapsing the essence into its function,[16] which undermines the larger ontological unity envisaged by Zongmi, whose interpretation hinges on an essentialist view of the mind based on the theory of original enlightenment.[17]

Zongmi's standpoint exemplifies a tendency to reify the self-nature or the true mind, postulating a notion of static essence (albeit one that is capable of emanating dynamic function) as that which is fundamental (*ben*). From that perspective, the experience of sudden enlightenment implies an epistemic shift that involves *seeing* the true nature, which is intrinsically pure and is the source of all mental functions.[18] In contrast, the Hongzhou school conceives of reality in terms of dynamic processes and shies away from the ontological assumptions that are at the core of Zongmi's analysis of mind and reality. From that point of view there is no self-existing essence to be grasped or realized, and thus there can be no experience of *seeing* the true nature, because no such substance exists.

Zongmi's advocacy of the sudden enlightenment followed by gradual cultivation paradigm represents a response to types of Chan radicalism that, from his perspective, fail to convey a positive vision of progressive path of practice.[19] This radicalism is epitomized by the "sudden awakening and sudden cultivation" (*dunwu dunxiu*) paradigm. In his writings, Zongmi makes no explicit statement that the sudden awakening and sudden cultivation paradigm corresponds to the teachings of the Hongzhou school. He only briefly notes that it is compatible with the approach propounded by Farong of the Niutou school, and he quotes Shenhui in the explanation of its basic features.[20] Nonetheless, Zongmi rebuffs the Hongzhou school's stance toward progressive cultivation, alleging that it considers practice to consist of "merely allowing the mind to act spontaneously."[21] He also dismisses the Hongzhou school's understanding of gradual practice as "mistaken and completely contrary."[22] According to Zongmi, the Hongzhou school's soteriological program places emphasis on sudden awakening and reduces practice to simply allowing the spontaneous functioning of the true nature. As can be seen from the writings of later figures such as Dahui (1089–1163) and Chinul (1158–1210),[23] this characterization led subsequent generations of Chan writers to perceive the Hongzhou school's approach as falling under the category of sudden awakening and sudden cultivation. We must ask, then, whether this is a fair and balanced assessment of the Hongzhou school's teachings.

A Vanishing Paradigm

Given the religious attitudes and doctrinal positions described in the previous two chapters, one might expect that the Hongzhou school would rebuff or gloss over the sudden/gradual polarity as just another duality. In fact, a closer look at the relevant textual sources reveals that terms and ideas associated with subitism are not nearly as prominent within the Hongzhou school's teachings as later generations of Chan teachers, writers, and scholars have presupposed. The term "sudden awakening" appears only once in Mazu's sermons, in a passage that mentions "sudden awakening to the original nature" (*dunwu benxing*), in reference to a practitioner with superior spiritual ability who achieves sudden awakening after receiving instructions from a qualified teacher: "There might be someone with superior capacity who meets a virtuous friend and receives instructions from him. If upon hearing the words he gains understanding, then without passing through the stages, suddenly he awakens to the original nature. That is why the [*Vimalakīrti*] scripture says, 'Ordinary people can still change, but not the *śrāvakas*.'"[24]

The term "sudden awakening" also appears in the title of Dazhu's *Dunwu rudao yaomen lun*. But although the treatise begins with a brief discussion of sudden awakening, the term appears in only three other passages, and it is fair to say that as a whole the text's focus is not on the idea of sudden awakening.[25] The presence of this term in the title of Dazhu's treatise represents another instance of its emblematic use: it functions as a catchphrase that evokes the mystique and uniqueness of Chan, reflecting a popular usage current in the aftermath of Shenhui's campaigns. The evidence of Shenhui's influence in the treatise offers further support for such an explanation.[26]

In *Baizhang guanglu*, the expression "sudden awakening" appears only once, in a question posed to Baizhang by a student.[27] It does not turn up in any statement attributed to Baizhang. Even the term *dun* by itself does not show up even a single time elsewhere in the text. The situation with Huangbo's two records is similar; there "sudden awakening" does not appear at all, although the character *dun* appears six times. In each instance, *dun* turns up as a part of two-character compounds, four in all: *dunliao* (sudden comprehension, twice), *dunchao* (sudden transcendence, twice), *dunxi* (sudden ending) and *dunfa* (sudden revealing). The paucity of relevant references and the manner in which they are employed suggest that the notion of sudden awakening was not a focal point and occupied a relatively minor position within the Hongzhou school's teachings. The idea of subitism was applied in reference to the sudden experience or realization of awakening, which was conceived of as the climax of a path of practice.

If the notion of sudden awakening was accepted but to some extent relocated to the margins, then what about the idea of "sudden cultivation"? Neither the exact term nor any similar compound appears in any text associated with the Hongzhou school. When the pertinent records explicitly take a subitist stance, it is associated with the experience of awakening, not with the process of spiritual cultivation. "Sudden" usually refers to the manner in which the experience occurs, namely as an all-at-once realization rather than a gradual unfolding of knowledge or awareness of reality. The same terminology is also used to talk about the nature of the experience, which is construed as an immediate realization of truth or reality that is an indivisible whole.

As was pointed out earlier, the term *dun* was often used in the sense of "unmediated," implying that the experience of awakening is realized independently of, or without the mediation of, spiritual practices, which constitute expedient means. In his anti–Northern school sermons, Shenhui accused his opponents of advocating misguided meditation techniques based on an inferior understanding of ultimate truth. In his writings, Zongmi presents a similar, albeit less emotionally charged, critique of the Northern school. He argues that the practices advocated by the Northern school are inauthentic because they are based on a mistaken understanding of the nature of the defilements (which are empty) and the mind (which is real), rather than on the direct realization of the true mind, which supposedly occurs at the point of the initial understanding awakening (*jiewu*). Zongmi's critique of the Hongzhou school also centers on its deficiencies in regard to practice, but with a notable difference. His indictment of Mazu and his followers is that they have mistakenly dispensed with all forms of gradual cultivation, not that they engage in flawed and inauthentic regimens of spiritual discipline along the line of those propounded by the Northern school.

In the Hongzhou school's writings, especially Huangbo's records, there are occasional criticisms of uncritical reliance on *upāya* (here used in the sense of methods of spiritual cultivation, including meditation), but they are rare. The story of Huairang's polishing a brick in front of the young Mazu is a case in point. There is also this example from Baizhang's record, followed by three more examples from Huangbo's records, all employing rhetoric that is more radical:

> Consulting virtuous friends [i.e., teachers] and seeking for certain knowledge or understanding is the demon of virtuous friends, because it engenders verbalizations and views. If one were to give rise to the four universal vows [of a bodhisattva], vowing to attain Buddhahood only after liberating all sentient beings, that is the demon of the wisdom of the bodhisattva teachings, because of not letting go of the vow. If one upholds the dietary regulations and precepts, practices meditation, and studies wisdom, those are afflicted roots of goodness.[28]

> Furthermore, as to [perfecting] the six perfections and [the rest of] the myriad practices, and [acquiring] merits [as numerous as] the

sands of [the Ganges] river, because you are already complete [with them], you need not add to [that perfection] through practice. You should perform them when there is an appropriate occasion, and return to stillness when the occasion has ended. If you do not definitely believe that this mind is Buddha, but want to practice by attaching to forms and seek rewards, all of that is false thinking and is not compatible with the Way.... To cultivate the six perfections and the myriad practices with the intention of seeking to become a Buddha implies gradualness. From the very beginning until now, there has never been a graduated Buddha.[29]

Even if you cultivate the six perfections and myriad practices for eons [as numerous as] the sands of Ganges [with the intention of] attaining the Buddha's enlightenment, that still contravenes the very truth. Why? Because they are karma-forming actions. When the [good] karmic causes are exhausted, you will still return to [this world of] impermanence.[30]

Awakening [occurs] within the mind, it does not involve the six perfections and myriad practices. The six perfections and myriad practices are all merely marginal things for instructing and liberating others in accord with circumstances. Even enlightenment (*bodhi*), suchness, ultimate reality, liberation, the dharma-body (*dharmakāya*), as well as the ten stages [of the bodhisattva path] and the four fruits of sagehood, all of them are expedient teachings, unconnected to the Buddha-mind.[31]

These comments problematize conventional interpretations of the Buddhist path and call into question the reification of its elements, in a manner that is distinctive and yet consistent with canonical teachings on the subject. We might better interpret them as warnings about the appropriate use of *upāya*, rather than as calls for their outright rejection. In that respect, the position of Mazu and his disciples is closer to that of the Northern school than to Shenhui, although even Shenhui could not avoid falling into gradualist slips and admitting the need for expedient means.[32]

From what we can tell, Mazu and his disciples were wary of doctrinal formulations and soteriological approaches that centered on unreflective use of *upāya*. They rejected the presupposition that mechanical performance of spiritual practices such as sitting meditation, without insight into their empty nature, can necessarily lead to the "attainment" of liberation. From their perspective, this viewpoint was problematic inasmuch as it reinforced a mistaken assumption that the realization of the unconditioned realm of Nirvāṇa is a direct result or consequence of religious practices. In itself, that is a sound doctrinal position not unique to Chan. Realization of absolute reality is not a product of spiritual discipline because, as Mazu points out, "it originally exists and it is present now, irrespective of cultivation of the Way or sitting in meditation."[33]

The Hongzhou school's stance toward practice is more nuanced than Zongmi's one-sided characterization makes it out to be. It is possible to assert that there is no direct correlation between the cultivation of spiritual practices and the realization of awakening and liberation, but only when such causal links are viewed from the perspective of absolute truth. Mazu makes that point when he states, "The Way does not belong to cultivation. If one speaks of any attainment through cultivation, whatever is accomplished in that way is still subject to regress. That is same as the [way of the] *śrāvakas*."[34] If that were Mazu's final statement on the matter, Zongmi might have a valid point. However, Mazu does not stop there, and his statement does not constitute an unqualified repudiation of the utility of spiritual practices.[35]

Mazu's sermon continues: "If one says that there is no need for cultivation, that is the same as ordinary people."[36] According to him, the bodhisattvas differ from ordinary people, who are caught up in their illusions and enslaved by their desires, and do not see the need to practice. At the same time, the bodhisattvas' practice differs from that of the *śrāvakas*, who are bogged down in a realm of dualistic opposites and are thus prone to becoming attached to their practices and reifying the ultimate goal.[37] Once again, the focus is on proper understanding of practice rather than on its outright rejection. This brings us back to the question of audience, for if these statements were directed to monks already engaged in spiritual cultivation, the main issue is not whether they should practice or not, but what is the proper attitude and manner of practice.

Ideas about spiritual cultivation such as these are closely related to the understanding of *upāya* discussed in the previous chapter. They also have parallels in canonical depictions of the bodhisattva path, such as those in the *Vimalakīrti* and *Prajñāpāramitā* scriptures. Canonical texts portray the bodhisattva as a tireless spiritual hero engaged in the cultivation of the perfections that constitute the path to Buddhahood. At the same time, the bodhisattva's spiritual training is grounded on the "taking up" of the perfection of wisdom, through which the bodhisattva realizes the emptiness of all dharmas, including the practices he or she is engaged in.[38] While the bodhisattva never abandons the practice of the other perfections, it is through the application of insight into their lack of self-nature, cultivated through the perfection of wisdom, that he or she avoids grasping all practices and misconstruing their true nature and function.[39]

From this vantage point, attachment to *upāya* and their indiscriminate rejection are both mistaken. The Hongzhou school's position on this issue is actually similar to the one advocated by Zongmi, with an important distinction. The critiques of all forms of grasping in the Hongzhou school's records also expose the problem of attachment to the notion of "original enlighten-ment," which is the cornerstone of Zongmi's "sudden enlightenment fol-lowed by gradual cultivation" paradigm. This distinction is expressed in Bai-zhang's record, which includes this passage: "To attach to original purity and original liberation, to consider oneself to be a Buddha, to be someone who understands Chan [without actually engaging in practice], that belongs to the way of those heretics who [deny cause and effect] and hold that things happen spontaneously."[40]

Mazu and Baizhang seem to argue that it is mistaken to presuppose that the realization of reality is a direct result of specific practices; however, the as-sumption that one can achieve awakening without engaging in arduous prac-tice is also problematic. A similar kind of dual sensitivity is evident in some early Chan texts, such as *Xiuxin yaolun* (attributed to Hongren).[41] The chal-lenge the Hongzhou teachers posed to their followers was to engage the two perspectives and strike a balance between them. The adept practitioner was supposed to exploit the creative tension engendered by the simultaneous com-prehension that spiritual practices lack self-nature and must not become ob-jects of attachment, and yet are indispensable expressions of authentic reli-gious life.

To sum up, the Hongzhou school adopted the idea of sudden awakening, but not the notion of sudden practice, especially in its more literalistic and radical forms. Practice inevitably involves temporality and process, which are associated with the gradualist perspective. From their standpoint, the idea of suddenness only affects actual practice in the sense that the adoption of a subi-tist perspective fosters an attitude of detachment toward the methods and goals of practice. In that sense, a sensible dose of subitism can serve as a cor-rective to ill-advised practice, shaping the manner in which various practices are understood and applied, instead of undermining their worth and rele-vance. If that is the case, then what about the Hongzhou school's conception(s) of the process of spiritual cultivation?

A Gradual Path of Practice

As the discussion moves into the sphere of spiritual cultivation and monastic training, predictably gradualist elements creep into it. One of the prime ex-amples comes from Baizhang's record. In a description of the path of prac-tice, Baizhang compares spiritual cultivation to the washing of a dirty robe (or cloth):

> You should study in the following manner: study is like washing
> dirty robe. The robe is originally there, while the dirt comes from
> outside. Having heard that everything existent or nonexistent, sound

or form, is like dirt and grease, do not settle your mind on any of it. The thirty-two characteristics and eighty minor marks [of the Buddha] under the tree of enlightenment all belong to [the sphere of] form, while the twelve sections of texts [in the Buddhist canon] belong to [the sphere of] sound. Right now, as you cut off the stream of everything existent and nonexistent, all forms and sounds, the mind become like empty space. You should study thus, like saving one's head when it is on fire . . . [42]

It is unclear from which source Baizhang adopted the analogy between religious practice and the washing of dirty robe. The simile is very ancient, and variations on the same theme appear in various canonical texts.[43] The same imagery appears in the *Vatthūpama Sutta* of the Pāli canon.[44] The Pāli scripture elaborates on a path of gradual purification that leads to the realization of Nirvāṇa, by means of which defilements that stain the mind are removed and the mind is purified. In this quotation, Baizhang adopts a similar perspective when he describes the process of spiritual practice as removal of impurities that stain the mind. Like the robe in the simile, the mind is intrinsically pure, whereas the impurities that sully it are extrinsic to it. Spiritual cultivation therefore consists of the abandonment or removal of extrinsic defilements that taint the mind, the origin of which is traced to the forming of attachment to external objects (literally, "sounds and forms"). When one abandons all mistaken attachments and deluded mental states, explains Baizhang, one's "mind becomes like empty space," free from the imperfections that arise when it is sullied by extraneous defilements.

The position expressed in Baizhang's text is analogous to the one implied by the first of the competing verses from the *Platform Scripture*, the verse (falsely) attributed to Shenxiu, which compares contemplative practice to a diligent effort to wipe dust from the surface of a mirror in order to keep it clean.[45] Like the robe mentioned in the simile, the mirror's surface is originally clean. The dust that needs to be removed comes from outside. It is therefore extrinsic to the mirror, whose essential characteristic is its ability to reflect images clearly. Yet, Baizhang's teaching is also in agreement with the second verse in the *Platform Scripture*, attributed (also falsely) to Huineng. That verse asserts that since the Buddha-nature is always pure, there is no place where any dust can gather.[46] Like the author of the second verse, Baizhang is aware of the danger of reifying defilements and misconstruing them as being real; he stresses, therefore, that practice involves the removal of defilements, but they are finally let go with the realization of the lack of intrinsic reality (i.e., emptiness), rather than by a gradual process of expunging them from the mind. Such an understanding prevents misguided efforts to obliterate mental defilements and purify the mind, based on a flawed assumption that there are real defilements that must be eradicated. This suggests a resolution of the allegedly contrasting doctrinal stances represented by the two verses from the *Platform Scripture*: the realization that there is nowhere for the dust to gather is precisely what is meant by removing the dust from the mirror.

While presumably Baizhang was not directly commenting on the competing verses from the *Platform Scripture,* his apparent acceptance of the two perspectives indicates that they need not be interpreted as diametrically opposed paradigms of religious practice, "gradual" and "sudden."[47] As has been pointed out, from the standpoint of the Northern school the two verses can be interpreted as summing up two complementary aspects of a balanced approach to religious practice. Baizhang adopts a similar perspective, asserting that one should engage in contemplative practice and sustain a state of mind that is "clear like empty space," maintaining mindfulness and letting go of impurities as soon as they arise. At the same time, one should not conceptualize or cling to the various mental states and experiences, attach to the meditative process, or reify the ultimate goal.

This point of view unavoidably conveys a sense of gradualism, as do a number of other passages in the Hongzhou school's records. For example, in one of his sermons Mazu encourages his disciples to nourish the womb of sagehood (a reference to the gradual perfection of the bodhisattva stages), even during everyday activities such as wearing their robes and eating food. Elsewhere, he urges them to keep the pure precepts and accumulate wholesome karma.[48] The gradualist perspective is also evident in the use of the image of ox-herding as an allegory for the path of practice. This allegory became popular during the Song period, as can be seen from the famous ox-herding poems and paintings, but it already appears in the Hongzhou school's records; mention of it can be found in the records of Shigong, Baizhang, and Da'an (a disciple of Baizhang).[49] In this example from Da'an's record, ox-herding serves as an allegory for gradual training that leads to realization of one's true nature:

> When Da'an arrived at Baizhang's [monastery], he paid his respects [to Baizhang] and asked, "I want to know the Buddha. What is he like?"
>
> Baizhang said, "It is like seeking an ox while you are riding on one."
>
> Da'an asked, "What shall I do after I know that?"
>
> Baizhang said, "It is like a man going home riding on an ox."
>
> Da'an asked, "How should I take care of it all the time?"
>
> Baizhang said, "It is like a man tending an ox. He looks after it with a stick in his hand, and does not let it intrude upon unripe crops."[50]

Just as the ox-herder tames the animal by watching over it and controlling its moves with a stick in his hand, the practitioner trains the mind by being constantly mindful and exerting control over all mental activity. In another passage, Da'an states that instead of studying Chan, all he did was look after a water buffalo. "If it went astray from the path and entered the grass, then I would pull it away. If it intruded on other people's crops, I would flog it with a whip in order to tame it." After a long struggle, the water buffalo "become a white ox in an open field, always on my side. Spending the day in the vast open fields, even if someone tries to take advantage of it, it does not go away."[51] Here the allegory of ox-herding evidently points to a gradual process of spiritual cultivation that involves mindful guarding of the mind and constant awareness of its activities.

The making of an allowance for gradual cultivation is also evident in the following passage from Guishan's records, which suggests parallels with the sudden awakening/gradual cultivation paradigm advocated by Zongmi:

> Once a monk asked the Master [i.e., Guishan], "Does a person who has had sudden awakening still need to cultivate?" The Master said, "When one has true awakening, attains to the fundamental, and knows other and self, then cultivation and non-cultivation are just dualistic opposites. Right now, though the initial inspiration is dependent on conditions, if within a single thought one awakens to one's own reality, there are still certain habitual tendencies that have accumulated over numberless *kalpa*s that cannot be purified in a single instant. That person should certainly be taught how to remove gradually the karmic tendencies and mental habits. That is cultivation. There is no other method of cultivation that needs to be taught to that person."[52]

The inclusion of gradualist elements and perspectives steers Chan rhetoric away from abstract ideas about arcane truths; instead it takes into account the needs and abilities of real people. The shift away from narrowly polemical uses of the terms "sudden" and "gradual" evident among Mazu's disciples is reflective of a sensitivity to an audience of monks engaged in religious training, along with the added audience of officials and literati. This did not lead to a total rejection of the subitist perspective, which by that time had become a permanent fixture of Chan discourse; rather, such an outlook was balanced by reintroducing gradualist elements that reflected the realities of spiritual life. Within this context, a modified form of the sudden teaching was employed in order to prevent monks engaged in Chan training from grasping or misconstruing their goals and practices. This vision of "suddenness" shaped attitudes about the process of spiritual cultivation—which was intrinsically gradual in character, notwithstanding the ingenious sophistry evidenced in some of the subitist rhetoric—and pointed to the inexpressibility of the final realization of awakening.[53]

Stages of the Path

A central theme in *Baizhang guanglu* is Chan practitioners' progression along stages that constitute a path of practice, which brings about spiritual transformation and culminates in the realization of awakening. Baizhang explains the path in terms of three propositions, which involve three distinct mental states (or conditions) that correspond to three stages of spiritual realization. These three propositions are hierarchical and progressive, and they explicate increasingly refined states of awareness and corresponding stages of religious perfection. With each successive stage, the practitioner's consciousness divests itself of increasingly subtle attachments and manifests a greater degree of accord with the Buddha's perfect and unobstructed vision of reality.

The process described by Baizhang involves a dialectical ascent to progressively more refined levels of detachment and transcendence, with each successive stage rectifying the limitations of the preceding stage and bringing about deeper insight into the final truth. The superior level of awareness realized by the practitioner at each higher stage is thus dependent on his renunciation of forms of clinging and imperfection evidenced at the previous stage. As the adept subdues his mind and abandons attachment, he is able to obliterate the ten states of impure mind, which Baizhang defines as "greedy mind, lustful mind, defiled mind, angry mind, clinging mind, dwelling mind, dependent mind, attached mind, grasping mind, and longing mind."[54]

At the initial stage of the path, the practitioner cultivates detachment from all things. When encountering all sorts of situations and coming in contact with various phenomena perceived though the senses, he is aware of their innate characteristics and is able to ascertain their purity or defilement. Yet, while adept at making such distinctions, he distances himself from everything and gives up all grasping and attachment. This mental state recalls the description of practice in *Erru sixing lun*, which includes an account of Bodhidharma's instructions about abiding frozen in "wall contemplation" (*biguan*). In this mental state, "self and other, ordinary person and sage, are one and the same," and the practitioner is "without discrimination, serene and inactive."[55] Baizhang describes the attainment of this detached frame of mind:

> One should distinguish the terms of purity and defilement. Defiled things have many names, such as greed, aversion, love, grasping, and so on. Pure things also have many names, such as awakening (*bodhi*), Nirvāṇa, liberation, and so on. Nevertheless, the present reflective awareness should, amidst the two streams of pure and defiled, profane and holy, amidst forms, sounds, smells, and physical sensations, amidst mundane and supramundane phenomena, have not even the slightest love or grasping for anything at all.[56]

The Chan practitioner clearly distinguishes between pure things, which include the elements of the Buddhist path, and impure things, which include all unwholesome mental qualities and predispositions that cause rebirth in saṃsāra—yet he is unattached to any of them. This constitutes the elementary level of practice and the first stage of the path, where the main concern is to "create a good state of mind":[57]

> When one no longer loves or grasps, but abides [in the state] of absence of love and grasping, and considers that to be correct, that is the elementary good. That is abiding in subdued mind. Such a person is [like] a śrāvaka, or [like] a person who has become so fond of the raft [that had taken him to the other shore] that he cannot give it up.[58] That is the way of the two vehicles [of śrāvakas and pratyeka-buddhas], and that is the result of meditation.[59]

Within Baizhang's overall scheme, the attainment of a subdued and dispassionate mind, brought about by the practice of meditation, is not the final goal of religious life. Indeed, the condition of utter detachment is an elementary rather than ultimate attainment because "abiding in subdued mind" entails clinging to nonattachment as an absolute state of numinous repose. Baizhang's first stage has parallels in the practice of Wuzhu and his Baotang school, which placed exclusive emphasis on nondiscrimination (wufenbie) as the "sublime way" that encompassed both practice and realization. This radical reinterpretation of the Chan teaching of no-thought (wunian) prompted Zongmi's critique of Wuzhu as teaching a mere "obliteration of consciousness" (mieshi) that led to the abandonment of all practices and ethical observances and elicited the charge of antinomianism.[60]

As a corrective to this one-sided grasping of nonattachment and nondiscrimination, Baizhang introduces the second stage, in which the practitioner "breaks through the good mind" cultivated at the first stage. Going beyond the inherent limitations of the initial stage, at the second stage the practitioner gives up the peaceful dwelling in a mental state of dispassion and detachment:

> Once one does not grasp anymore, and yet does not abide in nonattachment either, that is the intermediate good. That is the half-word teaching. [Nevertheless,] that is still [within] the formless realm. Although such persons avoid falling into the way of the two vehicles, and [also] avoid falling into the way of demons, that is still [a form of] meditation illness. That is the bondage of the bodhisattvas.[61]

At this second stage, which the text refers to as the "intermediate good," the practitioner forsakes dwelling in the state of nonattachment that was perfected at the previous stage and abandons the subtle form of spiritual clinging to the state of nondiscrimination and nonattachment. However, that is not yet the realization of complete freedom from all impediments. While at this stage the mind is disengaged from the habitual tendency to discriminate and attach to dualistic opposites, and there is attendant reflectivity that prevents reification and dwelling in nonattachment, there is still a subtle sense of self-awareness, as the practitioner is aware of himself as being someone who has relinquished all attachment without being stuck in an unadulterated state of nondiscriminating awareness.

A similar attentiveness to the danger of self-absorbed fixation on purity and detachment is evident in Dazhu's *Dunwu yaomen*. Dazhu first discusses the re-linquishment of all dualistic opposites and then goes on to add that the realiza-tion of their emptiness should not be accompanied by self-centered awareness, a state in which one thinks, "Now I see that dualistic opposites are empty," or "Now I have abandoned them all."[62] Elsewhere, Dazhu notes that when the mind attains spiritual repose and abides in a state of purity, it should do so with no attachment to purity and without thinking, "Now my mind is resting in a state of purity."[63] According to him, the appropriate response to this conundrum lies in the attainment of non-abiding mind (*wuzhu xin*), a state in which the mind is not affixed to anything and does not dwell anywhere, including the conditions of disentanglement and non-clinging to a detached frame of mind.   '

In order to free the mind from even the subtlest hindrances that prevent the arising of the Buddha's unobstructed vision and perfect wisdom, accord-ing to Baizhang's theoretical model, the advanced adept must discard the last vestiges of attachment and self-centered awareness. He must not even give rise to discernment or awareness that the subtlest forms of attachment have been forsaken. This final act of letting go constitutes entry into the third and final stage of the path:

> Once one does not abide in nonattachment any more, and does not even engender any understanding of not abiding in it either, that is the final good. That is the full-word teaching. Such a person avoids falling into the formless realm, avoids falling into meditation illness, avoids falling into the way of the bodhisattvas, and avoids falling into the condition of king of demons. Because of hindrances of knowl-edge, hindrances of stages, and hindrances of practice, seeing one's Buddha nature is [as difficult as] seeing shapes at night. As it has been said, at the stage of Buddhahood one obliterates two forms of ignorance: the ignorance of subtle knowledge and the ignorance of extremely subtle knowledge. Therefore, it has been said [in the *Huayan Scripture*] that a man of great wisdom smashes an atom to bring into the world a volume of scripture.[64]

At the third stage, the practitioner's mind finally goes beyond all impedi-ments and becomes completely free from even the subtlest forms of grasping. Spiritual ignorance is finally obliterated. The adept transcends even the most refined forms of knowledge and abandons all views, having realized that they obstruct the wisdom of Buddhahood from becoming manifest. Such a person, according to Baizhang, goes beyond all limitations and is free from all bondage. He finally actualizes the potential for perfection inherent in each person, and thus he is a "Buddha having Buddha nature."[65]

Prior to that realization, the Buddha is not truly known or realized because of attachment to Buddhahood as a religious goal and because of the self-centered seeking of its attainment. When that happens, according to Baizhang, the religious search itself becomes an insurmountable obstacle for the simple reason that "the Buddha is someone without attachments, with no seeking, and without resort." Therefore, adds Baizhang, "If you longingly search for the Buddha here and there, then you totally turn away from him."[66] Only when the notion of self is completely given up and there is no more seeking does the true Buddha manifest himself in his flawless purity and resplendent glory.

The realization of spiritual freedom described in Baizhang's record does not involve the attainment of a numinous state that is radically disjoined from each person's ordinary mind. The course of practice is not a process of acquiring special knowledge or exceptional ability; rather, it centers on liberating the mind from even the subtlest forms of attachment and conceptualization. A mind thus freed, Baizhang tells us, is able to intuitively apprehend "the principle that is originally present in everyone."[67] That principle cannot be cognized or conceptually apprehended because, as Mazu and Baizhang point out, "it is not a thing." It is no other than the principle of emptiness, which transcends the dualism of existence and nonexistence, and leaves no traces. "It is not something calculable, and being like empty space, it cannot be cultivated," Baizhang explains.[68] When that is realized, "then there is neither deficiency nor sufficiency; neither profanity nor holiness; neither light nor darkness." At that point, the Chan adept goes beyond having or not having knowledge, beyond bondage and liberation, entering a realm of reality where it is impossible to ascribe "any name or category."[69]

From this perspective, by transcending all views and abandoning all suppositions about the nature of reality, the Chan sage goes beyond self-imposed limitations and realizes a state of spiritual perfection in which dualistic opposites such as bondage and liberation, knowledge and ignorance, are no longer operative. "When one has no views of existence, nonexistence, or whatever, and yet does not lack vision, that is true vision," explains Baizhang.[70] At that point, having served their purpose, all teachings are abandoned, because "at the stage of Buddhahood there is neither observance nor transgression [of religious norms and practices], and neither the complete nor the incomplete teaching is admissible."[71]

To sum up, each of Baizhang's propositions elucidates a different stage of a three-tiered path in which each successive stage brings the Chan adept closer to a final realization. At the first stage, the emphasis is on perfect detachment from everything; at the second, on letting go of dwelling in the state of total detachment and nondiscrimination. The whole process culminates at the third stage, when even the understanding or awareness of this non-dwelling in detachment is abandoned and spiritual freedom is realized.[72]

Dazhu's treatise also employs an analogous threefold structure in its discussion of the nature of realization (*zheng*), although in contrast to the extensive coverage in Baizhang's records, it appears only in a brief section. Dazhu states that ultimate realization implies the absence of both realization and absence of realization (or no-realization, *wuzheng*). He then goes on to explain the tripartite structure of realization:

> (1) Externally, not to be defiled by forms, sounds, and so on, while internally not to give rise to a mind [filed with] false thoughts, when one is like that, that is called realization. (2) When one attains realization, not to give rise to the thought of realization is called no-realization. (3) When one attains this no-realization, also not to give rise to the thought of no-realization, that is called the absence of no-realization.[73]

The question that remains to be addressed is the relationship between the stages. Does each successive stage imply complete repudiation and rejection of the previous stage? Or do higher stages integrate the insight acquired at the previous stage or stages into a more complete and authentic vision of reality? A response by Baizhang to a question about the proper conduct of monastic life sheds light on this issue. The questioner wants to know what makes monks worthy of the offerings they receive from lay people. In his answer, Baizhang describes the proper frame of mind that makes one a true monk, who is precisely someone who has perfected the three stages:

> Just going by the present shining function, in each sound, form, fragrance, and taste, in the midst of all existent and nonexistent phenomena, and all external objects, if a person is without even the most minuscule impurity, grasping, or defilement, and yet does not abide in the non-grasping of defilements, and also has no understanding of such non-abiding, then such a person can, every day, consume offerings worthy ten thousand ounces of gold, and he will still be able to digest them all.[74]

This passage collapses the three stages into a single whole, a state of spiritual perfection that incorporates them all. The same idea of presenting the three stages as an integrated unit appears in a number of other passages, such as these two:

> Right now, do not abide in all phenomena, whether existent or nonexistent. Also do not abide in non-abiding, and do not give rise to

the knowledge that you do not abide [in all phenomena]. That is called great virtuous friend.[75]

Right now, do not be afflicted by greed, and do not abide in not being afflicted by greed, and do not give rise to the knowledge that you do not abide. That is called the fire of wisdom.[76]

As we have seen, the three stages represent three steps on a progressive path of freeing the mind from increasingly subtler forms of attachment. While each succeeding stage goes beyond the previous stage by overcoming its inherent limitations, a higher stage does not constitute a complete repudiation of the lower stage or stages. Instead, the second stage integrates the first stage, while the final stage integrates the other two in their entirety, as the above quotations show. Accordingly, Baizhang suggests that it is not advisable to teach only one stage, because it could be misunderstood by people, which might lead them to commit unwholesome acts that lead to bad rebirth.[77] Yet, Baizhang also cautions against teaching all three stages at once, presumably because each stage is suitable for a specific group of practitioners whose practice has reached a certain level of spiritual maturity.[78] Accordingly, the three stages have to be observed both as distinct elements and as integral parts of a whole that encompasses all three. In that sense, the three stages retain their distinct identity as they address specific levels of spiritual development; at the same time, they are closely connected and constitute an integrated totality. This, from Baizhang's point of view, represents the essence of a direct Chan path of practice and realization.

Comparable Conceptual Models

The format of Baizhang's three propositions has parallels in various categories of discernments (guan) found in the writings of medieval Buddhist scholiasts. Renowned examples from Huayan literature include the three general discernments of Fajie guanmen (Discernment of the Realm of Reality), traditionally attributed to Dushun (557–640), and the six broad categories of discernment (or contemplation) of reality explicated in Wangjin huanyuan guan (Discernment of Ending Falsehood and Returning to the Source), a treatise attributed to Fazang that deals with the philosophical and applied aspects of Huayan meditation.[79] In Fajie guanmen, the three general discernments are those of (1) true emptiness (zhenkong), (2) mutual unobstruction of principle and phenomena (lishi wuai), and (3) total pervasion and accommodation (zhoubian hanrong), and they are further subdivided into several narrower discernments.[80] In Wangjin huanyuan guan, the six main categories, each of which contains a progressively increasing number of specific discernments, are those of (1) revealing one essence (*xian yi ti*), (2) giving rise to two functions (*qi er yong*), (3) manifesting three universals (*shi san bian*), (4) cultivating four virtues (*xing si de*), (5) entering five cessations (*ru wu zhi*), and (6) giving rise to six contemplations (or discernments, *qi liu guan*).[81]

Another example, which reveals a similar penchant for theoretical complexity, is Kuiji's (632–688) five levels of discernment of *vijñaptimātrā* (*weishi*, or "representation only"): (1) dismissing the false and preserving the true; (2) abandoning the diffuse and retaining the pure; (3) gathering the branches and returning to the root; (4) suppressing the subordinate and manifesting the superior; and (5) dismissing appearances and realizing the nature.[82] These discernments are central to Kuiji's exposition of the Faxiang/Yogācāra path of practice and realization. Like Baizhang's three propositions, the five levels of discernment represent a structured and sequential model of realization of the true nature of reality. In each case, we are confronted with progressive stages of practice that entail increasingly subtler and more authentic levels of perceiving reality.

When set against the Huayan and Faxiang categories of discernments, however, Baizhang's propositions differ in terms of theoretical complexity, doctrinal perspective, and soteriological import. Closer in structure and content to Baizhang's three propositions are the three stages in the progressive realization of the two truths formulated by Jizang. Jizang's explanation of the two truths—conventional truth and absolute truth—is a major contribution to the evolution of Madhyamaka doctrine in China. The two truths represent two levels of religious discourse (or means of instruction) and two analogous ways of knowing reality. In medieval China, it was also not uncommon to interpret them as two distinct ontological levels. Part of Jizang's stated agenda was to present a critique of such views and demonstrate the fallacy of perceiving the two truths as objective realms of reality.[83]

By postulating three phases in the dialectical ascent of the realization of the two truths, Jizang created a theoretical model that mapped a process of spiritual transformation. Through it the individual moved from ordinary people's naive misapprehension of reality to a non-conceptual state of awareness realized by accomplished sages (*shengren*). In his commentary of the *Lotus Scripture*, he explains the three levels:

> At the first stage, existence is identified as conventional truth, while emptiness is the absolute truth. Next, emptiness and existence are both taken to represent the conventional truth, while neither emptiness nor existence is the absolute truth. At the third stage, both duality and nonduality are understood as conventional truth, whereas neither duality nor nonduality is the absolute truth.[84]

By reformulating the two truths in this manner, Jizang was able to avoid their reification and highlight the fact that neither truth is fixed and conclusive.

At the first stage, the conventional and the absolute truth are both affirmed as two ways of viewing reality. In order to prevent reifying emptiness and becoming attached to it, at the second stage both conventional reality and emptiness are treated as conventional truths, while their negation (or nonduality) is the ultimate truth. The last stage represents an antidote to that view, as both duality and nonduality are relegated to the level of conventional truth, while the simultaneous transcendence of both of them is the ultimate truth.

In Jizang's formulation, ascent to a higher stage of understanding/realization involves the refutation of dualistic constructs evidenced at the preceding stage, which serves as a corrective device that lessens attachment and leads to a subtler level of transcendence. The final soteriological goal is to free the mind from all views, extremes, and attachments, so that it can shine in a nonconceptual state of wisdom,[85] the same goal as the one postulated by Baizhang's three propositions. Although the three propositions make no recourse to the two-truths paradigm, the two models share a similar structure. Both represent dialectical ascents toward a nonconceptual understanding of reality, in which each successive stage serves as an antidote that overcomes a specific form of attachment or imperfection that is operative at the previous stage. In that sense, they are both heirs of the Madhyamaka tradition, inasmuch as they do not try to establish any particular view of reality or put forward arguments about how ultimate truth should be perceived or understood. Instead, in true Madhyamaka fashion, they advocate the abandonment of all views, concepts, and attachments.

A related example of the utilization of a tripartite structure are the three truths—emptiness, conventional existence, and the Middle—enunciated by Zhiyi, which form the centerpiece of his intricate and wide-ranging formulation of Tiantai doctrine. Zhiyi's three truths are a natural extension and refinement of the two-truths doctrine. They have their practical counterparts in the three contemplations, which articulate a general pattern of practice that leads to insight into the true nature of reality.[86]

An additional example of a tripartite structure in early Chan comes from *Jueguan lun*, which illustrates the influence of Jizang and the Madhyamaka tradition on the teachings of the Niutou school. Adopting the format of a dialogue between a fictional teacher and a disciple, this work structures its religious message in terms of a dialectical progression that involves thesis, antithesis, and synthesis. At the first stage, the student's questions about various aspects of doctrine are met with the teacher's consistent refusal to allow the postulation of fixed religious ideals or the engagement in deliberate activity. At the second stage, the student achieves obliteration of discriminative perception, but the teacher rebuffs this as cognitive nihilism. Finally, at the third stage, the student achieves enlightenment, a state of perfect wisdom.[87] While the text is filled with Madhyamaka-like negation and denial, their function is to counteract the tendency to discriminate or conceptualize the goals, methods, and ethical standards associated with spiritual cultivation, not to deny that there is a positive objective or goal to be reached.[88]

Baizhang's three propositions and Jizang's threefold analysis of the two truths, as well as *Jueguan lun*'s tripartite formulation of spiritual progress, reveal the continuing appeal of Madhyamaka ideas. Their formulations of paths of practice that incorporate progressive levels of detachment and transcendence represent ingenious adaptations of the Madhyamaka dialectic. Their adoption of this perspective modifies the notion that during the Sui-Tang period Chinese Buddhism moved away from the apophatic mode of religious discourse associated with the Madhyamaka doctrine and in its stead embraced a kataphatic approach centered on the tathāgatagarbha doctrine.[89] Undoubtedly, this argument is valid in the cases of many influential Tang thinkers, including Zongmi, but writings such as those of Jizang and Baizhang reveal the persistent influence of the emptiness and middle-way doctrines, accompanied by the rejection of metaphysical models and essentialist ontologies that reified the Buddha-nature.

Additional evidence for the continuing influence of the Madhyamaka dialectic during the Tang era comes from Daoism, especially the writings of *Daode jing* exegetes associated with the Double Mystery (Chongxuan) school.[90] This exegetical tradition flourished during the first half of the Tang; it was heavily influenced by Buddhist ideas, such as the tetralemma of Madhyamaka philosophy. The phrase "twofold mystery" that forms the name of the school—which first appeared in Buddhist sources—implies the double forgetting or repudiation of the beliefs in absolute existence (*you*) and nonexistence (or nothingness, *wu*).[91] The first mystery involves the abandonment of both existence and nonexistence, while the second involves the elimination of attachment to the first mystery. In other words, at the stage of the first mystery, the Daoist adept must cultivate detachment from existence and nonexistence and give up the attendant dualistic perception of the world. Then, at the second stage, he or she must become nonattached to the detachment realized at the first stage. The transformation of the mind of an ordinary person into the mind of a sage explicated by the twofold-mystery tradition closely parallels the first two propositions in Baizhang's threefold scheme. The process of double mystery is also explained in terms of the decrease and eventual elimination of desires: after all desires are discarded at the level of the first mystery, then one must abandon dwelling in the serene state of absence of desires.[92]

Awakening and Realization

Classical Chan records do not provide comprehensive and nuanced depictions of the realm of reality and the experience of awakening, especially when compared with the texts of scholastic traditions such as Huayan and Tiantai. This is largely a reflection of their contemplative orientation and distinct soterio-logical perspective, which allegedly prioritize an unswerving, pragmatic ap-proach over complex theoretical schemes and metaphysical speculations (im-portant as they might be for mapping the Buddhist path). This predisposition is also informed by the notion that both ultimate reality and the experience of awakening are indescribable and beyond the sphere of conceptualization. Ac-cordingly, Chan teachings are presented as tools for freeing the mind from dualistic views and one-sided perspectives, rather than as rational explana-tions of reality or instructions about how it is to be viewed or perceived.

The lack of detailed descriptions of ultimate reality and the experience of awakening is also influenced by the literary format of classical Chan texts. The pertinent records consist of excerpts from sermons and conversations, which do not readily lend themselves to the systematic exposition of complex ideas. Nonetheless, there are brief statements scattered throughout the extant records of the Hongzhou school that shed light on their conception of the "inconceivable" experience of awakening. To begin with, in Baizhang's record the descriptions of the simultaneous realization of the three stages, based on the three propositions, denote the final realization and perfection of the Bud-dhist path:

> If one penetrates the three propositions, then one will not be con-strained by the three stages. The doctrinal schools compare that to a deer getting out of a net in three leaps. That is called a Buddha who is beyond entanglements. Nothing can confine or bind him. He is among the Buddhas that come after Dīpaṃkara Buddha.[93] That is the supreme vehicle. That is the highest wisdom. That is standing atop the path of the Buddha. Such a person is a Buddha who has Buddha-nature. He is a guide, able to harness the unobstructed wind. That is called unobstructed wisdom.[94]

In this passage and elsewhere, Baizhang compares the perfection of the three propositions to the realization of Buddhahood. The state of liberation and the attainment of unimpeded freedom that entails are also touched upon in the following paragraph from Baizhang's record, which recalls some of the key themes we encountered in the passages cited in the preceding sections:

> When the pure and impure minds are both ended, there is no abiding in bondage, nor is there abiding in liberation. There are no ideas of conditioned or unconditioned, bondage or liberation. Although it is still within [the realm of] birth and death, such a mind is free. Ultimately, it does not commingle with all falsehood, empty illusions, sensual passion, mortal clusters, element of exis-tence, life, death, and the sense media. Transcendent and without

abode, nothing at all constrains it. It comes and goes through birth and death as through an open door.[95]

Here the actualization of spiritual freedom is mainly defined negatively, in terms of what is abandoned. The Chan adept transcends all dualities—such as purity and impurity, bondage and liberation—that shape human experience within the phenomenal realm. While he is free from all constrains of saṃsāric existence, he still remains within the sphere of birth and death. The text tells us little about what the experience or vision of the "mind without abode" is like, although it makes it clear that such a mind is purified from such defilements as ignorance and sensual desires, which cause each person to experience saṃsāric existence. The mind is set free as it abandons the inveterate tendency to misconstrue reality by bifurcating all things and experiences into conflicting and antithetical opposites.

From this point of view, once the mind is freed from all attachments and defilements, the Chan sage is able to engage the world freely and participate in all facets of everyday existence. Even as he transcends the world of dualistic opposites, he is still able to function within it and work for the welfare of others. In that sense, spiritual awakening and realization do not mark negative withdrawal from the world, but a playful, unhindered, and total participation in the wholeness of human existence. A passage from Baizhang's record briefly describes this sphere of unobstructed activity:

> After that, [the adept who has perfected the Path] is able to make free use of cause and effect, blessings and wisdom. It is to take a cart to carry cause and effect. Then, in life, one is not obstructed by life; in death, one is not hindered by death. Within [the realm of] the five *skandhas* [of form/matter, feeling, perception, volition, and consciousness], like an open door, one is not hindered by the five *skandhas*. One is free to go and stay, entering and exiting without difficulty. If one can be like that, there is no discussion of stages, of superiority and inferiority. Even down to the body of an ant, when one is like that, everything is a pure and sublime land. It is inconceivable.[96]

According to Mazu and Baizhang, the realization of spiritual freedom involves the transcendence of mundane existence, and yet this experience still takes place within the confines of phenomenal reality. As follows from the Huayan vision of a single unobstructed *dharmadhātu* (*fajie*, realm of reality), the enlightened sage supposedly realizes that in their essence "all phenomena are one with the ultimate principle."[97] The notion of awakening is introduced only because of deep-seated human ignorance about the true nature of reality. Once ignorance disappears, we are told, one simply sees things as they truly are. Going beyond all verbalizations and concepts, such a person does not even dwell in the realization of awakening. Mazu elaborates on that point:

> It is in contrast to ignorance that one speaks of awakening. Since originally there is no ignorance, awakening also need not be established. All living beings have since limitless eons ago been abiding in the samādhi of the Dharma-nature. While they are in the samādhi of the Dharma-nature, they wear their clothes, eat their food, talk, and respond to things. As they make use of the six senses, all their activity is the Dharma-nature. Because of not knowing how to return to the source, they follow names and seek forms. That gives rise to confused emotions and falsehood, thereby creating all kinds of karma. If one were able within a single instant to illuminate within, then the whole essence is the holy mind.[98]

All things and creatures partake of the true nature of reality, even if ordinary people are not aware of it. Thus Mazu posits a state of original perfection, a fundamental realm of reality that is there irrespective of human ability to awaken and realize it. The Buddhist sage is a person who realizes that universal truth, which is fully manifested all the time in every phenomenon in the cosmos. The sage becomes free without leaving the realm of everyday reality and remains aware of the manifold distinctions that shape ordinary life. Though able to function freely in the world, such a person is described as someone who goes beyond all limitations. As is pointed out in the last quotation from Baizhang's record, he "comes and goes through birth and death as through an open door," meaning he acquires the ability to control his coming and going in the continuous cycle of saṃsāra, an idea familiar from canonical Mahāyāna literature.

Although he supposedly possesses the ability to put an end to the sequence of future rebirths, we are told that, in accord with the bodhisattva ideal, the Buddhist sage chooses not to use that prerogative. He decides to stay in the world because the perfection of the path and the realization of awakening are not understood merely as private religious acts that bring about personal liberation. Following from the altruistic ethos of the bodhisattva ideal, the experience of enlightenment has wider social implications, as it sets the stage for selfless activity dedicated to the welfare and religious salvation of one's fellow human beings. Such a person, having cut off the causes that lead to continuous rebirth in saṃsāra, remains fully engaged in the world and immersed in its ways.

This depiction of a realized sage is in tune with canonical formulations of the bodhisattva ideal, another example of the already-noted sense of continuity and connection between the Hongzhou school and the canonical tradition. Baizhang also describes the realized sage as a spiritual benefactor, a religious teacher who "responds to all creatures with an unattached heart, opens all fetters with unhindered wisdom."[99] Having transcended the attachments to self

and things, he or she functions as a spiritual guide, enabling others to go beyond their self-imposed limitations and realize the sublime magnificence of
the realm of enlightenment, in all of its all-encompassing wholeness, lumi-
nosity, and perfection.

NOTES

1. In its usual sense, the term *ju* denotes a sentence, line, or part of a verse, and
it is used to translate the Sanskrit term *pada*. Here it is employed in the less common
meaning of a state or condition, found in phrases such as "the condition of enlightenment." An even closer usage is evident in phrases such as "the four propositions" of
Madhyamaka dialectic (Sanskrit: *catuṣkoṭi*; Chinese: *siju fenbie*), which constitute the
full range of logical possibilities on the basis of which it is possible to examine the
veracity of a given proposition. In his translation of Baizhang's record, Cleary
translates the term as "phase," which is an acceptable rendering. See the discussion
of the term in Cleary, *Pai-chang*, 104–5, n. 20, and Sharf, *Coming to Terms with Chinese
Buddhism*, 63.

2. See T 48.337b–338a and Yampolsky, *The Platform Sūtra*, 128–33.

3. McRae, "Shen-hui and the Teaching of Sudden Enlightenment," 228. There
are actually three verses, as there are two versions of Huineng's verse.

4. For an overview of the sudden/gradual polarity, see Gómez, "Purifying Gold:
The Metaphor of Effort and Intuition in Buddhist Thought and Practice." Additional
information is available in the other essays of the same volume (Gregory, *Sudden and
Gradual: Approaches to Enlightenment in Chinese Buddhism*).

5. See Whalen Lai, "Tao-sheng's Theory of Sudden Enlightenment Re-
examined."

6. McRae, "Shen-hui and the Teaching of Sudden Enlightenment," 256–57.

7. Faure, *The Rhetoric of Immediacy*, 33–36.

8. Ibid., 44.

9. T 47.589c.

10. Peter Gregory, "Sudden Enlightenment Followed by Gradual Cultivation:
Tsung-mi's Analysis of Mind," 308.

11. McRae, "Shen-hui and the Teaching of Sudden Enlightenment," 254.

12. Faure, *The Rhetoric of Immediacy*, 36. For Tiantai responses and resolutions
of such tensions, see Stevenson, "The Four Kinds of Samādhi in Early T'ien-t'ai
Buddhism," 80–81, 85.

13. For a discussion of Chengguan's writings on this topic, see Yoshizu Yoshihide, *Kegon zen no shisōteki kenkyū*, 249–64; there is also a brief summary in
Gregory, "Sudden Enlightenment Followed by Gradual Cultivation," 309–11.

14. T 48.407c; Gregory, "Sudden Enlightenment Followed by Gradual Cultivation," 282–84.

15. For a summary of Zongmi's critique of the Hongzhou school, see Gregory,
Tsung-mi, 236–44; for a translation of the relevant passages, see Jan Yun-hua,
"Tsung-mi: His Analysis of Ch'an Buddhism," 39–40, 45–47. While for reasons of
space and focus I do not go into the historical context of Zongmi's critique of the
Hongzhou school here, I plan to address this issue in a separate publication.

16. Gregory, *Tsung-mi*, 237.

17. According to Gregory, those concerns can be compared with Zongmi's ambiguous stance toward the Huayan doctrine of unobstructed interpenetration among phenomena (*shishi wuai*). Gregory, *Tsung-mi*, 250–52.

18. See Gregory, *Tsung-mi*, 194.

19. Gregory, "Sudden Enlightenment Followed by Gradual Cultivation," 307.

20. T 48.407c–408a.

21. XZJ 110.436a; Gregory, *Tsung-mi*, 238.

22. XZJ 110.438a; Gregory, *Tsung-mi*, 238.

23. See Robert Buswell, "The 'Short-cut' Approach of *K'an-hua* Meditation," 340.

24. MY, XZJ 119.406b; Cheng-chien, *Sun-Face Buddha*, 64.

25. See *Dunwu rudao yaomen lun*, in Hirano, *Tongo yōmon*, 24, 60, 90–91.

26. See the discussion of Dazhu's treatise in "Sources for the Study of the Hongzhou School's Doctrines" in the appendix.

27. See XZJ 119.411a. The pertinent section does not appear in the *Gu zunsu yulu* edition of the text, but it is added to the *Sijia yulu* edition. It might not have been part of the early edition of the record.

28. BGL, XZJ 118.83d; cf. Cleary, *Pai-chang*, 35.

29. *Huangboshan duanji chanshi chuanxin fayao*, T 48.379c–380a; cf. John Blofeld, *The Zen Teaching of Huang-po*, 30. Note the subtle difference between *jian* (gradual) and *cidi* (graduated).

30. *Huangboshan duanji chanshi wanling lu*, T 48.384b; cf. Blofeld, *The Zen Teaching of Huang-po*, 68.

31. T 48.384b; cf. Blofeld, *The Zen Teaching of Huang-po*, 69.

32. For Shenhui's gradualist slips, see Gómez, "Purifying Gold," 78, 87–88.

33. MY, XZJ 119.407a; Cheng-chien, *Sun-Face Buddha*, 68.

34. MY, XZJ 119.406a; Cheng-chien, *Sun-Face Buddha*, 63.

35. See Yanagida, "Goroku no rekishi," 498.

36. MY, XZJ 119.406a; Cheng-chien, *Sun-Face Buddha*, 63.

37. See MY, XZJ 119.406c; Cheng-chien, *Sun-Face Buddha*, 65.

38. See Conze, *The Perfection of Wisdom*, 103, 111, 188.

39. Consider the following scriptural passage: "Even if a Bodhisattva, after he has raised his mind to full enlightenment, would, for countless eons, give gifts, guard his morality, perfect his patience, exert in vigor, and enter the trances, however great may be his setting forth and the thought which he raises to full enlightenment, if he is not upheld by perfect wisdom and lacks in skill and means, he is bound to fall on the level of Disciple or Pratyekabuddha." Conze, *The Perfection of Wisdom*, 196.

40. BGL, XZJ 118.87b; Cheng-chien, *Sun-Face Buddha*, 22.

41. See McRae, *The Northern School*, 121–32.

42. BGL, XZJ 118.85a; Cleary, *Pai-chang*, 43.

43. The allegory of washing a dirty robe appears in the Chinese translations of the *Nirvāṇa Scripture*, T 12.793c, and T 12.548b, where it is used as a simile for bodhisattvas' cultivation of wisdom, which initially involves reading and recitation of scriptures, eventually followed by understanding of their meaning. For additional canonical references, see *Bailun*, T 30.170b, *Apidamo dapiposha lun* (*Abhidharma-mahāvibhāṣā-śāstra*), T 27.110a, and *Wenshushili wen jing*, T 14.503a. None of these

texts, however, corresponds closely to the passage in Baizhang's record, which might not be alluding to any specific canonical text.

44. See Ñāṇamoli and Bodhi, *The Middle Length Discourses*, 118–20.

45. See Yampolsky, *The Platform Sūtra*, 130.

46. Ibid., 132. For the traditional interpretation of the two "mind verses," see McRae, *The Northern School*, 1–7.

47. See McRae, "Shen-hui and the Teaching of Sudden Enlightenment," 228.

48. MY, XZJ 119.406a, 407a.

49. See MY, XZJ 119.407c; Cheng-chien, *Sun-Face Buddha*, 72.

50. CDL 9, T 51.267b; translation adapted from Cheng-chien, *Sun-Face Buddha*, 88–89, n. 46. Da'an is also sometimes regarded as a student of Guishan.

51. CDL 9, T 51.267c; Cheng-chien, *Sun-Face Buddha*, 89, n. 46. Considering the lack of earlier versions of this and the previous quoted passage, uncertainties remain about their origin and authenticity.

52. CDL 9, T 51.264c.

53. The Hongzhou school's responses to the challenge of balancing the subitist and gradualist perspectives was a new take on a perennial issue, which was previously tackled by other monks, both within the Chan movement (e.g. Shenxiu) and outside of it (e.g., Zhiyi). For Zhiyi's perspective on subitism and gradualism, see Neal Donner, "Sudden and Gradual Intimately Conjoined: Chih-i's T'ien-t'ai View."

54. BGL, XZJ 118.90c; Cleary, *Pai-chang*, 77.

55. McRae, *The Northern School*, 103.

56. BGL, XZJ 118.82d; Cleary, *Pai-chang*, 30.

57. BGL, XZJ 118.84d; Cleary, *Pai-chang*, 41.

58. For a classical version of the simile of the raft, see the *Alagaddūpama Sutta* of the *Majjhima Nikāya*, in Ñāṇamoli and Bodhi, *The Middle Length Discourses*, 228–29.

59. BGL, XZJ 118.82d–83a; Cleary, *Pai-chang*, 30–31.

60. See Hirai, "The School of Mount Niu-t'ou and the School of Pao-T'ang Monastery," 361.

61. BGL, XZJ 118.83a; Cleary, *Pai-chang*, 31. The phrase "bondage of the bodhisattvas" appears in the *Vimalakīrti Scripture* (T 14.545b); there it refers to the bodhisattva's attachment to the "flavor" of meditation, which is offset by the employment of expedient means.

62. Hirano, *Tongo yōmon*, 30; John Blofeld, *The Zen Teaching of Instantaneous Awakening*, 52.

63. Hirano, *Tongo yōmon*, 37; Blofeld, *The Zen Teaching of Instantaneous Awakening*, 55.

64. BGL, XZJ 118.83a; Cleary, *Pai-chang*, 31. The famous simile of a wise man engendering a volume of scripture from an atom comes from the "Manifestation of the Tathāgata" chapter of the *Huayan jing*. See T 10.272c and Cheng-chien, *Manifestation of the Tathāgata*, 105–6.

65. BGL, XZJ 118.83a; Cleary, *Pai-chang*, 31.

66. BGL, XZJ 118.86d; Cleary, *Pai-chang*, 55.

67. BGL, XZJ 118.83c; Cleary, *Pai-chang*, 34.

68. BGL, XZJ 118.84c–d; Cleary, *Pai-chang*, 41.

69. BGL, XZJ 118.83c; Cleary, *Pai-chang*, 34–35.

70. BGL, XZJ 118.87c; Cleary, *Pai-chang*, 59.

71. BGL, XZJ 118.84b; Cleary, *Pai-chang*, 38.

72. For additional passages where Baizhang explicates the three stages, see BGL, XZJ 118.84a, 84d, 86d, 87b; and Cleary, *Pai-chang*, 37, 41, 47, 55, 57.

73. *Dunwu rudao yaomen lun*, XZJ 110.426b; Hirano, *Tongo yōmon*, 108–9; Blofeld, *The Zen Teaching of Instantaneous Awakening*, 81. The last sentence in the XZJ text contains an additional four characters, which are probably a mistaken interpolation (see Hirano's note).

74. BGL, XZJ 118.86d; Cleary, *Pai-chang*, 55.

75. BGL, XZJ 118.84a; cf. Cleary, *Pai-chang*, 37.

76. BGL, XZJ 118.89b; cf. Cleary, *Pai-chang*, 70. There is also this similar passage: "Just detach from sounds and forms, do not abide in detachment, and do not abide in intellectual understanding. That is practice." See Cleary, *Pai-chang*, 47 (translation slightly changed from Cleary's version).

77. BGL, XZJ 118.84d; Cleary, *Pai-chang*, 41. This concern seems justified when we look at the history of Buddhism in East Asia. At times, unqualified repudiation of supposedly "elementary" teachings and practices that focus on purity and detachment, coupled with lofty rhetoric about the identity of defilements and enlightenment, served as a license to abandon traditional ethical observances. For an example from Japanese Buddhist history, see the discussion of the problems and justifications that surrounded the Tendai school's rejection of the Vinaya in Paul Groner, "The *Fanwang ching* and Monastic Discipline in Japanese Tendai: A Study of Annen's *Futsū jubosatsukai kōshaku*."

78. BGL, XZJ 118.84d; Cleary, *Pai-chang*, 41.

79. For an argument against Fazang's authorship of this text, see Kojima Taizan, "*Mōjin gengen kan* no senja o meguru shomondai."

80. See T 45.652b, T 45.672c; Thomas Cleary, *Entry into the Inconceivable: An Introduction to Hua-yen Buddhism*, 74; and Gimello, "Apophatic and Kataphatic Discourse in Mahāyāna," 120–28.

81. See T 45.637a–b and Cleary, *Entry into the Inconceivable*, 151–52.

82. *Dasheng fayuan yilin zhang*, T 45.258c–59a, and Alan Sponberg, "Meditation in Fa-hsiang Buddhism," 30–34.

83. Liu, *Madhyamaka Thought in China*, 140.

84. *Fahua xuanlun*, T 34.396a; cf. Liu, *Madhyamaka Thought in China*, 148. See also T 45.90c and Sharf, *Coming to Terms with Chinese Buddhism*, 64–65.

85. See Paul Williams, *Mahāyāna Buddhism*, 75–76.

86. Swanson, *Foundations of T'ien-t'ai Philosophy*, 115–56.

87. McRae, "The Ox-head School," 215–16.

88. Ibid., 217.

89. This argument is articulated in Gimello, "Apophatic and Kataphatic Discourse in Mahāyāna." The same line of interpretation is adopted and further elaborated in Gregory's *Tsung-mi and the Sinification of Buddhism*.

90. For more on this Daoist school, see Livia Kohn, *Early Chinese Mysticism: Philosophy and Soteriology in the Taoist Tradition*, 139–46, and Sharf, *Coming to Terms with Chinese Buddhism*, 52–71.

91. Isabelle Robinet, *Taoism: Growth of a Religion*, 194.

92. Kohn, *Early Chinese Mysticism*, 142.

93. Dīpaṃkara is among the mythical Buddhas of remote antiquity who preceded Śākyamuni Buddha. According to tradition, he predicted Śākyamuni's Buddhahood while the latter was still a bodhisattva. He appears in the *Lotus Scripture* and other canonical texts.

94. BGL, XZJ 118.83a; Cleary, *Pai-chang*, 31.

95. BGL (*Sijia yulu* ed.), XZJ 119.411b; Cleary, *Pai-chang*, 79.

96. BGL, XZJ 118.83a; cf. Cleary, *Pai-chang*, 31–32. This paragraph follows immediately the first passage quoted at the beginning of this section.

97. MY, XZJ 119.406a; Cheng-chien, *Sun-Face Buddha*, 62.

98. MY, XZJ 119.406b; Cheng-chien, *Sun-Face Buddha*, 64. In the last sentence, "illuminate within" is a somewhat free rendering of *fanzhao*, a term that refers to the mind shining back upon itself.

99. BGL (*Sijia yulu* ed.), XZJ 119.411c; Cleary, *Pai-chang*, 80.

Conclusion

Chan teachings such as Baizhang's three propositions (surveyed in the last chapter) invoke some of the central tenets of Mahāyāna and intersect with doctrinal outlooks shared by other Chinese Buddhist traditions, even as they express distinctive perspectives on practice and realization. Along with other Hongzhou school teachings, the three propositions exemplify the manner in which in their preaching Mazu and his disciples combined the familiar with the new, fusing them into distinct and readily comprehensible—even if at times rarefied—teachings about a Chan path of spiritual cultivation. Within the context of Tang Buddhism, their teachings were approachable in terms of established doctrinal and soteriological frames of reference; yet we learn from the recorded responses of monks and literati that they also came across as fresh and original. Evidently, the Hongzhou school's doctrinal and soteriological formulations evinced a sense of continuity with established creeds and received traditions, while also expressing distinct points of view and leaving a notable imprint on the evolution of Chan doctrine.

Mazu and his disciples distinguished themselves by the creative ways in which they adapted canonical principles and expressed time-honored monastic ideals, and by the manner in which they applied personal insights and perspectives in their explication of a direct approach to religious training and experience. By inventing or deftly adapting compelling catchphrases—such as "mind is Buddha," "it is not a thing," and "ordinary mind is the way"—they engagingly communicated key Buddhist insights and demarcated essential attitudes toward spiritual cultivation. Even as they formed a distinct, though loosely organized, group within the larger Chan movement, monks associated with the Hongzhou school embraced the cumulative wisdom and hallowed traditions inherited by virtue of their membership in the monastic order. They asserted—and presumably sincerely believed—that they were conveying an understanding of the most essential and central Buddhist insights and experiences and imparting soteriological tools for their realization. At the apex was the ineffable experience of awakening, which according to tradition took its perfect form when the Buddha sat under the *bodhi* tree in India. To that end, they articulated a way of reflection and practice that they believed would enable others to access those realizations, thereby fulfilling their innate potential for transcendence and the attainment of spiritual freedom.

Besides the appeal of its doctrines, the Hongzhou school's rise to prominence was predicated on the individual charisma of its leaders.[1] A conspicuous feature of the extant records is their focus on the singular personalities of leading Hongzhou school figures, although to some extent this was influenced by the genres in which they were written, which often privileged biographical narratives. Even so, it is apparent that the religious personalities and personal magnetism of prominent Chan teachers were important factors in the rise and popularity of the Hongzhou school. To borrow Max Weber's typology of authority, Mazu and his leading disciples aptly combined traditional and charismatic religious authority.[2] The exercise of traditional authority—based on conveying a religious message sanctified by established traditions and by holding an office—is evident in Mazu's position as the head of a state-sponsored monastery. His role as a respected monk who combined knowledge of canonical texts and traditions with contemplative prowess also fortified this aspect of his authority. The same can be said of his leading disciples, who were esteemed for their mastery of these two major spheres of monastic expertise.

Chan teachers such as Mazu and Baizhang also possessed charismatic authority, which relies on the person of the leader and disrupts established traditions. This aspect of their authority was predicated on a belief that they had special insight into the nature of reality, which they could impart or communicate to others. The potentially subversive force of their personal charisma was thus corralled by the responsibilities and privileges that went along with the exercise of traditional authority. As we saw in the examination of the Hongzhou school's attitudes toward canonical authority, the merging of these two was reflected in the image of the Chan teacher as someone who functioned both within and outside of prevailing norms and institutions, simultaneously challenging and embodying normative values and established traditions.[3]

Any assessment of the teachings of the Hongzhou school within the broader context of Tang Buddhism must also take into account what the records of Mazu and his disciples leave out or gloss over. They make very little reference to popular religious beliefs and practices that were integral to Tang Buddhism. For instance, there is scarcely a mention of the salvific powers of the various Buddhas and bodhisattvas or the cultic practices centered on them. Aside from a few passing references, thaumaturgy is similarly ignored, and the same can be said about prevalent notions of the law of karma[4] or the prospect of rebirth in the pure land of Amitābha Buddha. And there are very few practical instructions or depictions of procedures for the practice of meditation, such as those described in detail in Zhiyi's meditation manuals and treatises. These omissions do not necessarily attest that those elements were not part of the religious universe of Mazu and his disciples. The seemingly dismissive attitude toward popular beliefs and practices might be a function of who was doing the remembering, which was echoed in the sources about the Hongzhou school's teachings. Even so, we can safely assume that the main thrust of their teachings was centered on explicating a direct and unswerving—even though often abstruse—approach to Chan insight and practice, one that reflected the fundamental concerns and predispositions of what was essentially an elitist group of contemplative monks.

We can also discern in the extant records of the Hongzhou school's teaching an unstated but palpable aversion to convoluted metaphysical speculations or intricate exegesis of the finer points of Buddhist doctrine. This stands in contrast to the Buddhist scholastic traditions that flourished at the time, although it is reminiscent of general attitudes found within the Chan movement. When the Hongzhou school's teachings are compared with earlier Chan traditions such as the Northern and Niutou schools, however, we can detect a subtle shift toward a more distinctive Chan idiom, as well as a related conspicuous absence of the cumbersome strategies for bridging the gap between Chan and canonical Buddhism that were prominent in early Chan.[5] As we have seen, during the early Tang period these included the forced analogies of "symbolic exegesis" and the drawing of artificial connections between Chan teachings and specific canonical texts, especially the *Laṅkāvatāra* and *Diamond* scriptures. Such legitimizing strategies were initially used to bolster the Chan school's claims to authenticity and orthodoxy during a period of nascent growth. They were also employed to settle sectarian divides—real and imagined—in what at the time was still a nebulous movement that lacked a coherent center or clear source of authority. The eschewing of such legitimizing strategies by Mazu and his disciples symbolized the growing maturity and consolidation of the Chan movement, which by the early ninth century came to be primarily represented by the Hongzhou school.

All of these circumstances suggest that we can best understand the Hongzhou school's carving of a prominent space within the Tang religious landscape in terms of a subtle interplay between patterns of continuity and rupture with established Buddhist traditions. The school's emergence as a distinct but integral part of the Chan movement—and more broadly of Tang Buddhism—was a manifestation of the dialectical interplay between traditionalism and iconoclasm (albeit of a mild and placid kind) and their joint role in the construction of religious identity. The ingenious responses of Mazu and his disciples to the seeming paradoxes and frictions engendered by these divergent demands shaped the basic character of their tradition, as is reflected in their doctrines and practices. By employing the traditionalism/iconoclasm dichotomy, we can discern how the Hongzhou school was able to balance its adherence to established teachings and traditional mores (traditionalism) with the need to forge an identity by rejecting or reformulating aspects of received traditions (a mild form of iconoclasm). The ability to sustain this delicate balancing act contributed to the success of the Hongzhou school, which became the dominant tradition of Chan and thus left a significant mark on the religious history of Tang China.

The same set of issues is evident in the historical pattern of the Hongzhou school's incipient growth and its subsequent expansion, which was described in the first half of this volume. In contrast to the familiar images of rebellious radicals popularized by later Chan/Zen lore, in the stele inscriptions and other early records Mazu and his disciples come across as a group of monks grounded in the monastic ethos and canonical traditions of medieval Chinese Buddhism. The sources also convey an image of individuals attuned to the social realities and cultural norms of the world in which they pursued their monastic vocations. This is evident in the lives and monastic careers of individual monks, as well as in the general pattern of the Hongzhou school's growth. The school's responsiveness to concrete social and political predicaments is evident in its spread throughout the Tang empire and its formation of networks of patronage. This helped it to become the first empire-wide Chan tradition and to extend its influence as far as the Korean peninsula.

The extant evidence suggests that Mazu and his disciples displayed considerable skill and a sense of astuteness in communicating their teaching and reaching out to key audiences. They had considerable success in connecting and capturing the religious imagination of monks and laymen, with a focus (unintended or otherwise) on the elite members of both groups. The monastic disciples constituted the Hongzhou school's core, disseminating the teachings and providing a measure of group identity and institutional stability. Of almost equal importance was the Chan teachers' ability to appeal to the religious tastes and predilections of the sociopolitical and cultural elites. These included many sophisticated officials and literati who received religious instructions from Mazu and his disciples, along with a few emperors and a score of influential public figures. Taken together, they constituted an important audience for the Hongzhou school's teachings and an added source of socioreligious legitimacy, as well as a key supplier of economic support and political patronage.

The emergence of the Hongzhou school at the vanguard of the Chan movement during the mid-Tang period had significant ramifications for the growth of the Chan school and its gradual emergence as the main tradition of elite

Chinese Buddhism. As we saw in chapter 3, Mazu and his disciples appeared at a time when virtually all of the early Chan traditions were already defunct or in the final stage of their demise. Within the Tang context, then, the Hongzhou school played the historically important role of unifying a previously fragmented Chan movement. We may perhaps even speculate that with the demise of the early schools/lineages, the Chan movement might have come close to a premature demise, or at least a serious crisis with long-lasting ramifications, if it had not been not for the institutional dominance, renewed vigor, and creative energy infused by Mazu and his followers.

The Hongzhou school also put its stamp on an evolving conception of Chan orthodoxy. This was expressed in the construction of a multibranched Chan lineage that led to Mazu and his disciples, but also allowed for the inclusion of other lineages. The classical form of that lineage was first articulated in *Baolin zhuan*—compiled in 801, just as the Hongzhou school was evolving into the main representative of the Chan movement—and became accepted as normative throughout later Chan history. As the leading Chan figures of their generation, Mazu's disciples bolstered their tradition's prominent position within the Buddhist mainstream. They moved away from the radical excesses of some of their predecessors, exemplified by the antinomian teachings and attitudes of the Baotang school in Sichuan, and they adopted an ecumenical stance and promoted an inclusive vision of Chan orthodoxy. Although sectarian agendas never completely disappeared from Chan history, the kind of disruptive sectarianism evident during Shenhui's campaigns against the Northern school was for the most part left behind.

Later generations of Chan writers and adherents celebrated Mazu and his leading disciples as paradigmatic exemplars of the virtues and qualities they associated with the great Chan teachers of the "golden age" of Tang Chan. But their pious imagery of the Hongzhou school was formed on the basis of later apocryphal stories that portrayed Mazu and his disciples as the instigators of a new iconoclast ethos. These stories became the central motifs of popular Chan lore and a linchpin of official ideology, thereby obscuring the historical lives of their main protagonists. As a result, a monk such as Baizhang became chiefly known through the medium of popular, if somewhat outlandish, stories that depict him as crying after Mazu twisted his nose or becoming deaf for three days after Mazu shouted at him.[6] Baizhang was also celebrated as the patron saint of "Chan monasticism" and as the author of the mythical monastic code that supposedly ushered in the Chan school's institutional independence. On the other hand, the fairly comprehensive record of his teachings, one of the richest and most significant statements of Chan doctrine from the Tang era, was subjected to benign neglect. The selective approach to collective remembrance of the past evident in the world of Song Chan—or rather the creative reconstitution of the Chan school's early history in accord with a prevailing ideology—points to the significant gap between Tang and Song Chan, or more broadly between the different Buddhist traditions that flourished during these two major eras of Chinese history.

In terms of the broader evolution of Chan doctrine, the Hongzhou school's teachings are best understood as a culmination of doctrinal developments within Tang Chan. Notwithstanding their unique features, they must be interpreted within the religious and intellectual milieus of Tang Buddhism, including the rethinking of Buddhist theory and praxis initiated by the early Chan moment. This book argues that this more nuanced interpretative scheme should replace earlier views and interpretations about the emergence and character of the Hongzhou school, which was construed as a sudden paradigm shift that involved far-reaching and multifaceted transformations. We need to be especially wary of viewing Mazu, Baizhang, and other monks associated with the Hongzhou school as instigators of new developments that paved the way for the teachings and practices of Song Chan, especially as represented by the dominant Linji school that saw itself as carrying the mantle of Mazu and Baizhang. As this book shows, the Hongzhou school was historically important within the context of Tang Chan, but it was important in ways that were rather different from those assumed by later generations of Chan/Zen historians and adherents.

While some of Mazu's sayings, such as "everyday mind is the Way," were widely circulated within Chan circles during the Song and subsequent periods (including the present time), they were interpreted in the light of post-Tang ideas and traditions. The later traditions largely centered on exegesis of the encounter dialogue stories, expressed in a distinct literary idiom that appealed to the Song literati, and related to a new form of meditative praxis. It was also embedded in specific institutional structures and ideological constructs that became normative only during the Song era (and largely remained so during the ensuing periods). Teachings such as Baizhang's three propositions fared even worse, as they were all but forgotten. Thus the range of teachings promulgated by the Hongzhou school—important as they might be for the understanding Tang Chan—had limited impact on the theory and practice of Chan from the Song period onward. As the Chan tradition by and large coalesced around the *kanhua* (observing the critical phrase) approach championed by Dahui—which was linked to a new Chan literature represented by the classical *gong'an* collections—the putative sayings of the Tang masters assumed new meaning and significance, which had only tenuous links with their actual lives and teachings.

This book represents an attempt to take another look at the mid-Tang period and recover significant aspects of Tang religious history. Its portrayal of the Hongzhou school challenges popular views and prevalent notions about the history and character of Tang Chan, thereby further undermining the myth of Chan's uniqueness that still permeates many discussions of Chan/Zen history, literature, and teachings. Concerning the centrality of the Hongzhou school in subsequent historical narratives and demarcations of Chan orthodoxy, a re-thinking of its growth and character along the lines suggested in this volume has wide-ranging ramifications for reinterpreting the beliefs and ideologies of the later Chan/Zen traditions throughout East Asia. While in the preceding pages I have occasionally alluded to some of these implications, such later developments lie outside the scope of this volume, which focuses on a historical understanding of the mid-Tang period. The critical examination of the circumstances and issues that shaped the production of religious imagery and pseudo-historical narratives centered on the great Chan teachers of the Tang era—both as expressions of faith and tools of ideological dominance—takes us forward to the Five Dynasties and early Song periods. These remain fertile areas for future research, which might (among other things) clarify the historical developments that led to the transformation of the monks depicted in this volume into the iconoclastic heroes of later Chan lore.

A major challenge facing present-day Chan/Buddhist scholarship is the need to reexamine the various sources in relation to the applicable historical contexts and to produce studies that deal with Tang and Song Chan/Buddhism on their own terms and within the context of the societies and cultures in which they flourished. This will facilitate a reassessment of the broader historical trajectory of the Chan tradition and help us situate its wide-ranging and profound transformations in relation to the pertinent social and religious milieus. This book is a step in that direction. As we improve our understanding of the history and teachings of key traditions such as the Hongzhou school, we are in a better position to reassess the sweeping changes in the religious, social, and cultural spheres that took place during the Tang-Song transition, and to arrive at a more nuanced and complete picture of religious life in late medieval China.

NOTES

    1. Here I use the concept of charisma in the sense formulated by Max Weber, who defined it as "a certain quality of an individual personality by virtue of which he is set apart from ordinary men and treated as endowed with supernatural, super-human, or at least specifically exceptional powers or qualities. These are such as are not accessible to the ordinary person, but are regarded as of divine origin or as exemplary, and on the basis of them the individual concerned is treated as a leader." Max Weber, *The Theory of Social and Economic Organization*, 358–59.

    2. Ibid., 328.

    3. See "Use of Scriptures "in chapter 4.

    4. A notable exception is *Guishan jingce*, which often mentions the workings of the law of karma and warns its monastic audience of the dire karmic consequences of improper conduct and unwholesome behavior.

    5. See "Canonicity and Attitudes toward Scriptural Authority" in chapter 4.

    6. *Gu zunsu yulu* 1, XZJ 118.81b–c.

Appendix

The main primary sources for the study of Mazu's life—listed in chronological order—are as follows:

(1) A short stone inscription that was discovered in 1966 underneath Mazu's memorial pagoda—named Da Zhuangyan (Great Adornment) Pagoda—located on the grounds of Baofeng monastery in Jing'an county, Jiangxi province. The inscription was composed in 791, three years after Mazu's death, on the occasion of the formal opening of the pagoda. The full text of the inscription is: "On the seventeenth day of the seventh month of the seventh year of the Zhenyuan reign of the Tang (August 21, 791), a pagoda was build at this location for the golden relics of the great master, Rev. Daoyi. The great master entered Nirvāṇa on the first day of the second month of the fourth year of the Zhenyuan reign (March 13, 788). Recorded on that occasion by the Hongzhou governor Li Jian, the magistrate of Jiangzhang county Li Qi, the disciples from Falin monastery in Shimen, and others."[1]

(2) Mazu's stele inscription, composed by the famous official and literatus Quan Deyu (759–818) in 791. Its full title is *Tang gu hongzhou kaiyuansi shimen daoyi chanshi beiming bingxu*.[2]

(3) The memorial inscription written by Mazu's contemporary Bao Ji (dates unknown), the duke of Danyang, which was probably composed soon after Mazu's death. Though the original text is no longer extant, some of its contents are probably preserved in Mazu's biography in Zanning's (919–1001) *Song gaoseng zhuan*, compiled in 988 (see below).

(4) Mazu's biography in *Baolin zhuan*, composed in 801. Unfortunately, the last (tenth) fascicle of this text, which included Mazu's biography, is lost, and only a few brief fragments from Mazu's biography are extant.[3]

(5) Mazu's biography in *Song gaoseng zhuan*, which is primarily based on Quan Deyu's and Bao Ji's stele inscriptions, both of which are mentioned at the end of the biography.[4]

(6) Zongmi's (780–841) writings, especially his commentary on the *Yuanjue jing* (Perfect Enlightenment Scripture), *Yuanjue jing dashu chao* (fascicle 3b), and *Pei Xiu sheyi wen* (often referred to as *Zhonghua chuan xindi chanmen shizi chengxi tu*, following a mistaken reconstruction of its title by the *Zokuzōkyō* editors).[5]

(7) Mazu's biography in *Zutang ji*. This text includes some interesting hagiographic materials not found in the other sources.[6]

In addition, Yongming Yanshou's (904–975) *Zongjing lu* (compiled in 961) includes some of the earliest editions of Mazu's sermons (including excerpts from two sermons not preserved in any other source), but it does not contain any valuable biographical information.[7] All Song texts that belong to the transmission of the lamp genre, beginning with Daoyuan's *Jingde chuandeng lu*, also contain biographical materials about Mazu.[8] For the most part, however, they do not include any important information that is not already found in the earlier sources; when they do provide additional pieces of biographical data, they are of questionable provenance and accuracy.

Additional sources of information about Mazu's life are the biographies of his disciples. The earliest data of this kind can be found in his disciples' extant stele inscriptions that were composed during the early ninth century (see "Stele Inscriptions of Chan Monks" below). Pertinent information is also included in the biographies of his disciples recorded in *Zutang ji* and *Song gaoseng zhuan*. Last, information about people and sites connected with Mazu can be found in the local gazetteers of the areas where he resided, especially in gazetteers from his native Sichuan and Jiangxi, where he spent the second half of his life. Although this kind of information usually comes from fairly late sources, these local records provide interesting data about the history of the religious sites and local traditions that came to be associated with Mazu and afford insights into Mazu's stature in various local religious communities.

INFORMATION ABOUT MAZU'S DISCIPLES

The earliest information about Mazu's disciples comes from the list of prominent disciples in his stele inscription, which contains eleven names, including Xitang, Dazhu, Huaihui, and Weikuan.[9] Later sources provide various figures for the number of Mazu's close disciples. *Zutang ji* gives the number of his close disciples as eighty-eight, while *Baizhang yulu* and *Tiansheng guangdeng lu* state that he had eight-four disciples.[10] Mazu's biography in *Chuandeng lu*—which admittedly was compiled over two centuries after Mazu's death—asserts that he had 139 close disciples; the text also provides the names of all but one of them.[11] When we combine the information about Mazu's disciples available from all sources, we have the names of no less than 148 of them, although in a number of instances the lives of individual monks and their connections with Mazu are not well documented.[12] These listings of Mazu's disciples include only monks who distinguished themselves, either through their teaching or in some other way. We are thus primarily dealing with a monastic elite, rather than ordinary members of monastic congregations. Undoubtedly, the total number of monks who resided at Mazu's monasteries was significantly larger, and only a relatively small number of them were significant enough to deserve mention in the historical records.

As described in part I of this volume, Mazu had significant impact as a teacher who trained numerous prominent monks, including the leading Chan teachers of the next generation. His wide-ranging influence is evident when we compare the space Chan histories allocate to the biographies of his disciples with that given to the disciples of other noted Chan teachers from the Tang period. The biographies of Mazu's direct disciples alone take up three fascicles of *Chuandeng lu*, the most influential "history" of the Chan school, and comprise 10 percent of the whole text. If we were to exclude the biographies of the mythical Buddhas and putative Indian patriarchs, close to 13 percent of all biographies of Chinese monks included in the text belong to Mazu's direct disciples,[13] and they occupy a vastly larger space than the biographies of the disciples of any other Chan teacher, in a text that covers approximately the first half-millennium of the Chan school's history. Furthermore, a little more than two out of *Zutang ji*'s twenty fascicles are devoted to Mazu's disciples (fascicles 14–16), despite the apparent bias of the text's compilers in favor of Shitou's lineage.

For the sake of comparison, the disciples of all of Mazu's direct disciples (i.e., his second-generation disciples) taken together occupy only two fascicles of *Chuandeng lu* (fascicles 9 and 10). The difference becomes even more striking when we compare the space allocated to the disciples of Shitou, who together with Mazu is traditionally regarded as the main second-generation descendant of Huineng. The biographies of the disciples of Shitou occupy less than half a fascicle of *Chuandeng lu* (the first half of fascicle 14), even though Daoyuan, the text's compiler, was considered a member of Shitou's lineage. Moreover, half of the monks who are presented as Shitou's disciples were also disciples of Mazu, and they could easily have been included among Mazu's disciples. Mazu's disciples are also prominently represented in the section on Chan (meditation) practitioners (*xichan*) in *Song gaoseng zhuan*. A few disciples also appear in other sections of the same text.[14] In this historical work, Mazu also emerges as the most influential Chan teacher of the Tang period.[15]

Table A.1 provides basic data about forty-three of Mazu's leading disciples: their dates of birth and death, their province of birth, the location of their monastery, and their biographical records in four major collections.[16] In the table, the part of the name that is primarily used in the main body of the book is underlined.[17] For the sake of convenience, places of birth and monastery locations are listed by present-day Chinese provinces. The two Tang capitals, Chang'an and Luoyang, are listed separately. When a particular monk taught at more then one monastery (e.g., Dayi), the table lists the location of the monastery with which he is most closely associated, or it gives two locations. The references to monks' biographies in the last column are to four major collections—CDL, SGSZ, ZTJ, and QTW—which contain the bulk of the biographical materials; in the case of QTW, these mostly consist of stele inscriptions.[18]

YANAGIDA'S ANALYSIS OF THE HONGZHOU SCHOOL

Among scholars who have written about the history and literature of Tang Chan, the work of Yanagida Seizan has been among the most influential in terms of shaping current understanding of the Hongzhou school.[19] This in itself shows a lack of scholarly

TABLE A.1. Mazu's Disciples

Name	Dates	Place of birth	Monastery location	Biographies
Baizhang Huaihai	749–814	Fujian	Jiangxi	CDL 6, SGSZ 10, ZTJ 14, QTW 446
Baizhang Weizheng	d. 819	unknown	Jiangxi	CDL 6, ZTJ 14
Chaoan	unknown	Jiangsu	unknown	SGSZ 11*
Damei Fachang	752–839	Hubei	Zhejiang	CDL 7, SGSZ 11, ZTJ 15
Danxia Tianran	739–824	unknown	Henan	CDL 14, SGSZ 11, ZTJ 4
Dazhu Huihai	unknown	Fujian	Zhejiang	CDL 6, ZTJ 14
Deng Yinfeng	unknown	Fujian	Hunan, Shanxi	CDL 8, SGSZ 21
Dongsi Ruhui	744–823	Guangdong	Hunan	CDL 7, SGSZ 11, ZTJ 15
Ehu Dayi	746–818	Zhejiang	Jiangxi, Chang'an	CDL 7, ZTJ 15, QTW 715
Ezhou Wudeng	749–830	Henan	Hubei	CDL 7, SGSZ 11
Fenzhou Wuye	760–821	Shaanxi	Shanxi	CDL 8, SGSZ 11, ZTJ 15
Foguang Ruman	752–842?	unknown	Hunan, Luoyang	CDL 6, QTW 677
Funiu Zizai	741–821	Zhejiang	Henan, Luoyang	CDL 7, SGSZ 11, ZTJ 15
Furong Taiyu	747–826	Jiangsu	Jiangsu	CDL 7, SGSZ 11
Ganquan Zhixian	unknown	Fujian	Shanxi	SGSZ 9, CDL 6*
Guiyang Wuliao	unknown	Fujian	Fujian	CDL 8, ZTJ 15
Guizong Zhichang	unknown	unknown	Jiangxi	CDL 7, SGSZ 17, ZTJ 15
Hangzhou Zhizang	741–819	Jiangxi	Zhejiang	CDL 6*, SGSZ 6
Hongzhou Shuilao	unknown	unknown	Jiangxi	CDL 8
Huayan Zhizang	d. 815?	Zhejiang	Chang'an	SGSZ 11
Letan Changxing	unknown	unknown	Jiangxi	CDL 7
Letan Fahui	unknown	unknown	Jiangxi	CDL 6
Lühou Ningbi	754–828	Anhui	Zhejiang	CDL 8*, SGSZ 29
Lushan Fazang	745?–826?	Jiangxi	Jiangxi	CDL 8*, SGSZ 20
Magu Baoche	unknown	unknown	Shanxi	CDL 7, ZTJ 15
Nanquan Puyuan	748–834	Henan	Anhui	CDL 8, SGSZ 11, ZTJ 16
Nanyuan Daoming	unknown	unknown	Jiangxi	CDL 6, ZTJ 14
Pang Yun	d. 808	Hunan?	none	CDL 8, ZTJ 15
Qiling Zhitong	unknown	unknown	Jiangxu	CDL 6*
Shanshan Zhijian	unknown	unknown	Anhui	CDL 6, ZTJ 14
Shigong Huizang	unknown	unknown	Jiangxi	CDL 6, ZTJ 14
Tianhuang Daowu	748–807	Zhejiang	Hubei	CDL 14, SGSZ 10, ZTJ 4, QTW 691, 713
Tianmu Mingjue	d. 831?	Fujian	Zhejiang	SGSZ 11
Wuxie Lingmo	747–818	Jiangxu	Zhejiang	CDL 7, SGSZ 10, ZTJ 15
Xingshan Weikuan	755–817	Zhejiang	Chang'an	CDL 7, SGSZ 10, QTW 678
Xitang Zhizang	738–817	Jiangxi	Jiangxi	CDL 7, SGSZ 10*, ZTJ 15
Xiyuan Tanzang	758–827	unknown	Hunan	CDL 8, SGSZ 11
Yanguan Qi'an	752?–841	Zhejiang	Zhejiang	CDL 7, SGSZ 11, ZTJ 15, QTW 733
Yangqi Zhenshu	d. 820	unknown	Jiangxi	CDL 8, SGSZ 10, QTW 919
Yaoshan Weiyan	745–828	Shanxi	Hunan	CDL 14, SGSZ 17, ZTJ 4, QTW 536
Zhangjing Huaihui	755–816	Fujian	Chang'an (Shaanxi)	CDL 7, ZTJ 14, SGSZ 10, QTW 501
Zhaoti Huilang	738–820	Guangdong	Guangdong, Hunan	CDL 14, ZTJ 4
Ziyu Daotong	731–813	Anhui	Henan	CDL 6, SGSZ 10, ZTJ 14

focus on the Hongzhou school, since the bulk of Yanagida's prolific scholarship—which established him as a leading figure in modern Chan/Zen studies—deals with early Chan literature.[20] Yanagida has written only one short article (eight pages) on Mazu and the Hongzhou school, [21] and most of his views about it are expressed in larger works where the focus is on something else. Accordingly, Yanagida's comments are here introduced as an example of prevalent views about the Hongzhou school, and this should not detract from an appreciation of his seminal scholarly contributions to the study of other aspects of Chan history.

In the article devoted to Mazu and the Hongzhou school, Yanagida offers an assessment of the role played by Mazu and his followers in the history of the Chan school and Chinese Buddhism:

> The actual formation of the Chinese Chan school began with the multifarious activities of Mazu (709–788) and his disciples. First of all, the use of the appellation "Chan school," in a manner that clearly conveyed its meaning, was a characteristic of their sermons. Following the coming to the fore of early Chinese Chan, which started with Bodhidharma, the clear transition into the Chan school's period of real flourishing should be seen as occurring during the later period of Mazu's life. That is a conspicuous fact that can be recognized both in the doctrinal standpoint of their new Buddhist movement, as well as in its multifaceted social and institutional trends.[22]

According to Yanagida, the Hongzhou school formulated a unique approach to Buddhist spirituality characterized by immediacy, openness, and spontaneity. The Hongzhou school's reputed rejection of traditional models of religious praxis, introduction of a new rhetorical style, and use of unconventional pedagogical devices—such as shouting, beating, and engagement in "question and answer" (*wenda*) dialogues—are defining features of a new soteriological paradigm. Also, under Mazu and his disciples Chan fully embraced everyday life as a principal venue for spiritual practice, which mainly consisted of spirited interactions between Chan teachers and students, and precluded "any attachment to the traditional Buddhist religious practices of meditation and scriptural exegesis."[23]

In the course of their putative iconoclastic revolution, Mazu and his disciples established the foundations of patterns of religious life and practice that came to characterize Chan during its golden age. According to Yanagida, this was tantamount to a major paradigm shift in the history of Chinese Buddhism. The whole historical process involved four closely related developments: (1) the formation of a sectarian tradition centered on the notion of patriarchal lineage; (2) the establishment of a new model of institutionally independent Chan monasteries; (3) the emergence of the encounter dialogue as the main medium of religious instruction; and (4) the creation of new Chan literature, primarily represented by the *yulu* (records of sayings) genre.[24] The following paragraphs briefly summarize Yanagida's views on each of these developments.

First, there was the establishment of a sectarian tradition based on the notion of dharma lineage. It originated with the historical Buddha, and Bodhidharma transmitted it to China. After the invention of a range of early versions of the Chan lineage, the authors of *Baolin zhuan* (composed in 801) created the final version that contains the familiar list of twenty-eight Indian and six Chinese patriarchs, which the subsequent Chan tradition accepted as the orthodox lineage. Since Yanagida believes that *Baolin zhuan* was a product of the Hongzhou school, he assumes that the final codification of the "orthodox" version of the early Chan lineage, which ended controversies about the Chan transmission, reflects the emergence of Mazu's lineage as a bearer of the new Chan orthodoxy.[25]

Second, there was the establishment of independent Chan monasteries that signaled Chan's rejection of existing monastic mores and regulations, which led to its institutional independence from the rest of Chinese Buddhism. Baizhang purportedly initiated this development, as he codified the regulations for a new system of Chan monasticism first instituted at his monastery. Before long, the whole Chan school adopted Baizhang's regulations, and they served as the basis for the creation of a distinct denominational identity.[26]

Third, there was the creation of a new style of religious praxis centered on the "encounter-dialogue" model. Having rejected all traditional forms of Buddhist practice, including formal meditation, the Hongzhou school supposedly developed the new encounter-dialogue model of practice as the centerpiece of its novel approach to religious training. The spontaneous interactions, both verbal and physical, between Chan teachers and their disciples thus become the primary focus of spiritual discipline. This new paradigm of religious training purportedly stood in sharp contrast to the earlier soteriological schemata of Indian and Chinese Buddhism. Thus the spotlight shifted away from the teachings of canonical Buddhism and toward the actual words and actions of enlightened Chan teachers. This was tantamount to a revolutionary new approach to Buddhist spirituality, in which the truth was to be actualized in the context of everyday life and spiritual realization was readily accessible to anyone.[27]

Finally, the fourth main development was the creation of a new type of literature, principally represented by the Chan "records of sayings" (*yulu*) genre. There is a close connection between this and the previous point, because according to Yanagida the "attention to the Master's actions as models of enlightened behavior led directly to the development of the 'recorded sayings' genre."[28] These unique texts supposedly record Mazu's and his disciples' novel teachings, primarily delivered in the "question and answer" style described above, and as sermons presented in an original format instituted by them as part of their revolutionary transformation of Buddhism. These texts, which represented a new development in the history of Buddhist literature, were written in vernacular Chinese, and their direct manner of presentation became the model for later Chan records.[29]

Yanagida's writings are full of insightful observations and provide a wealth of valuable information for students of Chan history and literature. However, as was noted in the introduction, his specific views about the Hongzhou school are problematic and reflect the continuing influence of traditional Zen views and explanations. This observation applies to each of the four points just presented. His interpretations are frequently based on wrong types of sources, especially the encounter-dialogue stories; he also often accepts normative readings of Song era texts and the ideological stances of the later Zen traditions (especially Rinzai) in Japan.

SOURCES FOR THE STUDY OF THE HONGZHOU SCHOOL'S DOCTRINES

The historical study of Tang Chan is demarcated and constrained by the quantity and nature of the available textual sources. Methodological issues also shape research findings, influencing the ways ancient texts are read and utilized by scholars as they try to make sense of medieval religious worldviews, account for changing historical circumstances, and navigate complex socioreligious milieus. The need to differentiate and assess accrued layers of later Chan lore and interpretations—including those of the Song period historians, the sectarian traditions of Japanese Zen, and the contemporary scholarly and religious communities—further complicates the scholarly enterprise. In a sense, we can construe the history of Chan/Zen throughout East Asia as a series of interpretative distortions, linked with massive textual production by a tradition that claimed not to rely on words and letters. Within this milieu, subsequent generations of Chan monks legitimized nascent ideologies and emerging viewpoints by linking them with the great Chan teachers of the past, especially those of the Tang period.

The ongoing reinterpretation of the records of earlier Chan figures is evident in the manner in which later generations of writers recast the teachings of Mazu and his disciples by recourse to conceptual categories popular at the time. One such example is the reinterpreting of Mazu's teachings by means of the "great function and great essence" paradigm, which started during the Song period. Such exegetical exercises aimed at bringing the teachings of Mazu and the Hongzhou school in harmony with the doctrinal and soteriological outlook prevalent at the time, which was dominated by the *kanhua* model of Chan practice. The researcher of Chan doctrine thus faces the difficult challenge of decoding medieval religious doctrines and worldviews in reference to their pertinent historical contexts, without reading into them extraneous suppositions, ideological constructs, or interpretative schemata propounded by later generations of scholars and adherents, including those of the present time.

In addition to the issue of interpretation, the historical researcher of Tang Chan also confronts the problems of availability and reliability of sources. Not only is there a paucity of data, but also there are often uncertainties about the provenance and trustworthiness of the extant records. Even when dealing with the earliest texts, there is still potential for pious exaggerations and skewed facts, which we often cannot check against other sources. This is even more the case with the Chan chronicles and records of sayings compiled during the Song era, which reflect the historical realities and ideological orientations prevalent at the time.

As was noted in the introduction, the disparity between Song images of Tang Chan and the historical realities of the period is an essential starting point for understanding the broad historical trajectory of the Chan tradition. Nevertheless, we need to be careful about making sweeping generalizations regarding a Song invention of a Tang "golden age." The Song texts were not original works but were of complex origin in that they were compilations made from layers of earlier materials. We are thus dealing with hybrid literary artifacts that contain a fair share of historical misrepresentations and pious fictions, mixed with factual information. Often the two are all but impossible to disentangle, but this is not a straightforward case of wholesale manufacture of historical narratives. In view of that, we cannot simply stipulate that the Song editors invented a coherent storyline about the imagined glories of the bygone Tang era, although their texts obviously mirror an evolving Chan ideology and are not accurate records of earlier Chan history. We are basically confronted with a creative misrepresentation and an ongoing reinvention of an earlier tradition, which evolved over an extended period, but we must not assume that Chan writers and historians were completely unconcerned with issues of historical accuracy and sensible use of sources.

Even for scholars who are methodologically astute and use sources carefully, any analysis of Chan history and doctrine remains a contestable interpretative exercise. To complicate matters, the literary output of the Hongzhou school was limited; therefore, we have to rely on a few relatively short texts. Moreover, for the most part the records of Mazu and his disciples, unlike the writings of philosophical schools, do not contain careful definitions of key concepts or methodical expositions of tenets and theoretical arguments. Rather we deal primarily with transcripts of short sermons that introduce varied concepts and ideas, usually without defining their precise meanings and connotations or developing them in detail. While the sermons contain fascinating information about medieval religious attitudes and viewpoints, they are at times impressionistic, jumping from one topic to another without obvious connections and clearly defined lines of argument or narrative structure.

As was mentioned in the introduction, the conventional understanding that the Hongzhou school propounded an iconoclastic ethos is based on a problematic reading of the wrong type of literary sources. By focusing on the apocryphal encounter-dialogue stories, generations of Chan/Zen adherents and scholars have perpetuated normative views about the Hongzhou school's doctrines and practices. If the apocryphal stories from the post-Tang period are not reliable sources of information about the Hongzhou school's doctrines and practices, the use of much of traditional Chan lore is precluded. As a result, in the preceding pages there was hardly any discussion of the iconoclastic acts and peculiar "pedagogical" methods allegedly developed by Mazu and his followers—such as beatings, screaming, and outlandish verbal rumblings—that according to popular lore served as catalysts for the experience of Chan awakening.

Fortunately, a few significant records of Tang provenance contain information about the teachings of Mazu and his disciples. Important early documents include edited transcripts of Mazu's sermons, Dazhu's *Dunwu rudao yaomen lun*, Baizhang's *Baizhang guanglu*, and Guishan's *Guishan jingce*. Other valuable sources are the two records of Huangbo's lectures and discussions compiled by Pei Xiu.[30] These texts are supplemented by the records of Mazu's disciples preserved in Five Dynasties and early Song compilations, although the reliability of such later sources is often problematic and unverifiable, and they need to be used with care when no other sources are available.

Mazu's sermons—the main source for chapter 5—are of critical importance for the study of Chan doctrine. They introduce famous Chan adages, articulate key themes, and present doctrinal orientations emblematic of the Hongzhou school. Unfortunately, they are also rather brief and can hardly serve as a comprehensive source of information about the Hongzhou school's teachings and practices. Because of these limitations, they need to be supplemented with other texts, especially Baizhang's record. I have written elsewhere in some detail about the contents and provenance of Mazu's records[31] and about *Guishan jingce*,[32] so I will comment here only on two other principal texts, Dazhu's *Dunwu rudao yaomen lun* and Baizhang's *Baizhang guanglu*.

Dazhu's treatise *Dunwu rudao yaomen lun* is the earliest record associated with the Hongzhou school. In terms of its literary format and doctrinal orientation, it marks the transition between early and classical Chan. The present edition of the text was published in 1374 as the first part of *Dunwu yaomen* (The Essential Teaching of Sudden Enlightenment). The second part of this work consists of materials about Dazhu taken from *Chuandeng lu*, which are obviously from the Song period. There is also an earlier manuscript in the possession of Kanazawa Bunko, Japan.

Though the extant editions are quite late, the original text of Dazhu's treatise—not to be confused with the later materials derived from *Chuandeng lu*—undoubtedly goes back to the mid-Tang period. The treatise follows a question-and-answer format, although it is evidently a literary creation, as indicated by the character *lun* (treatise) in its title. This literary format is familiar from early Chan texts, such as *Xiuxin yaolun* and *Wu fangbian*; a similar format also appears in non-Chan texts from the same period. The laudatory verse at the beginning, another characteristic of early Chan texts, also points to the text's early origins.

Much of the Chan vocabulary that appears in Dazhu's treatise consists of phrases that were in vogue during the middle part of the eighth century, such as "non-created mind" (*wusheng xin*) and "non-dwelling mind" (*wuzhu xin*). A further indication of the text's early origins is the presence of quotations from early scriptures such as *Chanmen jing*, *Foshuo faju jing*, and *Fangkuang jing*, which are preserved only among the Dunhuang documents.[33] The text also shows the direct influence of the records of Shenhui, which helps to estimate roughly the date of its composition—probably sometime between Shenhui's death in 758 and Mazu's death in 788.[34] In light of the text's literary format, and considering the position of Dazhu within the Hongzhou school, it is possible to question the degree to which we can label it as belonging to the Hongzhou school, although undoubtedly its contents resonate with views expressed in the records of Mazu and Baizhang.

Baizhang's record, *Baizhang guanglu*—the main source for chapter 6—is the most wide-ranging statement of Chan doctrine from the mid-Tang period.[35] It presents the teachings of one of the Hongzhou school's leading figures, articulated in an idiom prevalent at the time. Because of its broad scope and extensive treatment of Chan doctrine, Baizhang's record is a unique source for the study of the Hongzhou school's doctrinal standpoints and its conceptions of spiritual practice and realization.

Baizhang guanglu is not to be confused with *Baizhang yulu*, which is obviously a Song period compilation. Confirmation of the compilation of Baizhang's record (*yuben*) can be found in his stele inscription, written by Chen Xu shortly after Baizhang's death. We cannot definitely ascertain the identity and contents of the original *yuben*, but a text titled *Baizhangshan heshang yaojue* (The Essential Teachings of the Reverent from Baizhang Mountain) is listed in Enchin's (814–891) catalogues of texts brought to Japan from China.[36] A comparison of its contents, language, use of technical terminology, and literary format with those of similar Tang texts, such as Huangbo's *Chuanxin fayao* and Dazhu's *Dunwuyao yaomen lun*, strongly suggests that *Baizhang guanglu* is a product of the early to mid-ninth century. Most of Baizhang's text consists of transcripts of sermons and discussions with his students about Buddhist doctrine and practice.[37]

Baizhang's record has been quietly neglected by modern scholarship. Although it is of great historical value as one of the most important Chan documents from the

mid-Tang period, and its author enjoys high esteem in the Zen world, Baizhang's record has yet to be translated into modern Japanese.[38] This compares poorly with the
treatment of other seminal Chan texts—especially popular Song texts, such as *Biyan
lu*, or records of sayings of Chan teachers that have sectarian significance in Japan,
especially *Linji yulu*—which have been translated into Japanese (and sometimes into
English as well) a number of times, and have been the subjects of numerous studies.
Nor has there been any serious effort to analyze the contents of Baizhang's sermons.[39]
Virtually all discussions about Baizhang and his place in Chan history are based on
images and ideas presented in later Chan texts, most of which have little or nothing to
do with him.[40] One of the ironies of Chan studies is that instead of analyzing Baizhang's extant record, Japanese Chan/Zen scholarship has concentrated on imagining
the contents of his mythical work on Chan monastic rules, "Baizhang Rules of Purity"
(*Baizhang qinggui*).

Suzuki Tetsuo has suggested that contemporary Japanese scholarship glosses
over Baizhang's text in part because it is perceived as being "difficult" to read.[41] Understanding Baizhang's record obviously requires grounding in canonical texts and
doctrines, but overall its contents pose fewer problems than the complex theoretical
discussions found in the writings of medieval Buddhist scholiasts such as Huiyuan,
Jizang, and Fazang, which has received extensive treatment by Japanese scholars.
Could it be that the difficulties have less to do with the text's contents and more with
the fact that its narrative style and ideas are fundamentally different from the standard Chan fare found in later sources? That is, the text might pose problems for scholars such as Suzuki because its contents are at odds with prevalent views about the
religious teachings, rhetorical strategies, and instructional methods attributed to the
Hongzhou school.

Instead of portraying Baizhang as an iconoclastic Chan teacher along the lines familiar from popular Chan/Zen lore, *Baizhang guanglu* reveals a thoughtful monk who is
eager to use his considerable learning in canonical texts and doctrines in order to communicate a coherent vision of a path of practice and realization. Moreover, as was noted
in chapter 6, Baizhang's vision of Chan praxis is infused with "gradualist" tendencies,
which were supposedly expunged from the Chan tradition after the Southern school established its orthodoxy by repudiating what they saw as the gradualist teachings of the
Northern school. In effect, Baizhang's text and other related documents are difficult to
interpret when we do not situate them within their proper historical context, and if we
are unwilling to question normative views about the doctrines, teachings, methods, and
religious practices of mid-Tang Chan. Once we overcome these obstacles, the texts afford
us tantalizing glimpses into a fascinating medieval religious world and fit well into
the overall historical narrative of the Hongzhou school's growth, as documented in this
volume.

STELE INSCRIPTIONS OF CHAN MONKS

Stele inscriptions (*beiming*) and similar types of commemorative writings usually
are the earliest and most reliable sources of biographical information about Chan
monks from the Tang period.[42] Customarily, well-known officials and literati wrote
the inscriptions not long after Chan teachers' deaths at the request of their surviving

disciples. In many instances, the literati who wrote the inscriptions knew personally the Chan teachers in question. Virtually none of the original stone inscriptions survived the ravages of history, but their texts were typically preserved in later literary collections, such as *Quan tang wen* (Complete Tang Literature). This, of course, brings the possibility of later editorial changes or even the creation of outright forgeries, given the need of later generations of Chan adherents to claim an illustrious spiritual ancestry. Admittedly, that is less of an issue with most of the inscriptions written for Hongzhou school figures, especially those composed by famous officials and literati. Because of their authors' fame, reliable editions of many of the inscriptions are available in their collected works and other pertinent collections. Nevertheless, even in such cases, we must use the texts with attention to the circumstances of their creation and the conventions of the genre in which they were composed.

In accord with an established tradition of Chinese commemorative writing, the epitaphs of noted Chan teachers were composed in refined literary prose and their authors were guided by a time-honored historical ideal of narrating accurate facts about main events in their subjects' lives. But we must also bear in mind that it was usually the disciples of the deceased monks who commissioned the inscriptions, and their function as public testaments to the exalted virtues and lofty accomplishments of the deceased prelates helps accounts for their pious tone and eulogistic character. We should also keep in mind that adulation of deceased Chan teachers enhanced the fortunes and standing of the religious communities they left behind. Thus the inscriptions may be seen as reflecting points of intersections between the value systems and religious ideals of the communities that commissioned them, and the prevalent intellectual, political, economic, and cultural milieus of Tang China.

The list of stele inscriptions presented here focuses on prominent monks featured in the present volume; it it is not an exhaustive listing of extant inscriptions of Chan teachers and other important monks from the Tang period.

Baizhang: *Tang hongzhou baizhangshan gu huaihai chanshi taming* 唐洪州百丈山
故懷海禪師塔銘, by Chen Xu 陳詡. (1) QTW 446.2014a–b; (2) in *Chixiu
Baizhang qinggui* 敕修百丈清規, T 48.1156b–57a.

Chengyuan: *Nanyue mituosi chengyuan heshang bei* 南嶽彌陀寺承遠和尚碑, by
Lü Wen 呂溫 (772–811). (1) WYYH 866.4568b–70b; (2) QTW 630.2814c–
15c.

Daowu: *Jingzhou chengdong tianhuangsi daowu chanshi bei* 荊州城東天皇寺道悟禪
師碑, by Fu Zai 符載. QTW 691.3137c. (See also QTW 713.3244a–b, for
Tianwang Daowu's stele inscription.)

Dayi: *Xingfusi neidaochang gongfeng dade dayi chunshi beiming* 興福寺內道場供
奉大德大義禪師碑銘, by Wei Chuhou 韋處厚 (773–823). QTW 715.3258a–
59a.

Huaihui: *Tang zhangjingsi baiyan dashi beiming bingxu* 唐章敬寺百巖大師碑銘並
序, by Quan Deyu 權德輿 (759–818). (1) QTW 501.2260b–c; (2) WYYH
866.4568a–b.

Huairang: *Hengzhou buoresi guanyin dashi beiming bingxu* 衡州般若寺觀音大
師碑銘並序, by Zhang Zhengfu 張正甫 (dates of birth and death unknown).
(1) QTW 619.2767b–c; (2) *Tang wencui* 唐文粹 62.5b–6b; (3) *Fozu lidai*

tongzai 佛祖歷代通載, T 49.595c–96a (the last version omits the closing verse section).

Guishan: *Tanzhou daguishan tongqingsi dayuan chanshi beiming bingxu* 潭州大潙山同慶寺大圓禪師碑銘並序, by Zheng Yu 鄭愚. QTW 820.3832b–34b.

Mazu: *Tang gu hongzhou kaiyuansi shimen daoyi chanshi beiming bingxu* 唐故洪州開元寺石門道一禪師碑銘並序, by Quan Deyu 權德輿 (759–818). (1) QTW 501.2261c–62a; (2) *Tang wencui* 唐文粹 64.1058–59; (3) *Quan zaizhi wenji* 權載之文集 28.167a–68a.

Ruman: *Foguang heshang zhenzan bingxu* 佛光和尚真讚並序, by Bo Juyi 白居易 (772–846). QTW 677.3054c.

Weikuan: *Xijing xingshansi chuanfatang bei* 西京興善寺傳法堂碑, by Bo Juyi 白居易 (772–846). (1) *Bo juyi ji* 白居易集 41.911–13; (2) QTW 678.3069c–70a; (3) *Boshi wenji* 白氏文集 41.11a–14a (*Sibu congkan* ed.); (4) WYYH 866.4570b–71b.

Wuxiang, Wuzhu, Mazu, and Xitang: *Tang zizhou huiyi jingshe nanchanyuan sizhengtang beiming* 唐梓州慧義精舍南禪院四證堂碑銘, by Li Shangyin 李商隱 (812–858). QTW 780.3608b–9c.

Xitang: *Gonggong shan xitang chishi dajue chanshi chongjian dabaoguangda beiming* 龔公山西堂敕諡大覺禪師重建大寶光塔碑銘, by Tang Ji 唐技. *Ganzhou fuzhi* 贛州府志 16.14a–15a, and *Ganxian zhi* 贛縣志 50.3a–4b. Reproduced in Ishii Shūdō 石井修道, "Kōshūshū ni okeru Seidō Chizō no ichi ni tsuite" 洪州宗における西堂智藏の位置について, IBK 40/1 (1991), 281.

Xuanxu: *Jingzhou nanquan dayunsi gu lanruo heshang bei* 荊州南泉大雲寺故蘭若和尚碑, by Li Hua 李華 (c. 715–774). (1) WYYH 860.4541a–42b; (2) QTW 319.1431a–c.

Xuefeng (a): *Fuzhou xuefengshan gu zhenjue dashi beiming* 福州雪峰山故真覺大師碑銘, by Huang Tao 黃滔. QTW 826.3857.

Xuefeng (b): *Xuefeng heshang taming bingxu* 雪峰和尚塔銘並序. In *Mingjue chanshi yulu* 明覺禪師語錄, T 47.673b–c.

Yangshan: *Yangshan tongzhi dashi taming* 仰山通智大師塔銘, by Lu Xisheng 陸希聲. QTW 813.3792a–b.

Yanguan: *Hangzhou yanguanxian haichangyuan chanmen dashi tabei* 杭州鹽官縣海昌院禪門大師塔碑, by Lu Jianqiu 盧簡求. (1) QTW 733.3354b–c; (2) WYYH 868.4578a–79a.

Yaoshan: *Lizhou yaoshan gu weiyan dashi beiming bingxu* 澧州藥山故惟儼大師碑銘並序, by Tang Shen 唐伸. QTW 536.2410c–11b.

Zhenshu: *Yangqishan zhenshu dashi beiming* 陽岐山甄叔大師碑銘, by Zhi Xian 至賢. QTW 919.4245a–b.

Zongmi: *Guifeng chanshi beiming bingxu* 圭峰禪師碑銘並序, by Pei Xiu 裴休 (787?–860). QTW 743.3408c–10a.

NOTES

1. For the discovery of the inscription, see Chen Baiquan, "Mazu chanshi shihan tiji yu zhang zongyan tianshi kuanji."

2. There are three extant editions of Mazu's stele inscription, preserved in the following collections: QTW 501.5106a–7a, *Tang wenzui* 64.1058–59, and *Quanzai zhi wenji* 28.167a–68a. The differences between the three editions are minor and appear to be mostly due to copyists' errors. The *Tang wenzui* edition is reproduced and rendered into a Japanese *yomikudashi* reading (which unfortunately is not accompanied by a modern Japanese translation) in Iriya Yoshitaka, *Baso no goroku*, 212–14. *Yudi jisheng* 26.1190 provides a slightly different title for the stele inscription: *Gu hongzhou kaiyuansi shimen daoyi chanshi taming*. While the accompanying note is not entirely clear, it seems to indicate that the original stele still existed during the Southern Song period, when this text was composed by Wang Xiang.

3. The contents of the last two missing fascicles of BLZ are discussed in two articles by Shiina Kōyū, "*Hōrinden* itsubun no kenkyū" and "*Hōrinden* makikyū maki-ju no itsubun."

4. SGSZ 10, T 50.766a–c.

5. XZJ 14.279a–b and XZJ 110.434b–d, respectively.

6. ZTJ 14.304–9.

7. See T 48.418b, 492a, 550c, and 940b. ZJL contains numerous quotations from early Chan texts (including the sermons of important Hongzhou school figures), some of which are no longer extant. For a listing of the quotations from the records of Hongzhou school monks found in ZJL, see Yanagida, "Basozen no sho mondai," 38–39.

8. See CDL 6, T 51.245c–46c.

9. See "Backgrounds of Mazu's Disciples" in chapter 2.

10. ZTJ 16.364 (Huangbo's biography), *Baizhang yulu*, XZJ 119.409d, and TGDL 8, XZJ 135.328c. On the other hand, Nanquan's biography in SGSZ states that Mazu had "over 800 disciples." SGSZ 11, T 50.775a. The large discrepancy between the numbers of Mazu's disciples given in SGSZ and in other sources can be explained in two ways: either SGSZ refers to all the monks who studied at Mazu's monasteries, instead of only to his close disciples (as other texts do), or the extant text might contain a misprint and need to be read as "over eighty" instead of "over eight hundred."

11. CDL 6, T 51.246b. Needless to say, not all information included in CDL is reliable.

12. The names of all these disciples are listed in a table format in Yanagida, "Goroku no rekishi," 526–30. Yanagida's table also provides references for sources about each disciple.

13. The biographies of Mazu's direct disciples comprise three of CDL's thirty fascicles (fascicles 6–8), but if we exclude fascicles 1 and 2, which include the hagiographies of the putative Indian Chan patriarchs, and fascicles 27–30, which do not include any biographies, the biographies of Mazu's disciples constitute about one-eighth of all biographies. This is quite remarkable when we consider that CDL covers all noted Chan teachers who lived from the early sixth century until the beginning of the eleventh century.

14. Mazu was also a teacher of monks who were not associated with the Chan school. Examples of such monks are Shenzhen (745–818), a Vinaya teacher whose stele inscription and biography in SGSZ record that he studied with Mazu during his

early monastic years, and the *Huayan Scripture*'s exegete Wushan Zhizang (741–819), a monk of Indian ancestry whose study with Mazu is recorded in his biography in the same text. For Shenzhen, see his stele inscription, composed by Bo Juyi, in *Bo Juyi ji* 41.917 (vol. 3), and his biography in SGSZ 16, T 50.807a; for Zhizang, see SGSZ 6, T 50.740c.

15. SGSZ presents full biographies for thirty-two disciples of Mazu, and additional two disciples (Chaoan and Xitang) are accorded minor biographical entries.

16. The data in table A.1 is based on a variety of sources, including the primary sources listed in the last column. Among secondary sources, I am especially indebted to a series of articles by Suzuki Tetsuo on the sources for the study of Tang Chan, which appeared in various issues of *Aichi gakuin daigaku bungakubu kiyō* (nos. 5, 8, 10, 12, 13, 14, 16) and *Aichi gakuin daigaku ronsō* (no. 3). Additional information about most of these monks can be found dispersed throughout Suzuki's two books on the history of Chan during the Tang and Five Dynasties, *Tō-godai zenshū shi* and *Tō-Godai no zenshū*.

17. The names of Chan monks usually consist of the name of the area where they resided, followed by monk's religious name (which is received upon entry into the monastic order). The first part is usually the mountain where the monk resided, but it can also be the name of the prefecture or the monastery. For example, in the case of Baizhang Huaihai we have the name of a mountain followed by a religious name, while in the case of Guizong Zhichang we have the name of a monastery (located at Lu mountain) followed by a religious name (in some texts he is also referred to as Reverend Lushan). There are exceptions to this pattern and variant usages (e.g., Mazu, literally, "Patriarch Ma," based on his lay surname).

18. The number after each title abbreviation refers to the fascicle number where the biography appears. An asterisk after a CDL fascicle number indicates that the monk in question has no biography and only his name is listed at the beginning of that fascicle; in the case of SGSZ, it means that the monk is not accorded a full biography and his brief biography is appended to one of the main biographies.

19. For a recent example (published in 2001) of the perfunctory treatment of Mazu and the Hongzhou school that attests to the continuing acceptance of conventional interpretations along the lines of those suggested in Yanagida's work, see Ibuki Atsushi, *Zen no rekishi*, 58–79.

20. Examples of that kind include *Daruma no goroku: Ninyū shigyō ron; Shoki no zenshi I: Ryōga shijiki, Denhōbōki; Shoki no zenshi II: Rekidai hōbōki; Sodōshu* (*Daijō butten: Chūgoku, Nihon hen*, vol. 13); and Yanagida's masterpiece, *Shoki zenshū shisho no kenkyū*.

21. Yanagida Seizan, "Basozen no sho mondai."

22. Ibid., 33.

23. Yanagida, "The 'Recorded Sayings' Texts of Chinese Ch'an Buddhism," 187, and "Zenshū goroku no keisei," 40.

24. The first three are noted in Okimoto Katsumi's brief summary of Yanagida's ideas, in his "Shingi kenkyū nōto," 407–9.

25. See Yanagida, *Shoki zenshū shisho no kenkyū*, 360–61, 405–16; "Shinzoku tōshi no keifu: jo no ichi," 34; and "Chūgoku zenshū shi," 56–58.

26. See Yanagida, "Chūgoku zenshū shi," 58–60; "Basozen no sho mondai," 34; and "Goroku no rekishi," 250, 472, 548. On this subject, Yanagida is following a widely accepted (but also erroneous) opinion about the establishment of an independent system of Chan monasticism. See "Baizhang Huaihai" in chapter 2 of this volume, especially n. 50, which contains references to works that elaborate on that subject.

27. See Yanagida, "Basozen no sho mondai," 37–38; "Chūgoku zenshū shi," 53–56; and "Zenshū goroku no keisei," 40. For further discussion of the encounter-dialogue model, see John R. McRae, "Encounter Dialogue and the Transformation of the Spiritual Path in Chinese Ch'an" and "The Antecedents of Encounter Dialogue." McRae's discussion resonates with much of Yanagida's views, but he rightly distances himself from Yanagida's assertion that the Hongzhou school developed this model of practice.

28. Yanagida, "The 'Recorded Sayings' Texts of Chinese Ch'an Buddhism," 187. The close relationship between the two developments is also stressed in Yanagida, "Shinzoku tōshi no keifu: jo no ichi," 19.

29. Yanagida has devoted the most sustained attention to this development. See Yanagida, "Goroku no rekishi," 457–548; "Zenshū goroku no keisei," 39–45; and "The 'Recorded Sayings' Texts of Chinese Ch'an Buddhism," 185–205.

30. Huangbo's two records—commonly known by the title *Chuanxin fayao* (Essential Teachings on Mind Transmission)—are in general agreement with the other sources mentioned above, although at times they employ more radical rhetoric and focus on concepts that are not prominent in the records of other Hongzhou school figures, such as "no-mind" and "one mind." In terms of their literary format, style, and contents, Huangbo's records are similar to *Baizhang guanglu*. While Huangbo's texts are occasionally cited in this volume, they are not used as extensively as the records of earlier figures, given the stated focus on Mazu and the first generation of disciples.

31. See Poceski, "*Mazu yulu* and the Creation of the Chan Records of Sayings."

32. See Poceski, "*Guishan jingce* and the Ethical Foundations of Chan Practice."

33. Hirano, trans., *Tongo yōmon*, 219, and Yanagida, "Goroku no rekishi," 239.

34. Suzuki Tetsuo, *Tō-godai zenshū shi*, 359–63.

35. The text is included in *Guzunsu yulu*, XZJ 118.82–90, a fairly late collection, with additional sections in XZJ 119.411a–b.

36. See T 55.1095a, T 55.1101a, T 55.1106c, and Yanagida, "The 'Recorded Sayings' Texts," 191–92. This text, compiled within a few decades of Baizhang's death, was probably an early version of the extant BGL (although there is no conclusive evidence to confirm that).

37. There is a possibility that some of Baizhang's letters, mentioned in a mid-Tang source, were included in his record. See Yanagida, "Goroku no rekishi," 546.

38. There is only an old Japanese *yomikudashi* rendering of BGL, published in 1927, in *Kokuyaku zenshū sōsho* 2/5, which is also reproduced in *Kokuyaku zengaku taisei*. There is also an English translation of Baizhang's records, which, though aimed at a general audience and lacking an extensive scholarly apparatus, is for the most part acceptable: Thomas Cleary, trans., *Sayings and Doings of Pai-chang*, 27–82.

39. The only partial exception is Suzuki Tetsuo's brief article, "Hyakujō kōroku ni mirareru shisō."

40. An example of this tendency is the chapter on Baizhang in Yanagida, "Goroku no rekishi," 537–48. The bulk of Yanagida's discussion is an analysis of different versions of fictional dialogues between Mazu and Baizhang that come from Song era texts, from which he tries to extrapolate information about Baizhang's religious experiences without making a serious attempt to consider the contents of Baizhang's sermons.

41. Suzuki, "Hyakujō kōroku ni mirareru shisō," 583.

42. For the general background of the Chinese steles and their Buddhist adaptations in medieval China, see Dorothy C. Wong, *Chinese Steles: Pre-Buddhist and Buddhist Use of a Symbolic Form*, 15–60.

Glossary

Anguo Lingzhuo 安國靈著
    (691–746)
Anguo monastery 安國寺
Anhui 安徽
An Lushan 安祿山 (d. 757)

Baizhang Fazheng 百丈法正
    (d. 819)
Baizhang guanglu 百丈廣錄
Baizhang Huaihai 百丈懷海
    (749–814)
Baizhang Niepan 百丈涅槃
    (d. 828?)
Baizhang qinggui 百丈清規
Baizhang yulu 百丈語錄
Baizhangshan heshang yaojue 百
    丈山和尚要決
Baizhang Weizheng 百丈惟政
    (dates unknown)
Bao Fang 鮑防 (723–790)
Bao Ji 包佶 (dates unknown)
Baofeng monastery 寶峰寺
Baolin zhuan 寶林傳
Bao Rong 包融 (dates unknown)
Baotang school 保唐宗
Baozhi 寶誌 (418–514)

Baxi 巴西
beiming 碑銘
Beishan lu 北山錄
ben 本
benjue 本覺
benlai wu yi wu 本來無一物
Biansong 汴宋
Biyan lu 碧巖錄
Bo Juyi 白居易 (772–846)
buke siyi 不可思議
Bukong 不空 (705–774)
buliaoyi jiao 不了義教
bushi wu 不是物

Caodong school 曹洞宗
Caoshan Benji 曹山本寂
    (840–901)
Caoxi 曹溪
Chan 禪
Chang'an 長安
changdaoshi 唱導師
Changlu Zongze 長蘆宗賾 (dates
    unknown)
Changsha 長沙
Changsha Jingcen 長沙景岑
    (d. 868)

Chanmen guishi 禪門規式
Chanmen jing 禪門經
chanshi 禪師
Chanyuan qinggui 禪苑清規
Chanyuan zhuquanji duxu 禪源諸詮
  集都序
chanzong 禪宗
Chaoan 超岸 (dates unknown)
cheng 誠
Chengdu 成都
Chengguan 澄觀 (738–839)
chengwu 證悟
Chinul 智訥 (1158–1210)
Chongxuan (school) 重玄
chuandeng lu 傳燈錄
Chuan fabao ji 傳法寶紀
Chuanfa temple 傳法院
Chuanxin fayao 傳心法要
Chuji 處寂 (684–734)
chujia 出家
Cien monastery 慈恩寺
cidi 次第
Cui Qun 崔群 (772–832)

Da'anguo monastery 大安國寺
Dabei 大悲 (709–816)
Dahui Zonggao 大慧宗杲 (1089–1163)
Daizong 代宗 (r. 762–779)
Daji chanshi 大寂禪師
Dali (era) 大曆 (766–779)
Damei Fachang 大梅法常 (752–839)
Da niepan jing 大涅盤經
Da zhuangyan pagoda 大莊嚴塔
Danxia Tianran 丹霞天然 (739–824)
Danyang 丹陽
dao 道
Daoan 道安 (312–385)
Daojun 道峻 (dates unknown)
Daosheng 道生 (c. 360–434)
Daoxin 道信 (580–651)
Daoxuan 道宣 (596–667)
Daoyuan 道原 (dates unknown)
Daoyuan 道圓 (dates unknown)

Daxingshan Monastery 大興善寺
Dayan pagoda 大雁塔
Dayu 大愚 (dates unknown)
Dazhong (era) 大中 (847–860)
Dazhu Huihai 大珠慧海 (fl. 8th c.)
Deng Yinfeng 鄧隱峰 (dates
  unknown)
Deshan Xuanjian 德山宣鑑 (782–865)
Dezong 德宗 (r. 779–805)
Dilun 地論
ding 定
Donglin monastery 東林寺
Dongshan famen 東山法門
Dongshan Liangjie 洞山良介
  (807–869)
Dongsi Ruhui 東寺如會 (744–823)
Dongting lake 洞庭湖
Du Fu 杜甫 (712–770)
Du Hongjian 杜鴻漸 (709–796)
dun 頓
Dunhuang 敦煌
dunwu 頓悟
dunwu benxing 頓悟本性
dunwu dunxiu 頓悟頓修
dunwu jianxiu 頓悟漸修
Dunwu rudao yaomen lun 頓悟入道要
  門論
dunxiu 頓修
Dushun 杜順 (557–640)

Ehu Dayi 鵝湖大義 (746–818)
Enchin 圓珍 (814–891)
Ennin 圓仁 (799–852)
Erru sixing lun 二入四行論
Ezhou Wudeng 鄂州無等 (749–830)

Fahua jing 法華經
fajie 法界
Fajie guanmen 法界觀門
Faju jing 法句經
fangbian 方便
fanzhao 返照
Farong 法融 (594–657)

Faru 法如 (638–689)
fashen 法身
Faxiang 法相
Fayan Wenyi 法眼文益 (885–958)
Fayan school 法眼宗
Fazang 法藏 (643–712)
Fazhao 法照
feixin feifo 非心非佛
Fenzhou Wuye 汾州無業 (760–821)
Foguang Ruman 佛光如滿
  (752–842?)
Fojiyan 佛跡巖
foxing 佛性
fozu 佛祖
Fu dashi 傅大士
Fuchong 府崇
Fujian 福建
Funiu Zizai 伏牛自在 (741–821)
Furong Taiyu 芙蓉太毓 (747–826)
Fuyan chansi 福嚴禪寺
Fuzhou 撫州

Ganquan Zhixian 甘泉志賢 (dates
  unknown)
gantong 感通
Gaoseng zhuan 高僧傳
Gaozu 高祖 (r. 618–626)
gong'an 公案
Gonggong mountain 龏公山
Gu zunsu yulu 古尊宿語錄
guan 觀
Guanding 灌頂 (561–632)
Guangdong 廣東
guanxin shi 觀心釋
Guanyin 觀音
Guifeng Zongmi 圭峰宗密
  (780–841)
Guishan Lingyou 潙山靈祐
  (771–853)
Guishan jingce 潙山警策
Guiyang school 潙仰宗
Guiyang Wuliao 龜洋無了 (dates
  unknown)

Guizong Zhichang 歸宗知常 (dates
  unknown)
Guoqing monastery 國清寺
guwen 古文

Han Yu 韓愈 (768–824)
Hangzhou 杭州
Hangzhou Tianlong 杭州天龍
Hangzhou Zhizang 杭州智藏
  (741–819)
Hanshan 寒山
Hanshan Deqing 憨山德清
  (1546–1623)
Hanzhou 漢州
Haozhi 好直
Heijian 黑澗
Hengyue 衡嶽
Heze Shenhui 荷澤神會 (684–758)
Hongch'ŏk 洪陟 (dates unknown)
Hongbian 弘辯 (781–865)
Hongjing 弘景 (634–712)
Hongren 弘忍 (601–674)
Hongzhou 洪州
Hongzhou school 洪州宗
Hongzhou Shuilao 洪州水老 (dates
  unknown)
Houhan shu 後漢書
Hu Shi 胡適
Huaiyang 襄陽
Huangbo Xiyun 黃檗希運 (d. 850?)
Huang Chao 黃巢 (d. 884)
Huangfu Bo 黃甫鎛 (c. 755–820)
Huanglong Weizhong 黃龍惟忠
  (705–782)
Huangmei mountain 黃梅山
Huayan school 華嚴宗
Huayan Scripture 華嚴經
hufa 護法
hui 惠
Huichang (era) 會昌 (841–845)
Huijiao 慧皎 (497–554)
Huike 慧可 (487–593)
Huineng 慧能 (638–713)

Huisi 慧思 (515–577)
Huiyuan 慧遠 (334–416)
Huizhao 慧照
Huizhen 惠真 (673–751)
Hyakujō ko shingi 百丈古清規
Hyech'ŏl 慧哲 (785–861)
Hyŏnuk 玄昱 (787–868)

jian 漸
Jianchang 建昌
Jianfu monastery 薦福寺
Jianke 劍客
jianxing 見性
Jianyang 建陽
Jianzhou 建州
Jing'an county 靖安縣
Jiannan 劍南
jiangshi 講師
Jiangsu 江蘇
Jiangxi 江西
Jiangzhou 江州
Jianzhong (era) 建中 (780–783)
jiaochan yizhi 教禪一致
jiaowai biechuan 教外別傳
jiewu 解悟
Jingde chuandeng lu 景德傳燈錄
Jingjue 淨覺 (683–750?)
Jingnan 荊南
Jingshan Faqin 徑山法欽 (714–792)
jingtu 淨土
jing yun 經云
Jingzhong 淨眾
Jingzhou 荊州
jingzuo buyong gong 靜坐不用工
jinshi 進士
Jiu tangshu 舊唐書
jixin jifo 即心即佛
jixin shi fo 即心是佛
Jizang 吉藏 (549–623)

Kaiyuan monastery 開元寺
Kanazawa bunko 金沢文庫
kanhua 看話

kien mondō 機緣問答
Kim heshang 金和尚 (684–762)
Kuiji 窺基 (632–688)

Lao'an 老安 (584?–708)
Laozi 老子
Lengqie jing 楞伽經
Lengqie shizi ji 楞伽師資記
Letan Changxing 泐潭常興 (dates unknown)
Letan Fahui 泐潭法會 (dates unknown)
Letan monastery 泐潭寺
Letian 樂天
li 理
Li Ao 李翱 (772–841)
Li Bo 李渤 (773–831)
Li Hua 李華 (c. 715–774)
Li Jian 李兼 (dates unknown)
Li Shangyin 李商隱 (812-858)
Li Tongxuan 李通玄 (635–730)
liangshui fa 兩稅法
Liang (dynasty) 梁 (502–557)
liaoyi jiao 了義教
Lidai fabao ji 歷代法寶記
liezhuan 列傳
lichu ji zhen 立處即真
Linde hall 麟德殿
Lingmo 靈嘿
Lingnan 嶺南
Linji Yixuan 臨濟義玄 (d. 866)
Linji school 臨濟宗
Linji yulu 臨濟語錄
Linchuan 臨川
lishi wuai 理事無礙
Liuzu tanjing 六祖壇經
Liu Zongyuan 柳宗元 (773–819)
Longan Ruhai 龍安如海 (dates unknown)
Longmen 龍門
Longya Yuanchang 龍牙圓暢 (dates unknown)
Lu Gong 魯恭 (dates unknown)

Lu Jianqiu 盧簡求 (789-846)

Lu Sigong 路嗣恭 (711-781)

Lü Wen 呂溫 (772-811)

Lühou Ningbi 呂后寧賁 (754-828)

Lujiang 盧江

lun 論

Lunyu 論語

Luofu Xiuguang 羅浮修廣

Luohan Guichen 羅漢桂琛 (867-928)

Luoyang 洛陽

Lushan 盧山

Lushan Fazang 盧山法藏 (744?-825?)

lüshi 律師

Magu Baoche 麻谷寶撤 (dates unknown)

Mazu Daoyi 馬祖道一 (709-788)

Mazu yulu 馬祖語錄

Mengzi 孟子

Miaofa lianhua jing 妙法蓮華經

Mijiao school 密教宗

ming 明

Mingyue mountain 明月山

Minyue 閩越

Moheyan 摩訶衍

Muyŏm 無染 (799-888)

Muzong 穆宗 (r. 820-824)

Nanchang 南昌

nanfang zhishi 南方知識

Nankang-jun 南康郡

Nanquan Puyuan 南泉普願 (748-834)

Nanyuan Daoming 南源道明 (dates unknown)

Nanyang Huizhong 南陽慧忠 (d. 775)

Nanyue (mountain) 南嶽

Nanyue Chengyuan 南嶽承遠 (712-802)

Nanyue Huairang 南嶽懷讓 (677-744)

nianfo 念佛

nishun yu 逆順喻

Niutou Farong 牛頭法融 (594-657)

Niutou Huizhong 牛頭慧忠 (683-769)

Niutou mountain 牛頭山

pai 派

Pang, Layman 龐居士 (d. 808?)

Pang Yun 龐蘊 (d. 808?)

panjiao 判教

Pei Du 裴度 (765-839)

Pei Kuan 裴寬 (681-755)

Pei Xiu 裴休 (787?-860)

Pei Xiu sheyi wen 裴休拾遺文

Pei Xu 裴諝 (719-793)

Pei Zhou 裴胄 (729-803)

pingchang xin shi dao 平常心是道

Pŏmil 梵日 (810-889)

Pŏmnang 法朗 (fl. 632-646)

Poyang 鄱陽

Puji 普寂 (651-739)

puqing 普請

puqing zuowu 普請作務

Qi Ying 齊映 (748-795)

Qian 虔

Qianhua 虔化

qi er yong 起二用

Qiling Zhitong 棲靈智通 (dates unknown)

qi liu guan 起六觀

qinggui 清規

Qingyuan Xingsi 青原行思 (d. 740)

Quan Deyu 權德輿 (759-818)

Quanzhou 泉州

Quzhou 衢州

rulaizang 如來藏

ru wu zhi 入五止

Sanjie jiao 三階教

sanju 三句

Sanlun 三論

Sengcan 僧璨 (d. 606?)

Sengyou 僧祐 (445–518)

Sengzhao 僧肇 (374?–414)

Shandao 善導 (613–681)

shangtang 上堂

Shannan-dao 山南道

Shanshan Zhijian 杉山智堅 (dates
  unknown)

Shaolin monastery 少林寺

Shaotan 紹曇

Shaozhou Ruyuan 韶州乳源

shengsi yu 生死語

Shenqing 神清 (d. 806–820)

Shenxiu 神秀 (606?–706)

Shenzhen 神湊 (745–818)

Shelun 攝論

shi 事

Shide 拾得

Shigong Huizang 石鞏慧藏 (dates
  unknown)

Shiji 史記

shilang 侍郎

Shimen mountain 石門山

shi san bian 示三遍

shishi wuai 事事無礙

Shitou Xiqian 石頭希遷 (700–790)

shizhong yun 示眾云

Shoulengyan jing 首楞嚴經

shouxin 守心

shouyi 守一

Shuitang 水唐

Shunzong 順宗 (r. 805)

si 嗣

Sichuan 四川

Sijia yulu 四家語錄

Silla (dynasty) 新羅 (668–935)

Sima Qian 司馬遷 (ca. 145–86 BCE)

Song (dynasty) 宋 (960–1279)

Song gaoseng zhuan 宋高僧傳

Song mountain 嵩山

Su Shi 蘇軾 (1037–1101)

sudi 俗諦

Sui (dynasty) 隋 (581–618)

sushi 素食

Taizong 太宗 (r. 626–649)

Tang (dynasty) 唐 (618–907)

Tang heshang 唐和尚 (684–734)

Tanran 坦然 (dates unknown)

Tanyu 壇語

tiyong 體用

Tianbao (era) 天寶 (742-755)

Tianhuang Daowu 天皇道悟
  (748–807)

Tiangong monastery 天宮寺

Tianmu Mingjue 天目明覺 (d. 831?)

Tiansheng guangdeng lu 天聖廣燈錄

Tiantai mountain 天台山

Tiantai school 天台宗

titou shi 剃頭師

Tongqing monastery 同慶寺

Tŏŭi 道義 (d. 825)

Toyun 道允 (797–868)

tupi 荼毘

Wang Wei 王維 (701–761)

Wangjin huanyuan guan 妄盡還源觀

wangnian 妄念

Wanling lu 宛陵錄

Wei Chuhou 韋處厚 (773–823)

weishi 唯識

Wei Xian 韋銑 (dates unknown)

wenda 問答

Wendi 文帝 (r. 581–604)

Wenshu shuo jing 文殊說經

Wenyuan yinghua 文苑英華

Wu Zetian 武則天 (r. 690–705)

wufenbie 無分別

Wujia zhengzong zan 五家正宗贊

Wumen guan 無門關

Wumen Huikai 無門慧開
  (1183–1260)

wuneng wusuo 無能無所

wunian 無念

Wushan Zhizang 烏山智藏
  (741–819)

wusheng 無生

wusuode 無所得

Wutai mountain 五臺山
wuwo 無我
Wuxi ji 武溪集
Wuxiang 無相 (684–762)
wuxiangjie 無相戒
wuxin 無心
Wuxie Lingmo 五洩靈默 (747–818)
wuyi 無意
wuyi 無憶
wuzhu 無住
Wuzhu 無住 (714–774)
Wuzong 武宗 (r. 840–845)

Xiangshan monastery 香山寺
Xiangyan Zhixian 香嚴智閑 (dates
　unknown)
xian yi ti 顯一體
Xianzong 憲宗 (r. 805–820)
xichan 習禪
Xili mountain 西裏山
Xin tangshu 新唐書
xingfu 興福
xinglu 行錄
Xingping 興平
Xingshan monastery 興善寺
Xingshan Weikuan 興善惟寬
　(755–817)
xing si de 行四德
Xitang Zhizang 西堂智藏 (735–817)
Xiuxin yaolun 修心要論
Xiyuan Tanzang 西園曇藏 (dates
unknown)
Xu baolin zhuan 續寶林傳
Xu gaoseng zhuan 續高僧傳
Xuansha Shibei 玄沙師備 (835–908)
Xuansu 玄素 (668–752)
Xuanzang 玄奘 (602–664)
Xuanzong 玄宗 (r. 712–756)
Xuanzong 宣宗 (r. 846–859)
Xuefeng Yicun 雪峰義存 (822–908)
Xuedou Zhongxian 雪竇重顯
　(980–1052)
Xujiang 須江

Yan Hui 顏回
Yang Jie 楊傑 (dates unknown)
Yang Yi 楊億 (974–1020)
Yangshan Huiji 仰山慧寂 (807–883)
Yanguan Qi'an 鹽官齊安 (752–841)
Yangqi Fanghui 陽岐方會 (992–1049)
Yangqi Zhenshu 陽岐甄叔 (d. 820)
Yaoshan Weiyan 藥山惟儼 (745–828)
Yifu 義福 (661–736)
yingshen 應身
yixin chuanxin 以心傳心
yixing sanmei 一行三昧
Yizong 懿宗 (r. 859–873)
yong 用
Yongming Yanshou 永明延壽
　(904–975)
Yu Chaoen 魚朝恩 (d. 770)
Yu Di 于頔 (d. 818)
Yuan (dynasty) 元 (1280–1368)
Yuan Zai 元載 (d. 777)
Yuanhe (era) 元和 (806–820)
Yuanjue jing 圓覺經
Yuanjuejing dashuchao 圓覺經大疏鈔
Yuanwu Keqin 圓悟克勤 (1063–1135)
Yuanwu xinyao 圓悟心要
yuben 語本
Yudi jisheng 輿地紀勝
Yuezhou 越州
yulu 語錄
Yunmen guanglu 雲門廣錄
Yunmen school 雲門宗
Yunmen Wenyan 雲門文偃
　(864–949)
Yuquan monastery 玉泉寺
yuyan 豫言
Yuzhang-wang 豫章王 (r. 551–552)
Yuzhou 渝州

Zanning 贊寧 (919–1001)
Zhangjing monastery 章敬寺
Zhangjing Huaihui 章敬懷暉
(756–815)
Zhangle Farong 長樂法融 (747–835)

Zhangqiu Jianqiong 章仇兼瓊 (dates unknown)

Zhangsong Ma 長松馬 (dates unknown)

Zhang Zhengfu 張正甫 (dates unknown)

Zhanran 湛然 (711–782)

Zhaoti Huilang 招提慧朗 (738–820)

Zhaozhou Zongshen 趙州從諗 (778–897)

Zhen Xu 陣詡 (dates unknown)

zhendi 真諦

zhengzuo duanran ru taishan 正坐端然如泰山

zhenkong 真空

zhenxin 真心

Zhenyan (school) 真言宗

Zhishen 智詵 (609–702)

zhishi 知事

Zhiwei 智威 (dates unknown)

Zhiyan 智儼 (602–668)

Zhiyi 智顗 (538–597)

Zhongzong 中宗 (r. 705–710)

zhoubian hanrong 周遍含容

Zhu Xi 朱熹 (1130–1200)

Zhuangzi 莊子

zhuke yu 主客語

zhuoyu 著語

Zimen jingxun 緇門警訓

ziti wuming 自體無名

Ziyu Daotong 紫玉道通 (731–813)

Zizhong 資中

zong 宗

zongchimen 總持門

Zongjing lu 宗鏡錄

Zongmen shigui lun 宗門十規論

zu 祖

zuochan 坐禪

Zuochan ming 坐禪銘

zuo jiutan yuanyuan 坐究探淵源

zushi 祖師

Zutang ji 祖堂集

Bibliography

PRIMARY SOURCES

Apidamo dapiposha lun 阿毘達磨大毘婆沙論 (*Abhidharma-mahāvibhāṣā-śāstra*), trans. by Xuanzang (656). T 1545, vol. 27.

Bailun 百論, attributed to Āryadeva (3rd century), trans. by Kumārajīva (404). T 1569, vol. 30.

Baizhang guang lu 百丈廣錄, by Baizhang Huaihai 百丈懷海 (749–814). In *Guzunsu yulu* 古尊宿語錄 1, XZJ vol. 118.

Baolin zhuan 寶林傳 (801). In Yanagida Seizan, ed. *Sōzō ichin hōrinden, dentō gyokuei shū* 宋藏遺珍宝林伝、伝灯玉英集. Kyoto: Chūbun shuppansha, 1975.

Beishan lu 北山錄, by Shenqing 神清 (d. 806–820). T 2113, vol. 52.

Biyan lu 碧巖錄, by Xuedou Chongxian 雪竇重顯 (980–1052) and Yuanwu Keqin 圓悟克勤 (1063–1135). T 2003, vol. 48.

Bo juyi ji 白居易集, by Bo Juyi 白居易, (772–846). 4 vols. Beijing: Zhonghua shuju, 1979.

Boshi changqing ji 白氏長慶集, by Bo Juyi 白居易. *Sibu congkan* 四部叢刊, vol. 92–94.

Chanyuan qinggui 禪苑清規 (1103), by Changlu Zongze 長蘆宗賾 (d. 1107?). (1) XZJ vol. 111; (2) Kagamishima Genryū, et al., trans. *Yakuchū: Zennen shingi*. Tokyo: Sōtōshū Shūmuchō, 1972.

Chanyuan zhuquanji duxu 禪源諸詮集都序, by Zongmi 宗密 (780–841). (1) T 2015, vol. 48; (2) Kamata Shigeo 鎌田茂雄, trans. *Zengen shosenshū tojo* 禪源諸詮集都序. ZG 9. Tokyo: Chikuma shobō, 1971.

Chōsen kinseki sōran 朝鮮金石総覧, edited by Chōsen sōtokufu 朝鮮総督府. 2 vols. Tokyo: Kokusho kankōkai, 1971 (original ed. published in 1919).

Chuan fabao ji 傳法寶紀 (c. 713), by Du Fei 杜朏 (dates of birth and death unknown). (1) T 2838, vol. 85; (2) Yanagida Seizan, ed. *Shoki no zenshi 1*. Tokyo: Chikuma shobō, 1971.

Chu sanzang jiji 出三藏記集, by Sengyou 僧祐 (445–518). T 2145, vol. 55.

Daban niepan jing 大般涅槃經. T 374, vol. 12.

Dafang guang fo huayan jing 大方廣佛華嚴經, (1) trans. by Buddhabhadra (359–429), T 278, vol. 9; (2) trans. by Śikṣānanda (652–710), T 279, vol. 10.

Da piposha lun 大毘婆沙論 (*Abhidharma-mahāvibhāṣā-śāstra*), trans. by Xuanzang 玄奘 (602–664). T 1545, vol. 27.

Dasheng fayuan yilin zhang 大乘法苑義林章, by Kuiji 窺基 (632–688). T 1861, vol. 45.

Dasheng qixin lun 大乘起信論. T 1666, vol. 32.

Da song sengshi lüe 大宋僧史略 (c. 978–999), by Zanning 贊寧 (919–1001). T 2126, vol. 54.

Dunhuang baozang 敦煌寶藏, edited by Huang Yongwu. Taipei: Xinwenfeng chuban gongsi, 1981–1986.

Dunwu rudao yaomen lun 頓悟入道要門論, by Dazhu Huihai 大珠慧海 (dates unknown). (1) XZJ vol. 110; (2) Hirano Sojo 平野宗浄, trans. *Tongo yōmon* 頓悟要門. ZG 6. Tokyo: Chikuma shobo, 1970.

Erru sixing lun 二入四行論, attributed to Bodhidharma. In Yanagida Seizan, ed., *Daruma no goroku: Ninyū shigyū ron*. ZG 1. Tokyo: Chikuma shobō, 1969.

Fahua xuanlun 法華玄論 by Jizang 吉藏 (549–623). T 1720, vol. 34.

Foxing lun 佛性論, (trans. or composed?) by Paramārtha (499–569). T 1610, vol. 31.

Fozu lidai tongzai 佛祖歷代通載 (1341?), by Meiwu Nianchang 梅屋念常. T 2036, vol. 49.

Fozu tongji 佛祖統記, by Zhipan 志盤 (fl. 1258–1269). T 2035, vol. 49.

Ganzhou fuzhi 贛州府志. Shanghai: Shanghai guji shudian, 1982.

Gaoseng zhuan 高僧傳 (519), by Huijiao 慧皎 (497–554). T 2059, vol. 50.

Guishan jingce 潙山警策 (c. 850), by Guishan Lingyou 潙山靈祐 (771–853). (1) XZJ vol. 111; (2) QTW 919.

Gu zunsu yulu 古尊宿語錄. (1) XZJ vol. 118. (2) Beijing: Zhonghua shuju, 1994 (2 vols.); (3) Yanagida Seizan, ed. *Zengaku sōsho*, vol. 1 禅学叢書之一. Kyoto: Chūbun shuppansha, 1973.

Hongzhou baizhangshan dazhi chanshi yulu 洪州百丈山大智禪師語錄. XZJ vol. 119.

Huangboshan duanji chanshi chuanxin fayao 黃檗山斷際禪師傳心法要, compiled by Pei Xiu 裴休 (787?–860). (1) T 2012a, vol. 48; (2) XZJ vol. 119; (3) Iriya Yoshitaka, trans. *Denshin hōyō, Enryōroku*. ZG 8. Tokyo: Chikuma shobō, 1969.

Huangboshan duanji chanshi wanling lu 黃檗山斷際禪師宛陵錄, compiled by Pei Xiu 裴休. (1) T 2012b, vol. 48; (2) XZJ vol. 119; (3) Iriya Yoshitaka, trans. *Denshin hōyō, Enryōroku*. ZG 8. Tokyo: Chikuma shobō, 1969.

Jianchang xianzhi 建昌縣志. Shenyang: Liaoning daxue chubanshe, 1992.

Jiangxi mazu daoyi chanshi yulu 江西馬祖道一禪師語錄. XZJ vol. 119.

Jiangxi tongzhi 江西通志. Taipei: Huawen shuju, 1967.

Jing'an xianzhi 靖安縣志. Nanchang: Jiangxi renmin chubanshe, 1989.

Jin'gang sanmei jing 金剛三昧經. T 273, vol. 9.

Jingde chuandeng lu 景德傳燈錄 (1004), by Daoyuan 道原 (dates unknown). (1) Taipei: Xinwen feng, 1988; (2) T 2076, vol. 51.

Jingzhou fuzhi 荊州府志. In *Zhongguo fangzhi congshu* 中國方志叢書 118.

Jiu tangshu 舊唐書 (945), by Liu Xu 劉昫 et al. Beijing: Zhonghua shuju, 1975.

Jueguan lun 絕觀論, attributed to Niutou Farong 牛頭法融 (594–657). In *Suzuki Daisetsu zenshū*, vol. 2. Tokyo: Iwanami shoten, 1980.

Lengqie jing 楞伽經. T 670, vol. 16.

Lengqie shizi ji 楞伽師資記, by Jingjue 淨覺 (683–750?). (1) T 2837, vol. 85; (2) Yanagida Seizan 柳田聖山, trans. *Shoki no zenshi I: Ryōga shijiki, Denhōbōki* 初期の禅史I―楞伽師資記, 傳法寶紀. ZG 2. Tokyo: Chikuma shobō, 1971.

Lidai fabao ji 歷代法寶記. (1) T 2075, vol. 51; (2) Yanagida Seizan, trans. *Shoki no zenshi II: Rekidai hōbōki* 初期の禅史II―歷代法寶記. ZG 3. Tokyo: Chikuma shobō, 1976.

Lidai sanbao ji 歷代三寶記, by Fei Changfang 費長房 (fl. 561–597). T 2034, vol. 49.

Linji yulu 臨濟語錄. T 1985, vol. 47.

Liuzu dashi fabao tanjing 六祖大師法寶壇經, attributed to Huineng 慧能 (638–713). T 2007 and 2008, vol. 48.

Lushan ji 廬山記, edited by Chen Shunyu (Song). T 2095, vol. 51.

Lushan guizongsi zhi 廬山歸宗寺志, compiled by Hanshan Deqing 憨山德清 (1546–1623). In Bai Huawen 白化文, ed., *Zhongguo fosi zhi congkan* 中國佛寺誌叢刊 16. Yangzhou: Jiangsu guangling guji keyinshe, 1992.

Lushan zhi 廬山志. In Du Jiexiang 杜潔祥, ed., *Zhongguo fosi shizhi huikan* 中國佛寺史志彙刊 16–19. Taipei: Mingwen shuju, 1980.

Miaofa lianhua jing 妙法蓮華經. T 262, vol. 9.

Mingzhou dameishan chang chanshi yulu 明州大梅山常禪師語錄. In *Kanazawa bunko shiryō zensho: Butten 1, zenseki hen* 金沢文庫資料全書、仏典、第一卷、禅籍篇.

Nanchang fuzhi 南昌府志. 6 vols. Taipei: Chengwen chubanshe, 1989.

Nittō guhō junrei gyōki 入唐求法巡礼行紀 (838–847), by Ennin 圓仁 (799–852). (1) *Dainihon bukkyō zensho* 大日本仏教全書 113.169–282; (2) Shijiazhuang: Huashan wenyi chubanshe, 1992.

Pang jushi yulu 龐居士語錄. (1) XZJ vol. 120; (2) Iriya Yoshitaka 入谷義高, trans. *Hō koji goroku* 龐居士語錄, ZG 7. Tokyo: Chikuma shobō, 1973.

Pei xiu shiyi wen 裴休拾遺文, by Zongmi 宗密. In ZK 60.

Quantang wen 全唐文 (1814), compiled by Dong Gao 董誥, et al. (1) Shanghai: Shanghai guji chubanshe, 1990; (2) Taipei: Huawen shuju, 1961; (3) Beijing: Zhonghua shuju, 1985.

Quan zaizhi wenji 權載之文集, by Quan Deyu 權德輿 (759–818). See *Xinkan quan zaizhi wenji* 新刊權載之文集.

Samguk yusa 三國遺史. T 2039, vol. 49.

Sanlun xuanyi 三論玄義, by Jizang 吉藏 (549–623). T 1852, vol. 45.

Shoulengyan jing 首楞嚴經. T 945, vol. 19.

Sichuan tongzhi 四川通志. 10 vols. Taipei: Huawen shuju, 1967.

Sifen lü 四分律. T 1428, vol. 22.

Sijia yulu 四家語錄. (1) XZJ 119 (incomplete); (2) Yanagida Seizan, ed. *Zengaku sōsho*, vol. 3 禅学叢書之三. Kyoto: Chūbun shuppansha, 1974.

Song gaoseng zhuan 宋高僧傳 (988), by Zanning 贊寧 (918–1001). (1) T 2061, vol. 50; (2) Beijing: Zhonghua shuju, 1987 (2 vols.).

Songzang yizhen 宋藏遺珍. Shanghai: Yingyin songban zangjing hui, 1935 (reprint: Taipei, 1978).

Song-yuan difangzhi congshu 宋元地方志叢書. 12 vols. Taipei: Dahua shuju, 1970.

Sŏnmun pojang nok 禪門寶藏錄 (1293), compiled by Ch'ŏnch'aek. XZJ vol. 113.

Tang wencui 唐文粹 (1011), by Yao Xuan 姚鉉 (Song). (1) Hangzhou: Zhejiang renmin chubanshe, 1986 (4 vols.); (2) Taipei: Taiwan shangwu yinshuguan, 1968 (2 vols.).

Tanzhou guishan lingyou chanshi yulu 潭州潙山靈祐禪師語錄. (1) T 1989, vol. 47; (2) XZJ vol. 119.

Tiansheng guangdeng lu 天聖廣燈錄 (1036), by Li Zunxu 李遵勗. XZJ vol. 135.

Wenshushili wen jing 文殊師利問經. T 468, vol. 14.

Weimojie jing 維摩詰經. T 474, vol. 14.

Weimojie suoshuojing zhu 維摩詰所説經註, by Sengzhao 僧肇 (374?–414). T 1775, vol. 38.

Wenyuan yinghua 文苑英華 (986), by Li Fang 李昉 (925–996). Beijing: Zhonghua shuju, 1966.

Wujia zhengzong zan 五家正宗贊 (1254), by Shaotan 紹曇 (d.u.). XZJ vol. 135.

Wumen guan 無門關, by Wumen Huikai 無門慧開 (1183–1260). T 2005, vol. 48.

Wuxi ji 武溪集, compiled by Yu Jing 余靖 (1000–1064). In *Siku quanshu* 四庫全書.

Xinkan quan zaizhi wenji 新刊權載之文集, by Quan Deyu 權德輿 (759–818). *Song shukeben tangren ji congkan* 宋蜀刻本唐人集叢刊 13 and 14. Shanghai: Shanghai guji chubanshe.

Xin tangshu 新唐書 (1060), by Ouyang Xiu 歐陽修 (1006–1072), at al. Beijing: Zhonghua shuju, 1975.

Xinxin ming 信心銘, attributed to Sengcan 僧璨 (d. 606?). T 2010, vol. 48.

Xiuxin yaolun 修心要論, by Hongren 弘忍 (601–674). T 2011, vol. 48.

Xu gaoseng zhuan 續高僧傳 (645), by Daoxuan 道宣 (596–667). T 2060, vol. 50.

Yuanjuejing dashu chao 圓覺經大疏鈔, by Zongmi 宗密 (780–841). XZJ vols. 14–15.

Yudi jisheng 輿地紀勝, by Wang Xiang 王象 (Song). 8 vols. Beijing: Zhonghua shuju, 1992.

Zhaolun 肇論, by Sengzhao 僧肇 (374–414?). T 1858, vol. 45.

Zhenzhou linji huizhao chanshi yulu 鎮州臨濟慧照禪師語錄. T 1985, vol. 47.

Zhongguo fosi zhi congkan 中國佛寺誌叢刊, ed. by Bai Huawen 白化文. 120 vols. Yangzhou: Jiangsu guangling guji keyinshe, 1992.

Zhongguo fosi shizhi huikan 中國佛寺史志彙刊, ed. by Du Jiexiang 杜潔祥. Taipei: Mingwen shuju, 1980.

Zhonghua chuan xindi chanmen shizi chengxi tu 中華傳心地禪門師資承襲圖, by Zongmi 宗密. XZJ vol. 110.

Zimen jingxun 緇門警訓 (1469?), by Rujin 如巹. T 2023, vol. 48.

Zizhi tongjian 資治通鑑 (1084), by Sima Guang 司馬光 (1019–1086). Beijing: Zhonghua shuju, 1987.

Zongjing lu 宗鏡錄, by Yongming Yanshou 永明延壽 (904–975). T 2016, vol. 48.

Zongmen shigui lun 宗門十規論, by Fayan Wenyi 法眼文益 (885–958). XZJ vol. 110.

Zutang ji 祖堂集 (952), compiled by Jing 靜 and Yun 筠. (1) Changsha: Yuelu shushe, 1996. (2) K 1503, vol. 45. (3) Yanagida Seizan, ed. *Zengaku sōsho*, vol. 4 禪学叢書之四. Kyoto: Chūbun shuppansha, 1984; (4) Taipei: Guangwen shuju, 1972.

Zuting shiyuan 祖庭事苑 (1108), by Muan Shanqing 睦庵善卿. XZJ vol. 113.

SECONDARY SOURCES: EAST ASIAN LANGUAGES

Akizuki Ryōmin 秋月龍珉, trans. *Rinzai roku* 臨済録. ZG 10. Tokyo: Chikuma shobō, 1972.

———, trans. *Jōshū roku* 趙州録. ZG 11. Tokyo: Chikuma shobō, 1972.

Aoyama Sadao 青山定雄. *Tō-Sō jidai no kōtsū to chishi chizu no kenkyū* 唐宋時代の交通と地志地図の研究. Tokyo: Yoshigawa hirobunkan, 1963.

Chen Baiquan 陈柏泉. "Mazu chanshi shihan tiji yu Zhang Zongyan tianshi kuangji" 马祖禅师石函题记与张宗演天师圹记. *Wenshi* 文史 14 (1982): 258.

Chŏng Sŏng-bon 鄭性本. *Silla sŏnjong ŭi yŏn'gu* 新羅禪宗의研究. Seoul: Minjoksa, 1995.

Dobashi Hidetaka 土橋秀高. *Kairitsu no kenkyū* 戒律の研究. Kyoto: Nagata bunshōdō, 1980.

Du Jiwen 杜继文 and Wei Daoru 魏道儒. *Zhongguo chanzong tongshi* 中国禅宗通史. Nanjing: Jiangsu guji chubanshe, 1993.

Hachiya Kunio 蜂屋邦夫. "Haku Kyoi no shi to bukkyō" 白居易の詩と仏教. In *Chūgoku no bukkyō to bunka* 中国の仏教と文化. Tokyo: Daizō shuppan, 1988: 657–85.

Han Kidu 韓基斗. *Silla sidae ŭi sŏn sasang* 新羅時代의禪思想. Iri: Wŏn'gwang taehakkyo ch'ulp'anbu, 1974.

———. "Keitoku Dentōroku ni miru Shiragi zen" 景徳伝灯録に見る新羅禅. ZBKK 13 (1984): 129–44.

Hanabusa Hideki 花房英樹. *Haku Kyoi kenkyū* 白居易研究. Kyoto: Sekai shisōsha, 1971.

Hirano Kensho 平野顕照. "Haku Kyoi no bungaku to bukkyō" 白居易の文学と仏教. *Ōtani daigaku kenkyū nenpō* 16 (1963): 119–187.

Hirano Sōjō 平野宗浄, trans. *Tongo yōmon* 頓悟要門. ZG 6. Tokyo: Chikuma shobō, 1970.

Hiraoka Takeo 平岡武夫. *Chōan to Rakuyō* 長安と洛陽. 3 vols. Kyoto: Jinbun kagaku kenkyūjo, 1956.

Hu Shi 胡適. *Shenhui heshang yiji* 神會和尚遺集. Taipei: Hu Shi jinianguan, 1968.

———. "Ba Pei Xiu de 'Tang gu guifeng dinghui chanshi chuanfa bei'" 跋裴休的唐故圭峰定慧禪師傳法碑. In Jiang Yihua 姜義華, ed. *Hu Shi xueshu wenji: Zhongguo foxue shi* 胡適學術文集 — 中國佛學史: 216–43.

———. "Bo Juyi shidaide chanzong shixi" 白居易時代的禪宗世系. (1) Huang Xianian 黃夏年, ed. *Hu Shi ji* 胡適集. Beijing: Zhongguo shehui kexue chubanshe, 1995. (2) *Hu Shi wencun* 胡適文存, vol. 3. Shanghai: Shanghai shudian, 1989.

Ibuki Atsushi 伊吹敦. *Zen no rekishi* 禅の歴史. Kyoto: Hōzōkan, 2001.

Iriya Yoshitaka 入谷義高, trans. *Baso no goroku* 馬祖の語録. Kyoto: Zen bunka kenkyūjo, 1984.

———, trans. *Denshin hōyō, Enryō roku* 伝心法要, 宛陵録. ZG 8. Tokyo: Chikuma shobō, 1969.

———, trans. *Hō koji goroku* 龐居士語録. ZG 7. Tokyo: Chikuma shobō, 1973.

———, ed. *Keitoku dentōroku* 景徳伝灯録. Vols. 3 and 4. Kyoto: Zen bunka kenkyūjo, 1993, 1997.

Ishii Shūdō 石井修道. *Chūgoku zenshū shiwa* 中国禅宗史話. Kyoto: Zen bunka kenkyūjo, 1988.

———. *Sōdai zenshūshi no kenkyū: Chūgoku sōtōshū to dōgen zen* 宋代禅宗史の研究：中国曹洞宗と道元禅. Tokyo: Daitō shuppansha, 1987.

———, trans. *Zen goroku* 禅語録. *Daijō butten: Chūgoku, Nihon hen* 大乗仏典 — 中国, 日本編, vol. 12. Tokyo: Chūo kōronsha, 1992.

———. "Enshū Yōgisan o meguru nanshūzen no dōkō" 袁州楊岐山をめぐる南宋禅の動向. IBK 38/2 (1990): 198–204.

———. "Hyakujō kyōdan to Isan kyōdan" 百丈教団と潙山教団. IBK 41/1 (1992): 106–11.

———. "Hyakujō kyōdan to Isan kyōdan (zoku)" 百丈教団と潙山教団, 続. IBK 42/1 (1993): 289–95.

———. "Hyakujō shingi no kenkyū" 百丈清規の研究. *Komazawa daigaku zenkenkyūjo nenpō* 6 (1995): 15–53.

———. "Isan kyōdan no dōkō ni tsuite—Fukushū Daian no shinjinki no shōkai ni chinande" 潙山教団の動向について — 福州大安の《真身記》の紹介に因んで. IBK 27/1 (1978): 90–96.

———. "Igyōshū no seisui (1–6)" 潙仰宗の盛衰 (1–6). KDBR 18–22, 24 (1985–1991, 1993).

———. "Kōshūshū ni okeru Seidō Chizō no ichi ni tsuite" 洪州宗における西堂智蔵の位置について. IBK 40/1 (1991): 280–84.

———. "Nanshū zen no tongo shisō no tenkai—Kataku Jinne kara Kōshūshū e" 南宗禅の頓悟思想の展開 — 荷澤神会から洪州宗へ. ZBKK 20 (1994): 101–49.

———. "Nanyō Echū no nanpō shūshi no hihan ni tsuite" 南陽慧忠の南方宗旨の批判について. In Kamata Shigeo hakushi kanreki kinen ronshu kankōkai, ed. *Chūgoku no bukkyō to bunka*: 315–44.

———. "Shinpukuji bunko shozō 'Hai Kyū shūimon' honkoku" 真福寺文庫所蔵《裴休拾遺問》翻刻. ZK 60 (1981): 71–104.

Ishikawa Rikizan 石川力山. "Baso kyōdan no tenkai to sono shijishatachi" 馬祖教団の展開とその支持者達. KDBR 2 (1971): 160–73.

———. "Baso zō no henka katei" 馬祖像の変化過程. IBK 20/2 (1972): 309–11.

———. "Basozen keisei no ichisokumen" 馬祖禅形成の一側面. SK 13 (1971): 105–110.

———. "Basozen ni okeru sokushin sokubutsu no rekishiteki kadai" 馬祖禅における即心即仏の歴史的課題. *Komazawa daigaku daigakuin bukkyōgaku kenkyūkai nenpō* 5 (1971): 153–83.

———. "Kanazawabunko-bon 'Minshū Daibaisan Jō zenji goroku' ni tsuite" 金沢文庫本《明州大梅山常禅師語録》について. *Komazawa daigaku daigakuin bukkyōgaku kenkyūkai nenpō* 6 (1972): 69–81.

Kagamishima Genryū 鏡島元隆. "Hyakujō shingi no seiritsu to sono igi" 百丈清規の成立とその意義. (Aichi Gakuin Daigaku) *Zen kenkyūjo kiyō* 6 and 7 (1976): 117–34.

Kagamishima Genryū 鏡島元隆 et al., trans. *Yakuchū Zennen shingii* 訳註 — 禅苑清規. Tokyo: Sōtōshū Shūmuchō, 1972.

Kajitani Sōnin, trans. "Isan kyōsaku" 潙山警策. In Nishitani Keiji 西谷啓治, ed. *Zen no koten: Chūgoku* 禅の古典—中国.

———, trans. "Isan kyōsaku" 潙山警策. In Nishitani Keiji 西谷啓治 and Yanagida Seizan 柳田聖山, eds., *Zenke goroku* 禅家語録, vol. 2.

Kamata Shigeo 鎌田茂雄. *Shūmitsu kyōgaku no shisōshiteki kenkyū* 宗密教学の思想史的研究. Tokyo: Tōkyō daigaku shuppankai, 1975.

————, trans. *Zengen shosenshū tojo* 禅源諸詮集都序. ZG 9. Tokyo: Chikuma shobō, 1971.

————. "Chūgoku zen shisō keisei no kyōgakuteki haikei: Daijō kishinron o chūshin to shite" 中国禅思想形成の教学的背景 — 大乗起信論を中心として. *Tōyō bunka kenkyūjo kiyō* 東洋文化研究所紀要 49 (1969): 98–109.

————. "Chūtō no bukkyō no hendō to kokka kenryoku" 中唐の仏教の変動と国家権力. *Tōyō bunka kenkyūjo kiyō* 東洋文化研究所紀要 25 (1961): 201–45.

Kamata Shigeo hakushi kanreki kinen ronshu kankōkai 鎌田茂雄博士還暦記念論集刊行会, ed. *Chūgoku no Bukkyō to bunka: Kamata Shigeo hakushi kanreki kinen ronshu* 中国の仏教と文化 — 鎌田茂雄博士還暦記念論集. Tokyo: Daizō shuppan, 1988.

Kawauchi Shoen 河内昭円. "Ken Tokuyo to Bukkyō" 権徳輿と仏教. (Ōtani daigaku) *Bungei Ronsō* 文芸論叢 20 (1983): 25–36.

Kojima Taizan 小島岱山. "*Mōjin gengen kan* no senja o meguru shomondai" 妄尽還源観の撰者をめぐる諸問題. *Nanto bukkyō* 南都仏教 49 (1982): 13–31.

Kondō Ryōichi 近藤良一. "Hyakujō shingi no seiritsu to sono genkei" 百丈清規の成立とその原形. *Hokkaidō Komazawa daigaku kenkyū kiyō* 3 (1969): 17–48.

————. "Hyakujō shingi seiritsu no yōin" 百丈清規成立の要因. *Indo tetsugaku bukkyōgaku* 2 (1987): 231–46.

————. "Tōdai zenshū no keizai kiban" 唐代禅宗の経済基盤. *Nippon Bukkyō gakkai nenpō* 日本仏教学会年報 37: 137–51.

Matsumoto Shirō 松本史朗. *Zen shisō no hihanteki kenkyū* 禅思想の批判的研究. Tokyo: Daizō shuppan, 1993.

Nakagawa Taka 中川孝, trans. *Rokuso dangyō* 六祖檀経. ZG 4. Tokyo: Chikuma shobō, 1976.

Nishiguchi Yoshio 西口芳男. "Baso no denki" 馬祖の伝記. ZK 63 (1984): 111–46.

Nishitani Keiji 西谷啓治 and Yanagida Seizan 柳田聖山, eds. *Zenke goroku* 禅家語録, 2 vols. Tokyo: Chikuma shobō, 1974.

Obata Hironobu 小畠宏允. "*Rekidai hōbōki* to kodai Chibetto no Bukkyō" 歴代法宝記と古代チベットの仏教. In Yanagida Seizan, trans. *Shoki no zenshi II: Rekidai hōbōki*: 325–37.

Ogawa Takashi 小川隆. "Jinne botsugo no nanboku ryōshū" 神会没後の南北両宗. SK 33 (1991): 193–8.

————. "Kataku Jinne no hito to shisō" 荷澤神会の人と思想. ZK 69 (1991): 29–59.

————. "Shoki zenshū keiseishi no ichi sokumen: Fujaku to 'Sūzan hōmon'" 初期禅宗形成史の一側面 — 普寂と崇山法門. KDBR 20 (1989): 310–25.

————. "Shūmitsu denbō seikei saikō" 宗密伝法世系再考. ZBKK 24 (1999): 67–82.

Ogawa Tamaki 小川環樹, ed. *Tōdai no shijin: sono denki* 唐代の詩人 —その伝記. Tokyo: Taishūkan shoten, 1975.

Okimoto Katsumi 沖本克巳. "Hyakujō kogi ni tsuite" 百丈清規について. ZBKK 12 (1980): 51–61.

————. "Hyakujō shingi to zenin shingi" 百丈清規と禅院清規. IBK 17/2 (1969): 773–75.

————. "Shingi kenkyū nōto" 清規研究ノート. In Sasaki Kyōgo 佐々木教悟, ed. *Kairitsu shisō no kenkyū* 戒律思想の研究: 405–37.

————. "Zen shisō keiseishi no kenkyū" 禅思想形成史の研究. (Hanazono daigaku kokusai zengaku kenkyūjo) *Kenkyū Hōkoku* 研究報告 5 (1997): 1–451.

Ōishi Morio 大石守雄. "Ko shingi ni tsuite" 古清規について. ZK 44 (1953): 81–88.

———. "Shingi no kenkyū" 清規の研究. ZK 54 (1964): 109–15.

Ono Katsutoshi 小野勝年. Nittōguhō junrei gyōki no kenkyū 入唐求法巡礼行紀の研究. 4 vols. Tokyo: Hōzōkan, 1988.

———. Nittō guhō gyōreki no kenkyū 入唐求法行歴の研究. 2 vols. Tokyo: Hōzōkan, 1982.

———. Chūgoku Zui Tō Chōan jiin shiryō shūsei: kaisetsu hen 中国隋唐長安寺院資料集成 — 解説篇. Kyoto: Hōzōkan, 1989.

———. Chūgoku Zui Tō Chōan jiin shiryō shūsei: shiryō hen 中国隋唐長安寺院資料集成 — 史料篇. Kyoto: Hōzōkan, 1989.

Ōnishi Ryūhō 大西龍峰. "Baso Dōitsu no henbō (1–5)" 馬祖道一の変貌 (1–5). Shunjū 春秋 5–7, 10, 12 (1994).

Sasaki Kyōgo 佐々木教悟, ed. Kairitsu shisō no kenkyū 戒律思想の研究. Kyoto: Heirakuji shoten, 1981.

Sato Tatsugen 佐藤達玄. Chūgoku Bukkyō ni okeru kairitsu no kenkyū 中国仏教における戒律の研究. Tokyo: Mokujisha, 1986.

Shiina Kōyū 椎名宏雄. Sōgenban zenseki no kenkyū 宋元版禅籍の研究. Tokyo: Daitō shuppansha, 1993.

———. "Hokushūzen ni okeru kairitsu no mondai" 北宗禅における戒律の問題. SK 11 (1969): 139–52.

———. "Hōrinden itsubun no kenkyū" 宝林伝逸文の研究. KDBR 11 (1980): 234–57.

———. "Hōrinden makikyū makijū no itsubun" 宝林伝巻九巻十の逸文. SK 22 (1980): 191–98.

———. "Nanshū no zazenkan to sono tokushoku" 南宗の坐禅観とその特色. SK 13 (1971): 134–46.

———. "Shotō zensha no ritsuin kyojū ni tsuite" 初唐禅者の律院居住について. IBK 17/2 (1969): 770–72.

———. "Sodōshū no hensei" 祖堂集の編成. SK 21 (1979): 66–72.

———. "Sūzan ni okeru hokushū zen no tenkai" 嵩山における北宗禅の展開. SK 10: 173–85.

———. "Tōdai zenshū no raisan ni tsuite" 唐代禅宗の礼懺について. IBK 20/2 (1972): 764–49.

———. "Tōzan hōmon keisei no haikei" 東山法門形成の背景. SK 12 (1970): 173–86.

Shinohara Hisao 篠原寿雄 and Tanaka Ryōshō 田中良昭, eds. Tonkō butten to zen 敦煌仏典と禅. Tokyo: Daitō shuppansha, 1980.

Shimosada Masahiro 下定雅弘. Hakushi monjū o yomu 白氏文集を読む. Tokyo: Benseisha, 1996.

Sun Changwu 孫昌武. Tangdai wenxue yu fojiao 唐代文學與佛教. Xi'an: Shaanxi renmin chubanshe, 1985.

———. Chansi yu shiqing 禅思与诗情. Beijing: Zhonghua shuju, 1997.

———. "Haku Kyoi to bukkyō: zen to jōdo" 白居易と仏教—禅と浄土, trans. by Soejima Ichirō. In Ōta Tsugio, et al., eds. Haku Kyoi kenkyū kōza 白居易研究講座, vol. 1. Kyoto: Benseisha, 1993.

Suzuki Tetsuo 鈴木哲雄. Chūgoku zenshū jinmei sakuin 中国禅宗人名索引. Nagoya: Kikōdō shoten, 1975.

———. *Chūgoku zenshūshi ronkō* 中国禅宗史論考. Tokyo: Sankibō busshorin, 1999.

———. *Sekkō kōzei chihō zenshū shiseki hōroku* 浙江江西地方禪宗史蹟訪録. Tokyo: Sankibō bushōrin, 1997.

———. *Tō-godai no zenshū: Konan, Kōsei hen* 唐五代の禅宗 — 湖南江西篇. Tokyo: Daitō shuppansha, 1984.

———. *Tō-godai zenshū shi* 唐五代禅宗史. Tokyo: Sankibō busshorin, 1985.

———. "Hyakujō kōroku ni mirareru shisō" 百丈広録にみられる思想. IBK 46/2 (1998): 583–88.

———. "Kōzei no zenshū ni kansuru shiryō" 江西の禅宗に関する資料. *Aichi gakuin daigaku bungakubu kiyō* 愛知学院大学文学部紀要 8 (1979): 135–85.

———. "Tongo nyūdō yōmon ron ni mirareru Kataku Jinne no eikyō" 頓悟入道要門論に見られる荷澤神会の影響. SK 12 (1970): 91–96 (reprinted in his *Tō-godai zenshū shi*: 359–69).

Tanaka Ryōshō 田中良昭. *Tonkō zenshū bunken no kenkyū* 敦煌禅宗文献の研究. Tokyo: Daitō shuppansha, 1983.

Tan Qixiang 譚其驤, ed. *Zhongguo lishi ditu ji* 中國歴史地圖集. 8 vols. Shanghai: Ditu chubanshe, 1982–87.

Tokiwa Daijō 常盤大定. *Shina ni okeru Bukkyō to Jukyō Dōkyō* 支那における仏教と儒教道教. Tokyo: Tōyō shorin, 1982 (original ed. published in 1930).

Tomitani Ryūkei 富谷龍渓, trans. "Butsuso sankyō kōgi" 佛祖三経講義. In *Sōtō-shū kōgi* 曹洞宗講義, vol. 3. Tokyo: Kokusho kankōkai, 1975 (original ed. published in 1928).

Tsukamoto Zenryū 塚本善隆. *Chūgoku jōdokyōshi kenkyū* 中国浄土教史研究. Tokyo: Daitō shuppansha, 1976.

———. *Tō chūki no jōdokyō* 唐中期の浄土教. Kyoto: Hōzōkan, 1975.

Ui Hakuju 宇井伯寿. *Zenshūshi kenkyū* 禅宗史研究. 3 vols. Tokyo: Iwanami shoten, 1939–43.

Yamaguchi Zuihō 山口瑞鳳, "Makaen no zen 摩訶衍の禅." In Shinohara Hisao 篠原寿雄 and Tanaka Ryōshō 田中良昭, eds. *Tonkō butten to Zen* 敦煌仏典と禅: 379–407.

Yamazaki Hiroshi 山崎宏. *Zui-Tō bukkyō shi no kenkyū* 隋唐仏教史の研究. Tokyo: Hōzōkan, 1967.

———. "Tōdai kōki no koji Hai Kyū ni tsuite" 唐代後期の居士裴休について. *Bukkyō shigaku* 14/4 (1969): 189–204.

Yanagida Seizan 柳田聖山, trans. *Daruma no goroku: Ninyū shigyō ron* 達磨の語録—二入四行論. ZG 1. Tokyo: Chikuma shobō, 1969.

———, trans. *Rinzai roku* 臨剤録. Tokyo: Daizō shuppan, 1972.

———, trans. *Shoki no zenshi I: Ryōga shijiki, Denhōbōki* 初期の禅史 I— 楞伽師資記, 傳法寶紀. ZG 2. Tokyo: Chikuma shobō, 1971.

———, trans. *Shoki no zenshi II: Rekidai hōbōki* 初期の禅史 II— 歴代法寶記. ZG 3. Tokyo: Chikuma shobō, 1976.

———. *Shoki zenshū shisho no kenkyū* 初期禅宗史書の研究. Kyoto: Hōzōkan, 1967.

———, trans. *Sodōshū* 祖堂集. *Daijō butten: Chūgoku, Nihon hen* 大乗仏典 — 中国、日本篇, vol. 13. Tokyo: Chūō kōronsha, 1990.

———, ed. *Sodōshū* 祖堂集. *Zengaku sōsho* (vol. 4) 禅学叢書之四. Kyoto: Chūbun shuppansha, 1974.

———, ed. *Sōzō ichin Hōrinden, Dentō gyokuei shū* 宋藏遺珍宝林伝、伝灯玉英集. Kyoto: Chūbun shuppansha, 1975.

———, trans. *Zen goroku* 禅語録. Tokyo: Chūō kōronsha, 1974.

———. "Basozen no sho mondai" 馬祖禅の諸問題. IBK 17/1 (1968): 33–41.

———. "Chūgoku zenshū shi" 中国禅宗史. In Nishitani Keiji 西谷啓治, ed. *Zen no rekishi: Chūgoku* 禅の歴史 — 中国: 7–108.

———. "Goroku no rekishi: Zen bunken no seiritsu shiteki kenkyū" 語録の歴史 — 禅文献の成立史的研究. TG 57 (1985): 211–663.

———. "Kosonshuku goroku kō" 古尊宿語録考. *Hanazono daigaku kenkyū kiyō* 花園大学研究紀要 2 (1971): 1–84.

———. "Mujū to Shūmitsu: Tongo shisō no keisei o megutte" 無住と宗密 — 頓悟思想の形成をめぐって. *Hanazono daigaku kenkyū kiyō* 花園大学研究紀要 7 (1976): 1–36.

———. "Shinzoku tōshi no keifu: jo no ichi" 新続灯史の系譜 — 叙の一. ZK 59 (1978): 1–39.

———. "Shinzoku tōshi no keifu: jo no ni" 新続灯史の系譜 — 叙の二. ZK 60 (1981): 1–70.

———. "*Sodōshū* no shiryō kachi" 祖堂集の資料価値. (Published under his original name, Yokoi Seizan 横井聖山.) ZK 44 (1953): 31–79.

———. "Zekkanron to sono jidai" 絶観論とその時代. TG 52 (1980).

———. "Zenseki kaidai" 禅籍解題. In Nishitani Keiji and Yanagida Seizan, eds. *Zenke goroku*, vol. 2: 445–514.

———. "Zenshū goroku no keisei" 禅宗語録の形成. IBK 18/1 (1969): 39–47.

Yanagida Seizan 柳田聖山 and Shiina Kōyū 椎名宏雄, eds. *Zengaku tenseki sōkan, betsukan* 禅学典籍叢刊、別刊. Kyoto: Rinsen shoten, 2001.

Yang Zengwen 楊曾文, ed. *Shenhui heshang chanhua lu* 神會和尚禪話録. Beijing: Zhonghua shuju, 1996.

———. *Tang Wudai chanzong shi* 唐五代禪宗史. Beijing: Zhongguo shehui kexue chubanshe, 1999.

———. "Tōdai zenshūshi no sho mondai" 唐代禅宗史の諸問題, trans. by Ogawa Takashi 小川隆. *Komazawa daigaku zen kenkyūjo nenpō* 9 (1998).

Yinshun 印順. *Zhongguo chanzong shi* 中國禪宗史. Taipei: Huiri jiangtang, 1971.

———. *Rulaizang zhi yanjiu* 如來藏之研究. Taipei: Zhengwen chubanshe, 1981.

Yoshikawa Tadao 吉川忠夫. "Hai Kyū den: Tōdai no ichi shitaifu to bukkyō" 裴休傳 — 唐代の一士大夫と仏教. TG 64 (1992): 115–277.

Yoshizu Yoshihide 吉津宜英. *Kegon zen no shisōteki kenkyū* 華厳禅の思想的研究. Tokyo: Daitō shuppansha, 1985.

SECONDARY SOURCES: WESTERN LANGUAGES

App, Urs, trans. *Master Yunmen: From the Record of the Chan Teacher "Gate of Clouds."* New York: Kodansha International, 1994.

Asad, Talal. *Genealogies of Religion: Discipline and Reasoning Power in Christianity and Islam.* Baltimore and London: John Hopkins University Press, 1993.

Barrett, Timothy Hugh. *Li Ao: Buddhist, Taoist, or Neo-Confucian?* Oxford: Oxford University Press, 1992.

Blofeld, John, trans. *The Zen Teaching of Huang-po on the Transmission of Mind*. New York: Grove Press, 1958.

————, trans. *The Zen Teaching of Instantaneous Awakening*. Leicester: Buddhist Publishing Group, 1987. (Originally published as *The Zen Teaching of Hui Hai on Sudden Illumination*. London: Rider, 1962).

Bodiford, William, ed. *Going Forth: Visions of the Buddhist Vinaya*. Honolulu: University of Hawai'i Press, 2005.

Bol, Peter Kees. *"This Culture of Ours": Intellectual Transitions in T'ang and Sung China*. Stanford: Stanford University Press, 1992.

Broughton, Jeffrey L., trans. *The Bodhidharma Anthology: The Earliest Records of Zen*. Berkeley: University of California Press, 1999.

————. "Tsung-mi's *Zen Prolegomenon:* Introduction to an Exemplary Zen Canon." In Heine and Wright, *The Zen Canon*: 11–51.

Brown, Brian Edward. *The Buddha Nature: A Study of the Tathāgatagarbha and Ālayavijñāna*. Delhi: Motilal Banarsidass Publishers, 1991.

Buswell, Robert E., ed. *Chinese Buddhist Apocrypha*. Honolulu: University of Hawai'i Press, 1990.

————. *The Formation of Ch'an Ideology in China and Korea*: *The* Vajrasamādhi-Sūtra, *A Buddhist Apocryphon*. Princeton: Princeton University Press, 1989.

————, trans. *The Korean Approach to Zen: The Collected Works of Chinul*. Honolulu: University of Hawai'i Press, 1983.

————. "The 'Short-cut' Approach of *K'an-hua* Meditation: The Evolution of Practical Subitism in Chinese Ch'an Buddhism." In Gregory, *Sudden and Gradual*: 321–77.

————. *The Zen Monastic Experience*. Princeton: Princeton University Press, 1992.

Buswell, Robert E., and Robert M. Gimello, eds. *Paths to Liberation: The Mārga and its Transformations in Buddhist Thought*. Studies in East Asian Buddhism 7. Honolulu: University of Hawai'i Press, 1992.

Chang, Chung-yuan, trans. *Original Teachings of Chan Buddhism*. New York: Vintage Books, 1971.

Chen, Jinhua. "One Name, Three Monks: Two Northern Chan Masters Emerge from the Shadow of their Contemporary, the Tiantai Master Zhanran (711–782)." *Journal of the International Association of Buddhist Studies* 22/1 (1999): 1–91.

Chen, Jo-shui. *Liu Tsung-yuan and Intellectual Change in T'ang China, 773–819*. Cambridge and New York: Cambridge University Press, 1992.

Ch'en, Kenneth. *Buddhism in China: A Historical Survey*. Princeton: Princeton University Press, 1964.

————. *The Chinese Transformation of Buddhism*. Princeton: Princeton University Press, 1973.

Cheng-chien Bhikshu [Mario Poceski], trans. *Manifestation of the Tathāgata: Buddhahood According to the Avatamsaka Sūtra*. Boston: Wisdom Publications, 1993.

————, trans. *Sun-Face Buddha: The Teachings of Ma-tsu and the Hung-chou School of Ch'an*. Berkeley: Asian Humanities Press, 1993.

Cleary, Thomas, trans. *The Flower Ornament Scripture*. 3 vols. Boston and London: Shambala Publications, 1984–1987.

————, trans. *Sayings and Doings of Pai-chang*. Los Angeles: Center Publications, 1978.

Cleary, Thomas, and J. C. Cleary, trans. *The Blue Cliff Record*. 3 vols. Boulder: Shambala Publications, 1977.

Conze, Edward, trans. *The Perfection of Wisdom in Eight Thousand Lines and its Verse Summary*. San Francisco: Four Seasons Foundation, 1973.

Dalby, Michael T. "Court Politics in Late T'ang Times." In Twitchett, *The Cambridge History of China, vol. 3: Sui and T'ang China, 589–906, Part I*: 561–681.

DeBlasi, Anthony Augustine. " 'To Transform the World:' A Study of Four Mid-Tang Intellectuals." Ph.D. diss., Harvard University, 1996.

Demiéville, Paul. *Le concile de Lhasa: une controverse sur le quiétisme entre bouddhistes de l'Inde et de la Chine au VIIIe siècle de l'ère chrétienne*. Paris: Collège de France, Institut des hautes études chinoises, 1987 (first edition published in 1952).

Donner, Neal. "Sudden and Gradual Intimately Conjoined: Chih-i's T'ien-t'ai View." In Gregory, *Sudden and Gradual*: 201–26.

Dumoulin, Henrich. *Zen Buddhism: A History*. 2 vols. New York: Macmillan Publishing Company, 1988.

Ebrey, Patricia Buckley, and Peter N. Gregory, eds. *Religion and Society in T'ang and Sung China*. Honolulu: University of Hawai'i Press, 1992.

Faure, Bernard. *Chan Insights and Oversights: An Epistemological Critique of the Chan Tradition*. Princeton: Princeton University Press, 1993.

———. *The Rhetoric of Immediacy: A Cultural Critique of Chan/Zen Buddhism*. Princeton: Princeton University Press, 1991.

———. *The Will to Orthodoxy: A Critical Genealogy of Northern Chan Buddhism*. Stanford: Stanford University Press, 1997.

———. "Bodhidharma as a Textual and Religious Paradigm." *History of Religions* 25/3 (1986): 187–98.

———. "The Concept of One-Practice Samādhi in Early Ch'an." In Gregory, *Traditions of Meditation in Chinese Buddhism*: 99–128.

Faurot, Jeannette L. *Ancient Chengdu*. San Francisco: Chinese Materials Center Publications, 1992.

Feifel, Eugene, trans. "Biography of Po Chü-i—Annotated translation from *chüan* 166 of the *Chiu T'ang-shu*." *Monumenta Serica* 17 (1958): 255–311.

Foulk, Theodore Griffith. "*Chanyuan qinggui* and Other 'Rules of Purity' in Chinese Buddhism." In Heine and Wright, *The Zen Canon*: 275–312.

———. "The Ch'an School and its Place in the Buddhist Monastic Tradition." Ph.D. diss., University of Michigan, Ann Arbor, 1987.

———. "The Ch'an *Tsung* in Medieval China: School, Lineage, or What?" *The Pacific World* 8 (1992): 18–31.

———. "Myth, Ritual, and Monastic Practice in Sung Ch'an Buddhism." In Ebrey and Gregory, *Religion and Society in T'ang and Sung China*: 147–208.

———. "Sung Controversies Concerning the 'Separate Transmission' of Ch'an." In Gregory and Getz, *Buddhism in the Sung*: 220–294.

Foulk, Theodore Griffith, and Robert H. Sharf. "On the Ritual Use of Ch'an Portraiture in Medieval China." *Cahiers d'Extrême-Asie* 7 (1993–94): 149–219.

Geertz, Clifford. *The Interpretation of Cultures*. New York: Basic Books, 1973.

Gernet, Jacques. *Buddhism in Chinese Society: An Economic History from the Fifth to the Tenth Centuries.* Trans. by Franciscus Verellen. New York: Columbia University Press, 1995.

Gimello, Robert. "Apophatic and Kataphatic Discourse in Mahāyāna: A Chinese view." *Philosophy East and West* 26/2 (1976): 117–136.

Gimello, Robert M., and Peter Gregory, eds. *Studies in Ch'an and Hua-yen.* Studies in East Asian Buddhism 1. Honolulu: University of Hawai'i Press, 1983.

Gómez, Luis O. "The Direct and Gradual Approaches of Zen Master Mahayana: Fragments of the Teachings of Mo-ho-yen." In Gimello and Gregory, *Studies in Ch'an and Hua-yen:* 69–167.

———. "Purifying Gold: The Metaphor of Effort and Intuition in Buddhist Thought and Practice." In Gregory, *Sudden and Gradual:* 67–165.

Gregory, Peter N., trans. *Inquiry into the Origin of Humanity: An Annotated Translation of Tsung-mi's* Yüan jen lun *with a Modern Commentary.* Honolulu: University of Hawai'i Press, 1995.

———. "The Problem of Theodicy in the *Awakening of Faith.*" *Religious Studies* 22/1 (1986): 63–78.

———, ed. *Sudden and Gradual: Approaches to Enlightenment in Chinese Thought.* Studies in East Asian Buddhism 5. Honolulu: University of Hawai'i Press, 1987.

———. "Sudden Enlightenment Followed by Gradual Cultivation: Tsung-mi's Analysis of Mind." In Gregory, *Sudden and Gradual:* 279–320.

———, ed. *Traditions of Meditation in Chinese Buddhism.* Studies in East Asian Buddhism 4. Honolulu: University of Hawai'i Press, 1986.

———. *Tsung-mi and the Sinification of Buddhism.* Princeton: Princeton University Press, 1991.

Gregory, Peter N., and Daniel A. Getz, Jr., eds. *Buddhism in the Sung.* Studies in East Asian Buddhism 13. Honolulu: University of Hawai'i Press, 1999.

Green, James, trans. *The Recorded Sayings of Zen Master Joshu: Chao-Chou Chan-Shih Yu-Lu.* Boston: Shambhala, 1998.

Griffiths, Paul J., and John P. Keenan, eds. *Buddha Nature: A Festschrift in Honor of Minoru Kiyota.* Tokyo: Buddhist Books International, 1990.

Groner, Paul. "The *Fan-wang ching* and Monastic Discipline in Japanese Tendai: A Study of Annen's *Futsū jubosatsukai kōshaku.*" In Buswell, *Chinese Buddhist Apocrypha:* 251–90.

———. *Saichō: The Establishment of the Japanese Tendai School.* Berkeley: Berkeley Buddhist Studies Series, 1984.

Hakeda, Yoshito S., trans. *The Awakening of Faith.* New York: Columbia University Press, 1967.

Halperin, Mark Robert. "Pieties and Responsibilities: Buddhism and the Chinese Literati, 780–1280." Ph.D. diss., University of California, Berkeley, 1997.

Hamar, Imre. *A Religious Leader in the Tang: Changguan's Biography.* Tokyo: The International Institute for Buddhist Studies, 2002.

Hartman, Charles. "Han Yu and the Chan Movement: Points of Contact." *Proceedings of the Second International Conference on Sinology.* Taipei: Academia Sinica, 1989: 289–306.

————. *Han Yü and the T'ang Search for Unity.* Princeton: Princeton University Press, 1986.

Heine, Steven, and Dale S. Wright, eds. *The Kōan: Texts and Contexts in Zen Buddhism.* Oxford: Oxford University Press, 2000.

————. *The Zen Canon: Undestanding the Classic Texts.* Oxford: Oxford University Press, 2004.

Henricks, Robert G., trans. *The Poetry of Han-shan: A Complete, Annotated Translation of Cold Mountain.* Albany: State University of New York Press, 1990.

Hirai Shunei. "The School of Mount Niu-t'ou and the School of Pao-T'ang Monastery." Trans. by Silvio Vita. *East and West* 37/1–4: 337–72.

Hu Shi. "Ch'an/Zen Buddhism in China: Its History and Method." *Philosophy East and West* 3/1 (1953): 3–24.

————. "The Development of Zen Buddhism in China." *Chinese Social and Political Science Review* 15/4 (1932): 475–505.

Hucker, Charles O. *A Dictionary of Official Titles in Imperial China.* Stanford: Stanford University Press, 1985.

Ishigami, Zenno, ed. *Disciples of the Buddha.* Tokyo: Kōsei Publishing, 1989.

Jan Yun-hua. "Conflict and Harmony in Ch'an Buddhism." *Journal of Chinese Philosophy* 4 (1977): 287–302.

————. "Tsung-mi: His Analysis of Ch'an Buddhism." *T'oung Pao* 58 (1972): 1–54.

Jia Jinhua. "Doctrinal Reformation of the Hongzhou School of Chan Buddhism." *Journal of the International Association of Buddhist Studies* 24/1 (2001): 7–26.

————. "The Hongzhou School of Chan Buddhism and the Tang Literati." Ph.D. diss., University of Colorado, 1999.

Jorgensen, John. "The Imperial Lineage of Ch'an Buddhism: The Role of Confucian Ritual and Ancestor Worship in Ch'an's Search for Legitimization in the Mid-T'ang Dynasty." *Papers in Far Eastern History* 35 (1987): 89–133.

Kieschnick, John. *The Eminent Monk: Buddhist Ideals in Medieval Chinese Hagiography.* Studies in East Asian Buddhism 10. Honolulu: University of Hawai'i Press, 1997.

King, Sallie B. *Buddha Nature.* Albany: State University of New York Press, 1991.

Kohn, Livia. *Early Chinese Mysticism: Philosophy and Soteriology in the Taoist Tradition.* Princeton: Princeton University Press, 1992.

Korean Buddhist Research Institute, ed. *Son Thought in Korean Buddhism.* Seoul: Donguk University Press, 1998.

Lai, Whalen. "Tao-sheng's Theory of Sudden Enlightenment Re-examined." In Gregory, *Sudden and Gradual:* 169–200.

Lai, Whalen, and Lewis Lancaster, eds. *Early Ch'an in China and Tibet.* Berkeley: Asian Humanities Press, 1983.

Lau, D. C., trans. *The Analects.* London: Penguin Books, 1979.

Liu, Ming-Wood. "The Doctrine of the Buddha-Nature in the Mahāyāna *Mahāparinirvāṇa-Sūtra.*" *Journal of the International Association of Buddhist Studies* 5/2 (1982): 63–94.

————. *Madhyamaka Thought in China.* Leiden: Brill, 1994.

Maraldo, John C. "Is There a Historical Consciousness in Ch'an?" *Japanese Journal of Religious Studies* 12/2–3 (1985): 141–172.

McMullen, David. *State and Scholars in T'ang China*. Cambridge and New York: Cambridge University Press, 1988.

McRae, John R. *Seeing Through Zen: Encounter, Genealogy, and Transformation in Chinese Chan Buddhism*. Berkeley: University of California Press, 2003.

———. *The Northern School and the Formation of Early Ch'an Buddhism*. Studies in East Asian Buddhism 3. Honolulu: University of Hawai'i Press, 1986.

———. "Encounter Dialogue and the Transformation of the Spiritual Path in Chinese Ch'an." In Buswell and Gimello, *Paths to Liberation: The Mārga and its Transformations in Buddhist Thought*: 339–69.

———. "The Antecedents of Encounter Dialogue in Chinese Ch'an Buddhism." In Heine and Wright, *The Kōan: Texts and Contexts in Zen Buddhism*: 46–74.

———. "The Ox-head School of Chinese Ch'an Buddhism: From Early Ch'an to the Golden Age." In Gimello and Gregory, *Studies in Ch'an and Hua-yen*: 169–252.

———. "Religion as Revolution in Chinese Historiography: Hu Shih (1891–1962) on Shen-hui (684–758)." *Cahiers d'Extrême-Asie* 12 (2001): 59–102.

———. "Shen-hui and the Teaching of Sudden Enlightenment." In Gregory, *Sudden and Gradual*: 227–78.

———. "Yanagida Seizan's Landmark Works on Chinese Chan." *Cahiers d'Extrême-Asie* 7 (1993–94): 51–103.

Ñānamoli, Bhikkhu, and Bhikkhu Bodhi, trans. *The Middle Length Discourses: A New Translation of the Majjhima Nikāya*. Boston: Wisdom Publications, 1995.

Nguyen, Cuong Tu, trans. *Zen in Medieval Vietnam: A Study and Translation of the Thiền Uyển Tập Anh*. Honolulu: University of Hawai'i Press, 1997.

Norman, K. R., trans. *The Rhinoceros Horn and other Early Buddhist Poems (Sutta-nipāta)*. Oxford: The Pali Text Society, 1996.

Ogata, Sohaku, trans. *The Transmission of the Lamp: Early Masters*. Wolfeboro: Longwood Academic, 1990.

Penkower, Linda L. "T'ian-t'ai During the T'ang Dynasty: Chan-jan and the Sinification of Buddhism." Ph.D. diss., Columbia University, New York, 1993.

Peterman, Scott Dennis. "The Legend of Huihai." Ph.D. diss., Stanford University, 1986.

Peterson, Charles A. "Court and Province in Mid- and Late T'ang." In Twitchett, *The Cambridge History of China, vol. 3: Sui and T'ang China, 589–906, Part I*: 464–560.

———. "The Restoration Completed: Emperor Hsien-tsung and the Provinces." In Wright and Twitchett, *Perspectives on the T'ang*: 151–91.

Poceski, Mario (see also under Cheng-chien Bhikshu). "Chan Rituals of Abbots' Ascending the Hall to Preach." In Steven Heine and Dale Wright, eds. *Zen Ritual*. Oxford: Oxford University Press, forthcoming.

———. "*Guishan jingce* and the Ethical Foundations of Chan Practice." In Steven Heine and Dale Wright, eds., *Zen Classics*. Oxford: Oxford University Press, 2005: 15–42.

———. "The Hongzhou School during the Mid-Tang Period." Ph.D. diss., University of California, Los Angeles, 2000.

———. "Mazu Daoyi (709–788) and Chan in Sichuan." *Komazawa daigaku zenkenkyūjo nenpō* 12 (2001): 1–26.

———. "*Mazu yulu* and the Creation of the Chan Records of Sayings." In Heine and Wright, *The Zen Canon*: 53–79.

———. "Xuefeng's Code and the Chan School's Participation in the Development of Monastic Regulations," *Asia Major, New Series* 16/2 (2003): 33–56.

Pulleyblank, Edwin. "Neo-Confucianism and Neo-Legalism in T'ang Intellectual Life, 755–805." In Wright, *The Confucian Persuasion*: 77–111.

Reischauer, Edwin O., trans. *Ennin's Diary: The Record of a Pilgrimage to China in Search of the Law*. New York: The Ronald Press Company, 1955.

———. *Ennin's Travels in T'ang China*. New York: The Ronald Press, 1955.

Robinet, Isabelle. *Taoism: Growth of a Religion*. Trans. by Phyllis Brooks. Stanford: Stanford University Press, 1997.

Sasaki, Ruth Fuller, trans. *The Recorded Sayings of Chan Master Linji Hui-chao of Chen Prefecture*. Kyoto: The Institute for Zen Studies, 1975.

Sasaki, Ruth Fuller at al., trans. *A Man of Zen: The Recorded Sayings of Layman P'ang*. New York: Weatherhill, 1971.

Schlütter, Morten. "Chan Buddhism in Song-Dynasty China (960–1279): The Rise of the Caodong Tradition and the Formation of the Chan School." Ph.D. diss., Yale University, 1998.

Sharf, Robert H. *Coming to Terms with Chinese Buddhism: A Reading of the* Treasure Store Treatise. Honolulu: University of Hawai'i Press, 2002.

———. "The Idolization of Enlightenment: On the Mummification of Ch'an Masters in Medieval China." *History of Religions* 32/1 (1992): 1–31.

Shih, Heng-ching. "T'ien-t'ai Chih-i's Theory of Buddha Nature—A Realistic and Humanistic Understanding of the Buddha." In Griffiths and Keenan, *Buddha Nature: A Festschrift in Honor of Minoru Kiyota*: 153–69.

Shinohara, Koichi. "Two Sources of Chinese Buddhist Biographies: Stūpa Inscriptions and Miracle Stories." In Phyllis Granoff and Shinohara Koichi, eds. *Monks and Magicians: Religious Biographies in Asia*. Oakville, Ontario: Mosaic Press, 1988: 119–228.

Solomon, Bernard S., trans. *The Veritable Record of the Tang Emperor Shun-ts'ung*. Cambridge: Harvard University Press, 1955.

Sponberg, Alan. "Meditation in Fa-hsiang Buddhism." In Gregory, *Traditions of Meditation in Chinese Buddhism*: 15–43.

Steinhardt, Nancy Shatzman. *Chinese Imperial City Planning*. Honolulu: University of Hawai'i Press, 1990.

Stevenson, Daniel B. "The Four Kinds of Samādhi in Early T'ien-t'ai Buddhism." In Gregory, *Traditions of Meditation in Chinese Buddhism*: 45–97.

Strassberg, Richard E. *Inscribed Landscapes: Travel Writing from Imperial China*. Berkeley: University of California Press, 1994.

Swanson, Paul L. "Apocryphal Texts in Chinese Buddhism: T'ien-t'ai Chih-i's Use of Apocryphal Scriptures." In A. van der Kooij and K. van der Toorn, eds. *Canonization and Decanonization*. Studies in the History of Religions, 82. Leiden: E J Brill, 1998: 245–55.

———. *Foundations of T'ien-t'ai Philosophy: The Flowering of the Two Truths Theory in Chinese Buddhism*. Berkeley: Asian Humanities Press, 1989.

———. "T'ien-t'ai Chih-i's Concept of Threefold Buddha Nature—A Synergy of

Reality, Wisdom, and Practice." In Griffiths and Keenan, *Buddha Nature: A Festschrift in Honor of Minoru Kiyota*: 171–80.

Suzuki, D. T. "Zen: A Reply to Hu Shih." *Philosophy East and West* 3/1 (1953): 25–46.

Takemoto, Melvin M. "The Kuei-shan ching-ts'e: Morality in the Hung-chou School of Ch'an." M.A. thesis, University of Hawai'i, 1983.

Teiser, Stephen F. *The Ghost Festival in Medieval China*. Princeton: Princeton University Press, 1988.

———. *The Scripture of the Ten Kings and the Making of Purgatory in Medieval Chinese Buddhism*. Studies in East Asian Buddhism 9. Honolulu: University of Hawai'i Press, 1994.

Thurman, Robert A. F., trans. *The Holy Teaching of Vimalakīrti: A Mahāyāna Scripture*. University Park and London: The Pennsylvania State University Press, 1976.

Twitchett, Denis, ed. *The Cambridge History of China, Volume 3: Sui and T'ang China, 589–906, Part I*. Cambridge: Cambridge University Press, 1979.

———. "Hsüan-tsung (reign 712–756)." In Twitchett, *The Cambridge History of China, Volume 3: Sui and T'ang China, 589–906, Part I*: 333–463.

Waley, Arthur. *The Life and Times of Po Chü-i*. London: G. Allen and Unwin, 1949.

Watson, Burton. "Buddhism in the Poetry of Po Chü-i." *Eastern Buddhist* 21/1 (1988): 1–22.

———, trans. *The Lotus Sutra*. New York: Columbia University Press, 1993.

———. trans. *Po Chü-i: Selected Poems*. New York: Columbia University Press, 1997.

———, trans. *The Vimalakīrti Sūtra*. New York: Columbia University Press, 1997.

———, trans. *The Zen Teaching of Master Lin-chi*. Boston: Shambala Publications, 1993.

Weber, Max. *The Sociology of Religion*. Trans. by Ephraim Fischoff. Boston: Beacon Press, 1964.

———. *The Theory of Social and Economic Organization*. Trans. by A. M. Henderson and Talcott Parsons. New York: The Free Press, 1964.

Weinstein, Stanley. *Buddhism under the T'ang*. Cambridge: Cambridge University Press, 1987.

———. "Imperial Patronage in the Formation of T'ang Buddhism." In Wright and Twitchett, *Perspectives on the T'ang*: 265–306.

Welter, Albert. "Lineage and Context in the *Patriarch's Hall Collection* and the *Transmission of the Lamp*." In Heine and Wright, *The Zen Canon*: 137–79.

———. *The Meaning of Myriad Good Deeds: A Study of Yung-ming Yen-shou and Wan-shan t'ung-kuei chi*. New York: Peter Lang, 1992.

———. *Monks, Rulers, and Literati: The Political Ascendancy of Chan Buddhism*. Oxford and New York: Oxford University Press, 2006.

White, Hayden. *Tropics of Discourse: Essays in Cultural Criticism*. Baltimore: Johns Hopkins University Press, 1978.

Wong, Dorothy C. *Chinese Steles: Pre-Buddhist and Buddhist use of a Symbolic Form*. Honolulu: University of Hawai'i Press, 2004.

Wright, Arthur F. *Buddhism in Chinese History*. Stanford: Stanford University Press, 1959.

———, ed. *The Confucian Persuasion*. Stanford: Stanford University Press, 1960.

Wright, Arthur, and Denis Twitchett, eds. *Perspectives on the T'ang*. New Haven: Yale University Press, 1973.

Wright, Dale S. *Philosophical Meditations on Zen Buddhism*. London: Cambridge University Press, 1999.

Xiong, Victor Cunrui, *Sui-Tang Chang'an: A Study in the Urban History of Medieval China*. Ann Arbor: Center for Chinese Studies, University of Michigan, 2000.

Yampolsky, Philip B., trans. *The Platform Sūtra of the Sixth Patriarch*. New York: Columbia University Press, 1967.

Yanagida, Seizan. "The *Li-tai fa-pao chi* and the Ch'an Doctrine of Sudden Awakening." Trans. by Carl W. Bielefeldt. In Lai and Lancaster, *Early Ch'an in China and Tibet*: 13–49.

———. "The 'Recorded Sayings' Texts of Chinese Ch'an Buddhism." Trans. by John McRae. In Lai and Lancaster, *Early Ch'an in China and Tibet*: 185–205.

Yifa. *The Origins of Buddhist Monastic Codes in China: An Annotated Translation and Study of the* Chanyuan Qinggui. Honolulu: University of Hawai'i Press, 2002.

Zou, Zongxu. *The Land Within the Passes: A History of Xian*. Trans. by Susan Whitfield. London: Penguin Books, 1991.

Index

abiding in subdued mind, 208
absolute truth, 176, 194, 196, 202,
    213, 214
Amitābha Buddha, 227
Anguo monastery, 64, 94
An Lushan rebellion, 3, 21, 22, 30,
    61, 68, 88, 90, 93, 95
antinomianism, 6, 9, 172, 186, 208,
    229
ātman doctrine, 172
attachment(s)
    Baizhang on, 162, 166, 168,
        214
    Buddha's lack of, 210
    as deep-seated, 158
    freeing mind from, 212
    Mazu on, 170, 178, 180, 185
    and "mind is Buddha" adage, 171,
        175–78, 182
    of ordinary people, 169, 185, 186
    See also nonattachment
awakening, 160–61, 163, 165, 168,
    185, 195–97, 200–202, 206–7,
    215–19, 226
Awakening of Faith, 170
awareness, 183, 209

Baiyan monastery, 67
Baizhang Fazheng, 51, 74n.44
Baizhang guanglu, 137, 146, 199,
    207, 241–42

Baizhang Huaihai
    call for relinquishment of views,
        176
    canonical sources, use of, 146–47,
        155n.72
    charismatic authority, 226
    childhood and education, 50
    on Daxiong mountain, 50, 74n.40
    death and funeral, 51, 74n.35
    on detached frame of mind, 207–8
    as disciple of Mazu, 7, 15n.1, 30,
        31, 46, 48, 49, 59, 71n.13
    disciples of, 51t, 113–14
    and emptiness, 204–5, 210, 215
    on ethical conduct and medita-
        tion, 138
    family background, 40, 144
    as founder of Chan monasticism,
        52, 95, 229
    in Jiangxi, 86
    and "mind is Buddha" adage,
        170, 173
    on monastic vocation, 131–32, 211
    on reality, 182, 191n.79, 203
    on realized sage, 218
    religious name, 79n.94
    sermons, 51, 96, 144, 182
    and spiritual lineage, 104, 105
    on spiritual well-being, 165–66
    as teacher, 50, 51, 73n.32,
        200–201

Baizhang Huaihai (*continued*)
  on teaching, 167–68, 173
  three propositions, 193–94, 207–16,
    225, 230
  on unobstructed activity, 217
  wood and stone metaphors, 162–63
Baizhang mountain, 50, 74n.40
Baizhang Niepan, 51, 74n.44
Baizhang Weizheng, 74n.44
Bao Fang, 31, 90, 91, 92
Baofeng monastery, 35n.3
Bao Ji, 91, 92, 115n.26
Baoji, 173
Baolin zhuan, 27, 29, 100, 101, 105,
    106, 111
Bao Rong, 92
Baotang school, 6, 8, 107, 110, 141,
    208, 229
Baozhi, 168
Biyan lu, 59, 121n.95
Bodhidharma, 7, 8, 16n.2, 100, 103, 105,
    135, 140, 142, 153n.52, 164, 171
bodhisattvas, 202, 205, 208, 220n.39,
    221n.61
Bo Juyi, 53, 64–66, 76n.66, 93, 102, 111,
    119n.71
Buddha, 22, 28–29, 46, 50, 100, 136,
    142–43, 147–48, 164, 165, 169,
    207, 226
  See also Buddhahood; Buddha-nature;
    Buddhism; "mind is Buddha"
Buddhahood, 127, 128, 165, 169, 200, 216
Buddha-nature (*foxing*), 51, 127–30,
    149n.1, 150n.6, 168–69, 171–73, 177,
    179, 185, 204, 210, 215, 216
Buddhism
  in Chang'an, 61
  and Chan school, 103, 105, 129, 135
  conceptions of sanctity, 132
  and Emperor Dezong, 42n.84
  under Empress Wu, 68
  of Hongzhou school, 46, 88–89, 111,
    158, 163
  kataphatic approach, 215
  Mahāyāna, 6, 64, 69, 99, 125, 126,
    129–30, 135, 148–49, 158, 163, 165,
    167, 179, 183
  main elements of, 66
  of Mazu, 90
  monastic regulations, 134

Sinification of, 139, 149
Tang, 85, 95, 118n.69, 125–28, 144,
    145, 149, 158, 169, 225–27, 230
  transcendence as goal of, 23
Buore monastery, 27
Buswell, Robert, 7, 17n.13

calming and contemplation (*zhiguan*), 64
canonicity, 139–44, 227
Cantongqi, 102
Caodong school, 112, 113
Caoshan Benji, 147
Caotang, 67
"Caotang ji," 53
Caoxi, 27
Chan
  and Buddha-nature, 129
  and concept of *upāya*, 164
  and Confucian scholarship, 149
  court-oriented outlook of, 85
  cultivation of nonattachment, 159
  formative development, 8, 125
  history, 4, 7–8, 9, 10, 17n.13, 95, 100,
    113, 136
  ideal of transcendence, 135
  and *Laṅkāvatāra Scripture*, 140–41,
    142
  and Mahāyāna doctrines, 129, 130
  mid-Tang, 85–121
  monasticism, 52, 95, 150–51n.16, 229
  monks, 23, 71n.9, 92, 95, 131–35,
    242–44
  orthodoxy, 63, 82n.142, 99, 101,
    106–8, 111–13, 150n.16, 194, 197,
    227, 229, 231
  practice of subtraction/elimination, 162
  radicalism, 198
  as school of Buddhism, 3, 5–6, 103,
    110, 135
  sermons, 146, 147
  and suddenness, 193, 194
  teachers, 86, 87, 88, 92, 96, 110, 147,
    148, 152n.51, 176, 226, 228, 231
  transitions in, 110–11
  transmission to Korea, 108–9, 111
  See also Chan lineage(s); Hongzhou
    school
Chan council (of 796), 63, 107
Chang'an, 55, 61–67, 87, 89, 94, 98
Changsha Jingcen, 184

Changxing, 52
Chan lineage(s), 5, 112–13
    definition of, 16n.2
    founders of, 16n.2, 112
    major, 99–101, 103
    and Mazu's Hongzhou school, 95–99,
        229
    patriarchs, 8, 100, 105
    pluralistic view of, 105–6
    and religious identities, 103–6
Chanmen jing, 141
Chanyuan zhuquanji duxu, 99, 102,
    169, 197
Chaoan, 30, 96
charisma, 226, 231n.1
Chengdu, 22, 24
Chengguan, 62, 80n.113, 91, 126
Chen Jinhua, 63, 107
Chen Xu, 73n.3
Chinul, 198
Chongtai, 46, 70n.3
Chuandeng lu, 9, 24, 25, 27, 28, 33, 47,
    49, 56, 57, 67, 100, 184
Chuanxin fayao, 146
Chuji, 23, 24, 25, 36n.11
Cien monastery, 62, 94
classical Chan, 17n.13, 59, 136, 216
compassion, 180
complete teaching, 167–68
conditioned origination, 126
Confucianism, 23, 149, 195
Confucius, 46
conventional existence, 214
conventional truth, 213, 214
convents, 61
Cui Qun, 55, 93
Cui Shenyou, 93
cultivation, 195, 197, 202, 206

Da'an, 205–6
Da'anguo monastery. See Anguo
    monastery
Dacien monastery. See Cien monastery
Dafo monastery, 31
Dahui Zonggao, 147, 198, 230
Daizong (emperor), 4, 30, 88, 94, 96
Dali period, 30, 31
Damei Fachang, 56, 57–58, 78n.89, 109,
    179–80
Damei mountain, 58, 179

Damei yulu, 181
Danrin, 112
Danxia Tianran, 9, 32, 60, 69, 71n.8,
    77n.69, 96, 98, 117n.51
dao, 191n.81
Daode jing, 215
Daoism, 129, 135, 195, 215
Daojun, 27
Daoqin. See Jingshan Faqin
Daosheng, 195
Daowu. See Tianhuang Daowu
Daoxin, 53, 87, 100, 102, 108, 135,
    150–51n.16, 168
Daoxuan, 60
Daoyuan, 25
Dasheng qixin lun, 144, 145. See also
    Awakening of Faith
Daxingshan monastery. See Xingshan
    monastery
Daxiong mountain. See Baizhang
    mountain
Dayan pagoda, 94
Dayi. See Ehu Dayi
Dazhidu lun, 146
Da Zhuangyan pagoda, 34
Dazhu Huihai, 7, 145, 170
    as disciple of Mazu, 30, 41n.67, 46,
        48, 56, 57
    Dunwu rudao yaomen lun, 57, 58,
        199, 241
    on nature of realization, 211
    ordination, 78n.87
    on purity of mind, 209
    quotations from Prajñāpāramitā
        scriptures, 155n.72
    on sudden awakening, 159, 199
    symbolic exegesis, 141
death premonitions, 33
deluded thoughts, 159, 169, 204
delusion of knowing, 175
Deng Yinfeng, 55–56, 87, 98
Deshan lineage, 113
desires, 157, 169, 173, 202, 215
detachment, 159–63, 165, 180, 183, 194,
    207–11, 215, 222nn.76–77
Deyang, 35n.4
Dezong (emperor), 4, 42n.84, 61, 62,
    91, 94
dharmadhātu (realm of reality), 160, 217
dharma inheritance, 103, 119n.72

dharmakāya (dharma body), 169–70, 191n.79, 201
dharma transmission, 72n.18, 104
dialectical progression, 214
Diamond Scripture, 60, 140–41, 145, 153n.55, 155n.72, 227
Dilun school, 127
discernment, 212, 213
disciples, 45–83, 114n.2
　of Baizhang, 51t, 113–14
　of Mazu, 45–47, 70–71n.8, 114n.1, 229, 234–35, 236t
　Mazu's in Chang'an, 61–67
　Mazu's second-generation Korean, 109t
　regional spread of Mazu's, 47t, 70n.7
　of Shenxiu, 87
　of Shitou, 98
　Suzuki on, 114n.1
　training in Hongzhou, 30–32
　See also specific disciples
doctrinal taxonomies, 129–30, 178–79, 195. *See also* panjiao
Donglin monastery, 53
Dong monastery, 55
Dongshan Liangjie, 98, 112
Dong Shuchan, 60
Dongsi Ruhui, 32, 55, 93, 96, 173
Double Mystery school, 215
dualism, 158, 161, 166, 176, 182, 183, 209, 214–17
Dumoulin, Heinrich, 10
dun, 195, 199, 200. *See also* suddenness
dunchao, 199
dunfa, 199
Dunhuang manuscripts, 7, 151n.23
dunliao, 199
Dunwu rudao yaomen lun, 57, 58, 199, 241
Dunwu yaomen, 30, 141, 209
dunxi, 199
Dushun, 16n.2

East Mountain (Dongshan) school, 8, 87, 127, 129, 135
Ehu Dayi
　background, 62
　Chan council of 796, 107
　in Chang'an, 62–63, 67, 87, 94
　conversations with emperor, 79n.109, 80n.114

as founder of new monastery, 86
　on meditation, 137
　stele inscription on Chan lineages, 99–101, 103, 104
　teaching on Ehu mountain, 55, 62
Ehu mountain, 55, 62, 63
emptiness, 126–29, 150n.6, 159, 161, 176, 179, 182, 204, 209, 210, 212, 214
Enchin, 111
encounter dialogues, 10–11, 18n.22, 29
enlightenment, 127–29, 138, 150n.16, 154n.67, 172, 179, 194, 201, 218–19, 220n.39. *See also* original enlightenment; sudden enlightenment
Ennin, 111
"entering the room," 45, 70n.2
Erru sixing lun, 164, 185, 207
Esoteric tradition, 126
essence/function paradigm, 195, 198
evil, 161, 172, 185
expedient means. *See upāya*
Ezhou Wudeng, 30, 56

Fahua xuanyi, 140
Fahui, 52
Fajie guanmen, 212
Faju jing, 141, 143
Fale monastery, 57
false thoughts, 128, 136, 162, 171, 211
Fanyun, 51
fanzhao, 223n.98
Farong, 96, 99, 101, 135, 153n.57, 198
Faru, 27
Faure, Bernard, 140, 195
Faxiang school, 126–27, 129, 130, 213. *See also* Yogācāra
Fayan Wenyi, 99, 113, 196
Fazang, 16n.2, 53, 60, 68, 126, 140, 179, 212
Fazhao, 50
Fenzhou, 60–61, 86
Fenzhou Wuye, 32, 60–61, 86, 94, 132–33
Five Dynasties period, 8, 17n.13, 113
Foguang Ruman, 63, 68–69
Fojiyan, 29, 41n.67, 57
Foshuo Foming Scripture, 143
Foulk, Griffith, 18n.24, 119nn.71–72
Four-Division Vinaya, 60
foxing. See Buddha-nature

Foxing lun, 150n.6
Fuchong, 67
Fu dashi, 145, 168
Fujian, 29–30, 46, 50
Funiu Zizai, 30, 60, 69, 96, 173
Furong Taiyu, 32, 59, 96
Fuzhou, 30, 50

Ganquan Zhixian, 30, 46, 60, 77n.71
Gaoying, 46, 70n.3
Gaozong (emperor), 60
Gaozu (emperor), 94, 100
gongan collections, 121n.95
Gonggong mountain, 30, 31, 41n.71, 48, 49, 50, 86, 92, 96
good, 161, 172, 185, 208
gradual (*jian*) approach, 193, 194–200, 203–6, 221n.53
"guarding the mind," 135, 206
"guarding the one," 129
Guifeng Zongmi
    approaches to practice and realization, 197
    on Buddha-nature, 128, 171, 185
    on Chan council of 796, 63, 107
    on Chan lineages, 99, 102, 103
    and Chan orthodoxy, 111
    classification scheme, 129–30, 179
    critique of Hongzhou school, 197–98, 200, 202
    critique of Northern school, 200
    critique of Wuzhu, 208
    departure from Sichuan, 25
    and kataphatic approach, 215
    on Mazu, 26, 28
    sudden enlightenment paradigm, 203, 206
    on true mind, 169
    use of term "Hongzhou school," 104
    writings, 8, 26, 28, 48, 98, 99, 102, 104, 128
    on Wuxiang, 37n.18
    on Xitang, 48
Guishan jingce, 133, 134, 135, 137, 138, 151n.23, 231n.4
Guishan Lingyou, 50, 93–94, 112, 133, 134, 137, 138–39, 206
Guiyang school, 112, 113
Guiyang Wuliao, 55
Guizong Chan monastery, 53

Guizong temple, 53
Guizong Zhichang, 32, 53, 54, 76n.66, 86, 93, 109
Guṇabhadra, 140
guwen movement, 149

Haichang-yuan temple, 57
Hangzhou Tianlong, 58
Hangzhou Zhizang, 59
Han Yu, 149
Hanzhou, 21, 22, 35n.4
Haozhi, 67
Hebei, 46
Heijian, 69
Henan, 60
Heze school, 129, 130, 198
Heze Shenhui, 25, 63, 92, 106–7, 110, 198, 201
    as author of robe bestowal story, 72n.18
    employment of *Diamond Scripture,* 140, 142, 153n.55
    invocation of subitism, 195, 196–97, 199
    as leader of Chan lineage, 8, 99, 106–7
    and meditation, 136, 200
    and "mind is Buddha" adage, 168
    records of, 7, 120n.80
    sectarianism, 6, 101–2, 111, 136
    and Shenxiu, 69–70n.1
Hongbian, 67, 82n.142
Hongch'ŏk, 49, 73n.31, 109*t*
Hongjing, 27
Hongren, 27, 46, 72n.18, 87, 100, 101, 135, 140, 150–51n.16
Hongzhou prefecture, 31, 46
Hongzhou school
    attitude toward meditation, 136, 137
    attitude toward monasticism, 133
    and Buddhist canon, 148, 158
    Buddhist influence, 127, 163
    canonical background, 145
    Chinese texts cited in records, 145*t*
    conception of awakening, 216
    conception of reality, 198
    Dayi's introduction of, 63
    doctrinal formulations, 6, 130
    as elite contemplative tradition, 165
    images of, 8–11

Hongzhou school (*continued*)
  leaders of, 226
  as major Chan lineage, 99, 111
  and Mazu Daoyi, 3, 4–6, 8–9, 21, 45
  monks of, 86, 87, 111, 226
  origination of term, 15n.1, 104
  and other Chan lineages, 95–99
  pattern of growth, 86–89
  position on religious language, 166
  prominent status in Chan history, 4, 6
  regional spread of, 45–83, 86
  religious identity, 10
  as revolutionary movement, 9
  romanticized image of, 4
  scriptural allusions, 145t, 148
  stance toward practice, 200, 202
  stance toward Vinaya, 150n.16
  style and ethos of, 9
  as successor of earlier Chan movement,
    111, 228–29
  and suddenness, 193, 199
  teachings, 226, 227, 230
  Yanagida's analysis of, 235, 237–38
  Zongmi on, 197–98, 200, 202
Huaihui. *See* Zhangjing Huaihui
Huainan, 55
Huairang. *See* Nanyue Huairang
Huaitao, 67
Huangbo Xiyun, 7, 50, 54, 72n.16, 93,
    146, 147, 159, 161–62, 170, 185, 199,
    200
Huanglong Weizhong, 25
Huangmei mountain, 53
Huayan school, 3, 16n.2, 109, 125, 126,
    129, 140, 195, 212, 215
Huayan Scripture, 60, 140, 143, 144,
    168, 169
Huayan Zhizang, 34, 67, 71n.11
Hui'an. *See* Lao'an
Huiguo, 62
Huike, 168
Huineng, 100, 101, 105, 136, 204
  disciples of, 46, 97
  as founder of Southern school, 16n.2,
    18n.21
  and Huairang, 39n.42
  as leader of Southern school, 48,
    102, 107
  "mind is Buddha" adage, 168
  "originally there is not a thing," 178

robe transmission, 72n.18
and Shitou, 117n.47
as sixth patriarch, 8, 69n.1, 72n.18,
    99, 112
as teacher, 26, 27
verse competition, 106, 194
Hŭiyang-san school, 108
Huiyuan, 53
Huiyun, 46, 70n.3
Huizhao, 50, 74n.37
Hunan, 46, 55
Huo Xianming, 62
Hu Shih, 10, 120n.80, 136
Hyech'ŏl, 49, 109t
Hyŏnuk, 67, 109t, 120n.87

iconoclasm, 11, 13, 141, 152n.51, 227–28
ignorance, 127, 150n.6, 157, 158, 160–61,
    166, 169, 217–18
immanence of enlightenment, 127
immediacy, 193, 195
imperfection, 157
imperial patronage, 89–95
impure mind, 185, 204, 207, 216
impurity, 167
Incense Fellowship, 69
inclusiveness, 101, 102
incomplete teaching, 167–68, 173
Indian scriptures, 139
insight, 159, 166, 194, 196, 201, 226
intermediate good, 208
intuition, 195
Ishii Shūdō, 7, 71n.10
"it is not a thing," 177, 178, 180, 191n.78,
    210

Japan, 4, 7, 111–12, 113
Jianfu monastery, 67
Jiangnan, 21–22, 29
Jiangxi, 29–30, 31, 46, 49, 51, 54–55, 85,
    86, 87, 88, 93
Jiangzhou, 54
Jiannan, 21, 22
Jianyang, 29
Jingde chuandeng lu. See *Chuandeng lu*
Jingjue, 23, 100
Jing mountain, 96
Jingshan Faqin, 55, 96, 97, 102, 107, 110
Jingzhong monastery, 24
Jingzhong school, 8, 107, 110

Jingzhou, 26, 27, 87, 131
Jizang, 128, 213–14, 215
ju, 219n.1
Jueguan lun, 129, 214, 215
Jueping, 67

Kaiyuan monastery, 30–33, 42n.76, 47,
    49, 50, 60, 86, 89, 90, 92
kanhua approach, 230
kataphatic approach, 215
Kim, Reverend. *See* Wuxiang
Korea, 4, 7, 25, 49, 73n.31, 108–9, 111, 113
Koryǒ dynasty, 108
Kuiji, 213
Kumārajīva, 126

language, 166–67
Laṅkāvatāra Scripture, 140–43, 145,
    153n.52, 154n.64, 227
Lao'an, 27
Lengqie shizi ji, 7, 23, 27, 100, 104, 140
Letan monastery, 33, 34, 52
Liang dynasty, 31
Liang Kai, 153n.51
Liang of Xishan, 25
Li Ao, 49, 62, 73n.27
Li Baozhen, 60
liberation, 201, 202, 203, 210, 218
Li Bo, 49, 53, 54, 71n.10, 76n.66, 93
Lidai fabao ji, 7, 100, 104, 107, 120n.81,
    141, 185
Li Hua, 107
Li Jian, 33, 34, 48, 49, 91, 92, 93, 115n.15
Li Jingrang, 93
Linchuan, 30
Linde Hall, 62, 64, 67
lineage, as term, 16n.10, 119n.72
Ling'ai, 51
Lingzhuo, 25
Linji Chan, 55
Linji school, 4, 16n.2, 52, 55, 112, 230
Linji Yixuan, 4, 16n.2, 147, 184
Li Shangyin, 48, 94
literati. *See* officials and literati
Liu Ke, 55, 98
Liu Taizhen, 62
Liu Zongyuan, 149
Liuzu dashi fabao tanjing. See *Platform
    Scripture*
Li Wanjuan. *See* Li Bo

Longan Ruhai, 96
Lotus Scripture, 60, 140, 141, 146, 213
Lühou Ningbi, 59
Lu Jianqiu, 93
Luofu Xiuguang, 55
Luohan monastery, 36n.11
Luoyang, 68–69, 87, 89
Lushan, 52–53, 86
Lu Sigong, 31, 42n.82, 90, 91, 92
Lý dynasty, 113

Madhyamaka, 126–27, 129–30, 141,
    153n.57, 164, 169, 176, 178–79,
    213–15
Magu Baoche, 60
Mahāparinirvāṇa Scripture, 127, 140
Mahāyāna (Moheyan), 146
Mahāyāna Buddhism, 6, 64, 69, 99,
    125, 126, 129–30, 135, 148–49, 158,
    163, 165, 167, 179, 183
Mahāyāna scriptures, 144
Mazu Daoyi
    adages, 177–78, 180–82, 191n.78,
        210, 230
    birthplace, 22, 35n.4
    and canonical tradition, 148
    charismatic authority, 226
    childhood, 22
    on detachment, 159
    disciples and lineages, 5, 45–83,
        86–89, 93, 94, 96, 111–12, 114n.1,
        229, 234–35, 236t
    distinctive perspectives and insights,
        158, 225
    doctrinal formulations and stance, 6,
        130, 165, 166, 179, 201, 228
    early years in Sichuan, 22–23
    family background, 22, 36n.8
    in *gongan* collections, 121n.95
    and Hongzhou school, 3, 4–6, 8–9, 21,
        45, 99, 200
    illness, death, and funeral, 32–35,
        35n.3, 43n.89
    meditation, 28, 136, 137, 201–2
    "mind is Buddha" adage, 168–70, 174,
        175, 177–82, 190n.69, 191n.78, 225
    monastic training, 23–25
    name, 22, 35n.5
    and Niutou school, 96–97, 110
    on ordinary mind, 183

Mazu Daoyi (*continued*)
  ordination, 24, 37n.15
  patrons, 89–93
  physical appearance, 22
  on principle and phenomena, 160
  radicalized image, 11, 89
  on reality, 161, 178, 203
  on realization of spiritual freedom, 217–18
  scriptures invoked, 145
  second-generation Korean disciples, 109*t*
  sermons, 136, 137, 142, 143, 146, 154n.70, 169–70, 202, 205, 240
  and Shitou, 97–98, 117n.51
  study with Huairang, 26–29, 40–41nn.61–63
  teaching in Fujian and Jiangxi, 29–30, 41n.67
  training of disciples in Hongzhou, 30–32
  travels east, 25–26
  on truth/reality, 184
McMullen, David, 148
McRae, John R., 7
meditation
  attitudes toward, 96, 135–39
  Baizhang on, 137–38, 208
  Chan, 135–38, 141
  Daoist, 129
  Huayan, 212
  main traditions of, 107
  of Mazu, 28, 136, 137, 201–2
  Shenhui on, 200
  as *upāya*, 164
  of Zhiyi, 227
  in *Zuochan ming*, 63
mental detachment, 132
mental purity, 65–66, 180, 196
metaphors, 146
Middle Way, 126, 128, 214, 215
"mind is Buddha," 58, 167–82, 190n.69, 191n.78, 201, 225
"mind without abode," 217
Mingyue mountain, 26, 40n.56
mirror metaphor, 144, 154n.67, 170
missionary work, 111
monasteries, 114n.2
  of Baizhang's disciples, 51, 111
  in Chang'an, 61–62, 94

in Hunan, 55
in Jiangxi, 46, 93
of Mazu's disciples, 86–87, 93, 94, 111
in Song period, 95
Suzuki on, 114n.1
See also specific monasteries
monasticism, 7, 23, 52, 131–35, 150–51n.16, 186, 203, 229
monks
  ascetic lifestyle, 132
  early predispositions for religious life, 22–23
  under Emperor Dezong, 42n.84
  exemplary, 131–35
  Guishan's advice to, 138–39
  heyday of, 69n.1
  of Hongzhou school, 86, 87, 111, 226
  in Jiangxi and South, 52–55
  knowledge of canonical texts, 144
  Korean, 25, 49, 109, 111
  missionary activities, 111
  productive lives of, 71n.9
  romantic images of, 95
  Sichuan, 25
  stele inscriptions of, 242–44
  See also disciples; *specific monks*
morality, 133
mountain schools, 108–9
Muzong (emperor), 49, 61

Nanchang, 31, 32
Nanquan Puyuan, 48, 59, 159
  anecdote about killing of cat, 9, 10
  critique of "mind is Buddha," 173–76, 180, 182
  as disciple of Mazu, 32, 71n.13
  radicalized image, 11
Nanyang Huizhong, 102, 110, 168, 172–73
Nanyuan Daoming, 54
Nanyuan mountain, 54
Nanyue Chengyuan, 26
Nanyue Huairang, 66, 87, 200
  biographical background, 27
  as disciple of Huineng, 18n.21, 39n.42, 112
  on meditation, 28, 136
  as teacher of Mazu, 13, 26–29, 40–41nn.61–63, 112
Nanyue mountain, 26, 27, 28, 29, 36n.8, 97

"neither mind nor Buddha," 178, 180, 181, 182, 190n.69, 191n.78
Nengren monastery, 31, 42n.81
"Nine Mountain schools," 108–9
Nirvāṇa, 168, 188n.21, 201, 204
Nirvāṇa Scripture, 141, 220n.43
Niutou Huizhong, 96, 97, 106, 107, 110
Niutou mountain, 96
Niutou school, 8, 96–97, 99, 101, 107, 108, 110, 129, 135–36, 141, 153n.57, 214, 227
no-mind, 161, 170, 185–86
non-abiding mind, 159–60, 209, 211
nonattachment, 159, 208–9
nonattainment, 162
nondiscrimination, 208, 211
nondualism, 158, 161, 164, 171, 183, 187n.19, 198, 214
no-realization, 211
Northern school, 34, 87, 96, 205, 227
  appropriation of Laṅkāvatāra Scripture, 140
  influence of Buddha-nature doctrine on, 127
  as Chan lineage, 8, 99
  court-oriented outlook, 85
  decline of, 70n.1, 108, 110
  and gradual approach, 194
  meditation, 135
  Niutou school as alternative to, 136
  after Shenhui's death, 107
  Shenhui's campaigns against, 195, 196
  Shenxiu as leader, 23, 27, 68, 70n.1
  stance toward Vinaya, 150n.16
  stress on monastic discipline, 131
  texts on, 7
  vis-à-vis Southern school, 101–2, 106
  Zongmi's critique of, 200
  in Zongmi's model, 129, 130
no-self, 127
no-thought, 141–42, 185, 208
nuns, 56

obliteration of consciousness, 208
officials and literati, 89–95, 147, 228
One Mind, 158, 160, 171
one practice samādhi (yixing sanmei), 135
ordinary mind, 182–86, 225
original completeness, 158
original enlightenment, 203

original liberation, 203
ox-herding allegory, 205–6

Pāli scripture, 204
Pang Yun, 117n.51, 183–84
panjiao, 178. See also doctrinal taxonomies
path of practice and realization, 178, 193–223
  awakening and realization, 215–19
  conceptual models, 212–15
  gradual path of practice, 203–6
  stages of, 207–12
  "sudden" and "gradual" paradigms, 194–98
  vanishing sudden paradigm, 199–203
patriarchs, 7, 8, 100, 105, 140–41
patronage, 89–95
Pei Kuan, 90, 115n.9
Pei Tong, 72n.23
Pei Xiu, 35, 72n.16, 93
Pei xiu sheyi wen, 48, 198
Pei Xu, 30, 42n.73, 42n.82, 72n.23, 89–90, 91, 92
Pei Zhou, 91
Penkower, Linda L., 80n.115
Perfect Enlightenment Scripture, 24
perfection, 158, 160, 165, 171, 179, 183, 202, 205, 207, 210, 211, 216, 218
phenomena (shi), 160, 212
Platform Scripture, 26, 27, 100, 101–2, 106, 107, 128, 136, 141, 172–73, 178, 185, 194, 195, 204–5
polemical discourse, 196
Pŏmil, 57, 109t
Pŏmnang, 108
Prajñāpāramitā scriptures, 145, 155n.72, 163, 168, 202
principle (li), 160, 212
Puji, 25, 87, 90, 92, 102, 106, 110, 131
Pure Land (Jingtu) tradition, 3, 34, 125, 126, 131
purity, 167, 180, 185, 203, 207–8
purity of mind, 127, 209, 216

Qianzhou, 30
Qiling Zhitong, 59
Qingyuan mountain, 97
Qingyuan Xingsi, 18n.21, 97, 106, 112
Qi Ying, 48, 93
Quan Deyu, 22, 26, 33, 34, 91–92, 115n.26

Ratnagotravibhāga, 127
reality
    absolute, 201
    all-pervasiveness of, 183
    Baizhang on, 182, 191n.79, 203
    Buddha's vision of, 207
    in Chan practice, 162
    conventional, 214
    essence of, 155n.79
    Hongzhou school conception of, 198
    insight into, 161, 166
    Mazu on, 161, 178, 203
    mind's pivotal role in, 129
    Nanquan on, 174–76
    nature of, 210, 213, 214, 217, 218, 226
    nonconceptual realization of, 135, 214
    and suddenness, 196
    and theory of two truths, 194
    ultimate, 128, 130, 157–58, 160, 164,
        170, 171, 179, 184, 187n.19, 191n.79,
        201, 216
realization (*zheng*), 211, 215–19
realized sage, 218
religious doctrines, 166
religious identities, 103–6
religious language, 166–67
religious perfection, 207
rhetoric, 196
robe, bestowal of, 48, 72n.18, 120n.81
rules of purity (*qinggui*), 52

Saga (emperor), 112
samādhi, 161
Samādhi of Single Practice, 153n.55
saṃsāra, 161, 167, 168, 170, 208,
    217, 218
sanctity, 131, 132
Sanlun school, 126, 141, 153n.57
Śāriputra, 137
school, as term, 16n.10, 119n.72
scriptural authority, 139–44
scriptural quotations, 144, 145t, 146, 147
scriptures, 144–49, 164
sectarianism, 6, 101–2, 107, 111, 136, 227
self, 128, 150n.6, 210
self-centered awareness, 209
Sengyou, 105
Sengzhao, 126, 145, 179
Shaanxi, 46, 60
Shandao, 34

Shandong, 46
Shangdang, 60
Shanshan Zhijian, 59
Shanxi, 46, 60
Shaotan, 36n.8
Shaozhou Ruyuan, 55
Sharf, Robert, 129
Shelun school, 127
Shengshan monastery, 69
Shenhui. *See* Heze Shenhui
Shenhui of Jingzhong, 24
Shenlong monastery, 63
Shenxing, 51
Shenxiu, 48, 69n.1
    as disciple of Hongren, 23
    disciples and lineages, 87, 99, 101, 131
    doctrinal positions, 130
    supporters of, 68, 92, 110
    verse competition, 106, 194, 204
    at Yuquan monastery, 27, 131
Shenzhao, 74n.37
Shigong Huizang, 41n.70, 54, 77n.69,
    205
Shiina Kōyū, 7, 136
Shili, 63, 80n.114
Shimen mountain, 32–33, 34, 43n.92, 50,
    52, 86
Shitou Xiqian, 8, 10, 55, 97–98, 102, 106,
    110, 112, 117n.47, 117n.51
Shuilao, 9
Shuitang, 55
Shunzong (emperor), 4, 62–63, 64, 68,
    80nn.113–14, 94
Sichuan, 22–23, 24, 25, 107
Sichuan tongzhi, 38n.30
Sifang, 22
Silla (dynasty), 24, 49, 57, 67, 108–9
sitting meditation, 135
six perfections, 200–201
Song Chan, 4, 8, 10, 18n.24, 99, 121n.95,
    229, 230
Song dynasty, 9, 11, 18n.24, 95, 113, 206
Song gaoseng zhuan, 24, 26, 27, 31, 34,
    47, 48, 52, 57, 60, 67, 98
Song mountain, 27
Sŏn schools, 49, 67, 108
Sōtō school, 113
Southern school
    as bearer of Chan orthodoxy, 8, 18n.21,
        63, 107–8

Buddha-nature interpretation, 128
and *Diamond Scripture*, 142
Huineng as founder of, 8, 16n.2,
  18n.21
lineages, 8–9, 99
and "mind is Buddha" adage, 172–73
Niutou school as alternative to, 136
and suddenness, 194, 195
and tathāgatagarbha doctrine, 128, 129
vis-à-vis Northern school, 101–2, 106
spiritual freedom, 158, 165, 210, 211,
  217, 226
spiritual lineage, 104
spiritual progress, 193, 215
Śrīmālādevī, 127
stele inscriptions, 66, 104, 223–24,
  242–44
stone metaphor, 162–63
subitism. *See* suddenness
sublime way, 208
suchness, 127, 128, 158, 160, 170, 201
sudden awakening, 135, 159, 198, 199,
  203, 206
sudden cultivation, 198, 199–200
sudden enlightenment, 193, 195, 197,
  198, 203
suddenness (sudden approach), 26, 193,
  194–200, 203, 205, 206, 221n.53
sudden practice, 203
suffering, 157
Sui dynasty, 3, 27, 94
Sui-Tang Buddhism, 125, 215
Suizhou, 24
Sumi-san school, 108
Suzuki, D.T., 10
Suzuki Tetsuo, 35n.3, 114n.1, 115n.26,
  190n.69, 242
symbolic exegesis, 141–42, 148,
  154n.60, 227

Taizong (emperor), 68, 94, 100
Tang, Reverend. *See* Chuji
Tang dynasty, 3–6, 11, 17n.13, 21, 27, 45,
  46, 61, 85–121
Tanran, 27
Tantric tradition, 126
Tanzang, 55
Tathāgata, 136
tathāgatagarbha doctrine, 126–30,
  149n.1, 168–72, 177–79, 197, 215

taxonomy of Chan teachings (by
  Zongmi), 197–98. *See also* doctrinal
  taxonomies
thaumaturgy, 64, 65, 126, 227
Thiền Uyển Tập Anh, 113–14
three contemplations, 214
three propositions (*sanju*), 193–94,
  207–16, 225, 230
three truths, 214
Tianhuang Daowu, 32, 46, 48, 96,
  98–99, 117–18nn.54–56
Tianmu Mingjue, 30, 41n.67, 59
Tiantai school, 3, 27, 58, 64, 104, 125,
  126, 129, 131, 140, 141, 195, 214, 215
Tibet, 24
Tongqing monastery, 93
Tongquanxian Xiu, 24
tongue, 22
Tŏŭi, 49, 109t
tradition, 149
traditionalism, 227–228
transcendence, 135, 159, 161, 165, 179,
  183, 186, 194, 207, 214, 215, 226
true mind (*zhenxin*), 169, 172, 173, 176,
  198, 200
truth, 138, 158, 160, 161, 164, 166, 176,
  182, 184, 186. *See also* absolute
  truth; two truths; universal truth
twofold mystery, 215
two truths (*erdi*), 126, 194, 213–15

Uighur troops, 61, 68
universal truth, 218
upāya, 163–68, 179, 182, 195, 200,
  201, 202

Vajrasamādhi Scripture, 129, 141.
Vietnam, 4, 111, 113–14
Vimalakīrti, 137, 164, 181, 187n.19
Vimalakīrti Scripture, 54, 60, 136,
  143–46, 164, 168, 183, 202
Vinaya regulations and teachings, 23, 65,
  27, 131, 150n.16, 222n.77
Vô Ngôn Thông, 113–14

wall contemplation (*biguan*), 207
Wang family, 50
Wangjin huanyuan guan, 212
washing of dirty robe metaphor, 203–4,
  220n.43

Weber, Max, 226, 231n.1
Wei Chuhou, 99
Weijian, 52–53
Weikuan. *See* Xingshan Weikuan
Wei Shou, 49
Wei Xian, 90
Wendi (emperor), 64, 94
Wenshu shuo jing, 135
wisdom, 153n.55, 158, 161, 163, 173, 181, 202, 212, 214, 216, 220n.43
wood metaphor, 162–63
words, 167
Wu fangbian, 164, 178
Wujia zhengzong zan, 36n.8
Wushan Zhizang, 71n.11
Wutai mountain, 60
Wuxiang, 24, 25, 37n.18, 48
Wuxie Lingmo, 59, 71n.8, 98
Wuxin lun, 185
Wu Zetian (empress), 21, 68
Wuzhu, 48, 107, 141, 208
Wuzong (emperor), 93

Xiangshan monastery, 69
Xianzong (emperor), 4, 61, 64, 66, 67, 82n.142, 89, 94
Xili mountain, 30
Ximing monastery, 60, 94
Xingping, 67
Xingshan monastery, 64, 65, 94
Xingshan Weikuan, 32, 46, 48, 61, 63–67, 69, 87, 94, 102–3, 105, 111
Xinjian, 31
Xinxin ming, 129
Xitang Zhizang
  background, 48
  death, 49, 72n.19, 72n.22
  as disciple of Mazu, 15n.1, 41n.67, 46, 48, 66, 71n.13, 72n.16
  and Faqin, 96
  inscriptions of, 71n.10, 72n.19, 72n.22
  in Jiangxi, 49, 86
  lay disciples, 93
  as leader at Gonggong mountain, 31, 48
  as leader at Kaiyuan monastery, 47
  and Mazu, 59, 72n.20
  ordination, 72n.22
  and Pei Zhou, 91
  religious name, 79n.94

Xiuxin yaolun, 164, 203
Xuanlang, 107
Xuansu, 90, 96
Xuanzang, 60, 94
Xuanzong (emperor), 21, 24, 31, 35, 57, 68, 89, 90, 93
Xuefeng lineage, 113

Yanagida Seizan, 7, 10, 24–25, 36n.8, 38n.30, 136, 235, 237–38
Yangqi Fanghui, 55
Yangqi mountain, 54–55
Yangqi Zhenshu, 54, 77n.71
Yangshan Huiji, 109, 112
Yanguan Qi'an, 30, 56, 57, 78n.83, 112
Yaoshan Weiyan, 50, 55, 98, 117n.54
Yifu, 87, 106, 110
Yikong, 111–12
Yogācāra, 126, 127, 129, 130, 154n.67, 213
Yongjia, 50
Youmin monastery, 31, 32
Youqing monastery, 31
Yuan (Vinaya teacher), 24
Yuanwu Keqin, 36n.8
Yuan Zai, 92
Yuanzhao, 62
Yu Chaoen, 94
Yunmen lineage, 113
Yunmen Wenyan, 99
Yu of Xiangzhou, 60
Yuquan monastery, 26, 27, 57, 58, 87, 131
Yuzhang (king), 31
Yuzhou, 24

Zanning, 47, 55, 92
Zechuan, Reverend, 25
Zen, 10
Zhangjing Huaihui, 32, 46, 48, 61, 63, 64, 66–67, 91, 94
Zhangjing monastery, 94
Zhangle Farong, 25
Zhangqiu Jianqiong, 24
Zhangsong Ma, 24–25
Zhangsong monastery, 38n.30
Zhangsong mountain, 24–25
Zhang Zhengfu, 66
Zhanran, 63, 80n.115, 126
Zhaoti Huilang, 41n.71, 98
Zhaozhou Zongshen, 9, 59
Zhejiang, 46, 56, 57, 59, 86

Zheng Yu, 93
Zhen Xu, 50, 73n.32
Zhiben, 60
Zhiguang, 46, 70n.3
Zhishen of Zizhou, 23, 120n.81
Zhitong, 46, 70n.3
Zhiyan, 57, 126
Zhiyi, 27, 135, 140, 214, 221n.53, 227
Zhongtiao mountain, 67

Zhongzong (emperor), 22
Zimen jingxun, 63, 151n.23
Ziyu Daotong, 30, 56, 98
Zizhong, 23, 36n.11
zong, 16n.10, 118n.69, 119n.72, 138
Zongmen shigui lun, 113
Zongmi. *See* Guifeng Zongmi
Zuochan ming, 40n.61, 63, 137
Zutang ji, 7, 11, 27, 28, 50, 54, 57

DATE DUE